Indigenous Law and the State

Bradford W. Morse and Gordon R. Woodman (eds.)

INDIGENOUS LAW AND THE STATE

1988
FORIS PUBLICATIONS
Dordrecht · Holland/Providence RI · U.S.A.

Published by:
Foris Publications Holland
P.O. Box 509
3300 AM Dordrecht, The Netherlands

Sole distributor for the U.S.A. and Canada:
Foris Publications USA, Inc.
P.O. Box 5904
Providence RI 02903
U.S.A.

CIP-DATA

Published for the Commission on Folk Law and Legal Pluralism of the International Union of Anthropological and Ethnological Sciences.

ISBN 90 6765 362 4

Printed in The Netherlands by ICG Printing, Dordrecht.

Contents

PART IV QUESTIONS OF STATUS: WOMEN; CHILD PLACEMENT

PART V ISSUES IN STATE CRIMINAL JUSTICE SYSTEMS

Preface

This volume originated in part from a series of symposia held by the Commission on Folk Law and Legal Pluralism in August of 1983 in Vancouver, Canada, as part of the XIth International Congress of Anthropological and Ethnological Sciences. Some of the essays are inspired by papers presented there, while others have been written for this book to address the themes discussed at the symposia. All of the chapters are intended to reflect the opinions and analyses of their authors as of late 1986.

As the title of the book indicates, every essay addresses some aspect of the relationship between the laws of indigenous peoples (that is, of their "folk", "customary" or "autogenous" laws), and the legal norms and processes of the states which have emerged upon their territories. As the individual titles of the twenty essays demonstrate, the subject is worldwide and varied. Ordering them into categories has been difficult. While acknowledging that any such ordering inevitably entails arbitrariness, we have sought a scheme which would stimulate constructive comparisons and contrasts.

An easy or rather, facile method would have been a geographical classification, according to the states or regions within which each indigenous people or group of peoples was located. We rejected this, because we believe that comparisons between states and regions can be revealing, and are not encouraged by a division which assumes the importance of mere geographic differences between them. Furthermore, this collection of essays is not intended to be comprehensive in global terms, although it does reflect considerable regional diversity. A variant, more tenable form of this ordering would have distinguished between the industrialised states in which indigenous peoples are small minorities, and other states. Such an ordering would have separated North America, Australia, and perhaps parts of South America, from the rest of the world, and have drawn attention to the similarities in the present circumstances of life of Indians, Inuit and Metis in the Americas and Aboriginals in Australia. We are convinced that the struggles of the indigenous peoples of these regions and their supporters can be strengthened by an acquaintance with each other s experiences. Nevertheless, we did not wish to stress these possibilities at the expense of implying that the experiences of the many other indigenous peoples in different parts of the world had little to offer those of the Americas and Australia, or vice versa.

Looking, consequently, to the widest comparative possibilities of the subject, our principal distinction has been between those studies which treat of the general relations between indigenous law and the state, and which aim to draw conclusions which are true of the entire field of social activity in a state, and those which explore more detailed questions about particular aspects of social activity. Within the former class, we distinguish between those general inquiries which advance evaluation and policy-arguments (Part I), and those which observe and analyse relations which exist or have existed in practice (Part II). The discussions of more specific issues have been grouped in three categories. Some concern the rules or practice of actual or potential constitutional laws (Part III). Some examine aspects of the law of the family and associated questions of personal status (Part IV). A further group focuses on the criminal justice systems of states, and the manner in which they deal with what they regard as deviancy issues rendered all the more sensitive and intractable by the fact that conduct characterised by the state as deviant is frequently not so viewed by indigenous law, whose subjects see no justification for the state s judgment. The essays collected in this last part reveal vividly the two features of the relationship between indigenous law and the state which form the underlying refrain of the entire collection: the universal experience of conflict, and the near-universal aspiration for mutual accommodation.

The Commission on Folk Law and Legal Pluralism was established in 1978 by the International Union of Anthropological and Ethnological Sciences, and affiliated with the International Association of Legal Science, on an initiative of Professor Geert van den Steenhoven, of the Institute of Folk Law, Nijmegen, The Netherlands. The Commission s primary purpose is to encourage greater knowledge and understanding of folk law and legal pluralism, with a focus upon theoretical and practical problems resulting from the interaction of folk law and state law. Its activities include assisting in making sympathetic and constructive contributions to the solution of problems connected with the interaction of folk law and state law, and thus to the future of indigenous, ethnic and social groups, governed by folk law, in the modern world. Lawyers, anthropologists, and other specialists from all regions of the world, concerned with folk law either in theory or in practice, participate in the work of the Commission. This volume is published on behalf of the Commission, which recommends the essays as worthy of consideration, while not holding itself committed to any particular views expressed therein.

This volume is the third to emanate from proceedings of the Commission. Others have been: *People's Law and State Law: the Bellagio Papers* (eds. Antony Allott and Gordon R. Woodman; Foris, Dordrecht; 1985); and the *Journal of Legal*

Pluralism, No. 23 (1985), a special number containing another selection of papers from the Vancouver symposia. A fourth volume is now in preparation, containing papers presented at a symposium on Formal and Informal Social Security held in 1986 in Tutzing, West Germany.

Readers interested in participating in the activities of the Commission are invited to write to the Secretariat, c/o Institute of Folk Law, Catholic University, Postbus 9049, 6500KK Nijmegen, The Netherlands.

The editors of this volume wish to thank the long-suffering contributors for their tolerance of and ready compliance with repeated requests for amendments and additional information, and their acceptance of our similarly repeated apologies for delays; and the publishers for their friendliness and skill in helping us along the road to completion of a work which, we hope, will contribute to an understanding of the requirements of justice for indigenous peoples around the world.

Bradford W. Morse
University of Ottawa
Canada

Gordon R. Woodman
University of Birmingham
Britain

April 1987

Introductory Essay: The State's Options

Bradford W. Morse and Gordon R. Woodman

INTRODUCTORY ESSAY: THE STATE'S OPTIONS

Bradford W. Morse and Gordon R. Woodman

I. Considerations in the construction of a comparative theory

The common feature of the papers in this volume is a concern with the policies of states toward the customary laws of indigenous peoples and the impact of these policies. Within this common frame they examine contrasting solutions and non-solutions to different problems in various societies. The practical utility of such studies within each country is great. Since the considerable variation in experience hinders comparison, little work has been done to date to build a comparative theory for state policies toward customary laws. It is necessary to start building such a theory, such as that which is being constructed for dispute institutions (e.g., in Abel 1973; F. von Benda-Beckmann 1985; Griffiths 1985), in order to learn from the experiences of other societies in a way that is translatable to one's own.

It is not difficult to designate, in very broad terms, the main policies regarding indigenous customary laws which may be pursued within state law. State law may replace, reform or conserve the norms and concepts of customary law. It may follow different policies for different areas of one system of customary law, for example, by replacing the customary law of wrongs, reforming that of marriage, and conserving that of land tenure. States may also choose to respect the continuing autonomy of indigenous peoples in part or in full so that their law remains intact, and possibly vital and independent of state intervention. This volume will concentrate largely upon situations in which states have sufficient authority, or strength, to be in a position to decide how their law will relate to customary law. Thus, we shall examine the state's options in this essay. This is, however, emphatically not intended to suggest that indigenous peoples do not also have their options a matter that receives some attention elsewhere in this collection.

Such a broad typology naturally needs refinement. Some possible schemes are indicated in the essays which follow: one may cite Burman's references to the possibility of customary laws being complementary to, indifferent to, or defiant of state law each a condition which can be affected, or indeed produced, by state law activity; or Havemann's distinctions between state law policies of indigenization and autonomization of social control institutions, and his consideration (citing Svenson 1978) of separation, assimilation, integration and accommodation of indigenous peoples; or Morse's four models of ways in which colonizers' legal systems may relate to indigenous legal systems. Furthermore, every paper demonstrates the possibility of focussing on limited, defined areas of legal activity in a society, such as alcohol control (Yamashiro; Tonkinson) or child care decision-making (Chisholm; Sansom and Baines).

Unfortunately, no detailed scheme for ordering their field is yet generally accepted by students of customary law in the modern state. They frequently find it necessary, in locating their chosen issues, to use somewhat vague, general indicators. Zion, for example, introduces his discussion by referring to the possibility of state law "using" Navajo custom, while the reference to the Australian Law Reform Commission on aboriginal customary law spoke of the possibility of Australian law "applying" customary law (Crawford, Hennessy and Fisher). Such general terms are useful as the means of preliminary indication of the general category of issue in question without foreclosing possible lines of exploration. They must, however, eventually be replaced by a more precise apparatus if we are to proceed to fruitful comparative studies using the findings of these specific investigations.

It is not yet possible to propose a full comparative theory of state policies toward customary law in a global sense. The considerable empirical research so far available demonstrates that there are many types of policies and very many gradations within these types. All will need to be specified, analysed and exemplified. This introductory essay attempts a preliminary, and relatively simple task. It starts from the obvious fact that every policy is implemented through a multitude of particular measures. We shall attempt to classify the types of measures which are the components of an operati?ve policy. It is hoped that this will serve as a first step in the development of a general theory of practical usefulness drawing upon the research and analysis represented by this volume as a whole. Although we realize that numerous motivations and objectives may underlie the option any particular state may select, this aspect remains for futher consideration in future.

The discussion will not primarily be directed to the measures which state laws may include with regard to non-indigenous groups, such as immigrant ethnic groups, nor to groups defined by non-ethnic features, such as the adherents of a religion, the members of a profession, trade or sporting club, or any of the other groups which flourish in human societies and have their own systems of customary laws (Galanter 1981).[1] Nevertheless, the typology may well be applicable to state laws' measures with regard to those other customary laws. Furthermore, it may be applicable to the initiatives taken within a customary law with regard to state law or with regard to any other laws with which that customary law co-exists. It may thus contribute to the development of a general theory of legal pluralism.

For the present purpose, following with some modification the analysis of Hart (1961), law will be considered to consist of two types of norms, namely: primary norms, "rules of obligation" in Hart's term, or imperatives (such as, killing is forbidden and subject to specified sanctions); and secondary norms, "power-conferring rules", or rules giving defined, valid effect to designated acts (such as, the performance of a specified ceremony forms a marriage).[2] These types of norms will be referred to respectively as "imperative norms" and "norms of validation". It will be necessary to consider the various forms of measures which state law may include with regard to each type of norm in customary law. It will also be convenient to classify some measures of state law as operating upon concepts (such as "family"), rather than upon complete norms of customary law. A concept is only one element of a norm, but in a legal system one concept may be an element in a number of norms. It will be clearer to consider a measure affecting such a concept as one measure affecting one (frequently-used) concept rather than as a series of (identical) measures affecting a number of norms.

A. Negative Measures

These are norms of state law which contradict those of customary law. They entail the use of state power actively to discourage social acceptance of customary law, and so tend against its continued existence. In most systems of state law this class of norms is the broadest in legal scope of all those which bear on customary law. It falls into two categories, of state norms which prohibit the observance of customary-law norms, and of those which negate the effects of customary norms of validation, respectively. Each category is subdivisible.

1. Prohibition

(a) This may be subdivided first according to the types of conduct prohibited.

(i) First, state law may prohibit conduct which is *required* by an *imperative norm* of customary law. This is the most direct form of conflict possible between state law and customary law. Instances given by Yamashiro and Tonkinson are cases where elders of a community, by performing their customary-law duties to maintain social order by preventing the importation of alcohol into the community, would in the view of state law be committing assaults and other wrongs. A further example is offered by Bell on Aboriginal Women, in which state law may prohibit women from entering land where they are required to perform customary ceremonies. This type of state norm may affect a portion only of a class of acts required by a customary-law imperative norm. For example, state law may prohibit obedience to some, but not all commands of a customary chief; or, in the British colonial practice, it may prohibit the observance only of those customs which are "repugnant to natural justice, equity and good conscience" (Morse; Richstone; Woodman).

(ii) Secondly, state law may prohibit conduct which is *permitted* by customary law as the conditioning conduct of a *norm of validation*. For example, in prohibiting a customary practice of child betrothal, state law prohibits acts which are permitted although not required by customary law, but which if done produce a legal status.

(b) An alternative subdivision of prohibitions is according to their mode of expression.

(i) First, state law may *directly* designate certain conduct, required by a customary imperative norm or having legal consequences under a customary norm of validation, as prohibited, such as infanticide of physically handicapped children, or precise ceremonies, such as the potlach and ghost dance in Canada.

(ii) Secondly, such conduct may be *incidentally* prohibited by a broad state norm which also applies to other forms of conduct. Such prohibitions are common in that type of state law which was originally formulated for application in another society (e.g., the mother country of a colony). The laws in force in colonial states frequently prohibit incidentally many of the customary-law practices of the colonized. For example, the common law of assault may incidentally make illegal the infliction of customary-law punishments (Crawford *et al.*). To avoid such prohibition while retaining the general rule, it is necessary to introduce measures which specifically exempt the customarily permitted practices. This may be referred to as "recognition" (Crawford *et al.*, also referring to it more particularly as "specific exclusion"), but in the present analysis is merely an absence of prohibition. When the implications of incidental prohibition are exposed and criticised, there may be attempts to defend them on the principle of equal treatment for all citizens. This may then lead to a policy of indigenization of the institutions of enforcement as an alternative method of accommodating the original population within the settler system (Havemann).

2. Denial of validity

By this type of measure state law negates a customary norm of validation by depriving an act of the legal consequences which would otherwise be conferred upon it by that customary norm. For example, state law may provide that conveyances of land according to customary law are not to effect transfers of title. Such a provision may be accompanied by another which prohibits the act (category 1(a)(ii) above), but need not. Equally it is possible, although less common, for an act to be prohibited but not deprived of legal consequences, as when for example persons are forbidden to exercise a legal customary power (e.g., practising traditional medicine within a state insured health scheme) without being deprived of that power. The present category of measure is different from that whereby an act which has a certain effect in customary law is merely denied a corresponding effect in state law: this is a case of denial of that particular type of incorporation, referred to below as recognition of norms of validation.

As in the case of prohibitions, a denial of validity may be made (i) *directly* or (ii) *incidentally.* The latter occurs inter alia when state law provides that a certain legal effect is to be produced exclusively by a given class of act, and thereby excludes the production of that effect in customary law by the act which has hitherto produced it. It is likely to occur only when some elements of customary law are already incorporated in state law. An instance would be a wills statute providing that no form of will other than that provided for should effect any disposal of property, when the system of state law recognised the validity of customary-law property titles.

Such negative measures of either type in state law may be socially ineffective in the sense that they may fail to change the actions and perceptions of validity of those who accept customary law. It seems likely that this is usually the case. (See, e.g., Elberg; Morse, on "the model of rejection".) In this event there will continue in that society an extensive and deep legal pluralism marked by contradictions between the legal systems. This is to be contrasted with types of legal pluralism internal to state law, to be mentioned in the next section, and deep pluralism accompanied by mutual acknowledgement of separate spheres of jurisdiction, mentioned in the last section.

B. Positive Measures

Here we consider the various ways in which state law may "recognise", "incorporate" or "acknowledge" customary laws. The implementation of any such measure requires the state to obtain information about the content of customary law, a process which is subject to difficulty and danger of error (various aspects of which are particularly discussed by Bell on Aboriginal Women; Grant; Woodman; and Zion). There are two main categories of which the second is extensive and susceptible of multiple subdivision.

1. Admittance as fact

This is a relatively superficial measure which some observers, and even those who administer it, may consider not to amount to an acceptance of the legal nature of customary law. It is effectuated in the process of applying a norm of state law which may have been formulated without reference to customary law.

Every legal norm requires the existence of certain facts as a condition for its application, and some norms provide further that the particular mode of their application is to depend upon certain details of those facts. The conditioning facts can be a category of social behaviour which includes the acceptance of customary-law norms. In such a case, the application of the non-customary norm requires the admittance of existing (accepted) customary law as a relevant fact. Examples are a court's taking into account the existence of customary law in sentencing a convicted person according to general state rules which require the social environment and beliefs of the criminal to be considered (Bell on Sentencing; Conn; Crawford *et al.*; Finkler; Morse), and the determination of whether proven conduct was "reasonable" when state law sets reasonableness as a criterion (Grant). Such recognition may be given not only to customary laws but also to customary practices which are not regarded as obligatory (Bell, id.). These, however, are not our present concern.

It might be thought that this form of "recognition" was nothing more than the consistent application of non-customary norms to fact-situations within their scope, and that it involved no adjustment of state law in response to customary law. It is indeed a type of measure which is often not accompanied by any full recognition of customary law of the type considered below, and it may, therefore, be viewed in some circumstances as an insignificant concession which may assist resistance to significant recognition (Conn). However, state laws have on occasion been blind to the facts of customary law when first encountered, even when, in the terms of their own norms, those facts were relevant to their application. In such circumstances, measures of the present type may tend to induce greater regard for customary law when they expressly assert that relevant social facts include customary law. (Grant advocates such a development, perhaps through case-law, as does Finkler in his "first approach".) Moreover, the existence of customary law may be a ground for advocating a change in the stated factual conditions of application of state law norms so as to include certain instances of customary law acceptance. Examples are: various changes in the rules of child placement reported and advocated by Chisholm, reported as having been recommended by Crawford *et al.*, and impliedly advocated by Sansom and Baines; the changes in the law on alcohol-induced crimes advocated by Yamashiro and Tonkinson; and possible changes towards "an entirely new correctional system, based on the traditional normative structure and system of sanctions", mentioned by Finkler. State laws changed in such ways may acknowledge the reasons for change by including express reference to customary law, as in the provisions of the statute discussed by Bell on Sentencing, and of the recommendation reported by Crawford *et al.*, but it is equally possible for the effect on customary law to be implied.

2. Incorporation as law

By this type of measure state law admits into its own body of norms a customary-law norm or portion of a norm. (Morse gives instances of this as "the model of incorporation".) A norm thus incorporated may be either an imperative or a validating norm. Incorporation would seem always to require some express statement, but the statement need not rehearse the terms of the incorporated norm.

(a) We may classify incorporation first according to the various elements of customary law which may be incorporated.

(i) Imperative norms are incorporated when acts required by customary law, such as observance of a dietary prohibition or the avoidance of adultery, receive enforcement by state legal prescription of sanctions. This may be called *enforcement of imperative norms.* Even if the imperative norm enforced by the state is identical to that of customary law, the degree and quality of compulsion are certain to differ, so that the effect of this measure is not to maintain unchanged the practice under customary law (as may be seen from Schechter).

(ii) Norms of validation may be incorporated by measures which give specified acts the same legal effect in state law as they have in customary law. This may be called *recognition of norms of validation,* and is exemplified when state law accepts performance of the customary-law requisites of a gift or a marriage as constituting a legally valid transfer of property or marriage. The latter is illustrated by a case referred to by Richstone.

A further refinement of this instance is needed. The immediate effect of a norm of validation is to establish that a particular type of act has a specified legal consequence in a general sense, such as the formation of a marriage. This consequence may in turn be a condition for the operation of various further norms of the system, which have more particular effects. In the example of the formation of marriage, instances of such further norms would be those imposing particular duties on spouses and those conferring state social welfare entitlements on married women. It is possible for these further norms to differ in this respect, however, so that for some the customary-law norm of validity provides a means of satisfying the conditions for their operation, while simultaneously for others it does not. Thus Australian law may come to recognise aboriginal customary marriage for some purposes but not for others (Crawford *et al.*). This may be referred to as *selective recognition* [of norms of validation]. The Australian Law Reform Commission's notion of "functional recognition" is a sub-type of this (id.). In the analytically simpler case of *total recognition,* the customary norm of validation is recognised for all the purposes of all norms of state law. Enforcement of imperative norms and recognition of norms of validation are referred to together as "recognition by translation of rules" by the Australian Law Reform Commission (id.).

(iii) A concept of customary law is incorporated when to a concept employed in a norm of state law there is attributed a meaning which is the same as or which includes that attributed to a concept in customary law. This *recognition of concepts* occurs, for example, when a state law employs the concept of "family", and it is accepted for the purpose of that norm that the term "family" either means exclusively or includes a family as defined in customary law (a possibility considered by Grant). It may seem to raise difficult questions as to whether the customary-law concept is in fact equivalent to the non-customary-law concept (Crawford *et al.*, referring to the provision as "recognition by translation of institutions"; Elberg). However, under the present scheme these questions may be classified as questions of choice between selective recognition and *total* recognition of norms of validation. Recognition of concepts also may be total, in which case the concept is interpreted to have or include the customary-law meaning on its every occurrence in the norms of state law, or *selective,* where on some occasions it does not.

(b) Another mode of subdividing the incorporation of customary law as law is according to the degree of detail of customary norms which is included in state norms.

(i) *Incorporation by reference* occurs in so far as the incorporating state law does not spell out the norms or meanings of concepts of customary law, but rather leaves them to be ascertained elsewhere. Thus British colonial law enjoined the courts generally to observe customary law in certain categories of cases, but they were required to ascertain its content by hearing evidence when such cases arose (Woodman).

(ii) *Incorporation by replication* occurs in so far as formal, authoritative statements of state norms themselves set out the content of norms of customary law. The clearest instance arises where a body of customary-law norms is reduced into a written code which is enacted as state legislation. The Greenland Criminal Code contains instances, although apparently in practice these are not always effectuated in accordance with the makers' intentions (Schechter). This type of incorporation may also be the eventual result of the research reported by Grant, who explains some of the difficulties in compiling such a code. However, it is possible that the people there would be content with a non-statutory code which was incorporated into state law by reference, or even which was authoritative only in the field of customary-law jurisdiction. The Australian Law Reform Commission noted that recognition of aboriginal law might be by specific words, or by reference (Crawford *et al.*). The process in the courts of common-law Africa of establishing customary law by precedent has produced a trend from incorporation by reference (mentioned in the last paragraph) to incorporation by replication as there has developed a body of binding judgments stating the norms of customary law (Woodman).

Any of these positive measures may be introduced by any institution with legislative competence in state law. Hitherto in the common law world much has occurred through judicial law-making (recounted by Woodman for instances of incorporation as law, and advocated by Grant for instances of admittance as fact). Much debate about future developments contemplates activity by legislative bodies of various ranks (e.g., Bayly; Crawford *et al.*). It is not unusual for broad measures to be enacted by central legislatures, which delegate their detailed elaboration to inferior legislatures.

Each type of incorporation as law may be applied to one norm or concept in isolation (Crawford *et al.*, referring to "specific" as distinct from "general" provisions). However, this rarely occurs because usually any such measure is taken as part of a programme of adjustment of state law which can be implemented only through a complex series of norms.

The analysis of positive measures in terms of admittance and incorporation is of measures under which state law undergoes no diminution of its scope, but changes its content, in that customary-law elements are added to or substituted for some of its existing elements. On each occasion some state law nearly always the vastly greater proportion of it remains unchanged. When the measures consist of the addition of norms, the process usually entails the creation or extension of legal pluralism within the body of state law, as, for example, when an additional form of marriage or type of family receives recognition. Consequently, questions of internal conflicts of laws, in the form of choice of law issues, arise (Richstone). Some of these, such as the classification of persons for the purpose of determining who is to be affected by the newly admitted or recognised customary laws, may become the subjects of acute controversy, as for example that in Brazil as to the proper criterion for classifying a person as an Indian (Conn; see also Bell on Sentencing).

There would appear to be no reason why any type of recognition of norms should not occur in respect of both procedural and substantive norms, assuming that both exist in any system of customary law. (This seems likely, even though procedural norms are sometimes said to predominate, e.g., by Zion. Both types receive prominence in the account of Sansom and Baines.) Thus the dispute settlement procedures of state law may incorporate procedural norms of customary law, and the substantive norms applied in state law adjudication may incorporate the rights and duties of the substantive norms of customary law. Since particular procedures are often inseparable in practice from the social institutions within which they operate, the incorporation of procedural norms is likely to be narrowly limited unless there is a profound reform of state institutions. For example, while state rules on the reception of evidence may be changed to incorporate certain of the rules which operate under customary procedures, it is not easy to reproduce a complete body of customary rules of adjudication within a framework of state law. Such may perhaps occur if, for example, it is provided that state adjudicatory procedures are not to begin until customary dispute settlement procedures have been followed. The effect of this in practice, however, may be largely to terminate the state procedures.

Thus, if it is desired to give full legal effect to customary procedures, this is likely to be attempted not by positive measures, but by measures of exclusive acknowledgement (discussed below), whereby the operation of certain state procedures is formally terminated and replaced by customary-law procedures outside the jurisdiction of state law. This observation leads one to feel some doubt about the possibility of "incorporating aboriginal customs and traditions" into newly designed forms of self-government (Bayly, reporting the advice of the Canadian Minister of Indian and Northern Affairs). If on the other hand customary procedures are not incorporated but customary substantive norms are, the latter, because they are implemented through non-customary procedures, will not perform functions closely comparable to those they fulfilled within the customary system (K. von Benda-Beckmann 1985; Woodman).

Caution is necessary in generalising about the effects in practice on a legal system of normative change, and even more in generalising about the social consequences. However, Woodman argues, on the basis both of example and of necessary effect, that the incorporation of norms of customary law invariably entails their distortion: that the norms as stated in the state legal system will not be coterminous with those of the non-state (folk) customary law, and cannot perform identical functions. The distortion may perhaps be more clearly envisaged when we consider cases where incorporated elements of customary law are closely related in the state system to non-customary norms. For example, the customary norm of validity providing for the formalities of marriage, or the customary concept of family, may be incorporated into a state law in which their interpretation and use may be in procedures which deeply contrast with customary procedures, and which give consequences to marriage and to family membership which are utterly different from those in customary law.[3] Sometimes the change becomes even more obvious through measures designed to strengthen the observance of customary law by its reform: examples would be the introduction by the state of registration requirements for (already recognised) customary-law marriages or land titles. Furthermore, it is because of this distortion and difference in function that some would argue that policies employing incorporation, such as those of "co-optation", will have inimical effects on the cultures out of which customary law emerges (Havemann).

3. Measures of Acknowledgement

Since there are relatively few examples of such measures in actuality this part of the discussion will not attempt a high degree of detailed precision.

These are measures by which state law expressly or impliedly provides that state institutions do not have an exclusive capacity to perform certain functions to do with law, which customary law is competent to perform. They are referred to variously as entailing "side-by-side existence" of customary and state law as compared with "incorporation" (Bell on Aboriginal Women), as "recognition by general exclusion" involving local autonomy or self-determination (Crawford *et al.*), and as "total avoidance" (Morse). Frequently they involve entrenchment of the measure in the state's constitution (Richstone). They may be compared with the provisions of a state's private international law which assert that specified types of functions are validly performed by the institutions of other states. Through a measure of acknowledgement state law accepts the capacity of customary law to constitute an institution with legal powers, such as a traditional assembly with power to enact law or to adjudicate in disputes. This is not intended to refer only to rigidly structured customary-law "institutions". In some cases the notion may need to be broadened to include the operation of very general social opinion, for example in creating norms of customary law (Richstone). In cases of clearly structured institutions, the use of this type of measure requires that they should have been established by customary law, not by state laws which incorporate customary laws. This requirement will be explained and illustrated in the first section.

The possible measures may be classified in three ways.

(a) The power which is the subject-matter of the measure may be either of two types.

(i) In the case of *legislative acknowledgement*, state law accepts that state legislative institutions do not have exclusive competence, and that an institution of customary law can have powers of law-making derived from customary law. Further measures may then provide that the norms made by the institution are to be incorporated into state law and so applied in state institutions. However, this is not necessary, and will not occur if concurrent measures of acknowledgement provide that the application of these norms is to be exclusively the function of customary-law institutions. (These would be measures of exclusive *norm-applying acknowledgement* as classified below).

It has been suggested above that measures of acknowledgement must all refer to power-bearing institutions constituted by norms of customary law. In the case of legislative institutions this means that acknowledgement does not occur when state law establishes an institution, even one which resembles a former customary-law institution, and confers on it legislative powers, even if they are the powers of that former customary-law institution. This is at most a measure of incorporation of norms of validity. For example, if the state establishes "native councils", defines their membership, and confers on them powers according to customary law to make by-laws, this amounts to defining the powers of a non-customary institution by incorporating (selectively or totally, by reference or by replication) customary-law norms of validation which defined the powers of a former customary institution. However, since state law may amend aspects of customary-law institutions without replacing them, it can be a question of degree whether an existing institution is a customary-law institution: the possibilites are noted by Zion, when he says that "traditional governments" may be, inter alia, so fully integrated into the state's governmental structure "that there is no difference", or may exist as a "formal and identifiable traditional government". (See also Morse, discussing the development of "carbon copies".) Therefore, policies of "accommodation" or "autonomization" (Havemann) may, but do not necessarily use measures of acknowledgement.

Perhaps the commonest instance of this measure is contained within provisions which also contain measures of incorporation as law. When a state institution, such as a court, is required to apply customary law, then, so long as customary law is expressly or impliedly defined as consisting of norms made in accordance with customary-law procedures, those law-making procedures are impliedly accepted as creating valid law. (Seen in these terms, there is no necessary difficulty in state institutions accepting the possibility of new norms replacing those which have already been incorporated by replication: Woodman 1985: 151.)

Legislative powers include powers to amend existing legislation. The powers referred to by this type of measure can in principle include the power to amend non-customary state law, if customary law confers such a power on the institution. A measure of acknowledgement may be qualified, however, and need not extend to all the customary-law powers of the institution.

(ii) Measures of norm-applying acknowledgement refer to all legal institutional powers other than that of legislation. The most apparent to the legal mind may be that of adjudication, but powers such as those of norm interpretation and norm enforcement are also included. An example of such acknowledgement arises if a state accepts the capacity of a customary court to adjudicate in a class of disputes. The requirement that the institution must have been established by customary law equally applies here. Thus in the case just put, it is necessary that the court be itself constituted by customary-law norms as opposed to state norms bearing some resemblance to former customary norms. The present instance does not include measures conferring customary-law powers of adjudication on "native courts" constituted by non-customary norms. Neither does it include the conferment of property rights on an "indigenous collective" if this institution is unknown to native custom (Bayly).

(b) The measures differ according to state law's characterisation of each.

(i) State law may assert that it has itself conferred the power on the customary institution. This may be called *acknowledgement by conferment of powers*. An example is contained in the *Alaska Native Claims Settlement Act* (Yamashiro, quoting Strickland 1982). It is the form of acknowledgement to be expected when the state claims a monopoly of legal authority, as most states do, whether in a written constitution or otherwise. After such a measure the state may continue to assert the power to amend or abrogate its acknowledgement, that is, to withdraw the powers from the customary institution. This is not essential, however, for legal doctrine can accommodate the notion of an irrevocable surrender of power. A different possible implication of acknowledgement by conferment of powers is that acts of state institutions will have overriding legal effect when they conflict with those of customary institutions. Thus, enactments of a state legislature may take effect in preference to conflicting legislation of a customary institution; or state courts may overturn the decisions of customary courts. However, this conclusion again need not necessarily be drawn as it is common for the constitutional law of a state to limit the powers of state legislatures and courts, even at the highest level.

(ii) An alternative characterisation of acknowledgement is to be made when state law asserts that it is recognising existing, legitimate powers. This may be called *acknowledgement by recognition of powers*. It implies abandonment of any dogma of a state monopoly of legitimate authority. It has existed in the past and continues in some limited instances today (Morse). Where it is introduced into an existing legal system it would seem to imply an admission of past error. A statement of the case for one demand for a measure of acknowledgement by recognition of powers, demonstrating the contentions on which it is based and indicating its implications, from an Australian Aboriginal perspective is made by Riley. An episode in another claim is recounted by Baxi (1985). The claims expressed by Riley refer primarily to legislative, while those by Baxi to adjudicative functions. The Dene "Agreement in Principle" of 1976 (Bayly) referred to both. Once such a measure has been provided, it would seem that state law cannot consistently claim to declare conclusively or to circumscribe the scope of the customary institution's powers, nor to abrogate them. However, the U.S. acknowledgement of the sovereignty of Indian nations (Morse) provides an exception to this: it is accompanied by a state claim to continue to hold overriding authority, although in practice little attempt is made to exercise this in such a way as to effect a total negation of customary law. Although this type of provision is discussed by theorists and by representatives of indigenous groups, its challenge to the state's monopolist claims renders it unlikely that there will as yet be widespread acceptance of it by state laws, as Havemann's historical account indicates. Thus the Dene Agreement in Principle was rejected, and the subsequent Denendeh Paper of 1981 claimed only a conferment of powers by state norms, with some limited incorporation of norms of validity (Bayly). That has also been the utmost effect of successfully negotiated comprehensive claims (Elberg).

These two types of claims regarding state authority are considered here as possible propositions of state law. Systems of customary law have their own norms, doctrines and claims to legitimacy. They may have their own provisions for the acknowledgement of state law (Morse; Tonkinson). Hence the customary-law characterisation of a measure of acknowledgement may differ from that of state law. A measure expressed by state law as a conferment of power may be viewed by customary law as a belated recognition of a capacity already existing (Richstone; Riley).

(c) The measures differ according to whether state law confers on a state institution powers concurrent with those granted to or recognised as held by the customary institution.

(i) A measure of *exclusive acknowledgement* provides that the customary institution is the sole holder of powers of the type designated. Thereby state law expressly or impliedly prohibits other institutions from, for example, enacting legislation on the designated subject-matter, or hearing disputes on the designated claims. (For example, the *Indian Child Welfare Act* of 1978 in the U.S.A. does this to some degree with child protection cases.) Past and present measures in constitutional statutes in India appear to be exclusive acknowledgement by conferment of powers of the customary laws of tribal communities (Burman).

(ii) A measure of *concurrent acknowledgement* permits non-customary institutions also to exercise the powers. As in every other instance of concurrent powers, it may be necessary to establish rules of priority of effectiveness in the event of the institutions seeking to exercise their powers in ways which conflict or simply exercising them simultaneously regarding the same parties and the same event. State law may establish such rules if there has been acknowledgement by conferment of powers. Acknowledgement by recognition of powers, however, poses the difficulty that the state law necessarily concedes its lack of competence to determine the scope of the powers of the customary institution. In this case conflicts can be determined only by some overriding law, based for example upon a notion of the binding force of agreement between populations of the two constituencies.

Acknowledgement of any type produces a "deep" legal pluralism. Whereas the pluralism of positive measures consists of the existence of different bodies of norms within state law, that of acknowledgement consists of the co-existence of state law with another law. This explains the difficulty of resolving conflicts in the latter case, where there exists no all-embracing law which can provide norms superior to those of the bodies in conflict. Some would contend that this is the only true legal pluralism (Griffiths 1986).

It may appear that measures of acknowledgement are less likely to change and distort the social reality of customary law, or to produce misrepresentations of it, and that it is more likely to be left to flourish uninfluenced by state activity. This may be correct in comparison with the effects of positive measures, but possibilities of induced change will not be absent. The social phenomenon of customary law will inevitably be affected by the multifarious and intrusive activities of the modern state (as can be seen from Elberg; Sansom and Baines; and Tonkinson). Moreover, all bodies of measures of state law with regard to customary law, even those of acknowledgement, include some statements of what are deemed to be elements of customary law. These, advanced with the authority of state law, and so likely to be believed by some, will inevitably sometimes be mistaken.

Conclusion

We have attempted in this introductory essay briefly to describe our perceptions of the various individual measures which state law may contain when a body of customary law exists among some or all of its subjects. In doing so, we have tried to draw upon the experience of a number of countries through the papers which follow in order to isolate certain basic elements of the relationship between state law and customary law.

One should not expect to find single, isolated measures in any category. Development starts with a baseline of measures taken, often unconsciously, at the date when the state law first comes into contact with the customary law. These initial measures will often be negative. Lawmakers of the colonizers are then likely to introduce bundles of measures. These will often be all in the same general category, although one may find them taking contrasting measures, for example negative measures being taken or extended at the same time as measures of acknowledgement, as during the missionary period in Jigalong (Tonkinson).

When the lawmakers are unaware of the customary law, or aware of and antagonistic toward it, the measures are likely to be of the negative class. Historically, a growing knowledge of and concern with customary law has often produced measures of the positive class. These are particularly likely in states where the customary law in question is that of the bulk of the population. In such states there is likely to exist both a desire for the continued existence of customary law, urging the rejection of negative measures, and a commitment to the development of the state, which tends to encourage the rejection of measures of acknowledgement. The story of customary law in many African states may illustrate this. An early period of negative measures after the colonial establishment of the state was followed by positive measures, both under those colonial administrations which conceded some claims to indigenous self-government, and under the early governments after independence. However, it is possible that these are being superseded today by new negative measures as popular commitment to the goals of nation-building and economic development grows, and produces a demand for the replacement of customary, traditional laws.

In contrast, in states where the adherents of customary law are ethnic minorities, the driving impulse for their claims regarding customary law is a demand for the human rights of those minorities as collectivities, advanced against states viewed with suspicion and bitterness. Such minorities are likely to demand measures of acknowledgement in preference to positive measures. The failure of governmental policies of assimilation and indigenization (Havemann) can create a favourable climate in which the state is prepared to relinquish a degree of its dominance.

To test and elaborate such generalisations would require a different analysis. This discussion has attempted to classify individual, formal legal measures. The next stage is a classification of the policies which may be manifested in these measures, along with a study of the relations of those policies to social, economic and political circumstances, perhaps developing the suggestive work of Allott (1980) or Fitzpatrick (1983). That in turn would form the necessary basis for further tasks, such as: cross-cultural comparisons (should they prove possible), both for their academic interest and to inform those concerned with the policies of particular states; and the evaluation of the various policies, first in particular circumstances and later, possibly, cross-culturally. It is hoped that the present overview may have made some contribution; and that the papers which follow will further assist in the search for greater understanding of this dynamic interaction through the wealth of diverse information and insights which they present.

Notes

1. We should acknowledge the perceptiveness in this respect of the much-criticised John Austin (another aspect of whose theory we shortly reject). He was acutely aware of the social presence of many bodies of laws other than those laid down by the political sovereign, and he considered the possible types of relationship between them and the law of the sovereign, although he declined to call them "laws strictly so called". Thus he analysed the possible relationships between (in his terminology) the law of God, positive law and positive morality, namely that they might coincide, not coincide, or conflict (Austin 1954: 159-163). He further considered what is called below the "incorporation" of customary law into state law, arguing that "customs" were a type of positive morality, but that if they were "clothed with legal sanctions [in the terminology below, 'enforced'] by the sovereign one or number", they became rules of positive law (Austin 1954: 163-164).
2. The Austinian notion that all legal norms could be regarded as imperatives is generally, and correctly rejected today (Hart 1961: 26-41). Further perspectives, of particular value in the anthropology of law, are provided by F. von Benda-Beckmann. According to his concept law evaluates situation-images (facts as construed by participants) for their legal relevance according to two "dominant standards": those of permissibility and of validity (F. von Benda-Beckmann 1979: 28-31). These two types correspond to the two classes of norms just mentioned above. However, he adds a third "main standard", which is identified as "indifferent". His example of the last is the evaluation of death in the law of inheritance, where the situation-image is not judged in terms of validity or permissibility, but nevertheless is "relevant" because it carries important legal consequences. It is not intended to dissent here from this view, an adequate critical appraisal of which would require a consideration of the problem of individuation of laws. It may suffice to suggest that for the present purpose the application of this third standard of evaluation can be regarded as the use of concepts as portions of other norms of the two types already mentioned. Thus, in the example given, various norms of inheritance law employ the concept of death. Some of these are imperative norms providing for evaluation by permissibility (such as the norm that, after the death of a property-holder, the successor is required/allowed to deal with the property in specified ways), and some are norms of validity (such as the norm that, after the death of a property-holder, certain specified acts by a specified person are valid disposals of the property).

3. It has been argued elsewhere that words such as "enforcement" and "incorporation" should not be used of processes whereby elements of customary law determine the content of emerging norms of state law, because they falsely imply an identity of content (Woodman 1985: 156). For the purpose of the present analysis it seems impossible to find any more accurate terminology. The observations in this paragraph will perhaps offset the misleading aspect of the words.

References

(Undated references in the text are to papers in this volume. The two papers by Bell are referred to as "Bell on Aboriginal Women" and "Bell on Sentencing".)

ABEL, R.L. (1973)
"A comparative theory of dispute institutions in society," 8 Law & Society Review 217-347.

ALLOTT, A. (1980)
The Limits of Law. Butterworths: London.

ALLOTT, A. and G.R. WOODMAN (1985)
People's Law and State Law: the Bellagio Papers. Foris: Dordrecht.

AUSTIN, J. (1954)
The Province of Jurisprudence Determined. H.L.A. Hart (ed.), Weidenfeld and Nicolson: London.

BAXI, U. (1985)
"Popular justice, participatory development and power politics: the Lok Adalat in turmoil," in Allott and Woodman 171-186.

BENDA-BECKMANN, F. von (1979)
Property in Social Continuity: Continuity and Change in the Maintenance of Property Relationships Through Time in Minangkabau, West Sumatra. Nijhoff: The Hague.

---------- (1985)
"Some comparative generalizations about the differential use of state and folk institutions of dispute settlement," in Allott and Woodman 187-205.

BENDA-BECKMANN, F. von (1985)
"The use of folk law in West Sumatran state courts," in Allott and Woodman 77-95.

FITZPATRICK, P. (1983)
"Law, plurality and underdevelopment," in D. Sugarman (ed.), Legality, Ideology and the State. Academic Press: London and New York.

GALANTER, M. (1981)
"Justice in many rooms: courts, private ordering, and indigenous law," 19 Journal of Legal Pluralism 1-47.

GRIFFITHS, J. (1985)
"Four laws of interaction in circumstances of legal pluralism: first steps towards an explanatory theory," in Allott and Woodman, 217-227.

---------- (1986)
"What is legal pluralism?," 24 Journal of Legal Pluralism 24.

HART, H.L.A. (1961)
The Concept of Law, Clarendon Press: Oxford.

STRICKLAND, R. (1982)
Felix S. Cohen's Handbook of Federal Indian Law, Charlottesville: Michie Bobbs-Merill.

SVENSON, K. (1978)
"Indian and Metis issues in Saskatchewan to 2001," (mimeo). Regina: Department of Indian Affairs and Northern Development.

WOODMAN, G.R. (1985)
"Customary law, state courts, and the notion of institutionalization of norms in Ghana and Nigeria," in Allott and Woodman 143-163.

Part I

General Relations Between Indigenous Law and The State: Policy Arguments

Aboriginal customary laws: proposals for recognition

James Crawford, Peter Hennessy and Mary Fisher

ABORIGINAL CUSTOMARY LAWS: PROPOSALS FOR RECOGNITION

James Crawford, Peter Hennessy and Mary Fisher

I. The Aboriginal customary law reference

The completion of the Australian Law Reform Commission's Report on the *Recognition of Aboriginal Customary Laws*[1] in 1986 marks the end of the longest and largest enquiry yet conducted by the Commission and the most extensive yet into many aspects of the law which affects Australia's Aboriginal people. It involved the Commission in much inter-disciplinary research, and consultation with judges, magistrates, lawyers, police, anthropologists, linguists, sociologists, historians and government authorities in Australia and many overseas countries. Extensive discussions took place with Aboriginal men and women and Aboriginal organisations around Australia.[2] Detailed research was undertaken into Australian law and its operation, and into the law and practice of overseas countries, especially Canada, the United States, Papua New Guinea, New Zealand and other Pacific countries.

The Commission's recommendations for the recognition of Aboriginal customary laws represent the Commission's response to questions referred to it on the 9th February 1977 by the then federal Attorney-General. Specifically the Commission was asked:

> *to inquire into and report upon* whether it would be desirable to apply either in whole or in part Aboriginal customary law to Aborigines, either generally or in particular areas or to those living in tribal conditions only and, in particular:

(a) whether, and in what manner, existing courts dealing with criminal charges against Aborigines should be empowered to apply Aboriginal customary law and practices in the trial and punishment of Aborigines;
(b) to what extent Aboriginal communities should have the power to apply their customary law and practices in the punishment and rehabilitation of Aborigines; and
(c) any other related matter.

The Commission was directed to have special regard in particular to 'the need to ensure that no person should be subject to any treatment, conduct or punishment which is cruel or inhumane'.

In refering this matter to the Commission, the Attorney-General set out a number of relevant matters, including:

- the special interest of the Commonwealth in the welfare of the Aboriginal people of Australia;
- the need to ensure that every Aborigine enjoys basic human rights;
- the right of Aborigines to retain their racial identity and traditional lifestyle or, where they so desire, to adopt partially or wholly a European lifestyle;
- the difficulties that have at times emerged in the application of the existing criminal justice system to members of the Aboriginal race; and
- the need to ensure equitable, humane and fair treatment under the criminal justice system to all members of the Australian community.

II. Questions for the Commission

The Terms of Reference were open-ended in that they did not assume that Aboriginal customary laws should be recognised. It would have been possible for the Commission to reject altogether the recognition of Aboriginal customary laws. It would also have been possible to recommend the exclusion of the general Australian law from Aboriginal people and its replacement by Aboriginal customary laws. Neither proposition was supported by the Commission. The Terms of Reference emphasised the use of customary law in criminal proceedings, but they did not exclude issues of recognition in areas of personal and economic law. In fact the Commission's recommendations extend to the recognition of traditional marriages and Aboriginal child care practices, and to the recognition of hunting and fishing rights.

The second part of the Terms of Reference asked whether Aboriginal communities should have the power to apply customary laws and practices in the punishment of Aborigines. This question raised issues of 'law and order', but it also raised fundamental issues of autonomy, the solutions to which are more likely to be found in economic, social and political changes than in proposals for the recognition of Aboriginal customary laws. The recognition of customary laws should not be seen as the channel through which Aboriginal self-determination is to be achieved, given that many of the Aboriginal demands for self-government cannot be satisfied through any form of recognition of customary laws. This is true more generally: the range of problems Aborigines experience with the legal system cannot be solved by a single set of proposals relating to Aboriginal customary laws.

III. Background to the reference

In referring the reference to the Law Reform Commission, the Attorney-General indicated several reasons why the recognition of Aboriginal customary laws should be the subject of an extensive examination by a body such as the Commission. These included:

- requests from, in particular, the people of Yirrkala (Northern Territory) to be empowered to set up a form of local justice mechanism, applying at least to minor law and order matters;
- the controversy aroused by the decision of Wells J. in the South Australian Supreme Court in the case of *R v Sydney Williams* (1976), where the Judge placed the defendant, convicted of the manslaughter of an Aboriginal woman, on a two year good behaviour bond on condition that he returned to the Yalata community and obeyed the lawful orders of his tribal elders. The decision, which was construed (or rather, misconstrued) as a form of licensing of traditional punishment (i.e., spearing in the thigh), aroused considerable controversy;[3]
- the lack of adequate statistics on Aboriginal criminality;
- problems that arise between Aboriginal legal services and other legal aid schemes;
- the report for the Western Australian Royal Commission into events at Skull Creek and Laverton;[4]
- the implementation of the Law Reform Commission's recommendations in its Report No 2 on *Criminal Investigation* (1975) relating specifically to Aborigines.[5]

IV. Consultation during the reference

The breadth and complexity of these considerations, which had already been emphasised in a number of official reports calling for further study of the issues[6], made it inevitable that the Commission would be involved in a long and complex study. But additional difficulties were created by the Commission's position as a non-Aboriginal body, as a relatively small federal law reform agency engaged in a considerable number of substantial projects, and by its practice of recruiting lawyers as Commissioners to lead particular projects for fixed periods of two or three years.[7] It was inevitable that the inquiry would last longer than this, and there was thus a considerable risk of discontinuity.

The Commission engaged in extensive formal and informal consultations throughout Australia. It conducted a number of rather longer field trips to particular areas, and prepared a series of consultative papers which were circulated widely for comment.

- *Public hearings* Formal public hearings were held in 38 centres around Australia, leading to over 3,000 pages of transcript. Less formal meetings, including some return visits, were held in at least as many other places. Many of the formal public hearings, and some of the informal meetings, were conducted in the form of separate men's and women's meetings, in an attempt to obtain input from Aboriginal women, who on some matters were reluctant to speak in the presence of the men. Women researchers from the Commission, and in one case a female Commissioner (Professor Alice E.-S. Tay of the University of Sydney Law School), together with consultants such as Dr. Diane Bell, assisted in this process.
- *Publications* Over the course of the Reference the Commission produced three Discussion Papers summarising its thinking on the Reference and setting out tentative proposals. In addition 14 detailed Research Papers and 9 Field Reports were prepared.[8] The Field Reports set out details of the major field trips undertaken by the Commission. The field trips were a means of gathering information about the scope of Aboriginal customary laws as well as providing a forum for discussing proposals for recognition. Simplified English versions of the Commission's Discussion Papers and translations of these summaries into some major Aboriginal languages, were made. These simplified versions were distributed in print, and read onto cassette tapes for distribution.

- *Submissions* The Commission received a large number (over 500) of written submissions from a wide variety of individuals and organisations, Aboriginal and non-Aboriginal. These vary from single page comments to extensive papers. In addition to such written comments, there was feedback from a wide range of people, including approximately thirty people appointed by the Attorney-General at the recommendation of the Commission as honorary consultants.[9] Meetings with consultants (Aboriginal and non-Aboriginal) were held in most of the capital cities.

The Commission as an official non-Aboriginal body did its best to try to come to grips in writing with an oral culture. A number of mistakes were made (e.g., in not engaging in practical experiment in certain areas such as community justice mechanisms, in failing to implement at an earlier stage better systems of consultation with Aboriginal women), although when these were pointed out attempts were made to correct them. At a more basic level the consultative problem is intractable, given the vast areas involved, the logistic and resource difficulties, and the inevitable complexity of many of the proposals. In these circumstances a considerable onus was cast on Aboriginal organisations (e.g., Aboriginal legal aid organisations), which possess the expertise in these areas and have a closer perception of Aboriginal needs and demands. Despite the difficulties, the Commission concluded that its consultations were sufficient to enable it to make the proposals set out in its Report. But it stressed that it did not represent Aboriginal opinion, and was cautious about making judgments about Aboriginal opinion.[10]

V. Historical context

The Reference needs to be seen in the context of the history of Aboriginal-/European relations in Australia. In 1788, the year of British settlement of Eastern Australia, the country was inhabited by indigenous peoples with their own established traditions, practices, social structures and laws. Aborigines are believed to have occupied Australia for at least 40,000 years before white settlement.[11] The Australian continent (including Tasmania) was divided into hundreds of tribal areas, with many different language units. There were possibly as many as six hundred distinct dialects or languages.[12] Official British policy stressed the importance of friendly relations with Aborigines, but the reality of the frontier frequently meant violence, dispossession and degradation. Conflicts between settlers and Aborigines, and the devastation of introduced diseases and alcohol, reduced the Aboriginal population during the first hundred years of settlement from an estimated 300,000 to 60,000.[13] Many who survived had their traditional way of life destroyed or suppressed. In Tasmania the effects of British settlement were particularly devastating.[14] Growing awareness within Australia of the mistreatment of Aborigines by colonial settlers and criticism of such mistreatment in England led to a policy of 'protection'. Aboriginal protectors were appointed and there was an increased missionary influence. This preceded a more formal policy of protection, resulting in the segregation of Aborigines into reserves, restrictions on the contact of other Aboriginal people with settlers, prohibitions on the use of alcohol and the removal of part Aboriginal children from their families. Later, during the 1930s and 1940s official policy began to favour the absorption or assimilation of all Aboriginal people into a 'white' Australia. Protectionism was phased out, to be replaced by health, education and housing programs designed to ensure that all Aborigines achieved the same manner of living as white Australians. Later still, in the 1960s and 1970s, such policies of paternalism were challenged and were ultimately reformulated under the label of 'integration'. Loss of Aboriginal identity was no longer proclaimed as the ultimate goal. Instead Aboriginal people were, it was argued, to a certain extent at least entitled to retain their racial identity, their languages, customs and distinct lifestyles, presumably including their customary laws. At present Australian policy is variously described in terms of self-determination or self-management for Aboriginal people. This has led to the granting of Aboriginal land rights in some parts of Australia, and the encouragement of Aboriginal self-management in programs such as housing, education, health, child care and the provision of legal services.

The legacy of some 200 years of European settlement is reflected in the disadvantages and low socio-economic status experienced today by many Aboriginal people. Apart from social and economic problems, the maintenance of order presents difficulties in many Aboriginal communities. This is in part due to the devastating effect of alcohol and the displacement of traditional social structures. New authority structures such as Aboriginal Councils have been created. Reliance on the payment of welfare benefits in cash and the availability of store-bought food affects kin obligations and responsibilities and reduces traditional forms of economic independence. Social structures are affected by western education. Cultural identity is likely to be affected in as yet unforseen ways by new technologies, particularly satellite communications.[15] Nevertheless, in many communities the holders of traditional authority still remain influential. In some areas the outstation movement has assisted in a revival of Aboriginal traditions and cultures; although some say the 'revival' is merely a trick of perception and publicity, involving the emergence into visibility of what was previously only suppressed or hidden.

It is tempting to present the impact of the European settlement on Aboriginal people in terms of statistics. Admittedly the statistics on Aboriginal disadvantage are inadequate, and those that do exist are frequently misinterpreted, or presented without adequate analysis. Nonetheless they do indicate that in terms of housing, education, income, unemployment, health and contact with the criminal justice and child welfare systems, Aboriginal people suffer far greater disadvantage than other groups within Australian society. To take several examples:

- In New South Wales, as at November 1985, 12% of children in substitute care (excluding adoption) were Aborigines, although Aborigines make up less than 1% of the population of the State.[16]
- In South Australia, as at August 1983, the Department of Community Welfare estimated that Aborigines represented 15-16% of all children under State care and control, although they made up 0.9% of the total population of the State.[17]
- National Prison Census figures for 1984 indicate that Aborigines comprise approximately 10.5% of the overall prison population.[18]

The same National Prison Census indicated that 14.3% of all persons imprisoned for 'offensive behaviour' offences were Aboriginal or Torres Strait Islander. Aborigines and Torres Strait Islanders are similarly disproportionately represented for other good order offences (26.5% of all prisoners).[19] The overall pattern is similar. Speaking of some earlier statistics, the then Director of the Australian Institute of Criminology stated:

> These are dramatic rates of imprisonment by any standards and for any community. Just to quote them is to question their justification. You have to believe either that Aboriginals are the most criminal minorities in the world or that there is something inherently wrong with the system which uses imprisonment so liberally.[20]

These figures reflect the disadvantage, dislocation and depressed socio-economic circumstances, against the background of which an examination of Aboriginal customary laws must take place. In common with many other indigenous people Aborigines share a problem of being an indigenous minority in a non-indigenous society:

> As a group, Aboriginals still cannot participate fully, effectively and equally in the day-to-day life of a community, notwithstanding the fact

that changes in the law and social attitudes have occurred. The recent history of Aboriginal people is one of hostile dealings with non-Aboriginals and with policies of governments which have had an extraordinary impact on the Aboriginal people's consciousness. This has helped separate Aboriginals as a group within Australian society.[21]

VI. The non-recognition of Aboriginal customary laws

Although Australia had been inhabited for some 40,000 years by an indigenous population with its own systems of laws, cultures and practices, the Colonial Office treated Australia in 1788 as uninhabited by a sovereign or sovereigns or by people with institutions or laws. No treaties were made with Aboriginal groups, as occurred in North America and New Zealand. Aborigines were treated as British subjects, subject to British law as individuals, not communities or nations despite the reality that they had no understanding of the general legal system and adhered to their own customary laws. The policy was stated, for example, by George Grey in 1837:

> [I]t is necessary from the moment the Aborigines of this Country are declared British Subjects they should, as far as possible, be taught that the British Laws are to supersede their own, so that any native, who is suffering under their own customs, may have the power of an appeal to those of Great Britain, or, to put this in its true light, that all authorised persons should in all instances be required to protect a native from the violence of his fellows, even though they be in the execution of their own laws. So long as this is not the case, the older natives have at their disposal the means of effectually preventing the civilization of any individuals of their own tribes, and those among them, who may be inclined to adapt themselves to the European habits and mode of life, will be deterred from so doing by their fear of the consequences that the displeasure of others may draw down upon them.[22]

Consistently with this policy the entire body of English law was applied throughout Australia without regard to the existence of Aboriginal customary laws. This non-recognition applied as much in civil as in criminal matters: it involved the non-recognition of traditional marriages[23] and the denial of land rights just as much as the refusal to recognise Aboriginal customary laws as a defence to crimes defined by British law.[24]

The injustice of this policy was noted at the time. In 1837 the British House of Commons Select Committee on Aborigines stated that to require from Aborigines 'the observation of our laws would be absurd and to punish their non-observance of them by severe penalties would be palpably unjust'.[25] These were strong sentiments, but ones which were not reflected in the actual recommendations of the Select Committee, or in any other action taken at the time or later. It became an axiom of British and then Australian law that Aborigines, whatever their actual lack of contact with or awareness of the law, were subject to it without qualifications or exception.

This policy of non-recognition was tempered in practice by the reluctance of law enforcement agencies to become involved in disputes between Aborigines, and by policies of non-prosecution and by mitigation of sentence. During the 1920s quite substantial attempts were made to accord recognition. In Western Australia a special court was created for Aboriginal cases.[26] In the Northern Territory an Aboriginal tribunal was proposed, though never implemented.[27] In Queensland Aboriginal courts and Aboriginal police were established in 1939, and in modified form these still operate.[28] In the Northern Territory juries for Aboriginal people were abolished except for capital offences.[29] The Supreme Court of the Northern Territory was given a discretion not to apply the death penalty to Aborigines convicted of murder, and Aboriginal customary laws were to be taken into account in sentence.[30] In Western Australia the death penalty for Aborigines was abolished and a maximum of ten years imprisonment was substituted: Aboriginal confessions and admissions were made inadmissible for any offence punishable by death.[31] But few of these provisions remain today.

Recognition as it exists today tends to be piecemeal and to take the form of specific responses to particular needs. For example, the courts have been prepared to take customary laws into account in determining a defendant's intent in criminal cases, in determining whether certain defences (e.g., provocation) are available and in passing sentence.[32] The courts have at times regarded the loss of traditional status and privilege as a compensable injury in motor vehicle accidents.[33] In one Northern Territory decision a traditional marriage was recognised for the purposes of adoption.[34] At the legislative level recognition has occurred through the granting of land to Aboriginal people on the basis of traditional association (in particular in the Northern Territory and South Australia)[35], recognition of traditional marriages for certain purposes (Commonwealth, Northern Territory and Victoria)[36], provisions recognising Aboriginal child care practices (Victoria and the Northern Territory)[37], sacred sites legislation[38] and exemptions from wildlife, conservation and fisheries laws to enable Aboriginal people to engage in traditional hunting and fishing.[39] Recognition, whether judicial or legislative, has been particular rather than general, has been confined to particular jurisdictions, and has often depended upon the exercise of discretions rather than existing as of right. It has been a piecemeal approach to the problems facing Aboriginal people rather than a reasoned response on the part of the general legal system. This constitutes an important aspect of the background to the Commission's Report.

VII. Some issues underlying the recognition debate

Arguments about recognition of customary laws tend to start with, and sometimes get no further than definitional questions, or the accumulation of general arguments for or against recognition. Many of the definitional problems, and some at least of the general arguments against recognition, can be avoided or minimised by adopting particular and specific rather than general measures of recognition. But something should first be said about the more general issues.

A. The definition of 'Aborigine'

An issue which has been a source of considerable difficulty in the United States and Canada is the definition of 'Aborigine' or 'Indian', that is, the criteria for membership of an indigenous minority. In Australia there has been no build-up of restrictive, technical or bureaucratic definitions of what constitutes such a member, for example, by reference to membership in a 'tribe' or 'band'. Although there are examples of earlier legislation defining Aboriginality by reference to degrees of blood (with phrases such as octoroon, quadroon, half-caste), the accepted Commonwealth administrative definition, which is also adopted widely in the States and Territories, is that an Aborigine is a person of Aboriginal descent, who identifies as an Aborigine and is accepted by other Aboriginal people as an Aborigine.[40] Clearly, framers of this definition preferred flexibility and breadth to any certain or exclusive definition. What was unclear until very recently was whether this broad definition corresponded with the constitutional definition of the 'Aboriginal race' for the purposes of s 51(26) of the Constitution. The High Court's decision in Commonwealth v Tasmania[41] indicates support for such a broad definition for constitutional as well as administrative purposes. As Deane J. expressed it:

> by "Australian Aboriginal" I mean, in accordance with what I understand to be the conventional meaning of that term, a person of Aboriginal

> descent, albeit mixed, who identifies himself as such and who is recognised by the Aboriginal community as an Aboriginal.[42]

Experience under State and Commonwealth legislation does not suggest that a more restrictive definition is necessary.

B. The definition of Aboriginal customary laws

This is a more complex question. Aboriginal customs and laws are part of an oral culture. There are no written codes or statements of customary laws such as are found in other countries. There is a considerable amount of general anthropological discussion on Aboriginal traditions and practices including especially marriage, kinship, hunting and fishing practices, relations to land and dispute resolution. There is however no agreement among anthropologists on certain issues, such as, for example, whether in Aboriginal traditional communities there were institutional authority structures for dispute resolution. There is however agreement amongst anthropologists that traditional societies had and continue to have a definable body of rules, practices and traditions accepted by the community. In *Milirrpum v Nabalco Pty Ltd*[43] (the *Gove Land Rights* case) in 1971 Blackburn J. had no hesitation in treating the system of land-holding and kinship rules of the North-East Arnhem Land people disclosed by the evidence as a system of law.[44] Blackburn J. commented that a recognisable sovereign or a separate territorial community with well-defined boundaries were not prerequisites for 'law'. He preferred to place emphasis on the processes of dispute resolution in traditional societies and to avoid a precise and exclusive definition of what constitutes Aboriginal customary laws. This would be to distort the reality:

> ... I do not think that the solution ... is to be found in postulating a meaning for the word 'law' .... What is shown by the evidence is, in my opinion, that the system of law was recognised as obligatory upon them by the members of the community which, in principle, is definable in that it is the community of Aboriginals which made ritual and economic use of the subject land. In my opinion it does not matter that the precise edges, as it were, of this community were left in a penumbra of partial obscurity.[45]

This view accords with overseas experience where the absence of a single all-purpose definition has not produced serious difficulties.[46] Difficulties which may arise can be minimised by particular forms of recognition.

C. Why recognise Aboriginal customary laws?

The Law Reform Commission was presented with a variety of arguments both for and against recognition. The principal arguments in favour of recognition, as outlined in the Report, are as follows:

- Non-recognition contributes to the continued undermining of traditional laws and authority structures. Aboriginal customary laws are a continuing reality in the lives of traditionally oriented people.
- Non-recognition can lead to injustice. It is unfair, for example, for an Aboriginal person to be punished by the general law for taking action required by his or her customary laws.
- Aboriginal people generally support recognition of their laws and, more specifically, have sought ways to enable the two laws, the general law and Aboriginal customary law, to work together. One concern, however, is their desire to maintain secret aspects of their law and to retain control over their law.
- Aboriginal customary laws assist in maintaining law and order within Aboriginal communities. Non-Aboriginal law and order mechanisms are often seen as ineffective and based on alien value systems.
- Recognition may also provide a way to compensate Aborigines for past wrongs, including the injustice of initial non-recognition.
- Australia's international standing would benefit from appropriate forms of recognition.

On the other hand a number of arguments against recognition were also made:

- recognition would involve endorsement of unacceptable punishments which cannot be tolerated by the general legal system;
- recognition would involve endorsing a system which discriminates against Aboriginal women and leads to other violations of basic rights;
- recognition would entail the loss of Aboriginal control over their laws and traditions;
- recognition requires reliable information about Aboriginal traditions, including secret matters, and this information is usually lacking;
- Aboriginal customary laws have ceased to exist in any meaningful form;
- Aboriginal communities are undergoing such change and the variety of Aboriginal experience is such as to preclude recognition altogether;

- recognition would create a form of legal pluralism which is discriminatory and divisive.

The Commission did not find the latter arguments persuasive, as arguments against any form of recognition whatever, for reasons made clear in its Report.[47] However the Commission took some of these arguments carefully into account in selecting the form of its proposals. The ways in which this was done are described briefly below.

Several matters were given careful consideration in the Commission's deliberations over the recognition of Aboriginal customary laws. The first is the variety of Aboriginal lifestyles and the right of Aboriginal people to make their own choices about their lives. Two further matters, partly related to the first, are the need to take account of Australia's international obligations, especially in the field of human rights, and questions about pluralism and equality before the law.

D. Diversity of Aboriginal lifestyles

There are among Aboriginal people enormous variations in experiences and circumstances. To some extent these variations must always have existed, but they also reflect the extent of European contact and the very different responses different groups have adopted to European contact. It was therefore essential for the Commission's proposals to take account of differences between Aborigines living in remote and relatively inaccessible areas, whose life is still predominantly traditionally-oriented, and those Aborigines who have been living for some considerable time in or around cities or larger country towns and who have modified their social organisation to a greater or lesser extent to reflect their changed circumstances and the new pressures upon them. These broad groups are commonly identified as: traditionally-oriented Aborigines, 'detribalised' or 'fringe-dwelling' Aborigines and urbanised Aborigines. However there are many difficulties in attempting to adopt classifications which do not take into account fluctuations in the composition and nature of the different groups, or the extent to which groups converge. Nor can it be assumed that there is any inevitable, one-directional movement away from more traditional ways of life. The situation varies markedly in different areas, and is influenced by such developments as land rights (especially in the Northern Territory and South Australia), the outstation movement, and the internal dynamics of particular communities. Many social, economic and legal difficulties are common to all Aboriginal people regardless of where they live. While the varying needs and demands of Aborigines in different areas called for care and flexibility in the development of the proposals for recognition, the available evidence does not support the view that Aboriginal customary laws and traditions are transitory. As the Commission concluded:

> What the position will be in 25 years time is unnecessary (even if it were possible) to predict. There are good arguments for action to be taken now to recognise aspects of Aboriginal customary laws and traditions which do now exist, and which are likely to continue to exist in much the same form for the foreseeable future.[48]

Arguments based on the fact that Aboriginal customary laws are undergoing change are not arguments against recognition so much as arguments for care to be taken in the form of recognition proposed.

E. Equality, discrimination and pluralism

A common argument against legislative, and even sometimes administrative recognition of indigenous minority rules and traditions is that such recognition would be discriminatory or unequal, or would violate the principle that all persons in a democratic society should be subject to 'one law'. These are powerful arguments, and, so far as basic standards of discrimination and equality are concerned, reflect fundamental values. However these standards are more difficult to apply than is commonly realised. The difficulties many common law judges have with the concepts of equality before the law and discrimination are shown by the struggle of the Canadian Supreme Court, in a series of cases from *R v Drybones* onwards,[49] to make sense of the principle in the light of established Canadian government policy towards Indians. In Canada, legislative distinctions, even if partly based on race, will be valid if they are directed at a 'valid federal objective', and do not penalise persons only on account of their race. These guarantees are consistent with special treatment of Canadian Indians, for whom there is a specific constitutional responsibility. In exercising its power with respect to Indians and Indian lands, parliament can use distinctions based on a 'legitimate legislative purpose in the light ... of long and uninterrupted history',[50] or on 'Indian customs and values',[51] provided that such distinctions do not exclude Indians from the enjoyment of basic rights and freedoms.

With some exceptions, the position in the United States, under the 'equal protection' guarantees in the Fifth and Fourteenth Amendments, is similar. Legislation will be consistent with equal protection if there is a rational basis for the legislative classification in the light of its legitimate purpose. Legislation which infringes basic rights (e.g., in the area of criminal procedure or the right to vote) or which adopts suspect categories as such (especially race or national origin) will be subject to stringent review, and will usually be unconstitutional. But, as in Canada, United States courts have been strongly influenced by the special federal responsibility for Indian tribes. Legislation for Indians and Indian tribes is based not on a suspect racial classification but on a 'political' classification, in view of the long-established special trust responsibility for Indians. Legislation for Indians is not immune from review under the Equal Protection Guarantee. But such legislation will be upheld 'as long as the special treatment can be tied rationally to the fulfillment of Congress's unique obligation towards the Indians'.[52]

In Australia, s 51(26) of the Constitution gives Parliament the power to pass special laws for the people of the Aboriginal race. In 1985 the High Court had to consider directly the application of a Commonwealth law prohibiting racial discrimination to a South Australian statute granting land rights to Aboriginal people. *Gerhardy v Brown*[53] involved a challenge to the Pitjantjatjara Land Rights Act (1981) (SA) s. 19 which provided that a person other than a member of the Pijantjatjara may not enter upon Pitjantjatjara land except with the permission of the body established to administer the land on behalf of the Pitjantjatjara. The Court held that while this provision involved a distinction on the basis of race, colour, descent or national ethnic origin as defined by the Racial Discrimination Act 1975 (Cth), the distinction constituted a special measure within s 8(1) of the Act and Art 1[54]) of the Racial Discrimination Convention and was accordingly justifiable. The Court accepted that reasonable steps can be taken for the recognition of Aboriginal claims or needs; provided these laws do not deny to members of the Aboriginal group basic rights, and provided they are designed to promote culture and cultural identity, they will be held to be special measures not prohibited by the Racial Discrimination Act 1975 (Cth) or the Convention. The Court also indicated that such laws need not be temporary. Special measures may be enacted for the economic or educational advancement of certain groups provided the measures are not continued after their objectives have been achieved.

Applying the standards of non-discrimination and equality in the light of the Racial Discrimination Convention and of other international and comparative experience in the field, the Commission concluded that special measures for the recognition of Aboriginal customary laws will not be racially discriminatory, or involve a denial of equality before the law or of equal protection, if these measures

- are reasonable responses to the special needs of those Aboriginal people affected by the proposals;
- are generally accepted by those people;
- do not deprive individual Aborigines of basic human rights or of access to the general legal system and its institutions.[54]

On the basis of this conclusion the Commission applied the following guidelines in making the recommendations in its Report:

- Aborigines should, wherever possible, retain rights under the general law (e.g., to enter into marriages).
- Legislation should be no more restrictive than necessary to ensure fidelity to the customary laws or practices being recognised.
- Measures of recognition should not unreasonably withdraw legal protection or support from individuals, whether Aboriginal or non-Aboriginal.
- Where the most appropriate remedy to a problem revealed by the Commission's inquiries is not a recognition of Aboriginal customary laws as such but some more general provision, it is necessary to consider if that provision can legitimately be applied to some class of Aborigines only or whether the reasons for the provision apply equally to all members of the community.[55]

These guidelines help to ensure that any proposals made are not discriminatory or unequal as between Aboriginal and non-Aboriginal Australians generally, or in relation to specific groups, including immigrant groups.[56]

F. Public opinion

Apart from basic arguments about discrimination and equality, the Commission was met by the argument that the recognition of Aboriginal customary laws would be divisive, or would create a form of backlash in terms of public opinion, thus causing more problems than it resolved. It is primarily for governments, not law reform commissions, to assess or represent this form of public opinion. But the Commission was not made aware of any upsurge of public opinion against the general idea of recognising Aboriginal customary law, although undoubtedly there will be members of the majority community who will have reservations about it. So much depends on the details of recognition, however, that it is fruitless to discuss these issues in the abstract. There is no doubt that Aborigines are in a special position. Quite clearly the effects of European settlement have been devastating on Aboriginal people. Their traditional ways of life have undergone enormous changes. Criminal statistics demonstrate the difficulties Aborigines face with the legal system. Special measures to deal with this situation are not merely justifiable but necessary. In this context each of the proposals made in the Report, the Commission concluded, were justified in their individual cases as necessary special measures.

G. The protection of basic human rights

As the Commission's Terms of Reference made clear, certain aspects of the recognition of Aboriginal customary law raise problems of the application and interpretation of basic human rights standards. It might be thought a sufficient reply to this to say that Aborigines themselves can determine and maintain adequate standards of human rights. A possible rejoinder to this is that the Commonwealth Parliament cannot abrogate its responsibility for ensuring the maintenance of the human rights of all Australians including Aboriginal Australians. But this does not dispose of the proposition that Aborigines themselves should assume responsibilities for the maintenance of human rights in their own communities. There are obviously tensions between the values of self-determination or self-management and other human rights standards, and their detailed resolution is not a simple or straightforward matter. What is true is that the Civil and Political Rights Covenant, which is the basis for the proposed Australian Bill of Rights and which is a widely-accepted formulation of basic civil and political rights, has to be interpreted and applied on a universal basis, in a wide variety of contexts and cultures. It is not to be assumed that its provisions are to be interpreted in the light of just one culture however influential. The Report concludes that the need for consistency with fundamental human rights does not preclude the recognition of Aboriginal customary laws. Whether human rights are preserved or infringed by a particular proposal depends on the detailed proposal in question. The Commission concluded that the recommendations in the Report are consistent with basic human rights.[57]

H. The Commission's approach

The Report is based on the premise that, whatever form of recognition is adopted, recognition should take place within the framework of the general law. But this leaves many questions unresolved. Recognition may be carried through in a number of ways. The scope for recognition of Aboriginal customary laws through common law rules is very limited, and is inadequate to deal with the questions raised by the Terms of Reference. The Commission also concluded that arguments for the recognition of Aboriginal customary laws through the re-examination of the status of Australia as a settled colony would not bring about appropriate forms of recognition of Aboriginal customary laws and traditions as these exist now. The primary alternative, accordingly, is legislative recognition. But legislative recognition of Aboriginal customary law can itself take several different forms, including:

- codification or specific enforcement of customary law;
- specific or general forms of 'incorporation' by reference;
- the exclusion of the general law in areas to be covered by customary laws;
- the translation of institutions or rules for the purposes of giving them equivalent effect;
- the accommodation of traditional customary ways through specific measures taken within the general legal system.

The Commission rejected codification and the general incorporation of Aboriginal customary law as appropriate forms of recognition.[58] Both carry with them the danger that Aboriginal people would lose control over their laws, and that there may be unwarranted intrusion into or disclosure of secret matters. Aboriginal people repeatedly impressed these concerns upon the Commission. In general they sought incorporation only of specific customary laws, usually as a protection against outside invasion or interference (for example the protection of sacred sites). The Commission preferred specific rather than general forms of recognition, but saw no need to adopt only one approach to recognition. Some of the recommendations are for measures in the form of translation of customary institutions or rules for the purposes of giving them equivalent effect (e.g., the proposals for the recognition of traditional marriage).[59] Other proposals would be best implemented by legislation requiring that the general legal system take Aboriginal customary laws into account (for example in the exercise of sentencing discretions). In other cases some specific exclusion of the general law may be an appropriate way to recognise the operation of Aboriginal customary laws (for example, exemptions to hunting or fishing legislation to recognise Aboriginal traditional hunting and fishing rights). The Commission took the view that the form of recognition should vary with the context.[60] This approach was in accordance with the Commission's view that problems of recognition would be minimised by approaching the Reference in a functional way, issue by issue. Wide-ranging categorical forms of recognition raise difficulties of definition, already referred to, and heighten problems of translation of the different concepts involved in the general legal system and under Aboriginal customary laws.

Adopting a functional approach, the Commission found, had the advantage of maximising the extent to which Aboriginal people would retain control over their laws. It also enabled specific proposals to be formulated to reflect the fact that Aboriginal customary laws continue to be subject to external pressures and to change, and that they vary from community to community both in strength and content. The criticism that functional recognition involves the general legal system dictating the extent to which it is prepared to recognise customary laws, rather than allowing full recognition, is a criticism that can be made of any form of recognition within the framework of the general law.

VIII. Areas for recognition

Against this background the Report examines, in Parts III-VII (Chapters 12-36) a series of areas of the law where recognition may be necessary. Some brief reference will be made to each of these.

A. Recognition of traditional marriage

Reference has already been made to the failure to recognise traditional Aboriginal marriage in any way, and to recent cases of legislative or judicial recognition of traditional marriage for particular purposes. Despite the long-standing failure to recognise them, patterns of traditional marriage continue to exist, and remain strong not only in the Northern Territory but also in parts of Western Australia, South Australia and Queensland.[61] Indeed there has been a tendency to revert to patterns of traditional marriage even in communities which had previously been subject to strong mission influence.

Responding to this situation is, however, another question. Traditional Aboriginal marriages are informal, non-ceremonial relationships, which can be entered into in a variety of ways, which are not infrequently polygynous (i.e., involving several wives), and which do not conform to the Marriage Act model in various other ways.[62] Consequently, it is sometimes suggested that the best way to deal with traditional marriages of this kind is to recognise them as de facto relationships, which also lack ceremonies or documents marking their commencement and conclusion, but which are nonetheless recognised for certain purposes in most States and Territories.[63] However this is very much a second class form of recognition, since the distinguishing feature of a de facto relationship in the wider society is that it is not a marriage. Aborigines do regard stable unions entered into within the appropriate kinship categories as marriages, rather than as de facto relationships.

On the other hand it is not appropriate to recognise such marriages as having all of the legal consequences of marriage under the Marriage Act. Most obviously, marriage under general Australian law is monogamous, requires a formal judicial termination and carries obligations of continuing maintenance which do not seem to have any direct analogue in Aboriginal tradition and which may well cut across other methods of providing for spouses. Under these circumstances, the Commission recommends the functional recognition of such marriages, that is their equation with Marriage Act marriage for certain specified purposes rather than generally. The aim is to avoid foisting on the parties to what is in most cases a rather informal relationship a set of rules and structures developed in a different culture and involving different assumptions about the status and consequences of marriage, while still offering appropriate forms of protection to traditional spouses consistent with Aboriginal marriage traditions. Thus it was recommended that parties to a traditional Aboriginal marriage, should be regarded as married persons for the purposes of Australian law relating to such questions as:

- status of children;
- adoption, fostering and child welfare laws, including questions of parental consent to adoption or fostering, and of qualifications to adopt or foster;
- distribution of property on death (intestacy, family provision);
- accident compensation (including workers' compensation, compensation on death, criminal injuries compensation and repatriation benefits);
- statutory superannuation schemes (and private superannuation schemes established in the future);
- the Social Security Act 1947 (Cth), with special provision being made for separate payment to spouses, and an associated regulation-making power;
- spousal compellability and marital communications in the law of evidence;
- unlawful carnal knowledge, provided both actual consent and traditional marriage are proved;
- spouse rebates under the Income Tax Assessment Act 1936 (Cth) and related legislation.

On the other hand, it was recommended that traditional marriages should not be recognised for the following purposes:

- variation of maintenance and property rights during a relationship or on divorce;
- bigamy;

- rape in marriage;
- the Family Court's jurisdiction with respect to principal and ancillary relief (including its powers with respect to domestic violence).[64]

Obviously the recommendations, though an acknowledgement of Aboriginal customary laws and traditions, only constitute recognition of Aboriginal customary laws in a rather special way. The proposals involve attaching consequences under the general law to a state of affairs which, under wholly traditional circumstances, would not attract many of the consequences simply because they would be irrelevant to the society. Conversely, the proposals do not involve the enforcement of Aboriginal marriage rules as such. To make these enforceable under the general legal system would be completely to change their character, and would tend to deprive Aboriginal communities of control over this aspect of their law. For these and other reasons this is one context in which 'recognition by translation' is to be preferred to 'recognition by incorporation', that is the enforcement or enactment of the indigenous rule as part of the general law.

B. Traditional distribution of property[65]

The idea of 'property' in Aboriginal tradition is very different to that adopted within the wider Australian community and by Australian law. This is so for both goods and land, but especially for land. Aboriginal society was not materialistic and placed little importance on wealth or possessions.[66] Much more important was the development, management and transfer of knowledge and skills. Aboriginal customary law is not static and has made significant changes to accommodate the wider Australian system. It has, in general, accepted the cash economy and its rules. But sometimes conflicts arise between Aboriginal ways of doing things and legal rules for transferring property. Problems arise, most obviously at least, in the area of the distribution of property upon death. There is the potential for conflict between the general rules for property distribution and claims upon death, based as they are substantially on an assumption of a nuclear family, and Aboriginal family structures and kinship obligations. So far this problem has surfaced only rarely, but a number of more traditional Aborigines are starting to acquire assets in various forms and problems may well arise in the future.

The Commission recommended, as well as the recognition of traditional marriage for the purpose of distribution of property upon death, including family provision, a reform of the general law relating to the distribution of property on death in the following form:

- Traditional marriages should be recognised for the purpose of intestacy legislation.
- Aborigines should be able to apply to have an intestate estate distributed in accordance with the traditions or customary laws of the deceased's community.
- State and Territory legislation for family provision (testator's family maintenance) should allow for applications for family provision by persons related by blood, kinship or marriage to a deceased member of an Aboriginal community and who could at the time of the deceased's death, have reasonably expected support (including material support) from the deceased in accordance with the customary laws of that community.
- Claims for family provision should prevail, in clear cases of need, over claims for traditional distribution on intestacy.[67]

C. Problems of Aboriginal child custody

On this issue at least, Aboriginal opinion is not hard to gauge. It would be difficult to find an Aboriginal person above the age of thirty who had not had some experience of State intervention in Aboriginal families. This makes the issue an extremely sensitive one for many Aboriginal people, and one of the stronger arguments for legislative reform is that it may provide a degree of security where security and confidence in the system up to now have been almost completely lacking. Like many other areas covered in the Report, this is an area of State administrative and legislative responsibility and it is necessary to ask who should take responsibility for delivery of child welfare services, and to what extent the Commonwealth's involvement in certain areas of funding (e.g., in funding Aboriginal Child Care Agencies) should carry with it some share in the determination of policy. It is also a question whether the Commonwealth's undoubted legislative power to make special laws for Aboriginal people (Constitution, s 51(26)) should be exercised. However it is important not to confuse federal issues with the substantive question of what should be done. Here, as elsewhere in Parts III-VII of the Report, a firm distinction is drawn between the two issues, with federal issues left to be resolved only after the substantive recommendations have been arrived at. On this basis, the Report recommends that:

- There should be an Aboriginal child placement principle established by legislation, requiring preference to be given, in decisions affecting the care or custody of children, and in the absence of good cause to the contrary, to placements with:

(a) a parent of the child;
(b) a member of the child's extended family;
(c) other members of the child's community (in particular, persons with responsibilities for the child under the customary laws of the community).

- Where such a placement is not possible, preference should be given to placement with families or in institutions for children approved by members of the relevant Aboriginal communities having special responsibility for the child, or by an Aboriginal child care organisation working in the area.
- In making these decisions account should be taken of the standards of child care and child welfare of the Aboriginal community to which the child belongs.
- Child welfare legislation should provide explicitly for consultation with the relevant Aboriginal custodians of a child and (unless they direct to the contrary) with the relevant Aboriginal child care agency, before placement decisions (except emergency decisions involving short-term placement) are made.
- Careful attention should be given to the possibility of devolving child care responsibilities to regional or local child care agencies by agreement, and with appropriate resources.[68]

D. Criminal Law and sentencing of Aboriginal offenders

As we have seen, the application of the general criminal law to Aborigines has long been established. This raises the possibility of conflict between that law and Aboriginal customary law rules adhered to by traditionally oriented Aborigines. But it would be wrong to assume that cases of direct conflict, or at least cases that come to court, are particularly common. While it is well-established that, for various reasons, Aborigines are grossly over-represented in the criminal justice system, the relationship between particular offences and Aboriginal customary laws is not a direct one. Examination of the limited evidence available suggests that:

- Even when traditionally oriented Aborigines are involved in criminal charges, the case will frequently involve non-traditional elements (especially alcohol) or a non-traditional offence.
- It is much more common, even for traditionally oriented Aborigines, that the act that resulted in the charge was a violation of both Aboriginal customary law and the general law, or was not specifically allowed or justified by Aboriginal customary law, than that it was so justified.

- The explanation for very high offence and imprisonment rates of Aborigines is not simply a product of non-recognition of Aboriginal customary laws by the substantive criminal law.
- The problems reflected by those exorbitant rates are not likely to be solved by the recognition of Aboriginal customary laws within the substantive criminal law. Indeed, if the characteristics of traditionally oriented Aboriginal offenders do not differ markedly from other Aborigines it may be that solutions will not be found directly through *any* form of recognition of Aboriginal customary laws.[69]

Nonetheless, particular conflicts do occur, and so too (more often) do problems of the interaction of the two systems. Such conflicts can to a certain extent be resolved by taking the operation of Aboriginal customary laws into account in determining criminal liability. In determining intent it appears that evidence of Aboriginal customary laws is admissible on the basis that the state of mind of a traditionally oriented Aboriginal defendant acting according to customary laws is something that is 'outside the supposed experience of ordinary people'. The courts have on occasions taken the customary laws of the defendant's community into account in determining whether a defence of provocation or duress was established sufficient to reduce charges of murder to manslaughter. To ensure that the law as represented by these decisions is applied fairly and consistently, the Report recommends legislation expressly providing that evidence of Aboriginal customary laws is admissible in such circumstances. Existing defences do not however completely cover the situation where an act sanctioned by customary laws comes to be considered by the courts. The fact that a defendant was impelled to do the act in question under his or her customary laws does not as such constitute a defence. The Report considered whether a customary law defence exonerating the defendant from liability in such cases should be created. While such a defence would constitute the most direct way of dealing with such situations its introduction was rejected for several reasons.

- A customary law defence would involve endorsing tribal killings, and would deprive persons, including Aboriginal victims of offences, of legal protection. The defence therefore raised serious problems of equal protection under the law.
- Evidence of Aboriginal customary laws can be taken into account sufficiently by the general criminal law by the exercise of sentencing and other procedural discretions.
- It is doubtful whether a customary law defence is necessary. It is relatively rare for cases of direct conflict between the general legal system and the

Aboriginal customary laws to come before the courts and even rarer for defendants to be severely punished in those cases where a customary law defence would apply. It was thought undesirable to create a controversial defence to deal with a small number of cases.

- A customary law defence carries the dangers of exposing Aboriginal customary laws for close analysis, definition and testing in order to establish a defence. In this way it was considered intrusive and as endangering Aboriginal control over their laws and traditions.[70]

The Commission did however support the creation of a partial defence, similar to a defence of diminished responsibility, which would operate to reduce the level of liability in particular cases from murder to manslaughter. This defence has several advantages:

- It does not involve condoning or endorsing payback killings or woundings.
- It represents a direct acknowledgment of conflicts that can occur between the general legal system and Aboriginal customary laws.
- It does not deprive victims of legal protection or the right of redress. It therefore does not raise questions of equal protection before the law in the way that a complete defence does.
- It allows the jury, as the representatives of the whole community, a role in mitigating the degree of culpability, and it operates as an adjunct to the sentencing discretion.[71]

E. Sentencing

After examination of numerous (mostly unreported) cases involving Aboriginal defendants, the Commission concluded that Aboriginal customary laws are to a considerable extent taken into account in sentencing. It is however necessary to strike the right balance between the requirement that the courts cannot incorporate or require traditional punishments or other customary law processes to occur as a condition to the release of offenders or in mitigation of punishment, and the need to take account of traditional Aboriginal dispute settlement procedures and customary laws. The Report draws on existing case law to establish certain principles which should guide the exercise of the sentencing discretion. For example, it was concluded that:

- A defendant should not be sentenced to a longer term of imprisonment than would otherwise apply, merely to 'protect' the defendant from the application of customary laws including 'traditional punishment' (even if that punishment would or may be unlawful under the general law).

- Similar principles apply to discretions with respect to bail. A court should not prevent a defendant from returning to the defendant's community (with the possibility or even likelihood that the defendant will face some form of traditional punishment) if the defendant applies for bail, and if the other conditions for release are met.
- Aboriginal customary laws are a relevant factor in mitigation of sentence, both in cases where customary law processes have already occurred and where they are likely to occur in the future.
- Aboriginal customary laws may also be relevant in aggravation of penalty, in some cases, but only within the generally applicable sentencing limits (what is commonly referred to as the 'tariff') applicable to the offence.
- Within certain limits the views of the local Aboriginal community about the seriousness of the offence and the offender are also relevant in sentencing.
- But the courts cannot disregard the values and views of the wider Australian community, which may have to be reflected in custodial or other sentences notwithstanding the mitigating force of Aboriginal customary laws or local community opinions.
- Nor can the courts incorporate in sentencing orders Aboriginal customary law penalties or sanctions which are contrary to the general law.
- In some circumstances, where the form of traditional settlement involved would not be illegal (e.g., community discussion and conciliation, supervision by parents or persons *in loco parentis*, exclusion from land) a court may incorporate such a proposal into its sentencing order (e.g., as a condition for conditional release or attached to a bond), provided that this is possible under the principles of the general law governing sentencing. Care is needed to ensure appropriate local consultation in making such orders, and flexibility in their formulation. In particular it is important that anyone into whose care the offender is to be entrusted, is an appropriate person, having regard to any applicable customary laws (e.g., is in a position of authority over the accused, and not subject to avoidance relationships), has been consulted and is prepared to undertake the responsibility.
- An opportunity to attend a ceremony which is important both to the offender and the community may be a relevant factor to be taken into account on sentencing, especially where there is evidence that the ceremony and its associated incorporation within the life of the community may have a rehabilitative effect. However initiation or other ceremonial matters cannot and should not be incorporated in sentencing orders under the general law.[72]

F. Community justice mechanisms

The Commission's Terms of Reference specifically required it to consider to what extent Aboriginal communities should have the power to apply their customary law and practices in the punishment and rehabilitation of Aborigines. Requests from the Yirrkala community and other Aboriginal communities in the Northern Territory for assistance in handling their law and order problems to a large extent prompted this question. Previously a number of reports and enquiries had considered the question of Aboriginal involvement in law and order matters. While the question as framed in the Terms of Reference appears to be limited to the empowering of Aboriginal communities to apply their customary laws, procedures and sanctions to offences defined by the general law, other matters such as the conferment of autonomy, the creation of Aboriginal courts and the use of Aboriginal personnel are relevant. Thus the Commission examined a broad range of issues, including the operation of Aboriginal courts in their various forms in Queensland, Western Australia and the Northern Territory. It considered the overseas experience, especially the village courts in Papua New Guinea and the United States Indian tribal courts. In making its recommendations the Commission adopted a number of criteria by which the suitability of local justice mechanisms for a particular community could be assessed. These included:

- the acceptability of the proposals to the local community as a whole;
- the extent to which the Aboriginal courts or other official structures reinforce or detract from local authority structures;
- the administrative feasibility of the proposed scheme; and
- the need to maintain basic individual rights in the administration of justice.[73]

The Commission commented that problems of 'law and order' in Aboriginal communities, and of local involvement in the criminal justice system, involve issues of local self-government or autonomy which extend beyond the recognition of Aboriginal customary laws, or of increasing Aboriginal participation in local courts or police forces. Schemes such as the Northern Territory Community Government Scheme are appropriate, although if Aboriginal communities are to exercise broader responsibilities, adequate support and enforcement powers are necessary. Furthermore, in many Aboriginal communities, unofficial methods of dispute resolution operate alongside the general legal system. Local resolution of disputes in these kinds of ways should be encouraged and supported. More specifically in relation to the creation of Aboriginal courts or similar bodies the Commission concluded that there should be no general scheme of Aboriginal courts established in Australia, although such courts or other official bodies may be appropriate for certain communities. If courts or similar bodies are set up it should only be at the instigation of and after careful consideration by members of the Aboriginal community concerned. In addition the Report sets out certain basic requirements for courts or similar official bodies:

- The Aboriginal group concerned should have power to draw up local by-laws, including by-laws incorporating or taking into account Aboriginal customs, rules and traditions.
- Appropriate safeguards need to be established to ensure that individual rights are protected, e.g., by way of appeal.
- The by-laws should, in general, apply to all persons within the boundaries of the community.
- If the court is to be run by local people, they should have power within broad limits to determine their own procedure, in accordance with what is 'seen to be procedurally fair by the community at large'.
- The community should have some voice in selecting the persons who will constitute the court, and appropriate training should be available to those selected. In minor matters there need be no automatic right to legal counsel, though the defendant in such cases should have the right to have someone (e.g., a friend) speak on his behalf.
- The court's powers should include powers of mediation and conciliation. A court which is receptive to the traditions, needs and views of the local people may be able to resolve some disputes before they escalate, perhaps avoiding more serious criminal charges. The power to order compensation of some kind in such situations is one way of achieving this.
- Such courts will need appropriate support facilities.
- There should be regular reviews of the operation of any such court, undertaken in conjunction with the local community.[74]

In establishing such courts care will need to be taken to minimise conflict with or the undercutting of local kinship and authority structures and special attention given to the composition of the court.

IX. Other issues

It is not possible in a paper such as this to give a detailed account of all areas of the Commission's work. A few examples will indicate the wide range of the Commission's inquiry, and the other matters dealt with in the Report. These other matters include a detailed discussion of questions of evidence and procedure as they affect traditional Aborigines coming before the courts. Aboriginal people experience particular difficulties in dealing with the police and in giving evidence in court. In this context, the Report proposes legislation to cover:

- The procedures to be followed by the police when interrogating Aborigines and rules relating to the admissibility of evidence obtained during such interrogations.[75]
- The right of certain Aborigines to make an unsworn statement.
- The protection of secrecy and confidentiality of evidence given by Aborigines of their customary laws.
- Power in the courts to protect a witness against self-incrimination under Aboriginal customary laws.
- Provision to cover the giving of group evidence by Aboriginal people and submissions from community members on sentencing.
- Amendments to certain rules of evidence (for example, the hearsay, ultimate issue and expert evidence rules) where these present obstacles for the admission of evidence of Aboriginal customary laws.[76]

In response to requests for recognition and protection of traditional hunting and fishing interests, the Report seeks to spell out ways in which an equitable balance can be struck between Aboriginal interests and other legitimate interests, including conservation, the effective management of natural resources, pastoral interests, commercial fishing and tourism. In doing so, the multitude of conflicting interests, the need for unitary management of resources and the extensive activities at State and Territory level combined led the Commission to conclude that it was not appropriate for comprehensive federal legislation to be enacted. Instead the Commission advocated a set of general principles to be adopted by the Commonwealth, State and Territory Governments. In articulating these principles the Commission sought information from Aboriginal people, anthropologists, marine biologists, conservation and wildlife authorities and others to demonstrate the significance of bush and sea foods, in terms of diet, way of life and in terms of customary laws and practices. The provisions of some 50 Federal, State and Territory Acts and associated regulations were examined and discussions were held with Federal, State and Territory lands departments, fisheries and national parks and wildlife authorities to assess the works of these provisions. Recommendations were made along the following lines:

- The determination of whether an activity was traditional should focus on the purpose of the activity rather than the method, so that the incorporation of new materials and hunting methods would not as such prevent an activity being classed as 'traditional'.
- Traditional hunting should not be limited to indigenous species but may extend to introduced feral animals.
- Traditional hunting should not be limited to the taking of food for sustenance but may include ceremonial exchange within the community concerned and the satisfaction of kin obligations.
- Traditional hunting and fishing must be subject to legitimate conservation and other identifiable overriding interests. In particular in the case of rare and threatened species it may be necessary to prohibit hunting or fishing altogether or to restrict the numbers taken or the methods by which or the areas in which they are taken.
- As a matter of general principle Aboriginal traditional hunting and fishing should take priority over non-traditional activities, including commercial and recreational activities, where the traditional activities are carried out for subsistence purposes.
- Aborigines should be accorded access to traditional lands for the purposes of hunting, fishing and gathering, whether these lands are unalienated Crown lands or are subject to leasehold or other interests. In doing so it is necessary to take account of interests of persons other than the Crown, whether by negotiated provisions or otherwise.
- Areas of sea adjacent to Aboriginal land should be preserved for traditional fishing.
- There needs to be consultation with Aboriginal people affected before steps are taken to restrict traditional hunting and fishing, to ensure that the views of those Aborigines affected are taken into account in reaching any decision on the management of resources.[77]

X. Implementing the Commission's recommendations

As already mentioned, in making its recommendations, the Commission adopted the approach of first determining what should be done, and leaving questions of implementation to be dealt with subsequently. At present legislation affecting

Aborigines is predominantly State or Territory legislation and legal and administrative involvement with Aboriginal people, in the areas dealt with in the Report, occurs mainly through State or Territory agencies. This is especially true in the criminal justice system. Thus very many of the Commission's recommendations concern existing fields of legal or administrative activities of the States or Territories. Section 51(26) of the Commonwealth Constitution gives the Commonwealth power to make special laws for the people of any race including the Aboriginal race if Parliament deems it necessary. That the Commonwealth has constitutional power to implement the Commission's recommendations is clear from the High Court decision in *Commonwealth v Tasmania*.[78] One area which can create constitutional difficulties is the creation of Aboriginal courts. The Commonwealth has no power to establish bodies exercising judicial power in a State other than in accordance with Part III of the Constitution, and furthermore the Commonwealth cannot alter the structure of State courts exercising federal jurisdiction. These limitations restrict Commonwealth involvement in proposals for community justice mechanisms, such as Aboriginal courts or bodies performing equivalent functions. But in any event the Report does not recommend a general scheme of Aboriginal courts.

More significant than questions of constitutional power are the administrative and political constraints of a federal system in which much of the involvement with Aborigines occurs through existing legislative or administrative activities in States and Territories. Despite this, the Report affirms that the welfare of the Aboriginal people of Australia is a national issue, and one that should be as far as possible dealt with through a coherent national policy. This is particularly so at the level of basic standards to be applied. According to this view the Commonwealth has a clear legislative responsibility, in cases where State or Territory laws do not establish adequate or appropriate rules, to legislate for the special needs of Aboriginal people. The Commission recommended that its proposals be implemented by Commonwealth legislation, but that this legislation should not exclude State or Territory legislation consistent with these provisions. The legislation would thus be concerned to establish minimum standards rather than uniformity of laws. But there are two exceptions to this conclusion. Federal legislation was not (for the reasons outlined already) recommended for the establishment of Aboriginal local justice mechanisms, or for the recognition of traditional hunting and gathering rights. In relation to hunting and fishing, special federal laws dealing with aspects of resource use in isolation from laws for the management of the resource in question are undesirable if not unworkable.

XI. The report in context

The Commission's recommendations are framed from the point of view of the general legal system, with the aim of achieving justice in cases where Aboriginal customary laws are relevant. In seeking to achieve this aim the Commission adopted certain critieria. Proposals for the recognition of Aboriginal customary laws should, in its view:

- be flexible enough to cope with change;
- interfere as little as possible with the way Aborigines choose to live their lives;
- allow maximum control over their customary laws;
- maintain basic rights, including basic individual rights, while avoiding, as far as possible, ethnocentric judgments about Aboriginal cultures and traditions.[79]

Adherence to these principles underlies the rejection of codification and of direct enforcement of customary laws as principal forms of recognition. It entailed a functional approach to the recognition of marriage. It follows from these principles that the Commission's proposals should be subject to continuing review. On the other hand it is not possible to avoid making judgments as to what should be done, even at the risk of a degree of ethnocentricity. Perhaps elements of ethnocentricity could only be avoided if the recognition of Aboriginal customary laws was part of wider negotiations for autonomy conducted between Aboriginal people and the government. The history of Australian indigenous policy to date has usually been regarded not as raising issues of local autonomy or self-determination so much as involving programs for Aboriginal advancement, attempts at resolving problems of Aboriginal welfare and the delivery of services to Aboriginal people. In Canada the position is otherwise. Developments in the area of self-government[80] indicate that the indigenous people of Canada no longer seek merely the provision of finance for particular projects or the provision of services from the Federal, Provincial or Territory Governments. Instead their claims are framed in terms of self-government or self-determination. The situation in Australia is different, as the giving of a reference about Aboriginal customary laws to a statutory law reform body might suggest. The Commission's recommendations for the recognition of customary law are not part of a negotiated or independent settlement of Aboriginal claims for self-government or self-determination. Nor does the Commission claim to speak for Aboriginal people. The Commission's recommendations are presented primarily as a response to a search for justice on the part of the legal system, in its dealing with Aboriginal people.

Notes

1. A.L.R.C. 31, *The Recognition of Aboriginal Customary Laws,* A.G.P.S., 2 vols. and 1 vol. summary (available separately), Canberra, 1986.
2. Id., vol. 2, Appendix B.
3. (1976) 14 S.A.S.R. 1.
4. Laverton Royal Commission 1976.
5. In particular, A.L.R.C. 2 recommended special protections for Aboriginal suspects under police interrogation: see id., para. 371-5. A version of these was included in the Criminal Investigation Bill 1981 (Cth) cl. 26.
6. For example, Commission of Inquiry into Poverty 1975 (Commissioner R. Sackville).
7. The Reference had three Commissioners in charge from 1977: the Chairman (Justice M.D. Kirby) on an interim basis until a Commissioner with particular responsibilities for the Reference could be appointed, Mr. B.M. Debelle Q.C. 1978-1981 and Professor James Crawford (1982--completion).
8. A full list is set out in A.L.R.C. 31, vol. 2, Appendix B.
9. For the list of consultants, see, id., vol. 1, xxxvii.
10. Id., para. 20.
11. Mulvaney, 1975:52.
12. Blainey, 1980:63.
13. Ibid.
14. See e.g., Ryan, 1981.
15. A.L.R.C. 31, para. 29-30.
16. Id., para. 345-6. Information provided by WELSTAT, Department of Social Security, Canberra.
17. Ibid. In Western Australia, 1983 figures indicate that while Aborigines represent 2.3% of the total population, some 54% of children in foster care placements were classified as Aboriginal and over 58% of children in residential care establishments were similarly classified.
18. Walker and Biles, 1985:22. Aborigines make up just over 1% of Australia's population.
19. Id., 66.
20. Clifford, 1982:8-9.
21. House of Representatives Standing Committee on Aboriginal Affairs, 1980: para. 25.
22. Report by Captain G. Grey on the Method for Promoting the Civilization of

Aborigines, Enclosure, Lord John Russell to Sir George Gipps, 8 October 1840, *H.R.A.* Series 1, Vol XXI, 35.

23. *R v Neddy Monkey* (1961), 1 W & W (CL) 40; *R v Cobby* (1883), 4 L.R. (N.S.W.) 355, 356.
24. *R v Jack Congo Murrell* (1836), 1 Legge 72. See Bridges, 1973a.
25. House of Commons.
26. A.L.R.C. 31, para. 53.
27. Id., para. 52, 56.
28. Id., para. 55-6.
29. Id., para. 52.
30. Ibid.
31. Id., para. 53.
32. Id., para. 72.
33. See, for example, *Napaluma v Baker,* (S.A. Supreme Court, 5 March 1982); (1982), 4 *Aboriginal Law Bulletin* 9; Dixon v Davies, (N.T. Supreme Court, 17 November 1982); (1983), 7 *Aboriginal Law Bulletin* 9; *Weston v Woodroffe* (1985), 36 N.T.R. 34.
34. A.L.R.C. 31, para. 276.
35. Aboriginal Land Rights (Northern Territory) Act 1976. (Cth); Pitjantjatjara Land Rights Act 1981 (SA); Maralinga Tjarutja Land Rights Act 1983 (SA).
36. See, A.L.R.C. 31, para. 80, 237-40 for details.
37. Id., para. 81, 359-64.
38. Id., para. 78.
39. Id., para. 79, 906-69.
40. See, for example, Fisheries Act 1905 (WA), s. 56(3); Aboriginal Land Rights Act 1983 (NSW) s. 4(1).
41. (1983) 46 A.L.R. 625.
42. Id., 817.
43. (1971), 17 F.L.R. 141.
44. Id., 267.
45. Id., 266-7.
46. On the other hand serious difficulties have been presented by attempts to codify customary laws, an attempt which leads to inflexibility and unreal assumptions about how customary laws operate.
47. A.L.R.C. 31, para. 127.
48. Id., para. 122.
49. See *R v Drybones,* [1970] S.C.R. 282; *Attorney-General of Canada v Canard* (1975), 52 D.L.R. (3d) 548. See, also, A.L.R.C. 31, para. 139.
50. *Attorney-General of Canada v Canard* (1975), 52 D.L.R. (3d) 548, 575.
51. A.L.R.C. 31, para. 142.

52. *Morton v Mancari*, 417 U.S. 535, 555 (1974); see also A.L.R.C. 31, para. 132-7.
53. (1985), 57 A.L.R. 472.
54. A.L.R.C. 31, para. 165.
55. Id., para. 158-69.
56. In view of the size and diversity of Australia's immigrant communities, the question of legal pluralism as it affects migrant groups is particularly sensitive. Some at least of the Commission's proposals might be applicable to members of immigrant groups with their own customs and traditions. In view of its Terms of Reference the Commission makes no recommendation to this effect: indeed in two areas (child care payments and right to an interpreter) it refrains from making a recommendation for legislation partly on the basis that these provisions are equally necessary for immigrants as Aboriginal peoples. However the Commission does stress the special justification for the recognition of indigenous customary laws, and the distinction between indigenous and immigrant groups: id., para. 163-4. The recognition of immigrant customary laws and traditions remains an open question. For a recent survey, see S. Poulter, English Law and Ethnic Minority Customs, Butterworths, London, 1986.
57. Id., para. 171-93.
58. Id., para. 200-2.
59. Id., para. 203, and generally chapters 13-14.
60. Id., para. 208-9.
61. Id., para. 226-9.
62. Berndt, 1961::338-9; Sutton, 1985.
63. A.L.R.C. 31, para. 238-40.
64. Id., 271-323.
65. See, A.L.R.C. 31, para. 326-43.
66. Id., para. 327-31.
67. Id., para. 333-42.
68. Id., para. 365-71.
69. Id., para. 399-400.
70. Id., para. 442-50.
71. Id., para. 451-3.
72. Id., para. 504-22.
73. Id., para. 804-8.
74. Id., para. 880.
75. See, id., ch. 22, and cf. note 5, *supra*.
76. Id., para. 677.
77. A.L.R.C. 31, para. 1001-3.
78. (1983), 46 A.L.R. 627.

79. A.L.R.C. 31, para. 1033.

80. For example, House of Commons, 1983; the introduction of the Indian Self-Government Bill (Bill C 52 of 1984); the constitutional initiatives culminating in the *Constitution Act,* 1982 (s. 35); and the land claims experience (*James Bay and Northern Quebec Agreement*, Editeur Officiel du Quebec, Montreal, 1976); Western Arctic Claim, *The Inuvialut Final Agreement Entitlement* (COPE), Department of Indian Affairs and Northern Development, Ottawa, 1984). See, also, Morse, 1985.

References

AUSTRALIAN LAW REFORM COMMISSION (1986)
Report. No. 31. The Recognition of Aboriginal Customary Laws. 2 Vols. Canberra: Australian Government Printing Service.

BERNDT, R.M. (1961)
"Tribal Marriage in a Changing Social Order," 5 University of Western Australia Law Review 326.

BLAINEY, G. (1980)
A Land Half Won. Adelaide: MacMillan.

BRIDGES, B. (1973)
"The Extension of English Law to the Aborigines for Offences committed inter se, 1829-1842," 59 J.R.A.H.S. 264.

CLIFFORD, W. (1982)
"An Approach to Aboriginal Criminology," 15 A.N.Z.J. Crim. 3, 8-9.

COMMISSION OF INQUIRY INTO POVERTY (1975)
Second Main Report, Law and Poverty in Australia. Cth. Parl. Paper No. 294.

HOUSE OF COMMONS (1837)
Parliamentary Paper No. 425.

---------- (1983)
Report. Special Committee on Indian Self Government.

HOUSE OF REPRESENTATIVES STANDING COMMITTEE ON ABORIGINAL AFFAIRS (1980)
Legal Aid. Australian Government Printing Service, Canberra.

LAVERTON ROYAL COMMISSION (1975-76)
Report. Perth, Government Printer 1976.

MORSE, B.W. (1985)
"The Resolution of Land Claims," in B.W. Morse (ed.), Aboriginal Peoples and the Law: Metis and Inuit Rights in Canada. Ottawa: Carleton University Press.

MULVANEY, D.J. (1975)
The Prehistory of Australia (revised edition). Ringwood: Penguin.

POULTER, S. (1986)
English Law and Ethnic Minority Customs. London: Butterworths.

RYAN, L. (1981)
The Aboriginal Tasmanians. St. Lucia: University of Queensland Press.

SUTTON, P. (1985)
"Aboriginal Customary Marriage Determination and Definition," 12 A.L.B. 13.

WALKER, J. and D. BILES (1985)
Australian Prisoners 1984. Australian Institute of Criminology, Canberra.

Aboriginal law and its importance for Aboriginal people: observations on the task of the Australian Law Reform Commission

Rob Riley

The National Aboriginal Conference was greatly indebted to the Australian Law Reform Commission for having, in the course of its work on the Reference on Aboriginal Customary Law, given the Conference the opportunity to address a number of bodies, including the Commission on Folk Law and Legal Pluralism at its symposia in Vancouver in August 1983. I must make it perfectly clear at the outset, however, that our acceptance of any such generous offer in no way indicated that the National Aboriginal Conference necessarily endorsed what the Law Reform Commission, its members or its consultants said at those symposia, in the Law Reform Commission's Final Report on the Reference, in any papers in this volume, or on any other occasion. They offered us time to speak, and we accepted, but that was the extent of the relationship.

The National Aboriginal Conference, which I and my colleagues represented in a number of discussions, existed since 1977 when it was formed to give Aboriginal Australians a political voice. It consisted of 36 members who were elected to ascertain and represent the views of the Aboriginal people and organizations within as many electorates. The election in Australia of a Federal Labour Government offered us hope that this political voice would be heeded in the development and implementation of policies favourable to Aboriginal progress and self-determination. Under the former Conservative Government this did not happen and the NAC found itself obliged to pursue its campaign for equality and justice in the international arena in the belief that world indignation would force a change of attitude.

The Reference on Aboriginal Customary Law led the Australian Law Reform Commission to engage in an evaluation of the past relationship between Aboriginal customary law and the Australian legal system and to seek to ascertain what kind of relationship could exist in the future. It sought the views of the NAC but because of limited financial and staff resources we had difficulty in responding. We hope that the government will provide realistic and adequate funding to enable us to respond more effectively in the future. In the meantime I would now like to express some personal views on the subject with the understanding that, though they would likely be supported by my colleagues in the NAC, they do not represent any official Conference position.

The question of legal pluralism - the dual existence and operation of two or more laws within a total society - is essentially one of right. The rights of different factions within that society must first be acknowledged if argument is to proceed on *how* the laws will function together. Unless right is acknowledged, and guaranteed, further discussion would be pointless. It would suggest patronization, and of course that is no basis on which to build a mutual and equal relationship. How do we approach the question of right? Is it doubted in the first place? Is there in the Australian situation really any firm and unshakeable belief on the part of the dominant white culture that Aborigines have a *right* to believe in and apply their own law to their own people? Or is it generally felt that, as a minority, they don't really have any rights at all or at best they have only those rights that the majority group will allow, those rights that will not interfere with the administration and development of the country in the best interest of this majority?

Aboriginals believe that nearly two hundred years ago they were subject to invasion by hostile forces. British sailors landed, hoisted the Union Jack, and claimed the 'Great South Land' for the British Crown. Were the Aboriginal people given any option? If they had approached those early explorers and said: "Look, we'd rather you didn't stop here", would those explorers have returned to Europe with a disappointed look saying "Back to the drawing board"? Hardly. In fact they didn't bother to ask, and doubtless they didn't care, what the Aborigines thought. And when Aboriginal opposition to their 'settlement' occurred they proceeded, without hesitation and with deadly resolve, to silence that opposition with a gun. Seldom, if ever, did they acknowledge the right of Aborigines to the land they themselves needed for their egotistical, economic progress. We must remember that the original settlers were the dregs of Europe who were sent to Australia simply because they didn't fit into their own society. They were desperate for status and knew that this only came through ownership of land. What they wanted, they took. There was no question of right about it. Aboriginal Australia was invaded, and the invaders embarked on a campaign of annihilation that was to decimate the Aboriginal population.

Historians, however, continue to believe that this occupation was as peaceful in intent, as it was inevitable. While abhorring the genocidal skills of Australia's first settlers they insist that the intention was never to dispossess the Aboriginal people brutally, and point out that the Monarch himself had instructed Captain Cook to seek Aboriginal approval for white settlement. The terrorism and slaughter that followed were 'terrible mistakes'. This rationalization, however, presents modern white Australia with a dilemma. If they assert that the settlement of Australia was not an aggressive invasion followed by forced occupation, then they must accept, in retrospect at least, a moral obligation to recognize the rights of the people who occupied the country beforehand. For only under the accepted terms of invasion and occupation would such rights inevitably be forfeited.

So, assuming that white Australia accepts that it has the moral obligation, if not the actual inclination, to acknowledge Aboriginal right, it must acknowledge, as included within that right, the right of Aboriginals to believe in and apply their own law to their own people. And this is an obligation that cannot be fulfilled with less than total commitment. The mentality of benevolent dictatorship is unacceptable. Humouring of the Aboriginal people, or a hedging of criticism is unacceptable. Half measures are not good enough. The commitment must be total, and it must involve a real endeavour to understand what customary law is, how it is practised and applied, and how integral it was, and remains, to the social, economic, cultural and political development of the Aboriginal people encapsulated within a dominant and alien society.

Let us consider for a moment what might have been the situation had not the outside world discovered Australia. What type of society would exist on the continent today? An archipelago of scattered and dwindling tribes, beset by crippling diseases, stupefied by alcohol, living in rusty iron humpies? Or a united and contented people, caring for each other and for their environment with skill and compassion? A proud and dignified people that had no need to own land because in fact it owned them? We know the answer and we know the reality. The white man came and conquered. And then in his acute shame at the bloody deeds he had done, he tried to remove the remnants of a broken and demoralized people by hiding them away on reserves and missions where all trace of their Aboriginality was to be wiped out. Not only had he all but murdered an entire race of people but he then tried to murder a cultural heritage and identity as old as time itself. It was a tragic chapter in the book of human development on this planet.

Today the descendants of those early settlers are puzzled and confused about the past and in a quandary about how to handle the present or prepare for the future. As they view with great discomfort their forefathers' handiwork they talk eagerly of conciliation and make what to them are magnanimous gestures of appeasement. They evince a mixture of guilt and resentment. And amazingly they wonder at our cynicism.

Nevertheless the Aboriginal people stand ready to co-operate in any genuine attempt to map out a positive plan for future development of a relationship with the white majority. They have shown remarkable resilience and tenacity throughout two centuries of abuse and will continue to foster these characteristics in this and future generations. The Aboriginal spirit that sustained them, sustains them still. They consider the question of acknowledgement, acceptance and tolerance of Aboriginal customary law within the confines of a dominant culture as a priority. They are prepared to assist those agencies which are grappling with the problems of how that law is to co-exist with the Australian legal system. And it must be appreciated that their involvement is a paramount necessity. For it would be the height of absurdity for anyone but an Aboriginal to attempt to understand the complexity of customary law: I know this, as an Aboriginal, and I wish to impress it upon others. Any wider understanding of Aboriginal customary law will require patient instruction by Aboriginal people themselves. For we are not talking about reams of parchment that hold the wisdom of a few hundred years of British justice but about a complex philosophical and religious way of living that has been carefully preserved and passed down through countless generations by Aboriginal men and women who, in anthropo?logical terminology, are known as persons of high degree.

Strictly and frankly speaking we should not be asking how this customary law can fit inside the parameters of the Australian legal system, but how the Australian legal system can fit inside the much wider and profound parameters of customary law. But of course that cannot be. Australian Aboriginals, thanks to the genocidal skills of European settlers, now number just two percent of the overall Australian population. So no matter whether my suggestion is correct, its adoption is not feasible and simply will not happen. Aboriginals know this. They have no option but to be realistic.

However, there are many principles that will not be prostituted for expediency. Foremost among these is the principle that Aboriginals and Aboriginals alone will consider, recommend or approve changes to that law in a spirit of accommodation of restrictions imposed by the inherent nature of the Australian legal system. The Aboriginal people are aware that progress towards ratification of a dual system of law must require compromise. But do not expect me to elucidate on these aspects of customary law that could be changed: this is for Aboriginals to decide alone and is not a subject for public argument.

There are aspects of customary law that are repugnant to the wider society. Tribal killings, for example, are regarded as murder by those who do not understand the complex reasoning behind them. By western law they are wrong.

By tribal law they are necessary. But on what ground are the mores of western law to predominate in the assessment of customary law? In terms of age alone, tribal law enjoys a seniority of many thousands of years. It has existed through the ages unchanged, understood and accepted by the people who created it, nurtured and refined till it was the purest and most profound system of legal control and justice on the face of the globe. Is this to be callously discarded because of the dictates of another society, no matter how strong in numbers, that came as unwelcome guests and stayed to take over the household? Again customary law provides for a system of tribal marriage that evolved from the intent and desire of the Aboriginal people to keep their race pure and strong. It worked successfully for millenia. Is it to be changed or abandoned simply because it offends the sensitivities of strangers?

These are considerations for Aboriginals to anguish over and to decide. They cannot be rushed to suit the timetables of government Commissions. You cannot condense thousands of years of wisdom into a "take it or leave it" package. There is more at stake than the physical manifestation of a law. There is meaning, there is reason, there is integrity to be considered.

Of course Aboriginals are aware that the situation has changed and changed irrevocably. They are not fools, my people. They have survived in union with nature for many generations in circumstances of primitive simplicity because they have a law that controls everything they do, everything they say and everything they think. They respect that law because it is based on an intimate contact with the land itself, their Mother. Therefore they appreciate fully that the changes in the physical situation around them that started so brutally and unexpectedly some two centuries ago will not stop. Their eminent adaptability is evidenced by their physical survival. But this confrontation could not, cannot, and will not change the basic Aboriginal character. Aboriginal culture has not been compromised by the materialist culture of the west. A Japanese transistor radio may increase our knowledge of the world outside, but it does not change the truth of our existence. And we as Aboriginals are the envy of others because we know that truth and through it we know ourselves.

The Australian Law Reform Commission, in its evaluation of the relationship between our law and that of white Australia, operated from the vantage point of power that was denied those it sought to influence and control by that evaluation. It was inevitable that the Commission would recommend that any changes it found necessary were more necessary for us than for them. It is fait accompli. Neverthe?less, we are willing to co-operate. We cannot lose our law. The law itself transcends any attempts by white Australia to come to terms with its own guilt. The law is sacred and forever; it will not change. The best that the Commission could have hoped for was that Aboriginals in their wisdom would adjust the administration of the law to accommodate dominant interests. And it is to this end that those charged with considering the Commission's recommendations should apply their energies.

If they require Aboriginal people to review the law, then they must be prepared to make available resources and facilities which will aid this process. They must discard the arrogance of presumed 'white superiority' and accept that they are dealing with something they do not and cannot understand. If, on the other hand, they pursue the course they have followed hitherto, then they will simply bring about the repression of the law by the people it serves. This occurred before, after the invasion, while the whiteman stumbled along the paths of protectionism, integration, assimilation and other management policies. Our law was there always to sustain and guide us, but we were not prepared to display it publicly to derision and scorn. It is there still and it is as strong as ever.

Certainly, as I encouraged the Commission to forge ahead so I encourage other like-minded bodies today: but in a spirit of understanding. I encourage them to seek Aboriginal involvement and interest: but in a spirit of commitment. Provide Aborigines with the wherewithall to meet and discuss these matters at length, and expect nothing. Then and only then may Australia come even remotely close to the objectives which motivated the Commission.

The indigenization of social control in Canada

Paul Havemann

I. Introduction

In 1982, the School of Human Justice of the University of Regina was commissioned by the Solicitor General of Canada to review the research findings of the past 10 years relating to "Natives and Justice" in Canada, in order to summarize and analyse the policy implications which could be derived from this body of research. This article is based on part of that Report which we entitled 'Law and Order for Canada's Indigenous People' (Havemann et al., 1984).

In agreeing to undertake that project we were aware of a major ethical conundrum. To quote Hugh Brody:

> It is never easy to know why research is being done, or whose interests in the end will be served. The accumulation of knowledge about colonial or tribal populations is often a facet of control and exploitation - even when the researchers firmly believe otherwise. To be neglected by science, therefore, might well be a blessing (Brody 1981:xii-xiii).

We were also determined to heed Kathleen Gough's injunction to those conducting research concerning indigenous people:

> to evaluate and analyse, as a world system and inter-connected political economy, the structure of western imperialism and the common and variant features of its impact on the non-western world (Gough 1968:147).

In order to resolve this ethical conundrum we focussed our attention upon the imposed legal system (Kidder 1979), that is, a system of the 'colonial' state (Burman and Harrel-Bond 1979) while trying to avoid the tendency, common among researchers, 'to blame the victims' (Ryan 1971) for their plight. Our critique of indigenization is not, however, an attempt to speak for indigenous people, but rather to analyse the motives and underlying assumptions of the 'colonial' system of social control for advocating 'indigenization'.

Moreover, we employed the conceptual vocabulary of 'colonization', 'pacification', and the 'development of underdevelopment' to highlight the inter-connected political economy which makes up the common and variant features of 'Western Imperialism' as it determines the relationship of Canada's indigenous people to the Canadian state. In this context, reform measures within the criminal justice system, the imposed system of social control, especially those concerning the police (the long-serving agents of militarized pacification) can be re-evaluated. What do these reforms contribute to the welfare state's compensatory rhetoric of self-government, self-determination and autonomy or to the alleviation of the concrete realities of pacification, assimilation and poverty?

Our conclusion is that a reform such as indigenization, i.e., the recruitment of indigenous people to enforce the laws of the colonial power, can rarely be a satisfactory measure. The benefits to the colonial criminal justice system gained from recruiting indigenous people to enforce its rules must be weighed against the burdens which this may entail for indigenous people. These include short-term personal ones such as the threat to identity and the necessity of managing conflicting loyalties, and the long-term political cost of participating in a hybridized (Abel 1982) system which may serve to retard the process toward increased autonomy.

It may be that once upon a time small, stable, homogeneous communities had the capacity to exert real social control through informal and indigenous means, i.e., non-sovereign power. In such a community, the formal or state system of social control is a mere adjunct. Presumably, this is the ideal role of 'consensus' policing (Cowell, Jones and Young 1982). Like the urban poor of the metropole, the indigenous people of the hinterland have experienced, almost since the inception of the process of colonization, a different reality - that of 'militarized' policing. An essential dimension of the colonization process employed by western imperialism has been the subjugation and pacification of the indigenous community by military means. The North West Mounted Police and their successors, the Royal Canadian Mounted Police, were, along with the missionaries, in the vanguard of pacification aimed at creating a disciplined, orderly hinterland suitable for the most efficient mercantile exploitation. This has resulted in the 'development of underdevelopment' of the hinterland.

Indigenization is a bureaucratic reform measure and part of the process of underdevelopment. Underdevelopment has forced indigenous people into limbo between hinterland and metropole. In both metropolitan centres and the hinterland, whether they be in Central, South (Petras 1978), or North America, Australia, New Zealand, or South Africa, indigenous people join the ranks of those marginal to the mode of production dictated by modern, patriarchal captialism. As marginals, their plight is analogous to that of blacks in the U.S. and U.K., 'pieds noirs' in France, and Turkish guest-workers in Sweden and Western Germany who occupy the poverty-ridden ghettos of the large, declining, de-industrializing conurbations. As the global economic crisis (Amin *et al.*, 1982) deepens, such groups are increasingly the targets of militarized policing or pacification which is apparently required to control these 'alien' reserve or surplus armies of labour and their dependents (Hall *et al.*, 1978, Benyon 1984) in the declining welfare state (O'Connor 1973, Panitch 1977, Gough 1981).

The 'indigenization of policing' in Canada is both an attempt to address the historical problem of militarized policing always experienced by hinterland people and the contemporary trend toward militarization of policing in the metropolitan centres. As such, its intent is benign. During the decades of economic growth from the Second World War until the 1970s, policies such as 'indigenization' arose to promote consensual rather than coerced co-operation from marginal classes. In the deepening crisis of authority, legitimacy and economic viability of the welfare state, the function of indigenization has become more significant and also more contradictory. The crisis leads inexorably to the centralization of control and away from pluralistic legal and political processes. This chapter, therefore, examines 'indigenization' against such a backdrop.

II. Indigenization in lieu of legal pluralism

> ... the task of theorists of legal pluralism [is] to identify the nature and forms of power relations which pre-exist and co-exist and the 'meta' or sovereign power of the state, in interaction with the micro-mechanisms of social (non-sovereign) power operating at all levels of society (Baxi 1986:13).

The study of the 'indigenization' of policing is an attempt to examine the interaction between the sovereign power of the state as exerted through the imposed system of social control and the use of the 'micro-mechanisms of social (non-sovereign) power' as manifested in the knowledge, authority and identity of indigenous people to enhance the power of the imposed system.

In Canada, the sovereign power of the State has been absolute. The Canadian state's legal system acknowledges no other legal system either in terms of indigenous norms or dispute resolution mechanisms. 'Indigenized' police, by definition, must always serve within the imposed system of social control backed by the sovereign power of the state and enforce the criminal law of that state. The Canadian state, a federal version of the 'Westminster' model of government, has, despite the presence of Treaties with Indian Nations, never been sufficiently pluralistic to tolerate autonomy for the indigenous nations within its territory (Lyon 1985). The creation of reserves and the violent subjugation of the Metis Nation under Louis Riel in the nineteenth century provide the historical and constitutional context for any contemporary call for recognition of a non-state legal system in Canada.

Even the grudging and ambiguous affirmation of "existing aboriginal and treaty rights" in the new Canadian constitution under section 35 of the *Constitution Act, 1982* represents recognition of rights in the state legal system rather than rights to recognition of indigenous non-state legal systems or elements thereof, since none of them 'exist' at present. It is arguable that existing rights might be re-interpreted in terms of international declarations (Lyon 1985:419). In Canada and Australia, the state legal systems have cautiously recognized indigenous custom (Grant 1982, Zlotkin 1984, Hennessy 1984:336) as one small concession to the existence of autonomous normative systems located within the culture of indigenous people.

Ironically, in North America it is the U.S.A. which, despite an official policy of genocide for most of the nineteenth century, and the twentieth century's assimilationist rhetoric of the melting pot, has in its constitutional framework accommodated a more pluralistic approach to non-state legal systems. Tribal courts and codes of law, such as the *Indian Child Welfare Act*, are accepted features of the governance of Indian nations in the U.S. (Morse 1980). In Canada, despite the rhetoric of a 'cultural mosaic', the indigenization of social control and regulation seems an end in itself rather than a transitional stage towards a more pluralistic legal system. Indigenization serves as a cheap substitute for some measure of autonomy, self-government or, indeed, sovereignty. It assimilates indigenous people into the imposed social control apparatus rather than autonomizing the social control apparatus for the benefit of indigenous people.

A case study of the indigenization of policing provides an insight into the process of indigenization paralleled in nearly every other component of the criminal justice system. 'Indigenization' in Canada involves the affirmative recruitment of indigenous individuals as police officers in federal, provincial and municipal police forces. Indigenization has emerged as an aspect of the solution to the problem of the 'over-involvement' of indigenous people with the criminal justice system over the last twenty years in policing (Canada, DIAND 1973; Hale 1974; Harris 1977; Bryant, Hawkes and Machan 1979; Singer and Moyer 1981); as Justices of the Peace (Mewett 1982; Maracle, McCormick and Jolly 1982); in correctional services (NCSA 1980b; National Conference 1975); in the appointment of Native court workers to offer special interpreter/advocacy services within the formal court system (NCSA 1982, Fearn and Kupfer 1981); and even as lawyers (Maclean 1977). Government-sponsored reviews and research reveal that indigenization is the preferred means of 'integrating' indigenous people into the imposed system of social control. Indeed, 'indigenization' is presented as the progressive means to manage the conflictual relationships at the interface between indigenous people and the criminal justice system.

In contrast, indigenous spokespeople have not advocated 'indigenization', calling instead for the development of 'Indian institutions' or 'Indian service delivery systems' (Brass:1979; NCSA 1980a; Maracle, McCormick and Jolly 1982).

III. The political economy of indigenization

The debate over the merits and demerits of 'indigenization' is one concerning the distribution of political and economic power. We must start with 'pacification' as the basis upon which the relationship between indigenous people and the Canadian state rests (Kellough 1980). Leopold Pospisil describes pacification accordingly:

> Whenever a colonial power moves into new territory it inevitably effects immediate and profound changes in the native political structure. "Pacification" the word used for establishing colonial control over a territory usually means not only eliminating native warfare and enforcing intra-as well as inter-tribal peace, but also taking away the people's independence and limiting or completely abrogating the powers of native political leadership (Pospisil 1979:131).

The denial of their independence and the limitation upon or abrogation of indigenous leadership in Canada has had disastrous results for indigenous people. A critical feature of this outcome is their "over-involvement" with the Canadian criminal justice system. Most explanations of this outcome are based upon the findings of government-sponsored, positivist researchers who simply quantify and describe the dimensions of the problem. This approach leads to the conclusion that the path to social order and, therefore, consensual conformity with the law, lies in assimilation (Reasons 1977; Michalis and Badcock 1979; Verdun-Jones and

Muirhead 1979-80) and not the sharing of power by the state. The maldistribution of power in the existing social order is, therefore, not challenged or built into our understanding of the problem. Solutions such as indigenization which have merely 'tinkered' with existing arrangements have maintained their appeal:

> For the politician and the planner, positivism provides a model of human nature which, in its consensual aspects, allows the world 'as it is' to remain unquestioned and, in its determinist notion of human action, offers the possibility of rational planning and control (Taylor, Walton and Young 1973:35).

It is our contention that no appropriate policy concerning law enforcement among indigenous people can be developed from perspectives which allow 'the world as it is' to remain unquestioned. Reasons describes the characteristics of this perspective:

> The order/assimilationist perspective minimizes the significance of power and coercion in everyday life between subordinate and superordinate groups, emphasizing the social psychology of individual and group adaptation to dominant group values and practices. Society is viewed as made up of competing individuals who carry out their competition within the context of neutral social institutions. Thus, everyone is equal and has equal opportunity (Reasons 1977:255).

We argue that indigenization must be understood in terms of the tensions between consent and coercion as a means of social control. James O'Connor suggests:

> ... that the capitalistic state must try to fulfill two basic and often mutually contradictory functions - accumulation and legitimization .... This means that the state must try to maintain or create the conditions in which profitable capital accumulation is possible. However, the state also must try to maintain or create the conditions for social harmony. A capitalist state that openly uses its coercive forces to help one class accumulate capital at the expense of other classes loses its legitimacy and hence undermines the basis of its loyalty and support (O'Connor 1973:6).

Indigenization masks the reliance of the contemporary welfare state upon coercion and hence the consequential over-involvement of indigenous people as a class with the criminal justice system can be explained in terms of the deficiencies of indigenous people. Indigenous people constitute approximately a mere 3.5%

of the Canadian population and are marginal to the major economic and political forces in the state. For this reason, their discontent seldom represents a threat to social harmony and government has little need to legitimize itself in their eyes. Indigenous people become a relevant group only as political footballs used to secure electoral advantage, or when their presence impedes resource exploitation, land appropriation or urban development.

As Ponting and Gibbins (1980:xvi) conclude, indigenous people are 'irrelevant' in a political sense. In particular, they have been victims of the process of the development of underdevelopment, a process involving the systematization of an unequal exchange of power, goods and control between the metropolitan centres and the hinterland. Indeed, the denial of 'aboriginal' rights, and indigenous autonomy as well as the refusal to settle land claims and an emphasis upon 'law and order' for Indians purchase electoral advantage and 'legitimacy' in the eyes of the majority.

Theories about the development of underdevelopment in the Third World, derived from models developed by A.G. Frank (1976), S. Amin (1976) and James Petras (1978), have considerable application to the Canadian situation (Dosman 1972; Elias 1975; Watkins 1977; Kellough 1980; Havemann 1982; Frideres 1983). Such models help to explain the development and persistence of underdevelopment wherever an economy consisting of a developed capitalist sector, for example, that dominated by the Hudson's Bay Company or uranium mining multi-nationals, exists alongside the essentially pre-capitalist economy of hunters, gatherers, trappers and fishermen. In such a dual economy the "developed" sector will always exploit the pre-capitalist sector. Such an exploitative relationship results in an uneven exchange between the metropole, the capitalist sector, and the hinterland, the largely pre-capitalist sector.

Petra's work articulates the linkage between 'modernization', i.e., the post-military phase of pacification, and 'indigenization' of control in the overall context of underdevelopment:

> Through imperial-directed modernization, wide strata have been incorporated into a hierarchical society of subordination and consumerism; the entourage of clients has been tied to the lifestyle of the imperial patron and largely earns the residual surplus by performing non-productive work, i.e., policing the local population .... Population movements in the periphery can best be understood in terms of the flow of capital: from areas of surplus appropriation to areas of surplus disposal - from hinterland to capital city, from periphery to core (Petras 1978:75).

IV. The human costs of pacification

> In a socio-economic sense, Native people are the most disadvantaged group of any population segment in Canada ... and because of a combination of cultural, jurisdictional, logistical, financial and administrative barriers, the Native people of Canada often do not receive the socio-economic benefits promised by Canadian Law (Michalis and Badcock 1979:9).

Such jurisdictional barriers involving the imposed law of the state legal system, and logistical, financial and administrative barriers to a fair exchange of the wealth derived from the hinterland is explicable in terms of the processes of pacification/modernization and underdevelopment.

In 1980 the federal Department of Indian Affairs and Northern Development published a survey which assembled specific comparative data for social planners wanting to make adjustments to the management and delivery of the social, economic and political programs offered to indigenous people in Canada. The document is a damning indictment of the Canadian state's failure to manage its contradictory functions, and in particular of government's complicity in and failure to prevent the hinterland from being 'pacified' and modernized as a mere adjunct to the metropolitan marketplace:

> Approximately two-thirds of the Indian population live in remote or rural areas, a large proportion of which are accessible only by water or air.
>
> The proportion of Indians living in high unemployment regions is slightly more than twice the national proportion.
>
> The increasing problem of finding adequate jobs on reserves is reflected in the increased migration off reserves - from 16% in 1966 to 30% in 1979 (Canada, DIAND 1980:63).
>
> One in three families lives in crowded conditions. 11,000 new homes are required and 9,000 need repair. Less than 50% of Indian houses are properly serviced, compared to a national level of over 90% (ibid, 1980:3).

The survey states that recent estimates of Indian unemployment have ranged from 35% to 75% of the labour force age population. No figures were available giving the number of indigenous people still pursuing a "traditional" (i.e., non-wage) hunting and gathering existence in the non-capitalist sector of the regional economy, but estimates range between 10% and 15% of the population between 15 and 64 years old (Canada, DIAND 1980:58-59).

At the same time, the dominant segments of the Canadian state accumulate enormous wealth from the renewable and non-renewable resources extracted from the hinterland, such as lumber, oil, gas, uranium, fish and furs. Indicators of the human costs of this unequal exchange are even more telling illustrations of the impact of coerced underdevelopment:

> Life expectancy, a reflection of health standards, is still ten years less than the national proportion.
>
> Violent deaths are three times national levels; suicides particularily in the 15-24 age group, more than six times national rates.
>
> The strength and stability of family units appear to be eroding, with higher divorce rates, more births outside marriage, and more children in care (Canada, DIAND 1980:3).

V. Pacification by consent and coercion

Typically, social order among majority groups has been achieved through programs and policies of legitimization involving social spending. The control or containment of marginals, such as members of minority groups from or in the hinterland, has been achieved by coercion. Coercion, by definition, results in an over-involvement with the imposed social control system, namely, the criminal justice system.

Public expenditure patterns in the Canadian welfare state reveal that government appears to devote considerably greater public funding to policing, that is coercive social control, for indigenous populations, while spending proportionately more creating consensual social control among the dominant metropolitan population. For example:

> During the past 10 to 20 years, expenditures on Indians have been relatively stable since 1970, growing in real terms 14% per capita, compared to 128% per capita growth in other federal social services (Canada, DIAND 1980:98).

In the hinterland territories which have the largest proportions of indigenous people, spending on policing in the Yukon is 171% and, in the Northwest

Territories, 244% above the per capita national average. The Yukon population consists of 13% registered Indians and the Northwest Territories 18%, but both include further indigenous peoples who are not registered Indians. These high levels of expenditure mean that the hinterland territories have the highest number of police per 1000 people. Similarly, the province with the largest indigenous population, Saskatchewan, has the highest number of police per 1000 people for a jursidiction in southern Canada. These are not, however, the jurisdictions with the highest crime rates.

Some of the research reveals that police are in fact the only form of 24-hour 'social' service available to people in both remote and rural areas (Singer and Moyer 1981), and in urban ghettos. One must conclude that the policing of indigenous communities fulfills a hybrid function of order maintenance and social service to a much greater degree than it does in other communities. The indigenization of policing is entirely consistent with this hybridized - order maintenance/social service - mode of social control for indigenous communities. Such an allocation of resources and form of delivery system, however, must inevitably result in the over-involvement of indigenous people with the criminal justice system.

The appearance of consensual social control is achieved by offering policing by indigenous people for indigenous people. Indigenized, social service-oriented policing of indigenous people is not necessarily benign. It highlights the territorial injustice of their unequal treatment by the waxing and waning welfare state as the fiscal crisis deepens. Such territorial injustice is both rural and urban. Policing is being used as a substitute for coherent urban social planning in Canadian cities. The saturation of poorer neighbourhoods with police to corral and ghettoize indigenous people into certain districts is an emerging trend. In one Prairie city a large canine unit was developed for this purpose. An independent review (Faris and Currie 1983) revealed that 58% of those injured by police dogs were of Indian ancestry!

The mixing of social services and order-maintenance has a 'net-widening effect' which inevitably leads to the over-involvement of indigenous people with correctional services. Police are the gatekeepers of the criminal justice system - it is in large part their activities which dictate the size of the prison population. Registered Indians, i.e., those whose status is recognized under the federal *Indian Act*, make up only 1.3% of the total Canadian population, 2% of the Alberta population, 5% of the Saskatchewan population, and 4.3% of the Manitoba population, yet they constitute 19% of the Alberta, 22% of the Saskatchewan and 30% of the Manitoba penitentiary population (Canada, DIAND 1980:37).

Statistics which include all indigenous people, that is all those of Indian ancestry, and which cover the population of provincial jails holding petty offenders confirm this gruesome modern manifestation of cultural genocide. In Saskatchewan, for example, where 16% of the population is calculated to be of Indian ancestry, well over 65% of the inmates in the provincial correctional system are from this population! John Hylton estimated from these figures that in the population over age fifteen, a registered Indian male was 37 times, and a Metis or non-registered Indian 12 times, more likely to be admitted to a correctional centre than a white male. The situation for women was worse still; a registered Indian female was 118 times, and a Metis or non-registered Indian 25 times, more likely to be incarcerated than a white female (Hylton 1980:16).

Such social indicators reveal how coerced underdevelopment has tragically affected the indigenous people of Canada. Their share of social spending is much smaller than their share of police costs. Jail appears to be a 'rite of passage' for extraordinary numbers. Fiscal logic and humanitarian principle would seem to demand that preventive measures be devised within the criminal justice system, but even more urgently and drastically in the constitutional, social and economic systems.

Indigenization of policing has evolved as an ameliorative policy within the criminal justice system. We believe it compounds the net-widening effect of the hybridized social service and order-maintenance policing which indigenous people experience. Ultimately, this contributes to their over-involvement in the criminal justice system. We now turn to its negative symbolic impact in the development of policy toward indigenous people.

VI. Colonial policy since 1969: assimilation, integration and accommodation

The infamous 1969 Federal Government White Paper, which proposed the abolition of Indian status and thereby crystallized 100 years of assimilationist federal policies, served as a catalyst for the development of indigenous people's organizations. Since that time these organizations have become progressively more Pan-Indian, more nationalistic and more militant in their rhetoric and dealings with government (Boldt 1980; Frideres 1983:246-49). A basic plank in the platform of indigenous organizations since 1969 has been the demand for greater or even total autonomy, i.e., self-determination or sovereignty, and the end of the policy of assimilation. Such demands include autonomous control over the delivery of services and ultimate recognition of the non-state Aboriginal legal systems.

Ken Svenson has identified four patterns of government response to these demands. These can be classified in terms of a spectrum ranging through separation, integration and accommodation to assimilation. The demand for autonomy implies a policy of separation. Options at this end of the spectrum have aroused little government support. Compromises, however, between government and indigenous people have increasingly revealed that government no longer seeks to pursue overt 'assimilation' as its primary operating principle. Instead, Svenson found the increasing adoption of 'accommodation' and 'integration' policies. 'Accommodation' is reflected in the creation of autonomous but government-funded agencies.

> The accommodation alternative means facilitating the separate development of a number of Indian institutions in those areas which are key to the maintenance of Indian identity such as education and government and some economic institutions (Svenson 1978:15).

'Integration', Svenson suggests, has been the principle post-1969 compromise:

> ... integration involves combining two entities with the result being different than either one of the original entities (Svenson 1978:14).

He argues that the implementation of integrative policies in decision-making arenas has given Indians only token involvement. Co-optation at an organizational level and indigenization at the level of front-line service delivery workers are the dominant integrative tactics. Admittedly, 'integration' and 'accommodation' represent a form of pacification which is preferable to assimilation. Our question is: does the shift represent sufficient possibilities for a transition to autonomous social control to off-set the disabling and dependency-inducing features of co-optation or indigenization?

Outside the realm of the criminal justice system, a considerable degree of 'accommodation' and 'integration' has taken place since 1969, particularly in the field of Indian local government at the band level:

> During the past 10 to 20 years bands have assumed increased responsibility for the administration of government programs. $227.2 million is now administered directly by bands (1/3 of the Indian Affairs Program budget) compared to $34.9 million in 1970-1 (13% of the budget) (Canada, DIAND 1980).

and the political level:

> There are now established political organizations to act as policy and program interlocators with government. These organizations are supported through consultation, program and research funding by government (now $19 million, compared to $4.4 million in 1971-2) (ibid. 1980:99).

Autonomous health care, education programs, local governments and political organizations have been 'accommodated' by state policy. Policing policy has been much more timid; yet police remain key actors at the interface between indigenous people and the colonial welfare state:

> [T]he prototype of imposed law as it seems most generally understood is the colonial situation where legal systems are imported from dominant cultures and forced upon indigenous populations (Kidder 1979:289).

The military phase of colonial pacification in Canada followed this prototypical model of imposed social control. The indigenous non-state social control or legal system was destroyed and the state legal system, especially the crime control apparatus, was forced upon Indian people.

The contemporary modernization phase of pacification involves the 'integration' model of imposed social control which includes 'indigenization.' Research by authors studying colonial regimes where the settler or colonial minority government seeks to control the majority of the population provide evidence of the highly disruptive impact of even the integrative model (Kidder 1977; Galanter 1968; Fitzpatrick 1980). Despite its appearance as more benign than the model of pure imposition, the integrated or indigenized model is one in which the colonizer preserves aspects of the indigenous social control system, primarily in order to utilize its authority to support the new pattern of domination.

Such a strategy may have unintended consequences. Co-optation of indigenous people's social control systems may fail to procure the level or form of pacification desired by the colonizer. The policy may sometimes provide a colonized people with some leverage to enable them to mitigate the full impact of colonization and preserve some identity and autonomy. Or, as Massell (1968) shows, indigenization as an aspect of co-optation has sometimes simply reinforced the power of patriarchical and reactionary groups within the indigenous society against the wishes of the "reform-minded" colonizer. The contemporary anti-reform position of male-dominated, government-funded Indian organizations with respect to Indian women's rights may be a current Canadian example (Jamieson 1978). There are obviously no simple answers for those seeking to make Canada's imposed social control system more relevant to indigenous people but it seems imperative that indigenization is not casually accepted as a panacea.

VII. The integrative model of imposed social control

Our review of the evaluative literature on Canada's criminal justice system and its programmes relating to indigenous people (Havemann, *et al.*, 1984) revealed that the integrative model of imposed social control employs an order/assimilationist perspective in which the problem of indigenous crime is defined and solved using a conceptual framework which appears to contain the following assumptions:

1) the law and criminal justice system are inherently just for all Canadians;

2) the disproportionate numbers of indigenous people caught in the criminal justice system can be explained by:

> i) their conspicuous criminality, the culture of poverty, alcoholism:
> In general, relationships between the police and the Indian people in these parts of Canada [B.C., the Prairies, and the Territories] are less amicable and, in many areas, have reached a stage where bitterness prevails on both sides. This is particularly true where police officers have rural detachments containing many Metis settlements or Indian reserves. The constant surveillance sometimes required by the Indian and Metis people can, under these circumstances, harden into open dislike on the part of the police (Canadian Corrections Association 1967:36).
>
> ii) the element of prejudiced discretion exercised by decision-makers throughout the imposed system of social control:
> Underlying all problems associated with Indians and Eskimos in this country are the prejudice and discrimination they meet in the attitude of non-Indians (ibid:55).
>
> iii) indigenous people's ignorance of their legal rights (and presumably obligations) and their mystification by the imposed system of social control.

The solutions derived from these explanatory assumptions are that the problem of the prejudiced exercise of discretion can be alleviated by: a) the 'cross-cultural' education of the bulk of decision-making officials in the criminal justice system who are not indigenous; b) the indigenization of decision-making and especially front-line service delivery roles by programmes of affirmative recruitment of indigenous people into policing, prosecuting, defence, legal representation, summary adjudication as justices of the peace, interpreters and workers in the correctional system. The problem of indigenous people's ignorance of their rights (and duties) and their mystification by the system can be reduced by public legal education targeted to their communities, by the provision of legal representation, and by the provisions of indigenous interpreters and mediators, i.e., Native court workers to explain the imposed criminal justice system to them.

This conceptual model has some elements of superficial validity but it is derived largely from the findings of evaluations which have been sponsored by government and not by indigenous people. Such findings support a 'monist' rather than a pluralist view of the desirable character of a legal system and an order/assimilationist ideological perspective. This rationalizes integrationist policies such as indigenization as progressive. As a result, few of the contradictions between the integrative approach to social control and the post-1969 Federal Government rhetoric of accommodation and self-government are explored.

VIII. The contradictions of indigenization

We would argue that the indigenization of policing mirrors these contradictions. The personal, political and symbolic nature of these contradictions must be acknowledged. Indigenous communities must be offered increased opportunities for autonomous policing and there must be checks and balances in the system of social control so that they will be less compromised. Our argument is that despite the benign intent and apparent value of indigenization, it will simply compound oppression of indigenous people. We must therefore evaluate the symbolic and practical impact of indigenization in terms of its likely contribution to the liberation of the individual and the collective expression of personal and political identity and the empowerment of indigenous people.

The experience of indigenous people in Canada parallels that of the American Indian:

> ... the effect of some 200 years of imposition of American law has been the steady compression of Indian identity in both its individual and collective forms through the systematic suppression of both personal and political expression (Svensen 1979:85).

In the United States (Hagan 1966) and Australia, the indigenization of policing began in the nineteenth century.

> ... coping with renegades and common criminal elements was the original reason for organizing the Indian Police ... the appropriation bill authorizing them ... provided that they should be employed also 'for the purpose of' civilization of the Indians (Hagan 1966:69).

Hagan describes some aspects of the contradictory role of Indian Police:

> As an advance agent of the whiteman's way he frequently found himself opposed by most of his fellow tribesmen especially the old respected leaders. Cast as an informer, a petty police spy, he had to report on the work habits of bands to determine whether they merited ... rations (ibid.:71).

A study of indigenous people recruited into the Royal Canadian Mounted Police's Special Constable Program asked the question:

> How much time is allocated to under cover work on reserves in an attempt to clearly identify and be able to prosecute the ringleaders that constitute the negative element in the community? (Bryant *et al.*, 1979:54).

A Cree social scientist, discussing the poor relationship between indigenous people and regular law enforcement agencies, says:

> The problem is therefore not a 'cross-cultural' conceptual disagreement but rather one relating to police attitudes and methods (Brass 1979:33).

Brass' paper points out that indigenous people have always had social control mechanisms. Thus, the integration of indigenous people into the imposed social control system as Indian Special Constables is a particular target for Brass' criticisms. As one would anticipate, he found that in the process of modernization the indigenous people recruited as Special Constables came from the "affluent," i.e., "upwardly mobile class" (defined in assimilationist terms), not from the poor or "traditional" families. Another of his findings was that all recruits are under enormous "peer" pressure to identify with the values and attitudes of their white fellow-officers. So much for altering the way discretion is exercised. He suggests that cultural relativism and racial stereotyping are reinforced by the double standard with respect to lower qualifications and lower pay which is a component of this "special" affirmative action program (Brass 1979:34-35).

The indigenous person employed in the imposed system of social control must manage a number of major contradictions impinging upon his/her identity and political loyalty. A Mohawk social worker summarizes both the negative aspects of this role and those considered a key justification for indigenization:

> The social and psychological distance between the affluent, well-integrated Indian field-worker and the self-destructive, transient alcoholic is as great as the distance which exists between their white counterparts .... What Indians have to offer to their own is an approach which is saddled with fewer prejudices arising from cultural difference (Castellano 1971: 361).

The indigenization of the police through the Indian Special Constable Program has been consistently applauded in a series of federal and provincial government studies since the early 1970s (Canada, DIAND 1973; Hodges 1974; Harris, 1977; Bryant *et al.*, 1979; Kirby 1978). The first of these was a Federal Government study in 1973 of policing on reserves, which started from the premise that:

> Indian communities or reserves have a right to expect as good policing as other Canadian communities (Canada, DIAND 1973:5-6).

This report, however, lamely explained the over-involvement of Indian people with the criminal justice system in terms of a lack of deterrence to their criminal tendencies:

> ... a variety of reasons, some of which stem from the isolated and remote nature of some reserves, policing has been less than adequate, and one of several consequences has been the disproportionately high incidence of petty crime (ibid.:5-6).

This study forms the basis for the contemporary process of indigenization.

The Policing on Reserves Study Task Force had explored three options. One was autonomous indigenous police forces with unlimited jurisdiction (Option 3a), which Indian organizations in both New Brunswick and Saskatchewan advocated. This option was rejected because of:

> ... the present lack of police experience among Indians to administer and operate such a service .... [and] the problem of recruiting to the required standard would present difficulties (DIAND 1973:16).

Another option (Option 3c) involving the outright purchase of regular policing services for Indian reserves from the province or municipality, was rejected because it was assimilationist not 'integrationist'. The compromise option adopted involved indigenization of policing through the recruitment of indigenous individuals into a separate category of Special Constable within the RCMP or provincial or municipal police (Option 3b). The rhetoric of the Task Force which conducted the study led participants to believe that all three options were equally viable. Nevertheless, the bias of the Task Force reveals that 'indigenization' via 'integration' was the officially desired policy. An immediate evaluation of the implementation of Option 3b in Ontario (Hodges 1974) confirmed the Task Force's view. The Hodges report recommended the downgrading of powers and reduction in numbers of the few band constables employed by Indian Bands, which were a component of autonomous local government. This report concluded by recommending the 'integration' of band constables into the provincial police forces (Hodges 1974:60), i.e., indigenization.

In 1978, the Alberta Government asked Mr. Justice Kirby to conduct a review of the administration of justice and Native people in Alberta (Kirby 1978). His report also recommended indigenization, although it was highly critical of the band constable scheme. Among the grounds for this criticism were the very constraints imposed upon Native constables by Federal and provincial governments. For example, they could not carry fire-arms, regularly needed outside help, and had very limited jurisdiction and salaries, and training was found to be poor. In other words, their situation compared very poorly with that of regular RCMP and municipal police. Kirby also found that band constables lacked the respect of band elders and were subject to excessive politicization and personalization in the exercise of their discretion (Kirby 1978:28). Thus, the denial of full-fledged status to band constables and their involvement with their communities served to fulfill the prophesy that they were not ready for autonomy. The ancient colonial argument against self-determination was perpetuated.

In 1980, the first evaluation of indigenized policing conducted by an indigenous people's organization appeared. The Native Counselling Service of Alberta concluded:

> In Alberta, Option 3b cannot now be regarded as a viable program for reserves. Although it was conceptually solid and there was potential for its constructive development, the program has become politically defunct. The current trend is clearly towards autonomous Indian policing (NCSA 1980a:23).

This study raised a number of problems; its report was not simply a quid pro quo to Kirby's. The integration of special constables into the regular RCMP in Alberta was found to have resulted in constables spending inadequate time on reserves. Some special constables, the review found, chose not to live on reserves suffering ostracism and conflicts of identity as a result. This tends to confirm that there are contradictions inherent in the indigenization of the pacification process which the official evaluations have ignored (Canada, DIAND 1973; Bryant *et al.*, 1979; Harris 1977; Kirby 1978).

The Bryant, Hawkes, Machan (1979) and Harris (1977) evaluations of indigenized policing confirmed indigenous people's demands for more accessible policing. However, they also tended to pre-empt the discussion about what form this policing should take. The plea for access to policing was not construed as a plea for access to other forms of informal dispute settlement, social services or crisis intervention. It was just interpreted as a request for more of the same order-maintenance.

The Federal Government's rhetoric of self-government prompted it to experiment cautiously with 'accommodating' autonomous policing. Two projects, the Amerindian Police Force in Quebec and one in Manitoba were initiated. The evaluation of policing undertaken by the Dakota-Ojibway Tribal Council (D.O.T.C.) in Manitoba, which was conducted for the federal Solicitor General, concluded:

> It is possible that by sharing the same or a similar culture and knowing the disputants personally, the D.O.T.C. officers are better able than regular members of the RCMP to deal with conflict situations by finding alternative remedies to maintain order. There is no evidence that the quality of life on reserves has changed as a result of this practice by the D.O.T.C. Police (Singer and Moyer 1981:20).

It is notable that this evaluation found that the D.O.T.C. tended to perform a social service or informal dispute settlement role while order-maintenance functions were performed by the RCMP from the local detachment. The evaluators seem to regard this as a neutral outcome. However, one could either construe this as an argument in favour of autonomous policing since it is a manifestation of 'consensus' policing, or as evidence of territorial injustices in the provision of social welfare which the Dakota-Ojibway people have been forced to remedy through police funding.

The indigenous people's own interpretation of the value of the Tribal force has been inadequately canvassed. It would be inappropriate, therefore, to draw a definitive conclusion. Even semi-autonomous police are employed in the hybrid function we have discussed in the meting out of 'informal' justice, while regular federal, provincial and municipal police mete out formal "justice" (i.e., crime control). Such a trend also serves to mask the lack of autonomy in the field of social control characterized by indigenization of the legal system. Equally, the institutionalization of a social service function in this way is no substitute for real community-controlled social services.

As the popularity of diversion, mediation, and neighbourhood justice centres attests, government is increasingly viewing community-based informal justice measures with favour. Motives involving both a financial saving and the promotion of legitimacy contribute to this positive attitude. Nevertheless, informal justice approaches can harbour dangers and advantages. Richard Abel describes some desirable attributes of "informal justice" approaches as their dissociation from state power, their non-coercive (dependent on rhetoric rather than force), consensual, non-bureaucratic, decentralized, democratic, and flexible nature. These attributes, one might argue, are the basic virtues of consensual, autonomous social control mechanisms. Abel, however, warns that:

> Where parties are unequal which ever has the law on its side prefers to appeal to formal authority ... disputants prefer true formality or true informality, not a hybrid .... And just as coercion undermines the consent that is supposed to be the foundation of informal justice, so central control undermines the autonomy of local institutions. The upshot is that the State, in the name of informality, destroys indigenous traditional informal justice and substitutes institutions that serve to extend central control, implement national programs, enhance the legitimacy of the official legal system by appearing to improve them, and undermine the local community (Abel 1982:5).

Thus, both indigenization and the creation of semi-autonomous police within the imposed social control systems are examples of hybridization - the mixing of formal with informal justice and social service with order maintenance. The reluctance to develop autonomous police forces, the consistent attack on band constable programs, and the inadequate powers and funding of these programs all illustrate that hybridized, integrated services with some semblance of 'informality' yet under the centralized control of the state are the reality concealed by government rhetoric.

Are semi-autonomous services or indigenous services even an option worth considering? Evaluations of those semi-autonomous services, such as Native court worker schemes in Ontario and Alberta, where indigenous people mediate and act as advocates for indigenous people, reveal that they experience considerable stress and confusion produced by role and loyalty conflicts arising from their demystifier/interpreter/advocate function for both indigenous people and the courts of the imposed system (Obonsawin and Jolly 1980; N.C.S.A. 1982; Fearn and Kupfer 1981). Not surprisingly perhaps, the judiciary was found to be extremely pleased with their contribution (Fearn and Kupfer 1981:59-65).

This may be compared with the utilization of Indian justice of the peace (J.P.) schemes to provide adjudication of a limited range of criminal and civil matters on reserves and in remote areas. Recent research reveals that Indian J.P.s have been consistently under-utilized. A significant reason for this state of affairs emerging from the Ontario Native Council on Justice's studies was a reluctance on the part of indigenous individuals to compromise themselves by serving as Justices of the Peace (Maracle et al, 1982:xxiv-xxxi) in the imposed system.

The Ontario Native Council on Justice, an indigenous people's organization, saw the Indian J.P. scheme as a transition toward much greater accommodation of autonomous adjudicatory institutions in that autonomy would include giving band councils the right to choose their own J.P.s. An evaluation compiled for the Ontario Attorney General, however, found it unacceptable that:

> a duly appointed Native Justice of the Peace [be] in any way subservient to or answerable to a Band Council or clan elders (Mewett 1982:218).

Conclusion

The rhetoric of self-management, self-government, and the accommodation of indigenous agencies working according to indigenous rules will involve trust and the sharing of power. Few colonial policy-makers seem prepared to abandon or modify their notions of one state-one law, and independent law enforcement and judicial institutions in order to accommodate the authority of the gerontocratic, subjective, community-based justice and the recognition of an indigenous common law. The Canadian multi-cultural mosaic is a cosmetic mask concealing the absence of cultural and legal 'pluralism'.

Indigenization and the creation of semi-autonomous entities must be acknowledged for what they are - hybrids of the imposed system of social control which appropriate indigenous personnel to enhance legitimacy. Indigenization might constitute a potentially useful 'transitional' phase for criminal justice service delivery, especially if it began at both the most senior decision-making levels and among frontline staff. It must not become an end in itself. What seems more likely is that 'indigenization' of the policing function will create serious conflicts of loyalty and personal identity, and undermine existing non-state forms of social control such as traditional informal justice.

A transition from 'assimilationist' and 'integrationist' policies to policies of accommodation and, ultimately, self-government will have to encompass the totality of government, law, legal institutions, and social and political rights, and not merely service delivery. At this stage we would urge that, rather than indigenizing policing, alternative checks and balances on the exercise of discretion by law enforcement personnel should be explored. Indigenous communities, however, are not homogeneous in terms of the needs and expectations they have of central government. Considerable choice as to the form of policing must, therefore, be offered to them. At the present time, few independent complaint procedures exist and the self-policing of police has engendered a deep distrust among indigenous people in rural, remote and urban settings. Police/community liaison committees should be explored and given greater power to publicize and discipline police agenices. Indigenous people could serve as mediators and ombudspersons by attending at the scene of incidents and participating in dispute resolution and crisis intervention. They might even monitor the conduct of police by patrolling in patrol cars. Indigenous diversion/mediation schemes could be set up to keep people away from the formal criminal justice system and so on.

A largely neglected check upon the prejudiced exercise of discretion in the crime control process is the development of the due process, advocacy capacity of indigenous communities (Morse 1976; Havemann 1982; Frewin and Maunula 1980). The Native court worker schemes have been defined as interpreter services and are primarily aimed at assisting the criminal justice system to treat indigenous people in a humane fashion and to speed the flow of cases. Other than some Indian legal service programs in British Columbia, there are no Indian legal services corresponding to the robust Aboriginal Legal Services found in Australia. Youth advocacy centres, ghetto grievance mechanisms and other services for indigenous people are sadly lacking. The federal *Young Offenders Act*, 1981 offers the potential to develop advocacy services to guarantee indigenous youth due process rights, now reinforced by the new *Canadian Charter of Rights and Freedoms* (Constitution Act, 1982). The *Young Offenders Act* also contains the potential for indigenous people to set up diversion and community service order schemes, and to participate on Youth Justice Committees. Thus, indigenous people could make a modest contributuion to defining the form of justice their youth would receive within this aspect of the imposed system. To date, few of these opportunities have been utilized.

As this brief review attests, there are numerous ways of combatting the negative exercise of discretion in the criminal justice system. The due process dimension of the adversary process must be greatly strengthened instead of concentrating upon the relatively crude option of indigenizing the gate-keepers of the system.

We would argue that the symbolic effect of co-opting indigenous people into a hybridized process of pacification, coupled with the negative personal, familial and political implications of serving in this capacity, are a contradiction of the Canadian welfare states stated goal that it seeks to allow and facilitate greater dignity, autonomy and self-government for indigenous people.

The problem of the over-involvement of the indigenous people in the imposed criminal justice system will take courage to understand and solve. Timidity about relinquishing power and accepting responsibility has characterized our thinking at all points while the problem remains and grows. Having recognized the ineffectiveness of our attempts to understand and solve the problem we have created, how can we deny indigenous people the opportunity to do better? They surely will not do worse.

References

ABEL, Richard L. (ed.) (1982)
Informal Justice. Comparative Studies, Vol. II. New York: Academic Press.

AMIN, Samir (1976)
Unequal Development. New York: Monthly Review Press.

AMIN, Samir, G. ARRIGHI, A.G. FRANK and I. WALLERSTEIN (1982)
Dynamics of Global Crisis. New York: Monthly Review Press.

BAXI, U. (1986)
"Discipline, Repression and Legal Pluralism" in P. Sack and E. Minchin (eds.), Legal Pluralism: Proceedings of the Canberra Law Workshop VII. RSSS, Australian National University.

BENYON, J. (ed.) (1984)
Scarman and After: Essays Reflecting on Lord Scarman's Report, the Riots and their Aftermath. Oxford: Pergamon Press.

BOLDT, M. (1980)
"Canadian Native Indian Leadership: Context and Composition," 12 Canadian Ethnic Studies 15.

BRASS, Oliver (1979)
"Crees and Crime: A Cross-Cultural Study," mimeographed. Regina, Saskatchewan: University of Regina.

BRODY, Hugh (1981)
Maps and Dreams. London: Penguin.

BRYANT, V.M., F.J. HAWKES and J.S. MACHAN (1979)
"Evaluation of the RCMP Special Constable Program Option 3b." (C.N.P.) Evalucan Ltd.

BURMAN, Sandra, Barbare E. HARREL-BOND (eds.) (1979)
The Imposition of Law, in Studies in Law and Social Control. New York: Academic Press.

CANADIAN DEPARTMENT OF INDIAN AFFAIRS AND NORTHERN DEVELOPMENT (1973)
Policing on Reserves. Ottawa: Department of Indian Affairs and Northern Development.

---------- (1980)
Indian Conditions: A Survey. Otttawa.

CANADIAN CORRECTIONS ASSOCIATION (1967)
Indians and the Law. Canadian Corrections Association, Ottawa.

CASTELLANO, M. (1971)
"Out of Paternalism and into Partnership: An Exploration of Alternatives in Social Service to Native People," in James. A. Draper (ed.), Citizen Participation: Canada. Toronto: New Press.

COWELL, D., T. JONES and J. YOUNG (1982)
Policing the Riots. London: Junction Books.

DOSMAN, E. (1972)
Indians: The Urban Dilemma. Toronto: McClelland and Stewart.

ELIAS, Peter, Douglas (1975)
"Metropolis and Hinterland in Northern Manitoba," mimeographed. Winnipeg, Manitoba.

FARIS, D. and W. CURRIE (1983)
"Review of the Regina Police Service Canine Unit Regional Board of Police Commissioners," Regina, Saskatchewan.

FEARN, L. and G. KUPFER (1981)
"Criminal Courtworker: Native Counselling Services of Alberta: A Program Review & Evaluation Assessment." Ottawa: Department of Justice.

FITZPATRICK, P. (1980)
Law and State in Papua New Guinea. New York: Academic Press.

FRANK, Andre Gundar (1976)
Capitalism and Underdevelopment in Latin America. New York: Monthly Review Press.

FREWIN, C.C. and F.A. MAUNULA (1980)
"A Process Evaluation of the Thunder Bay District Native Legal Counselling Service." Thunder Bay, Ontario: (n.p.).

FRIDERES, James A. (1983)
Native People in Canada: Contemporary Conflicts. Scarborough, Ontario: Prentice-Hall.

GALANTER, Marc (1968)
"The Displacement of Traditional Law in Modern India," in Journal of Social Issues 24.

GOUGH, Ian (1981)
The Political Economy of the Welfare State. London: MacMillan.

GOUGH, Kathleen (1968)
"World Revolution and the Science of Man," in Theodore Rozak (ed.), The Dissenting Academy. New York, Pantheon.

GRANT, Peter R. (1982)
"Role of Traditional Law in Contemporary Cases," in 5 Canadian Legal Aid Bulletin 107.

HAGAN, William (1966)

Indian Police and Judges: Experiments in Acculturation and Control. Connecticut: Yale University Press.

HALE, E.B. (1974)
Task Force on Policing in Ontario: Report to the Solicitor General.

HALL, Stuart, Chas CRITCHER, Tony JEFFERSON, John CLARKE and Brian ROBERTS (1978)
Policing the Crisis: Mugging, the State, and Law and Order. London: MacMillan.

HARRIS, R.E. (1977)
"Evaluation of the Indian Policing Program." Toronto: Ontario Provincial Police.

HAVEMANN, Paul L. (1982)
"The Regina Native Counsel Project: A Civilian Perspective on the Delivery of Legal Services to People of Indian Ancestry in the City," 5 Canadian Legal Aid Bulletin 69.

HAVEMANN, Paul, Keith COUSE, Lori FOSTER and Rae MATONONVITCH (1984)
"Law and Order for Canada's Indigenous People." Regina, Saskatchewan: University of Regina, Prairie Justice Research.

HENNESSY, Peter (1984)
"Aboriginal Customary Law and the Australian Criminal Law: An unresolved conflict," in B. Swanton (ed.), Aborigines and the Criminal Justice System. Australian Institute of Criminology, Woden, ACT.

HODGES, J.E. (1974)
Policing on reserves, a study group on the Role of the R.C.M.P. in Ontario.

HYLTON, John (1980)
"Admissions to Saskatchewan Provincial Correctional Centres: Projections to 1993." Regina, Sask.: Prairie Justice Research Consortium, University of Regina.

JAMIESON, Kathleen (1978)
Indian Women and the Law in Canada: Citizens Minus. Ottawa: Ministry of Supply and Services.

KELLOUGH, Gale (1980)
"From Colonialism to Economic Imperialism: The Experience of the Canadian Indian," in John Harp and John R. Hofley (eds.), Structured Inequality in Canada. Scarborough, Ontario: Prentice-Hall.

KIDDER, Robert L. (1977)
"Western Law in India: External Law and Local Response," 47 Sociological Inquiry 155.

---------- (1979)
"Toward an Integrated Theory of Imposed Law," in S. Burman and B.E. Harrel-Bond (eds.), Studies in Law and Social Control. New York: Academic Press.

KIRBY, W.J.C. (1978)
Native People in the Administration of Justice in Provincial Courts (report No. 4) Alberta Board of Review, Provincial Courts, Attorney-General. Edmonton.

LYON, Noel (1985)
"Constitutional Issues in Native Law," in B. Morse (ed.), Aboriginal Peoples and the Law: Indian, Metis and Inuit Rights in Canada. Carleton University Press.

MacLEAN, H. (1977)
"The Native Law Student Program: An Evaluation Report." Department of Justice, Ottawa.

MARACLE, S., C. McCORMICK and S. JOLLY (1982)
The Native Justice of the Peace: An Under-employed Natural Resource for the Criminal Justice System. Ontario Native Council on Justice, Toronto.

MASSELL, G. (1968)
"Law as an Instrument of Revolutionary Change in a Traditional Milieu: The Case of Soviet Central Asia," 2 Law and Society 79.

MEWETT, A. (1982)
Report to the Attorney-General of Ontario on the Office and Function of Justices of the Peace. Attorney-General, Ontario, Toronto.

MICHALIS, G. and W.T. BADCOCK (1979)
Native People and Canada's Justice System: Programmes and Issues. Department of Indian Affairs and Northern Development, Ottawa.

MORSE, Bradford (1976)
"Native People and Legal Services in Canada," 22 McGill Law Review 504.

---------- (1980)
Indian Tribal Courts in the United States: A Model for Canada? Saskatoon, Saskatchewan: Native Law Centre, University of Saskatchewan.

NATIVE COUNSELLING SERVICES OF ALBERTA (NCSA) (1980a)
"Policing on Reserves: A Review of Current Programs in Alberta," NCSA, Edmonton.

---------- (1980b)
"Factors Affecting the long-term Future of Correctional Service of Canada," NCSA, Edmonton.

---------- (1982)
"Native People and the Criminal Justice System: The Role of the Native Courtworker," 5 Canadian Legal Aid Bulletin 55.

OBONSAWIN, Robert and Stan JOLLY (1980)
Review of the Ontario Native Courtworker Program: Final Report to the Ontario Native Council on Justice and the Ontario Federation of Indian Friendship Centres. Toronto, Ontario Native Council on Justice.

O'CONNOR, James (1973)
The Fiscal Crisis of the State. New York: St. Martin's Press.

PANITCH, Leo (1977)
"The Role and Nature of the Canadian State," in Craig Heron (ed.), Imperialism, Nationalism and Canada. Toronto, Ontario: New Hogtown Press.

PETRAS, James (1978)
Critical Perspectives on Imperialism and Social Class in the Third World. New York: Monthly Review Press.

PONTING, J. Rick and Roger GIBBINS (1980)
Out of Irrelevance: A Socio-Political Introduction to Indian Affairs in Canada. Toronto, Ontario: Butterworths.

POSPISIL, Leopold (1979)
"Legally Induced Culture Change in New Guinea," in S. Burman and B.E. Harrel-Bond (eds.), Studies in Law and Social Control. New York: Academic Press.

REASONS, Charles E. (1977)
"Native Offenders and Correctional Policy," 4 Crime et/and Justice 255.

RYAN, William (1971)
Blaming the Victim. New York: Pantheon Books.

SINGER, C. and S. MOYER (1981)
The Dakota-Ojibway Tribal Council Police Program: An Evaluation 1979-81. Ministry of the Solicitor General, Ottawa.

SVENSEN, Frances (1979)
"Imposed Law and the Manipulation of Identity: The American Indian Case," in S. Burman and B.E. Harrel-Bond (eds.), Studies in Law and Social Control. New York: Academic Press.

SVENSON, K. (1978)
Indian and Metis Issues in Saskatchewan to the year 2001: The explosive years. Regina, Sask.: Department of Indian Affairs and Northern Development, Mimeographed.

TAYLOR, Ian, Paul WALTON and Jock YOUNG (1973)
The New Criminology: For a Social Theory of Deviance. London: Routledge & Kegan Paul.

VERDUN-JONES, Simon N. and Gregory K. MUIRHEAD (1979-80)
"Natives in the Canadian Criminal Justice System: An Overview," 7 Crime et/and Justice 1.

WATKINS, Mel (1977)
"From Underdevelopment to Development," in M. Watkins (ed.), Dene Nation - the Colony Within. Toronto, Ontario: University of Toronto Press.

ZLOTKIN, Norman (1984)
"Judicial Recognition of Aboriginal Customary Law in Canada: Selected Marriage and Adoption Cases," 4 Canadian Native Law Report 1.

Indigenous law and state legal systems: conflict and compatibility

Bradford W. Morse

I. Introduction

In this essay I hope to address two basic objectives. Firstly, it is designed to provide an overview of the relationship between indigenous law and the subsequently developed state legal system in selected countries. Secondly, it is intended to suggest that this relationship has been sufficiently unsatisfactory that various options for changing the present situation should be considered. In this latter regard, the possibilities of state legislation, constitutional entrenchment, and separate indigenous legal systems will be summarily analyzed. These issues will be addressed primarily in the context of the current position of the indigenous populations in Australia and Canada. Consideration will, however, be given to the similar circumstances existing in the U.S.A. and, to a lesser degree, in Papua New Guinea and New Zealand.

Before embarking upon a discussion of the substance of this paper, it is appropriate to elaborate several underlying premises. The author accepts as proven that the indigenous or aboriginal peoples in the countries under discussion all possessed their own laws and systems of resolving disputes in accordance with those laws (which will be labelled as traditional or customary laws in reflection of their existence and evolution since time immemorial). Further, these indigenous societies were sovereign nations enjoying the full attributes of sovereignty, including self-government and foreign relations.[1] It is also the author's opinion that the original inhabitants of Australia (the Aborigines and Torres Strait Islanders), the USA and Canada (the Indians, Metis, and Inuit) still retain at least some degree of sovereignty and still abide by elements of their customary law.

The author also accepts as self-evident that the indigenous peoples of these three countries, along with many others, have suffered extensively and disproportionately from the negative effects of the application of state laws and legal apparatuses to them. It is no longer necessary, in my view, to prove the accuracy of this assessment by reciting a litany of tragic indices: such as child welfare apprehension rates, poverty levels, unemployment percentages, poor health records, arrest and conviction statistics, and rates of incarceration. It is now sufficient to state the obvious - namely, that the legal system has taken a heavy toll in human misery from indigenous peoples throughout the former Brtish Empire, especially in those countries where the original inhabitants were overrun by colonizers.[2]

Finally, the author assumes that it is possible to make comparisons of developments in different countries. Although one must always appreciate the dangers inherent in such an effort due to cultural, historical, political and legal variances, nevertheless there are sufficient similarities in these common law countries and in the positions and aspirations of the indigenous populations to make comparative analysis fruitful.

II. State law responses to indigenous law

A. Initial responses

The act of colonization of inhabited lands immediately presents two basic and related questions to the colonists and their legal system. Firstly, what law (including legal institutions) will govern the human activities of the colonists? Secondly, how will the legal system of the colonists relate to the indigenous population?

The colonists could choose (perhaps through the persuasion of military arms, or otherwise) to accept the application of the indigenous law to them as the lex loci. All modern states now expect immigrants to accede to the prevailing domestic law as the sole source of law. Therefore, one can easily suggest that the same option was available during the colonial era. There is in fact a wealth of information indicating that early travellers, traders and colonists willingly chose to accept local Indian law as governing their affairs in the Canadian Prairies.[3] If the first question is answered in this manner, then the second one doesn't arise as no separate colonial legal system would be created.

The nature of colonialism is such, however, that the colonizing power inevitably wants its form of government, including the legal system which supports it, to prevail, at least in regulating the affairs of the colonists. It is unfortunately beyond the scope of this essay to do more than state this fact and go forward to examine the second issue raised.

The colonizer's legal system, whether it be founded in the common law, civil law or socialist law, may relate to the indigenous legal system in four distinct ways, any one of which may be chosen. It could select what might be called the "total avoidance" approach in which the two systems would both function without any, or only negligible, interaction. Neither system would then assume jurisdiction over the activities of the adherents of the other. A parallel could be drawn with this situation by pointing to the position of neighbouring states whose governments deal with each other on the international level. Their domestic legal systems are only invoked when an individual attempts to flee one jurisdiction to the other (e.g., extradition and hot pursuit laws) or where the inhabitants interrelate generating a conflict of laws problem (e.g., inter-marriage or business dealings). This option was selected by some of the British colonies in North America in the 17th century regarding certain Indian nations. Treaties were signed pledging the parties to turn over any escapees found in their territory to the proper authorities of the other signatory for handling in accordance with the latter's criminal law.[4]

The Treaty of Fort Albany is a good example of this phenomenon. The British in the colony of New York were confronted by the larger and militarily more powerful Iroquois Confederacy. Thus, the treaty of peace and friendship negotiated on September 24-25, 1664 addressed criminal jurisdiction over incidents involving the members of both nations. Thus, it was assumed that each nation would continue to deal internally with disputes exclusively among their own citizens. The Treaty included the following provisions:

> That if any English, Dutch, or Indian (under the protection of the English) do so any wrong, injury, or violence, to any of ye said Princes, or their subjects, in any sort whatever, if they complained to the Governor at New York or to the Officer in Chief at Albany, if the person so offending can be discovered, then that person shall suffer punishment and all due satisfaction shall be given, and the like shall be done for all the other English Plantations.
>
> That if any Indians belonging to any of the Sachims aforesaid, do any wrong, injury or damage to the English, Dutch or Indians under the protection of the English, if complaint be made to ye Sachims, and the person be discovered who did the injury, then the person so offending shall be punished and all just satisfaction shall be given to any of His Majesties subjects in any Colony of other English Plantation in America.

A second possibility could be labelled the "co-operation" model. Here, once again, both systems function side-by-side, but this time they formally interrelate by dividing their jurisdictions along clearly defined boundaries such that specific circumstances determine which system has authority in a given case. The dividing lines could consist of any or all of the three traditional criteria for assessing judicial jurisdiction, namely, territorial or geographic limits, the subject matter of the legal issue in question, and the location, residence or citizenship of the person. For example, it could be decided that colonial courts and law would govern all matters in colonial settlements affecting both the colonial and indigenous populations whereas indigenous law would regulate all legal matters in what remained of aboriginal territory.

One natural mechanism of implementing this approach is by way of a formal agreement or treaty that would clearly articulate the jurisdictional dividing lines. Past experience has not generally demonstrated such orderly planning. This approach was initially chosen in some of the British colonies in North America.[5]

With the defeat of the French and consolidation of English domination in British North America, a gradual shift took place in this prior pattern in that it became a one- way "hot pursuit" arrangement. The Royal Proclamation of 1763, which was read to many Indian nations at gatherings with the Crown's representatives and accepted by the Indian nations as a treaty, contained the following clause:

> And We do further expressly enjoin and require all Officers whatever, as well Military as those employed in the Management and Direction of Indian Affairs within the Territories reserved as aforesaid for the Use of the said Indians, to seize and apprehend all Persons whatever, who, standing charged with Treasons, Misprisions of Treason, Murders, or other Felonies or Misdemeanors, shall fly from Justice, and take Refuge in the said Territory, and to send them under a proper Guard to the Colony where the Crime was committed of which they stand accused, in order to take their Tryal for the same.[6]

Despite the alteration from the Fort Albany Treaty approach, the recognition of separate exclusive legal regimes was maintained.

The co-operation model has slowly evolved, albeit somewhat erratically, since then in establishing the relationship among the federal, state and tribal courts in the U.S.A.[7] Although there is great variety in the natures of the over 100 Indian tribal courts functioning today in the United States and many circumstances unique to individual states, the situation may be cautiously summarized. Tribal courts have full jurisdiction in all civil and criminal matters (other than fourteen offences withdrawn from their scope by federal law) arising within the reservation and exclusively involving tribal members. The tribal courts are required to adhere to certain basic human rights standards imposed by the *Indian Civil Rights Act*.[8] Events arising outside of the territory of tribal courts can only be heard by tribal courts if the case is transferred by consent of the parties (for example, the *Indian Child Welfare Act* requires all child welfare cases to be transferred from state courts to the tribal court of the parents' reservation, whether they reside there or not, if the parents and the tribal court consent). Jurisdiction over non-Indians has varied over time. The prevailing view at present is that tribal courts are limited to cases where the parties are all Indian people. Therefore, tribal courts have concurrent or exclusive jurisdiction over a defined group of persons (tribal members), in limited territory (the reservations) in subjects set out by tribal statute law or custom unless expressly withdrawn by Congressional enactment.

Another option could be described as the "incorporation" route. Owing to various factors, one society can come to dominate the other to such a degree that the dominant society can choose to incorporate selected portions of the indigenous law or all aspects of it which do not fundamentally conflict with its own. This can occur indirectly as a function of the exceptions to the reception of law doctrine in the common law system whereby the entire common law is received by the colony so long as it is neither inapplicable to nor in conflict with local circumstances. An example would be acceptance of the application of indigenous customary family laws as governing marriages among the indigenous population and marriages between colonists and aboriginals. Many Canadian judges have ruled that requirements for licences and ceremonies solemnized by members of the clergy under English or colonial law simply could not possibly be met in rural and remote regions of the country.[9]

Mr. Justice Monk ruled, in the leading Canadian case of *Connolly v Woolrich*, that nothing in the Treaty of Paris or the Royal Proclamation of 1763 had the effect of

> ... abolishing or changing the customs of the Indians or the laws of the French settlers, whatever they may have been; nothing which introduced the English common law into these territories. When Connolly went to Athabaska, in 1803, he found the Indian usages as they had existed for ages, unchanged by European power or Christian legislation.[10]

He went on to describe his interpretation of the law in these terms:

> There is besides, one answer to all this, and a very plain one. lst, The supreme authority of the empire, in not abolishing or altering the Indian law, and allowing it to exist for one hundred years, impliedly sanctioned it, and 2nd, The sovereign power in these matters, by proclamation has tacitly acknowledged these laws and usages of the Indians to be in force, and so long as they are in force as a law in any part of the British empire or elsewhere, this Court must acknowledge and enforce them.
>
> This Indian custom or usage is, as regards the jurisdiction of this Court, a foreign law of marriage; but it obtains within the territories and possessions of the Crown of England, and until it is altered, I cannot disregard it. It is competent it has been competent during the last hundred years, for the parliament of Great Britain to abrogate those Indian laws, and to substitute others for them. It has not thought proper to do so, and I shall not.[11]

A more direct approach is simply to accept the appropriateness of indigenous law continuing to control the affairs of the original population but to have it administered by the courts established by the dominant society. This option has been used in New Zealand by the federally created Maori Land Court, which is designed to ascertain the owners of Maori lands under Maori law, translate their customary title into a form recognized by western law, and resolve all legal disputes regarding its administration.[12] Canadian judges have also adopted this view with some regularity, especially in family law.[13]

The incorporation model was a particularly common practice in British colonies in Africa and Asia. It is interesting to note that this approach has often been retained upon independence and occasionally entrenched in constitutions or special legislation.[14] For example, Papua New Guinea's Constitution expressly includes customary law with English common law and equity as the "underlying law". Customary law can be altered or overridden by statutes, but it will otherwise continue to exist and prevail over the imported law in cases of conflict.

The final model is outright rejection of the validity of indigenous law by the colonial governments and/or their courts. This may be thinly veiled as non-recognition due to the desire to establish a single legal system for all.[15] It also can more bluntly reflect a racial or ethnocentric bias by declaring the indigenous law to be so "primitive" and "uncivilized" as to be unrecognizable as a system of law at all, but merely so-called "lewd practices".[16]

One must remember, of course, that what occurs in reality may differ greatly from legal theory. For example, recognition of Indian and Inuit customary marriage law by Canadian courts is relatively little known by the Indian peoples and has had little effect upon their lives. Rejection of the traditional law of Aboriginals by Australian courts has not caused its disappearance as many Aborigines and Torres Strait Islanders continue to adhere to its tenets, even if this causes conflict with state law. Geographic isolation can further restrict the impact of judicial and legislative decisions.

B. Reconsidering initial responses

Initial decisions regarding such questions may also change over time. Increasing colonization may result in the disappearance of any initial willingness to ignore traditional law (option #1) or to co-operate with it (option #2), as it did in Australia by the 1850s. This can reflect rising racism or stem from the greater military and numerical might of the colonizer. A decline in the economic importance of the indigenous population can effect this change as well. In Canada, the decline in the fur trade meant that interest in preserving the traditional lifestyle of the Aboriginal peoples (including their legal system) dissipated. Changes in the economic objectives of the colonists cannot be discounted either. A demand for aboriginal lands can create an interest in destroying traditional society, as it did in Australia, New Zealand and Canada. A desire to transform the indigenous population into cheap labour, for example, as workers on cattle stations in Australia, can foster the same goal.

We are witnessing today a different kind of example of this process of reconsideration. The aboriginal populations in many countries are actively struggling to obtain greater respect for their traditional laws, lands and governments. Aboriginal people in Canada have made the recognition of customary law an issue in constitutional negotiations through presentation of proposed amendments to the Constitution of Canada that would respect indigenous customs along with their languages, cultures and beliefs.[17] Customary law has also been placed on the table as an item for negotiation in several major land claims in the North.[18] Aborigines and Torres Strait Islanders have been involved in pursuing the matter through the Australian Law Reform Commission's Reference on Aboriginal customary law, through discussions with the Commonwealth on Makarrata (which have ceased) and by seeking legislative changes from the Government of the Northern Territory. The Commission's Report contains extensive recommendations for statutory initiatives to validate specified types of customary laws in a number of substantive fields.[19] Governments are becoming more receptive to suggestions that they reverse their positions as a result of this pressure. Moreover,they are faced with the fact that integrationist policies have generally failed abysmally, especially in the criminal justice and child welfare areas.[20]

C. The present legal position

1. Australia

The Australian courts had initial reservations about their authority to apply the common law to the indigenous population. On several occasions in the early nineteenth century,[21] the South Australia and Western Australia Supreme Courts refused to accept jurisdiction in criminal trials involving Aboriginal accused. Although the correctness in fact and in law of the leading decisions on this point can be disputed,[22] it nevertheless became the settled view that Aboriginal customary law had no legal force.

Ironically, this situation began to change in part as a result of a celebrated decision in which aboriginal land rights were rejected by the Northern Territory Supreme Court.[23] Mr. Justice Blackburn acknowledged the traditional law of Aborigines "as a system of law" which could be recognized by the general courts,[24] while asserting that Aboriginal concepts of property could not fit within common law notions of real property law. The existence of customary law is now accepted by numerous courts in Australia. Furthermore, the courts of several jurisdictions view customary law as a factor to be considered in criminal sentencing.[25] This does not mean, however, that customary law has been recognized as incorporated within the common law or can be applied either by the general courts or Aboriginal communities themselves as "law" in its own right. The only exceptions are provided by those aspects of customary law which have received legislative support in the Northern Territory.[26]

2. Canada

There is relatively little Canadian jurisprudence on the validity of Indian and Inuit customary law and absolutely none concerning Metis law. What does exist is restricted largely to questions concerning family law and estates. The clear weight of the decisions supports the validity of Indian and Inuit customary law concerning marriage, divorce, and adoption, as well as their impact upon inheritance, spousal immunity in evidence, and related matters. Canadian courts, thus, have recognized the traditional law and incorporated it within the common law as applied by them.[27]

It must be noted, however, that the continued validity of this proposition may depend upon the ambit of contradictory legislation applying to these legal fields.

It is beyond the scope of this paper to embark upon an analysis of the arguments for or against such an effect stemming from individual provincial or federal statutes.[28] It is sufficient to identify the problem and to indicate that such legislation presently in force as does contradict the continuing vitality of customary law is not applicable to all parts of Canada. Traditional law is still very much alive and well in some jurisdictions within this country, particularly in the Northwest Territories. Furthermore, the entrenchment of aboriginal and treaty rights may generate a resurgence of customary law if the general courts rule that traditional law is encompassed within the phrase "existing aboriginal and treaty rights" of s. 35(1) of the Canadian Constitution.

Finally, it should be noted that the sole example of express legislative recognition of customary law by the dominant society in Canada is confined to subsections of the Indian Act.[29] These provisions accept custom adoptions as lawful for the purposes of determining the eligibility of children to register as Indians and to inherit from estates. The Spallumcheen Indian Band of British Columbia has carried this a step further by incorporating customary law as an essential element in their own duly enacted child welfare law.[30] The Indian Act also permits Indian bands to select their local political leaders according to customary methods as articulated by the First Nations concerned. Recent amendments have also recognized the right of each Band to determine their own membership. Initial experience with membership codes drafted to date suggests that traditional laws governing group definition are being resurrected in a modified form. Many bands also allocate land within their reserves according to custom despite the explicit language of the *Indian Act* to the contrary.

Pressure is clearly mounting in both countries for further and express recognition of customary law through federal and provincial/state legislation. Conferences have been held, reports written and submissions made to government for action.[31] One can anticipate that some positive results are near at hand.[32] The question next becomes, what kind of changes can and should be made?

III. Options for change

A. Validation of traditional law

It is obviously possible to recognize indigenous customary law, or expand its recognition, as part of the prevailing state law. This could occur through what might be called test-case litigation. The acceptance of traditional law considerations in establishing the proper quantum of damages in tort cases in Australia[33] and Canada[34] is a recent example. Clearly, however, such a process is very slow and uneven. Moreover, in Australia's case, a fairly dramatic shift in the jurisprudence would be required.

A more effective, thorough and uniform approach would be to enact appropriate legislation declaring customary law to be part of state law. The passage of specific statutes dealing with concrete aspects of traditional law, as the Australian Law Reform Commission is proposing and the Northern Territory has already undertaken, or the enactment of a general statute, would produce the desired result. The latter method would require careful consideration of repercussions upon the dominant legal regime of any such general enabling statute that would have the effect of validating all customary law. How would conflicts between indigenous law and state law be resolved? Which court would be authorized to settle any such conflicts that did arise? Would the indigenous population automatically be covered by the precepts of traditional law based solely upon their race; or would there be an element of choice; or would an aboriginal person have to prove his/her "entitlement" to the application of customary law by evidence of adherence to traditional values or lifestyle? Would there be geographic limits? Minimum standards?

These, and many other fundamental questions, would naturally have to be addressed in the process of deciding to enact either subject specific or general statutes. Opting for legislation that would give broad recognition to customary law is obviously a more dramatic move. As such, it holds certain attractions over and above its simplicity, but on the other hand, it may also be viewed as very threatening by significant segments of the general society - not to mention the legal profession. One possible formulation would allocate to traditional indigenous law the same status as that of traditional western common and civil law, namely, that of constituting part of the legal foundation of the society or its core of law. It could then be relied upon as a vital part of the total law of the country to be used when applicable at the choice of litigants. It would thus be the source of the governing law in certain cases, be used to interpret relevant statutes in others, or have no application at all in yet other situations. It would also, however, be necessary to determine the priority between western and indigenous law in cases of conflict. This could be done by making indigenous law subject to overriding specific legislation while enacting a statutory rule of precedence between the customary law of the original population and that of the colonists as has been done concerning the dominance of equity over the common law.

A further related question concerns the impact of modern human rights principles. Both indigenous and western societies have changed dramatically over the last two centuries in terms of the prevailing attitudes concerning sexual and racial discrimination, popular participation in decision-making, and the rights of the individual. Although this has largely been a situation in which Europeans have unwittingly adopted indigenous values, aboriginal societies have also evolved in this regard. As a result, some sectors have suggested that customary law should only receive full force and effect where its principles do not violate internationally accepted standards of human rights. If one presumes that such a threshhold is equally applied to the imported law by a nation state (which is clearly not always the case at present), then the suggestion has considerable appeal. For example, Papua New Guinea has adopted this as a fundamental criterion for the application of any customary law rule.[35]

Nevertheless, the requirement that customary law not violate human rights principles generates some negative reaction. Firstly, it does sound analogous to the statements made several generations ago by the Privy Council about aboriginal law being primitive and socially repugnant to Europeans. More fundamental, however, is the potential clash between the importance placed upon individual freedoms by the western view of human rights with the Fourth World's emphasis on the paramountcy of collective rights. This is becoming an internal dilemma for the West also regarding its favoured collective groups (such as trade unions, religions, social clubs) when the exercise of their objectives conflicts with the desires of some individuals. This is likely to be a source of continuing tension and debate for the next few decades at least within each country, able to be resolved only by a domestic determination of where the appropriate balance lies.

Another possibility for validating traditional aboriginal law is to incorporate precise provisions within a land claims settlement which is itself incorporated within specific legislation giving the settlement full effect as law. The James Bay and Northern Quebec Agreement[36] contains sections directing that the rules of practice (s. 18.0.15 concerning the Cree and s. 20.0.7. regarding the Inuit) and provisions of the *Code of Civil Procedure*, the *Criminal Code* and the *Canada Evidence Act* be amended so as to take into account "the circumstances, usages, customs and way of life" of the Cree and Inuit (s. 18.0.19 for the former group and s. 20.0.20 for the latter).

A further method would be to entrench such recognition in the constitution of the country, following the lead of Papua New Guinea. This has been proposed in Canada as part of the First Ministers Conference process (originally via s. 37 and now through s. 37.1) of defining and elaborating the "aboriginal and treaty rights" already entrenched in section 35(1) of the Canadian Constitution. It was also suggested by the National Aboriginal Conference as a component of a treaty to be negotiated (or Makarrata[37]) in Australia. Although that initiative appears to have died, the current thrust to reform the Australian Constitution through the appointment of a Royal Commission to investigate possible areas of reform may give rise to a similar proposal in the future. There is also some movement to include this issue within a revision of the Treaty of Waitangi in New Zealand.

B. Indigenization of the state legal system

A completely different strategy would be to fill the general legal institutions with trained Aboriginal people. The theory here is that the justice system would be more likely to meet the needs of indigenous populations and be more respected by them if it were staffed by indigenous judges, lawyers, police officers, etc. In those countries in which the original inhabitants have become a minority such attempts have been minimal.

Both Canada and the USA created programmes in the early 1970s to encourage and facilitate the entry of Aboriginal peoples into law schools. Although this has now led to a quantum leap forward in the number of Indian and Metis lawyers,[38] it cannot be suggested that the face of North American justice has changed as a result. There is still just one lower court judge of Indian ancestry and only small numbers of indigenous police, probation and correctional officers. The number of Indian and Metis justices of the peace even appears to have declined somewhat in recent years in Canada.[39]

The development of special legal aid programmes designed to meet the needs of the indigenous populations in Canada, the USA, Australia and New Zealand has been a positive step.[40] It too, however, has not been sufficient to address the scope of the unmet needs, nor has it generated any greater protection for and respect of customary law in those countries. It also must be realized that these initiatives can very easily be directed toward assimilating and pacifying the indigenous population rather than respecting their unique legal position within the nation as a whole.[41]

C. Development of carbon copies

A further possibility is to create a separate regime which is largely a mirror image of the state justice system. That is, the national or regional governments could authorize the constitution of indigenous courts with a prescribed mandate designed to function similarly to the general courts. Some tribal courts in the USA, particularly those established pursuant to the Code of Federal Regulations, are criticized for being almost as formal, legalistic, and misunderstood as the state court system.[42] The Canadian *Indian Act* provides for the possibility of a special court system on Indian reserves,[43] while the Government of Queensland has created Aboriginal community courts to function on Aboriginal and Torres Strait Islander reserves within that state.

Inherent in this approach is the fact that it is the representative government of the dominant society which determines the jurisdiction of these courts and the legislative powers of the indigenous governments affected by the court. Experience with the aforementioned examples tends to demonstrate active state involvement in the selection and qualifications of the judiciary as well as state control of the resources necessary for the court to operate. Recognition of customary law and the desires of the indigenous population have generally been stifled.

D. Development of separate but equal systems

A completely different theoretical base underlies the position of traditional courts and some other tribal courts in the United States. Albeit grudgingly, the American government has accepted the inherent and continuing sovereignty of Indian nations. This sovereignty, however, is residual in that it is subject to the ultimate control of Congress through express legislation. This has meant that the rights of self- government and self-determination are not dependent upon Congressional legislation or largesse for their creation, but that their continuance is dependent upon inaction by Congress.

Therefore, a separate yet roughly equal legal system has developed upon certain Indian reservations in the USA. Tribal governments have generally had the freedom to choose the type of dispute resolution mechanism to use, how it will operate and in accordance with what laws. This does not inevitably mean that customary law will be preserved, as it could be discarded in favour of newly created law or a blending of old and new. Nor does it mean that the traditional methods of settling disputes will be utilized. In fact, most of the tribal courts have been heavily influenced by the white system and have adopted much of its style and procedure perhaps far too much. Nevertheless, this decision, and the right to alter it in the future, rest with the Indian tribes themselves.

Viewing indigenous law as one facet of self-government permits indigenous people to make these choices as well as to learn from the mistakes of the past, including their own. It also allows customary law to evolve and to adapt, (which it must do out of necessity as circumstances keep changing in our global village) rather than to become static and fossilized. Aboriginal peoples in Canada have clearly determined that they are seeking recognition of their right to self-government as the cornerstone to the development of their future. Respect for customary law and its evolution will be one component of the exercise of this right.

IV. Conclusions

I have assumed throughout this paper that customary law largely functioned effectively and positively in pre-colonial times. I further submit that it has remained alive since contact and will continue to have a valuable role to play in the future. Thus, my concern here has been its present scope and how it can be further nurtured through direct initiatives.

There is no one great answer for every country and every indigenous population as conditions differ far too dramatically from nation to nation and within each nation. Interaction between the original inhabitants and what has become the dominant society, along with increasing urbanization of Aboriginal peoples, means that things have, to some degree, changed irreversibly.

The challenge today is to find a mix of solutions which can respond to the different needs and circumstances of indigenous peoples. To do so will require the support of the general community, which means that some minimum standards must be adhered to in order to gain that approval and tolerance. Customary law can and should be an integral part of this movement, as should respect for the rights of self- government and self-determination. It will not, however, be the customary law of several centuries ago any more than the common law of today is the same as it was in the seventeenth century.

My opinion is that customary law has evolved over the years and can continue to demonstrate the adaptability and flexibility necessary to meet future pressures if only given a chance to do so. I wish I were as confident about the ability of modern nations to do the same.

Notes

1. See, e.g., Opekokew 1982; Cohen, 1971; and *Worcester v State of Georgia* (1832), 31 U.S. (6 Petrers) 515 at 542 (U.S.S.C.).
2. See, e.g., DIAND, 1980; Morse, 1985; Department of Aboriginal Affairs, 1982.
3. See, e.g., Morse, 1980a, and the early Canadian cases cited therein.
4. For more information on this point, see Williams, 1982.
5. Ibid.
6. *Royal Proclamation of 1763,* R.S.C. 1970, App. I, p. 127. The Royal Proclamation is now entrenched by the *Constitution Act, 1982.*
7. For more information on how this operates in the USA regarding tribal courts, see, e.g., Small, 1980; Hall, 1981; Morse, 1980b.
8. 25 U.S.C. ss. 1301-1303 (1985).
9. Morse, note 3, supra.

10. *Connolly v Woolrich,* [1867] 11 L.C.J. 197, at 214 (Que. S.C.); aff'd [1869] 1 R.L. 253 (Que. C.A.).
11. Ibid., at 249.
12. See, e.g., McHugh, 1983.
13. Morse, 1980a. See also Zlotkin, 1984.
14. See, e.g., Weisbrot, et al., 1982.
15. See, e.g., *Regina v Jack Congo Murrell* (1836), 1 Legge 72 (N.S.W.S.C.).
16. See, e.g., *Re Southern Rhodesia,* [1919] A.C. 211 at 233-234; and *Hamlet of Baker Lake et al.* v *Minister of Indian Affairs and Northern Development et al.* (1980), 107 D.L.R. (3d) 513 at 542-544 (F.C.T.D.).
17. See, e.g., the proposals of the Native Council of Canada and the Inuit Committee on National Issues; see also, the contributions by John Bayly and Jeff Richstone contained herein.
18. The Labrador Inuit Association, the Committee of Original Peoples' Entitlement, the Dene and the Council of Yukon Indians have particularly submitted this as an issue for discussion in land claims negotiations.
19. Australian Law Reform Commission, 1986; and the contribution by Crawford et al. herin.
20. See, e.g., the chapter by Chisholm contained herein.
21. Morse, 1983 and sources cited therein.
22. *Regina v Jack Congo Murrell*, note 15, supra, and *Cooper v Stuart* (1889), 14 A.C. 286.
23. *Milirrpum v Nabalco Pty Ltd. and the Commonwealth of Australia* (1971), 17 F.L.R. 141 (N.T.S.C.).
24. Ibid., at 268.
25. For a partial review of this area, see, Rees, 1982.
26. For further information on this point see the discussion and research papers of the Australian Law Reform Commission.
27. Morse, 1980a, and Zlotkin, 1984.
28. For an analysis of the impact of the federal *Divorce Act* and provincial adoption and marriage statutes, see, Morse, 1980a:239-250 and 254-256.
29. R.S.C. 1970, c.I-6, as amended, ss. 2(1) and 48(16) expressly recognize customary laws while s.10 is permissive concerning membership rules:
    2. (1) In this Act,
    "child" includes a child born in or out of wedlock, a legally adopted child and a child adopted in accordance with Indian custom;

    "council of the band" means
    (a) in the case of a band to which section 74 [which deals with the

imposition of an elected form of Indian government] applies, the council established pursuant to that section,
(b) in the case of a band to which section 74 does not apply, the council chosen according to the custom of the band, or, where there is no council, the chief of the band chosen according to the custom of the band;

10.(1) A band may assume control of its own membership if it establishes membership rules for itself in writing in accordance with this section and if, after the band has given appropriate notice of its intention to assume control of its own membership, a majority of the electors of the band gives its consent to the band's control of its own membership.

(2) A band may, pursuant to the consent of a majority of the electors of the band,
(a) after it has given appropriate notice of its intention to do so, establish membership rules for itself; and
(b) provide for a mechanism for reviewing decisions on membership.

48(16) In this section [which deals with the distribution of property on intestacy], "child" includes a child born in or out of wedlock, a legally adopted child and a child adopted in accordance with Indian custom.

30. *A By-law for the care of our Indian Children,* Spallumcheen Indian Band of British Columbia, 1980, By-law No. 3.
31. Chartier and Mercredi, 1982; Morse, 1984; and, most importantly, Australian Law Reform Commission, 1986.
32. For example, the Province of Ontario has implemented the possibility of legally sanctioning a form of custom adoptions and providing financial support where necessary, *The Child and Family Services Act,* S.O. 1984, c. 55.
33. See, e.g., *Jabanardi v AMP Fire and General Insurance Co. Ltd. et al.* (1981), 1 *Aboriginal Law Bulletin* 7; and *Napaluma v Baker* (1982), 4, *Aboriginal Law Bulletin* 9.
34. *Gawa v Horton and Watson,* (1982, Unreported, B.C.S.C.). For further information on this case, see the chapter herein by Grant, as well as his case comment in Grant, 1982.
35. See, e.g., Weisbrot et al., 1982.
36. Editeur officiel du Quebec, 1976.
37. Keon-Cohen, 1981.
38. For a detailed description of the Canadian programme, see, Purich, 1982.

39. Ontario Native Council on Justice, 1982.
40. See, e.g., Greg Lyons, 1984; Kirby, 1982; Gardner, 1982; Native Counselling Services of Alberta, 1982; Morse, 1976; Sutherland, 1973.
41. For a far more detailed discussion on this point, see, Morse, 1976; and the chapter by Haveman contained herein.
42. Morse, 1980b.
43. Morse, 1982.

References

AUSTRALIAN LAW REFORM COMMISSION (1986)
The Recognition of Aboriginal Customary Laws. 2 vols., Report No. 31, Canberra, Australian Government Publishing Service.

CHARTIER, Clem and Ovide MERCREDI (1982)
"The Status of Child Welfare Services for the Indigenous Peoples of Canada: The Problem, the Law and the Solution," 5 Canadian Legal Aid Bulletin, Nos. 2 & 3, 163-174.

COHEN, Felix (1971)
Handbook of Federal Indian Law. 1942, Washington, D.C., United States Government Printing Office; reprint (ed.), Albuquerque: University of New Mexico Press.

DEPARTMENT OF ABORIGINAL AFFAIRS (1982)
Aboriginals in Australia today. Canberra: Australian Government Printing Service.

DIAND (Department of Indian Affairs and Northern Development) (1980)
Indian Conditions: a Survey. Ottawa.

GARDNER, Eddie (1982)
"Le Programme de Conseilleurs Para-Judiciaires au Quebec," 5 Canadian Legal Aid Bulletin, No. 1, 47-53.

GRANT, Peter (1982)
"Role of Traditional Law in Contemporary Cases," 5 Canadian Legal Aid Bulletin, Nos. 2 & 3, 107-110.

HALL, Gilbert T. (1981)
An Introduction to Criminal Jurisdiction in Indian Country. American Indian Lawyer Training Program, Inc.

KEON-COHEN, Bryan (1981)
"The Makarrata: A Treaty Within Australia Between Australians," 57 Current Affairs Bulletin, No. 9, 4-19.

KIRBY, Peter (1982)
"The Use of Native Paralegals," 5 Canadian Legal Aid Bulletin, Nos. 2 & 3, 35-38.

LYONS, Greg (1984)
"Aboriginal Legal Services," in Peter Hanks and Bryan Keon- Cohen (eds.), Aborigines in the Law. Sydney: George Allen & Unwin Ltd., 137-159.

McHUGH, Paul G. (1983)
Maori Land Laws of New Zealand. Saskatoon, University of Saskatchewan Native Law Centre.

MORSE, Bradford W. (1976)
"Native People and Legal Services in Canada," 22 McGill Law Journal 504-540.

---------- (1980a)
"Indian and Inuit Family Law and the Canadian Legal System," 8 American Indian Law Review 199.

---------- (1980b)
Indian Tribal Courts in the United States: A Model for Canada?, Saskatoon, Native Law Centre.

---------- (1982)
"A Unique Court: S. 107 Indian Act Justices of the Peace," 5 Canadian Legal Aid Bulletin, Nos. 2 & 3, 131-150.

---------- (1983)
"Indigenous Peoples and the Law: Cross-Cultural and Transnational Comparisons," 8 Legal Services Bulletin 104-108.

---------- (1984)
"Native Indian and Metis Children in Canada: Victims of the Child Welfare System," in Gajendra K. Verma and Christopher Bagley (eds.), Race Relations and Differences: Educational and Interpersonal Perspectives London: Croom-Helm Ltd., 259-277.

---------- (1985)
"Aboriginal Peoples and the Law," in Bradford W. Morse (ed.), Aboriginal Peoples and the Law: Indian, Metis and Inuit Rights in Canada. Ottawa: Carleton University Press, 1-15.

NATIVE COUNSELLING SERVICES OF ALBERTA (1982)
"Native People and the Criminal Justice System: the Role of the Native Courtworker," 5 Canadian Legal Aid Bulletin, No. 1, 55-63.

ONTARIO NATIVE COUNCIL ON JUSTICE (1982)
The Native Justice of the Peace: An Under-employed Natural Resource for the Criminal Justice System. Toronto, Ontario Native Council on Justice.

OPEKOKEW, Delia (1982)
The First Nations: Indian Governments in the Community of Man. Regina, Federation of Saskatchewan Indians.

PURICH, Donald J. (1982)
"The Native Law Centre, University of Saskatchewan," 5 Canadian Legal Aid Bulletin, Nos. 2 & 3, 39-43.

REES, Neil (1982)
"Police Interrogation of Aborigines," in John Bastien, et al. (eds.), The Criminal Injustice System. Sydney, Australian Legal Workers Group and Legal Service Bulletin.

SMALL, Carrie (ed.) (1980)
Justice in Indian Country. Oakland, American Indian Lawyer Training Program, Inc.

SUTHERLAND, O.R.W. (1973)
Maori Participation in Pakeha Justice. Wellington, New Zealand Race Relations Council.

WEISBROT, David, Abdul PALIWALA and Akilagpa SAWYERR (1982)
Law and Social Change in Papua New Guinea. Sydney: Butterworths.

WILLIAMS, Paul (1982)
The Covenant Chain. LL.M. Thesis, York University.

ZLOTKIN, Norman (1984)
"Recognition of Aboriginal Customary Law in Canada: Selected Marriage and Adoption Cases," 4 Canadian Native Law Reporter 1-17.

Searching for Indian common law

James W. Zion

I. Introduction

The Indian and Native Peoples of North America have shown they will continue to survive as independent and unique groups, and for reasons which are not immediately apparent, national governments around the world have taken a sudden interest in ways in which the laws of indigenous peoples may be used in various forums, including state (i.e. national) and Native forums. In Greenland, the government is attempting to utilize Inuit customs as an instrument of criminal law.[1] The Australian Law Reform Commission has undertaken an ambitious study of a possible integration of Aboriginal customary law in the Australian state

---

*) This paper relies primarily upon the author's involvement with the study of Indian common law over a four-year period. This includes work for and with Indian judges, lawyers and policymakers of the Cree, Navajo, Pima and Blackfeet Peoples, discussions of custom law at formal conferences and many lengthy and informal discussions with students, both Indian and non-Indian, of the Indian common law. There are many items of information or judgment which are not readily citable as to individual, time or place. The author has had many kind and patient Indian teachers throughout a ten-year career in Indian law, and this article attempts to communicate what has been learned.

system.[2] The Canadian Government has made a joint study of possible methods of using Indian laws and procedures in both state and Indian fora, in cooperation with the Province of Saskatchewan and the Federation of Saskatchewan Indian Nations.[3] The more recent Australian and Canadian studies have actively involved the subjects of their studies, the Native Peoples themselves, properly making legal anthropology a participatory and policymaking process. In contrast, the United States has largely ignored these developments, leaving the Indian governments to go forward with their own programs to use customary law.[4]

The new-found interest in the indigenous laws of Native Peoples is concerned with the development of both national and international policies. In addition to the work of bodies which are organs of national government, private and public international bodies, such as the North American Working Group of the Commission on Folk Law and Legal Pluralism,[5] and the Working Group on Indigenous Populations of the United Nations Human Rights Commission,[6] are studying issues surrounding the use of customary law. The international perspective is important, and a study of the Sub-Commission on the Prevention of Discrimination and Protection of Minorities (of the UN Human Rights Commission) suggests that the new concern over indigenous law is a matter of international law, since Native Peoples have the right to use their own law as an aspect of enjoying one's own culture, which is guaranteed by international human rights law.[7] While the right of ethnic, religious and linguistic minorities to enjoy culture is protected by the International Covenant on Civil and Political Rights, it is also guaranteed by international customary law, which binds countries such as the United States, which has yet to ratify the Covenant.[8]

However beneficial the new interest in the use of Native customary law may be, many pitfalls and dangers are to be found in the present efforts to "find" and use that law. Some national governments and their organs have taken the position that they may judge indigenous law, assessing it against their own standards of "barbarity" or "national policy", and accepting or rejecting Native customary law in accordance with those standards.[9] Non-Native researchers and policymakers have insisted upon framing the principles of particular Native legal systems in non-Native terms, using non-Native legal structures. A certain degree of romanticism has also been harmful to a proper approach to non-European law.[10] Despite these problems, there have been some very sincere efforts by governments and international organizations to work with Native Peoples and governments to find practical ways of integrating aboriginal legal systems and procedures into the state legal system.

The problem common to all these efforts is the proper way to "search for," "find" and successfully "use" the laws of Native Peoples. This is but one attempt to articulate standards and guidelines for that process. It may be greatly flawed, but it seeks to encourage discussion and the search for better ideas. It is largely the product of the views of American and Canadian Indian lawyers, that is, those who are a part of the Indian legal structure on reservations or reserves. Today many people are actively engaged in the search for aboriginal customary law but all too often their work, which could be a shining light, is hidden by the obstacles of limited funding, ignorance of the work of others and official neglect or obstructionism. This rather opinionated attempt to articulate standards for the search for Indian common law will suggest some approaches and tools of analysis.

II. The common law model

Many legal systems can be found in the dominant states of the world.[11] The major ones include the common law system of English-speaking nations, the Civil Law system of many of the Latin-language states, and the Soviet Law system, found in many Socialist countries.[12]

This discussion is concerned with the Indians of North America, excluding the Hispanic countries, and the common law systems of the United States and Canada. Since these two nations largely follow the common law tradition, it makes sense to speak to Indian law in terms of that method. This method of analysis is also useful in the international law context because many of its principles are based upon an international common law.[13] This is not a matter of yet another imposition of alien forms of analysis on Indian cultures because the analysis is aimed at the non-Indian who needs to be convinced that Indians indeed have their own law. The comparison between Anglo-European common law and Indian common law demonstrates that Indian law has foundations which are understandable to the non-Indian.

While there are peoples in North America who are generally classified as "Indian," "Inuit," "Eskimo," "Metis" or "Half-Breed," these terms designate ethnological or legal classifications which need not concern us here.[14] Although this discussion focusses upon those peoples called Indians, the approach is the same for all Native Peoples of North America.[15]

For the purpose of a rational discussion of Indian customary law, it is best to use the term "Indian Common Law." Indian government, law and daily life are founded upon long-standing and strong customs, and since the stated rationale for the English Common Law is that it is a product of custom, that approach may be used for Indian law as well.

Indians have every right to assert that their law stands on the same footing as the laws of the United States and Canada. It is unfortunate that the term "custom" implies something that is somehow less or of lower degree than "law."

There are connotations that a "custom" is somehow outside the "law" of government, which is powerful and binding. This is an ethnocentric view, since punishment by an Indian judicial system is as binding as that of an Anglo-European judicial system, and often may be equally or more severe. Given Indian family ties and the reverence for one's home, a community sentence of banishment can be more severe than a prison sentence, and punishment by shaming or humiliation can have severe consequences.[16]

What, then, are the shared elements of the common law concept which indicate that Indian common law stands on the same footing as English, Canadian and American common law?

The common laws of England (excluding the civil law tradition of Scotland), the United States and Canada have the same origins. The legal tradition that the common law originated in custom and was the product of custom may be questioned, and it may be said to be a myth or legend.[17] The tradition is important, however, because the justification of a customary origin has been used over the centuries to give legitimacy to the common law. Indian stories and legends have often been called myth too, but they also illustrate base values.

According to our myth or legend, the common law is nothing more than an articulation of the common customs of the English People. English legal writers from Fortescue (who published his major works between 1468 and 1471) to Blackstone (who, in 1753, gave the lectures which were to become Anglo-European, American and Canadian legal scripture) said, very simply, that the common law is custom. St. Germain, writing the First Dialogue of *Doctor and Student* in 1523, proclaimed:

> The thyrde grounde of the lawe of Englande standeth vpon dyuerse generall Customes of old type vsed through all the realme: which haue ben acceptyd and approuyd by our soueraygne lorde the kynge and his progenytours and all theyr subgettes. And bycause the sayd customes be neyther agaynst the lawe of god nor the lawe of reason & haue ben alwaye taken to be good and necessarye for the common welth of all the realme. Therfore they haue in so mouche that he that doth agaynst them doth agaynst Iustyce *and law* And these be tho customes that proprely be called the common lawe.[18]

Sir Matthew Hale, writing in the latter half of the 17th century, spoke of "some of those laws (which) have obtained their force by immemorial usage or custom" and were called "common law, or the general custom of the realm."[19] Blackstone, whose *Commentaries* were carried to the frontiers of the United States as *the* law, defined the common law as a collection of "maxims and customs" of antiquity.[20]

This myth that the common law is composed of customs and usages gave judges and lawyers the flexibility to formulate a very plastic, adaptive and responsive form of law which fitted national needs and could be adapted to changing conditions. It was a living law whose heritage is viewed with pride in English-speaking North America. The term "common law" can equally be used to describe Indian legal systems, which are also the product of custom and which are plastic, flexible and responsive to today's conditions. Indian law reflects traditional and contemporary custom which changes and adapts to accommodate the new of the dominant culture while tenaciously clinging to and deferring to the old.

Indian law does not simply state principles which may be called "legal." It is a product of relationships and experience which form custom. Indian law is common law, and it is alive and well.

III. The characteristics of Indian common law

The non-Indian searchers after Indian common law have a great deal of difficulty approaching and "finding" that law. This is sometimes due to language problems, sometimes to the fact that many Indians do not speak of their common law in articulated ideal legal norms,[21] and sometimes to constraints created by non-Indian thinking patterns. The lawyer or government planner is continually looking for something concrete, something that can be written down; in other words "rules." This is the sort of thinking Jerome Frank labelled "rule-fetishism,". He criticized as a myth the idea that law is composed of authoritative rules and urged us to rid ourselves of it.[22] Frank agreed that usages, customs and mores in all parts of society are "legal," but that the word "law" is most often used to indicate governmental control.[23] However, law is in fact controlled by factors which are common to all sorts of administration, whether governmental or not.[24]

While Mr. Justice Frank was not discussing or thinking of the search for Indian common law, his observations are correct in this context. One cannot use the structure of the Anglo-European common law, its language, or its approach, and successfully identify, conceptualize and use Indian common law. Indian common law is not stated in terms of rules, and the researcher will be disappointed when he or she finds an Elder who knows it but cannot or will not state it. The better approach is to get some idea of the nature and flow of Indian common law.

First, one must be careful not to assume that the structure of the law is the same for all Indian Peoples. There are many practices and approaches among the various tribes which are the same or similar,[25] but there are also many differences which make different groups unique.[26]

Second, the searcher must have a feel for the infrastructure of the common law for each group studied. An excellent example of this is to be seen in the background of the Plains Cree of Montana, Alberta and Saskatchewan. These peoples were organized for survival on the plains of the Western United States and Canada. The plains constituted a hostile environment without the horse, and even with the horse the Cree had to organize every level of their society for survival. There were two institutions which aided survival, religion and an interlocking government.

The Cree are animists, and animism underlies their legal thinking. Animism assumes that the Creator, the Great Holy, created a universe in which everything has a soul. One Cree educator explained that people, animals, rocks, trees and even the ashtray before him have a soul.[27] Since, in reality, each thing has a soul, there are both interlocking obligations and sources of assistance with all things. The obligations are expressed in terms of respect for things. For example, one is required to have a good reason for cutting a tree, and to ask the tree's permission before cutting it.[28] One can also call upon the Spirits (ideal "master souls") of other beings for assistance. This can be in the form of using an eagle feather in prayer to request the assistance of the Eagle Spirit for various enterprises, or other ceremonials. Animism is a very logical and sensible religion because it recognizes the interdependence of people and the environment an interdependence which involves all parts of the environment.

The Cree, and many other Indians, believe that religion is a central part of life. As one Cree woman puts it, "It is very hard being an Indian because each day is one long prayer ceremony."[29] Unlike the secular cultures of the United States and Canada, many Indian Peoples cannot and do not separate religion and religious belief from their everyday activities. This is an important part of Indian common law. The legal nature of Indian belief becomes very apparent upon close examination. The Cree have a saying that "everything has consequences." This saying is taught to children, and told and retold as a reminder that everything people do will come back to them. When evil things or bad conduct are discussed, someone may interject: "Don't call it to you," or "don't call evil down on to you."[30] Thus, if one person is angry at another and speaks of doing harm to him, he may be quickly reminded not even to speak of it, for it will "call evil to you." The Cree also speak in terms of "taking pity" upon others. The term "to take pity" is a bad translation of the Cree concept, which really expresses the idea that we all have obligations to see those around us who are in need and reach out to help them. The Great Holy is said to have taken pity on People by seeing the harshness of their lives and giving them children to make them happy. When one "takes pity," for example by helping a widow in distress, there is a consequence. Each good deed gives the doer the luck of the person who is helped. For example, a friend helped a stranded man from a distant tribe by giving him enough money to get home, and he smiled and told her she would have his luck. She used this luck in gambling and won about five times the amount she had given him. She explained this in terms of the consequences of "taking pity."[31] What is involved in these religious concepts is immediate supernatural punishment or reward. There is a specific and identifiable belief in the immediacy of supernatural intervention in daily life, and this is a reason that many cultures rely upon the spiritual world as a primary agency in law. This is also why petty crime is dealt with by leaving it to supernatural intervention, and why the Cree have a saying, when another injures them, to "leave it alone" and not take action in revenge. "Leaving it alone" means that the Spirits will take care of things. Thus religious belief is a strong element of Cree common law and that of other Indian tribes.

Cree common law is also expressed in terms of relationships and community structure. It is a pyramidal structure with the family at the base and the leaders at the apex. The family unit is more important to Indians in general than it is in the overall societies of the United States and Canada. A person thinks of family not only in terms of the nuclear family of parents and children, but in terms of the extended family. Cousins by blood may be as important as natural brothers and sisters, and there are strong ties even to adoptive relations. Non-Indians working with Indian Peoples are often confused by the Indian use of blood relationship terms, such as "brother" and "sister," "grandparents," or "aunt and uncle," to refer to relationships by religious tie, clan or society. All these extended relationships are important to the Cree common law. For example, a young woman owes a duty to her brother to act in a way that will not bring shame upon him. In turn he is responsible for helping and protecting her. Likewise each person has "grandparents" (parents' parents) and "Grandparents", who are the Elders. The Elders are at the heart of the Cree community. They are not "elders" in the sense of being older members of the community, rather they have demonstrated the achievement of spiritual power through good works and prayer and have thus earned respect as persons who are wise and from whom guidance should be sought. The holding of this office is by common consent and acknowledgement, and its powers may be taken away by the people as they gave them. An Elder has various constituencies to serve. He (or she) is important as a representative of those around him (or her) who rely upon him (or her) for protection. The Elder may also represent a particular faction or society within the community. There are groups of male and female Elders who have their own religious societies, and there is a "men's Law" and a "womens' Law".[32] Some Elders may be responsible to the community for the Sun Dance, the most important Cree ceremony. Others may represent the modern Native American Church, the Shaking Tipi Society or other societies. The Plains Cree warrior society still survives in various forms today.

These groups in turn select, by consent and consensus, the leaders of the community. In modern times these can be elected members of a tribal council, a band council or some other modern structure which has been imposed upon Indians by the outside world. In addition, there are intertribal structures which deal with universal concerns.

A look at the structure of Cree government reveals a distinction which varies from place to place and group to group between the apparent Indian government and the underlying traditional government. Sometimes the traditional government is so integrated into the governmental structure created by the national law of the United States or Canada that there is no difference. Sometimes, as with the Fort Belknap and Blackfeet Tribes of Montana and the White Mountain Apache of Arizona, there are formal and identifiable shadow governments of Elders. Sometimes there appears to be no traditional structure such as the religious or warrior society, and sometimes there is an informal structure which coexists with a formal government. There are many patterns, but the important thing for the searcher is to be able to identify what the real infrastructure is.

The infrastructure is important because it is the law. The religious outlook described above and the interlocking pattern of families and Elders constitute the court, the flow of the law. Legal relationships are family and religious relationships, and the law operates in accordance with the structure found. If a legal problem cannot be resolved in the immediate family, it is taken to the Elders for the family. If they cannot resolve the problem, sometimes a group of Elders, forming a society, will intervene to resolve the matter and mete out the appropriate punishment. The structure responds to the problem depending upon its seriousness and its impact on the community at large.

The flow of the Cree common law, as it is with the flow of the common law of many tribes, is structural and procedural, rather than substantive and rule-oriented. The non-Indian may have an impression of anarchy, given the absence of observable and obvious mechanisms and rules which he is used to as "law," but if one understands the base values of the people and sees how those base values are enforced through an interlocking structure of obligation to person and thing through the Animist Way, then the law becomes apparent.

IV. Difficulties in the search for indian common law

The conceptual framework of Indian common law is the product of a given people's religious values as expressed in its Scripture. The "law" is contained in that Scripture but it is not expressed as law in the form to which the general society is accustomed. Researchers among Indians are often frustrated by the inability of individual Indians to discuss their law or verbalize legal concepts. This is because the nature of Indian legal systems is quite different from the Anglo-European system. Nevertheless, the law is there and can be found if legalistic terminology and classifications are avoided.

Many university-educated Indians involved in documenting the common law of their people also have conceptual difficulties due to the rule orientation of the general society. Some Indians will simply explain their "law" by saying that it is the sum total of their education, experience and culture. Indian common law is, with respect to procedure, contained in the community structure described above.

With respect to substantive law, it is contained in teaching and memory devices, such as the tribe's Scripture, legends, myths and even humorous stories about what happened to individuals who erred.

First and foremost, the Indian common law is procedural. It deals with relationships, mutual obligations and the ways in which the particular tribe and its people survive. During the pre-horse and horse eras, survival depended upon a very sophisticated and tight structure. Today, survival remains a very real problem. The various studies of Indidans conducted in the United States and Canada broadcast, echo and re-echo conditions of poverty, unemployment, social distress and hardship. Outside intervention and efforts have ignored the existing community structure, with the result that the structure very quietly and effectively resists the outside. Indian common law operated through this structure which is at the heart of the law. Albert Angus, a Cree attorney from a very traditional reserve in Saskatchewan, observed that if you want to study Indian common law, you must know Indian civil procedure.[33] This statement sums up the nature of the Indian legal structure and its diversity in the most accurate way possible.

This is not to say that there is no substantive law. It exists in a form that is not always easily recognized, consisting of the sayings taught in childhood, the prayers of ceremonies, hero stories, animal stories and humorous tales about members of the community. These form, in the mind of the adult Indian, a body of law which he or she may be hard-pressed to articulate in terms of actual rules, but which are there in the mind. This is why Indians, and only Indians, can truly have a comprehensive knowledge of their law.

A legal revolution has taken place on the reservations of the United States, and is about to break out in Canada. The American tribal court system, whatever its shortcomings and whatever its detractors may say, is a success because it is operated by Indians for Indians. A growing number of Indian legal practitioners are very sophisticated in their knowledge and use of law. The American Indian Bar Association is growing in strength and effectiveness as more Indian practitioners join, and a number of tribal bar associations have been formed. The Navajo Nation Bar Association has approximately 250 members, approximately 175 of whom have gained entry to the bar without attending law school through a difficult examination and either community college training or apprenticeship. The Pima and Papago tribes of Southern Arizona have formed NATBA (the Native American Tribal Bar Association) to administer a common entrance examination and regulate practice in their courts. Difficult law examinations are held in the tribal courts of the Blackfeet, Fort Peck, Navajo and other bars. Recently, a non-Indian retired Montana District Court judge failed the Fort Peck tribal bar examination, apparently because he did not know the general principles of American Indian law and did not immerse himself in the tribal code.

These practitioners are largely responsible for experimentation in the law. While they have received training in the general principles of American law, there is a growing awareness and admission that what they are actually doing in tribal court is practicing their own common law within the framework of general American law. Most of the tribal court system, which has existed in the United States since the 1880s, was founded specifically as an instrument to destroy Indian culture, religious practices in particular.[34] This attitude has been taught for so many years that many tribal court practitioners have come to accept the idea that "the White Way is the right way." It is difficult, however, to train an individual to know a foreign system well, such that many Indian practitioners, recognizing that one cannot simply adopt an alien system, are now advocating a return to the use of traditional common law. This process is not easy as it is difficult to reconcile systems which have very different goals and methods. Nonetheless, the transition is being made, and made well.[35]

Many projects have now begun the process of defining Indian common law, "finding" it and using it. In Canada, the Federation of Saskatchewan Indian Nations has conducted a joint study of Indian common law as a preliminary step to setting up Indian-controlled justice systems for its sixty-nine member bands.[36] The Saddle Lake Tribe of Alberta is investigating the possibility of a judicial system by focusing upon serving modern legal needs through a traditional structure. The Navajo Courts have utilized different approaches to Indian common law, creating an experimental traditional court and publishing opinions using Navajo common law. The White Mountain Apache Tribe of Arizona is experimenting with an advisory body of Elders who will make the tribal court more responsive to traditional principles. Many other tribes and bands are conducting their own searches. The problem is *how* to approach a search which, given the very different nature of Indian common law, is a difficult task.

Indian informants are valuable for non-Indian researchers, particularly if they happen to be Indian judges or practitioners. The practitioner informants can be difficult to deal with if they are preoccupied with English common law legalisms, non- Indian legal structures and the feeling that "the White Way is the right way." Nevertheless, many Indian judges and practitioners are interested in finding their own common law, and lengthy discussions of what law "is" can be useful as a prelude to hard fieldwork. Hoebel's approach to field research is particularly useful, and it should be discussed with an Indian research partner.[37] An informant must be a good interpreter and have a great deal of patience. It is difficult to shift gears from Anglo- European legal thinking to the receptivity that is required to understand Indian common law. A patient research partner with a good sense of humour can tolerate you while you attune your mind to a new way of thinking. A good research partner can also make necessary introductions to the Elders, explain what you want and obtain their blessing for your work. The key to using Indian informants is understanding that anyone who has been steeped in his or her traditions knows the law already, such that it is a matter of building the type of working relationship that the person will become educated to your needs and approach and respond with the information that is needed. These are the people who know the law and, if they are respected leaders in the community, they *are* the law.

The Elders, selected by common consent, are the law and they know it well. Many peoples have their own Scripture, and this is a key as well. Some Scriptures have been written down.[38] This can pose problems, in that often a Scripture will have different forms, will be incomplete or inaccurate in translation, or require some interpretation by one who follows it in order to find out what is "legal." Moreover, many Indians believe that the Scripture should not be written, disclosed to a non- Indian, or sometimes even disclosed to many members of the particular tribe. Sometimes a "deviant" who disregards the non-disclosure belief will be the source of a translation, raising questions of whether he or she truly knows the Scripture or can relate it accurately.[39] Sometimes, where the Scripture is not written, a knowledgable informant will recount portions relating to a legal concept, and it is here that a close and genuine partnership with a sophisticated informant is necessary and helpful. For example, Associate Justice Homer Bluehouse and Chief Justice Tom Tso of the Navajo Supreme Court are very aware of the legal nature of much of the Navajo Sacred Scripture and frequently use portions of it to relate and explain a legal concept under Navajo common law.

Stories are case law. Just as the English common law was a body of stories collected to show the application of custom (prior to enshrinement in law codes for rule-worship), the common law of many Indian Peoples is in the form of instances applying the law. These stories can be in the form of what appears to be fiction, such as the Coyote stories common to most North American tribes. They are told (sometimes only at specific times of the year due to religious restrictions) for the purpose of teaching legal principles. Other stories told as case law have a grounding in reality. One form of Cree punishment for wrongdoing is the telling, and enthusiastic retelling, of the tale of a person who has had consequences visited upon him. One recent case from the Rocky Boy's Reservation in Montana, involved the conduct of a tribal councillor who liked women much older than he. One day an elderly man came before the full council and asked to be heard. He said: "Please tell this man (indicating the councillor with a sign) to return my wife who he borrowed from me; I want her back now." The council collapsed in laughter and ordered the council member to return the wife. The story is now told and retold on the reservation (as it will be for many years) because it is not only case law showing the foolishness of taking another man's wife, but case law illustrating the foolishness of being attracted to a much older woman.

Other sources of law are the manuscripts now being collected by Indian cultural programs, contemporary Indian writers and Indian researchers. For example, many of the Navajo Medicine Men are now either writing about legal topics or having their addresses to their people recorded and transcribed. These are invaluable sources of law. A recent Navajo Court opinion on the Navajo law of adoption was based upon this sort of material, and some tribal courts are building a body of modern case law through written opinions. These types of opinions may not be what the anthropologist wants, but if we are searching for Indian common law, the written opinions of contemporary tribal judges are important. These opinions may not "accurately" state a tradition. Often the tribal judge is reaching to justify a decision on a modern legal question by invoking the common law, but Indian judge-made law is law nonetheless. It adapts to fit present circumstances.

One question which arises in the process of "finding the law" is who is finding it and for what purposes. Indian leaders are interested in using their own common law for a very important political purpose to gain control over their own affairs. Thus, Indian judges, lawyers and leaders will use their own traditions for advocacy purposes. In the United States, where tribal law "pre-empts" outside law,[40] Indian judges and legislators want to find their own law in order to keep alien law out. For a tribal judge, this may involve identifying and articulating a principle of tribal common law in a decision so as to reject an offered principle of outside law. The legislator may want to justify an enactment in terms of a base value taken from his own law. This is sometimes hard to do, however, as some judges or legislators are not able to conceptualize a principle taken from their own law in terms of the legal problem before them. This was so in the case of Navajo adoption, for the meaning of the term as expressed in modern codes is completely alien to the Navajo concept.[41] Some Indian decisionmakers have turned to anthropological and ethnological literature,[42] and although many Indians laugh at such literature about them as being incomplete, inaccurate, told out of turn or, simply, just not "it", Indian decisionmakers are now using it as an advocacy tool. It seems ironic that Indians are using materials written about them by non-Indians to persuade the non-Indians to let them make their own decisions, but this is a political reality. It is, perhaps, departure from "finding" the true Indian common law, yet it highlights an important part of the search.

The law is being "found" for various reasons, and we must identify the actors in the process, their motives and their political goals if we are to have an idea of what we should be doing.

V. Who are the searchers?

There are many searchers for Indian common law. There are international bodies, national governments, Indian leaders and scholars. Each has its own goals and motivations which compel participation in the search, rendering it important to know who each is and why they are doing what they do.

A. International Bodies

Since World War II, the United Nations and other international bodies have been very active in the area of human rights. On December 10, 1948, the United Nations General Assembly, by a vote of 48 to 0, adopted the Universal Declaration of Human Rights.[43] Between 1945 and 1980 forty major global and regional human rights instruments were adopted and circulated for ratification by UN member states.[44] Twenty-one multilateral human rights instruments are now available for ratification.[45] While knowing that fundamental human rights are an international concern is cause for some optimism about the human condition, these documents have dangerous implications for Indian Peoples. Most of them contain the "equality principle," which requires signatories to guarantee and insure complete equality before the law. However, Indian Peoples feel their right to self-determination is endangered by this principle, and indeed in Canada, Indian governments are being told they must comply with the sexual equality principle whether they like it or not. The justification for Canada's policy is its ratification of the International Covenant on Civil and Political Rights, which contains the principle of sexual equality. However, Article 27 of that covenant, which came into force in 1966, guarantees "ethnic, religious or linguistic" minorities the right to "enjoy their own culture," and thus there is a clash in the application of the covenant.[46]

The United Nations is beginning to see that there are distinct problems with the equality principle as it applies to Native Peoples. The United Nations Human Rights Commission, established under the authority of the covenant, hears complaints against states which have adopted it and an optional procedural protocol.[47] Thus, the conflict is being highlighted.

Indians have been frustrated by the non-responsiveness and destructive decisionmaking of their own countries and have begun to see the UN Human Rights Commission as a possible forum. After a great deal of lobbying, the Commission and the UN Economic and Social Council established the Working Group on Indigenous Populations in 1982 to look into the protection of Native Peoples.[48] Among the issues this body is examining is the right to use customary law as an incident of the right to enjoy culture.[49]

It is obvious that Indian groups will seize upon Article 27 of the Covenant and use international fora to try to embarrass national governments into guaranteeing self- determination. Where a state (e.g., the United States) has not ratified the Covenant, Indians will argue that it is only a codification of international common law. Perhaps this is a dangerous undertaking, for East-West conflicts, Capitalist-Socialist ideologies and Third World power consolidation are all motivations which prompt UN action. The claim will thus be argued in the context of the world mood, and while Indians will be able to use the UN for leverage, they may not be able to control what they begin.

B. National bodies

There is a definite interest on the part of some modern, industrialized nations in the common law of their Native Peoples. Denmark, Australia and Canada have shown particular interest in finding practical means to integrate Native common law into the State system, but the motivation, goals and interests of these governments will determine the role of Native Peoples in the process.

The record of what has happened shows four motivational patterns. It appears these governments are seeking: (1) prestige in light of international human rights law and policy; (2) means to clear the way for economic development by resolving land and resource entitlement questions; (3) a way to solve the "Indian" or

"Native" "problem" for both prestige and economic gain; and (4) fulfillment of romantic attitudes toward Native Peoples.

For example, Canada was humiliated by the UN Human Rights Commission decision in *Lovelace v Canada*, which held that Canada's sexually discriminatory law regarding membership within Indian bands and standards for official legal recognition as Indians was violative of the International Covenant on Civil and Political Rights.[50] As a leader in promoting international human rights, Canada immediately tried to refurbish its tarnished image by proposing retroactively to make many Indian women and their children "Indians" under the law. When consulted about the content of the policy, many Canadian Indian bands and organizations responded that their traditional law required sex differentiation for membership and other matters, but the government's response was firm the law would be changed. Rather than discussing the nature of Indian government in Canada, the non-applicability of certain international and national legal principles to Indians or the equality principle in international law, the Canadian Government moved to repair its wounded pride.[51] This example suggests that international human rights prestige may prove injurious to Indian law unless the focus of that prestige can be shifted to the right to enjoy culture under Article 27 of the Covenant. The United States has a good approach to the use of Indian law by Indians, but since it has failed to ratify the covenant it will be difficult to argue the protection of Article 27 there. Indian leaders in both countries will need to prepare full arguments on the true meaning of equality and their natural right to self-government.

The desire to clear the way for economic development is a very serious factor in looking at Indian common law. Australia, Canada and the United States all wish to settle Native claims in order to "clear title" to lands and resources.[52] The scheme in the United States aimed not only at resolving old claims, clearing title and giving compensation, but at terminating completely the legal relationship between Indian tribes and the national government.[53] Fortunately for American Indians, that scheme backfired because Indians were not willing to be "terminated" or assimilated. Although claim negotiations may encourage the finding and use of Indian common law, a problem lies in the fact that there is a lot of money involved and powerful economic interests are pushing for quick settlements. Perhaps, however, this may be used to advantage in securing the right to use Indian common law; but it has dangers if Indian leaders themselves do not recognize the protection of their own power as a clear goal.

The third motivation, the desire to take care of the "Indian problem", is an old one and closely related to the previous explanation. The United States has been attempting to do this over almost three centuries of colonial and national history. U.S. policy has fluctuated and shifted between assimilationist policies and those which would allow Indian Peoples to maintain their cultural identities. Underlying these changes in sentiment are the racism which created the "Indian problem" and which continues today, and a romanticism about Indians. The claims process is a product of the past policy which viewed Indians in an international law context and used treaties to gain resources, as well as of the feeling for "the noble savage", engendered by novels and pious manifestos. If Indian common law is to be protected, then the foundations of the "Indian problem" must be discussed. It is time for a fresh look at the basis of Indian peoples' rights and a new articulation of a doctrine which enshrines those rights. Perhaps the retained sovereignty doctrine of the United States would serve, as long as it is clear that the United States or Canada cannot unilaterally change the rules. An extensive articulation of the right to enjoy one's own culture could be a doctrinal vehicle as well. The open charter model of local government, in which a governmental body can do anything which it is not specifically (and consensually) prohibited from doing, would be effective for the use of Indian law. The current model whereby Indians are prohibited from doing anything that is not specifically permitted has failed, and as the experience of modern municipal corporations has shown, the open charter model is more workable.

Romanticism about Indians is something which has been with us for a long time.[54] From St. Thomas More to Aldous Huxley there has been a fascination with the "noble savage" theme, and while it is an unrealistic approach to intercultural relations, it has persisted. It is found in film portraits of the "dumb" or "stoic" Indian, and in the many romantic novels sold at supermarket checkout stands. This romanticism continues to invade policy discussions about the use of Indian common law, and one court, perhaps because the Indian litigants did not appear in buckskins, beads and feathers, declared that the Blackfeet common law was dead.[55] Sincere non-Indian policymakers will recognize this tendency in themselves, as non-Indian common law researchers are trying to do, and deal with it openly.

There are, of course, other motives causing non-Indian policymakers to do what they do. The question most Indian leaders have when invited to talk about Indian common law is, "Can this person be trusted?" In the field of Indian common law a willingness to avoid taking strong policy positions at the outset will engender trust. One cannot forcefully demand to know rules when the legal system is not expressed in terms of rules. One cannot take a strong position on the limits of a body of law unless that law is first understood. There are reasons to be suspicious of policymakers who are tied to a national government, particularly in light of the motivations discussed above, unless there is free, open and patient discussion. In other words, governmental policymakers should be prepared to take part in the search with an open mind and reach decisions on the use of or limitations to Indian common law after getting a feel for it.

C. Indian groups

The various Indian groups mentioned share the same broad goals. The formal customary and common law initiatives undertaken by the Indians of the United States and Canada are geared to self-government and to excluding an alien system.

The goal of self-government is quite apparent, but there are dangers. If an Indian government copies standard codes used in state fora, it can expect to be second-guessed by the outside. Thus, when American Courts were reviewing disputes under the *Indian Civil Rights Act*, "traditional" tribal policies were upheld while those adopted from the outside were used to overturn elections.[56] If an Indian government or court system uses its own common law, as expressed in its own language by its own members (who are the only ones who can really "know" the law), then the outside will have no say in the matter. When Navajo policy-makers, either tribal council members or judges, wish to discuss a decision among themselves in the presence of a non-Indian adviser, they switch to Navajo, knowing that very few non-Navajo can speak the language. This is jokingly referred to on reservations in the U.S. as an "OIT" (old Indian trick). There are many such devices for promoting independent action and decision making. The Navajo Courts began their program of finding ways to use Navajo common law in April of 1981, and discovered many ways to defeat laws which are culturally inappropriate to the Navajo through the use of that law.

The Indian common law revolution is understandable when viewed in terms of a demand for self-government and a return to community values. Many Indians see the disintegration of their society around them and recognize that reintegration will have to involve the legal values still present in the structure described earlier. A sympathetic attitude toward Indians using their own law has as a corollary support for Indian government.

VI. The barbarism principle

One factor which contributes to a lack of communication and trust is the insistence of national governments that they may judge Indian law and reject any practice which they deem to be "barbaric." This attitude is universal and is typical of European colonialism.[57] In the United States, Indian law has been rejected as being "barbaric" or as being "contrary to national policy."[58]

The barbarity principle must be eliminated for several reasons. First of all, it is racist and discriminatory for one people to judge another and declare that a part of their culture is unacceptable. While there may need to be discussions of specific aspects of Indian culture as they may conflict with national policies (e.g. the possession and use of peyote, possessing eagle feathers, dealing with non-Indians on reservation), the process must be bilateral and not unilateral. The paternalism of the past, where Indians were "heathen savages" to be punished and assimilated into a "superior" culture, is clearly contrary to modern democratic thought, as is the "noble savage" approach in which Indians are thought to have lost their "Indianness" because they wear modern clothes and hold modern jobs.[59]

The barbarism principle is also unrealistic Indian peoples are going to follow their own ways in any event. The Sun Dance and other ceremonies survived vicious repression in the United States. Polygamy and the killing of witches continues within the Navajo Nation today, demonstrating that local justice operates in spite of legalities.

If there is a modern international right guaranteeing a person's enjoyment of his or her own culture, then it is the particular culture which defines what is acceptable or unacceptable, otherwise the right has no meaning. Who is the judge of a culture? Do I have a right to pronounce something silly if I am culturally or linguistically unable to understand it fully?

It is inevitable that there will be clashes between Indian cultures and the dominant culture. These clashes affect religious values, expectations and practices. The American and Canadian hunting cases offer a good example of this, with the national governments pointing to the surrender of lands and the exclusion of hunting upon them due to settlement or public use, and Indian people arguing that their ancestors could not have had the power to surrender such rights.

In Flagstaff, Arizona, a District Court judge rejected the plea of the family of a Navajo rape victim to require the Navajo defendants to make restitution in the traditional way in exchange for their freedom.[60] The rape victim was thus left without compensation and without honour. The decision was that of non-Indian people who failed to ask about and understand what the expectations of the different culture are and why. If Indian common law is to have a place of dignity in Canadian and American jurisprudence, the barbarism principle must be abandoned and Indian law must be upheld, even when it offends the non-Indian.

VII. The art of ethnojurisprudence

The work of the searchers is so recent in time that it is difficult to know what to call them. "Anthropologist" does not fit, while "ethnologist" is still too broad. The searchers are not all lawyers, although they are studying law, and yet they are so numerous that a special term is appropriate. I like to use the term "ethnojurist" to describe work in the field of "ethnojurisprudence."[61]

Ethnojurisprudence is a study unlike any other. It requires a knowledge of law, anthropology, ethnology, political science, psychology, sociology, and human relations. Its students travel from one discipline to another, trading ideas and giving support. The ethnojurist is likely to be an activist, with distinct political goals and sympathies. Very often the ethnojurist is not a member of the culture he or she supports, and is very careful to define his or her role in terms of the desires of Indian leaders.

The ethnojurist is often working in the dark. Legal anthropology is a fairly recent study, with few scholars and little in print for guidance. What has been published is often of limited use, because the classic studies of Indian law do not deal with the everyday modern legal problem.

Ethnojurisprudence is frequently a very practical discipline. A tribal court wants to use the traditional common law in its proceedings and there is nothing to say how that is to be done. The lawyer-ethnojurist tries to explain to a Federal court precisely why a proposed dam will violate religious freedom, and is told by the Elders he can't explain "why" because that would violate religious precepts. One needs to know a particular principle of Indian common law. The anthropological studies don't mention it and you have to find a "reliable" source. Who is that person? How do you approach him or her? How do you ask the question in an understandable way? Should you approach a woman as well as a man because the question involves "women's knowledge?" The ethnojurist asks not simply as a scholar or scientist, but as a practitioner, advocate and adviser.

The ethnojurist is an intercultural communicator, a reconciler of values, a fixer, an arranger, an author, and many other things. He or she is a factotum.

It is impossible at this stage to declare authoritatively and precisely what the art of ethnojurisprudence is and what its techniques are. However, a few guidelines can be offered:

1. There must be a clear understanding of the goals of your work. If you are working for an Indian tribe, band or group you must speak with your principals to find out exactly what they want. It may be setting up a tribal court so members can take care of criminal or child welfare problems. It may be negotiating a claim. It may be many things, but the goal will often give practical guidance for finding the means.

2. You must have Indian partners, guides and friends. Indian ethnojurists are frequently as lost as the rest, but lengthy discussions in a relaxed atmosphere often lead to mutual insights and exciting schemes. Ethnojurists are educators and students, with the roles changing as the discussion progresses.

3. You have to write things down immediately, without regard for form, footnotes and formality. A very useful device is to maintain a ring-binder dedicated to a particular culture and to write down the jokes, stories, thoughts and sayings as you hear them. This is a valuable resource for future use, as this article has shown in its use of many stories recorded for various tribes.

4. You must be prepared to innovate while not being afraid of failure. Some ideas work, others don't and you may look back at something you wrote previously and wonder why you were so stupid. Innovation and experimentation open the way for new ideas.

5. You must be a thief of ideas. Again, the notebook preserves ideas which can be retrieved and works of comparative law, philosophy, and even novels have much wisdom in them.[62]

6. You must have both patience and a lively sense of humour. Many informants are suspicious and must be cultivated over time, and poking fun at oneself will often smooth the way in field work.[63]

It may be presumptuous for a person who is not formally trained in the science of studying Man to suggest guidelines for the art of ethnojurisprudence, but a nice thing about trying to coin a new term is that you get to say what it means.

Conclusion

Indian common law is valuable for everyone. Its study leads to a new appreciation of the problems of the general legal system and suggests new approaches to them; as well as to the problems of the culture where the particular law is used. At the heart of the new worldwide interest in the law of Native peoples is the attitude of the various searchers. This is not simply a legal or an anthropological process but a very political one, and each searcher must examine the policies that are to be developed through the search.[64] It is an exciting pursuit.

Notes

1. Bentzon and Brondsted, 1973; Schechter, in this volume.
2. Crawford et al., in this volume.
3. Government of Canada, et al., 1985.
4. The National American Indian Court Judges Association, which represents approximately 300 American Indian judges, has been unable to obtain support from either the Bureau of Indian Affairs or the Department of Health and Human Services in order to carry out an Indian common law project. To date, customary or Indian common law has been ignored by the American government.
5. The Working Group is effective because it fosters communcation within a network of individuals who are dealing with Indian common law on a practical professional basis.
6. Resolutions 1589(L) and 1982/34, UN Economic and Social Council.
7. Capotorti, 1979:66-67.
8. Id., Par. 212, 36.
9. See, Lopez, 1984 (Article on the rejection of a Navajo custom in a rape case); *National Farmers Union Ins. Co. and Lodge Grass School District No. 27 v Crow Tribe of Indians et al.* (1985), 105 S. Ct. 2447, 53 LW 4649 (June 3, 1985) (Civil jurisdiction over non-Indians limited by policy); Yabsley, 1984:17 (English rule).
10. Berkhofer, 1979.
11. Opekokew, 1982; Davies, 1985:16, 24-28 (Indian communities are "states" too).
12. Patterson, 1953:154-159.
13. See, Sieghart, 1983.
14. Both the American and the Canadian law affecting Native Peoples is concerned with denying or extending benefits on the basis of definitions in which the subject peoples have no say.
15. The term "Indian" is used because that is what the author hears the people use when identifying themselves. See Berkhofer, 1979:304, concerning the use of the term.
16. See, *R v Malboeuf,* [1982] 4 C.N.L.R. 116 (Sask. Court of Appeal) for a discussion of banishment. Judge Homer Bluehouse of the Navajo Courts indicates that under Navajo tradition persons who are banished would frequently commit suicide.
17. Patterson, 1953:224, Harding 1966:203, 289.
18. St. Germain, 1974:xi, 45, 47-91.
19. Hale, 1974: 2, 6.
20. Blackstone, undated: 67.

21. Hoebel, 1954:140.
22. Frank, 1963:283-306.
23. Id. 293.
24. Ibid.
25. In July of 1983 Indian judges, lawyers and practitioners from the Cree, Klallum, Blackfeet, Salish-Kootenai, Pima, and Navajo tribes met in Browning, Montana, to discuss Indian custom law. As the participants to the meeting began speaking of specific practices, they realized that there are many common elements to the laws of the various tribes. They agreed that there should be a general study to explore the most common elements.
26. The classic comparison is that of Benedict, 1959.
27. The informant was a Canadian Cree educator who was explaining animism to a reporter preparing an article on the meaning of the Pow-wow, Rocky Boy's Reservation, Montana, July, 1984.
28. G. Stump, (Cree) Rocky Boy's Reservation, July, 1984.
29. Ibid.
30. This concept has been expressed by members of the Navajo, Pima, Chippewa and Cree Tribes and it appears to be common Indian usage.
31. G. Stump in a bingo parlor in Saskatoon, Saskatchewan, October, 1984. Kenneth Ryan, the chairman of the Fort Peck (Assiniboine-Sioux) Tribe of Montana explained the concept of luck and good consequences for good acts in much the same way: Ryan, 1985.
32. Compare this finding with that of Bell and Ditton, 1980. The concepts of "men's knowledge" and "women's knowledge" may be widespread and should be carefully examined.
33. Comments to the Canadian Native Law Student Association, August, 1984.
34. For a fuller description, see, Zion, 1984.
35. Ibid.
36. Government of Canada et al., 1985.
37. Hoebel, 1954:29-45; Llewellyn and Hoebel, 1983:20-40.
38. E.g., Waters, 1963; Locke, 1976; Haile, 1981a and 1981b; Bloomfield, 1934; Zolbrod, 1984. Also, see, Claire R. Farrer's review of this last work for a good critique of such collections, Farrer, 1985. There are many published verions of Indian Scripture in the form of narratives, summaries and stories, but works such as those by Haile and Bloomfield are particularly useful because they are published in both the tongue of the Scripture and English. Since they are precise translations, they are more useful as statements of law. Waters' work is an excellent general narrative, but we must put our trust in his accuracy in summarizing the Hopi Scripture. Works such as those by

Locke are less reliable because the Scripture may have suffered in a cultural as well as a linguistic translation.

39. Waters was very careful about this and tells how he went about receiving clearance for his work, Ibid; xii-xiv.
40. *Fisher v District Court* (1976), 424 U.S. 382; See also, Lynaugh, 1977.
41. In the case of *Navajo Nation ex rel Div. of Social Welfare In the Interest of JJS*, (1983), 4 Navajo Rep. 192, the Window Rock District Court faced two sets of adoptive parents vying for the adoption of a Navajo child. The court found that adoption was a rarity in Navajo common law, at least in the modern sense, because a child always had family or clan members other than the parents who were responsible for a child and who would care for it in the event of parental incapacity. The court noted this pattern and ruled that the Navajo adoptive parents who were extended relatives would be preferred over the non-Navajo parties.
42. See, Navajo Reporter (1984-1985); and Zion, 1985.
43. General Assembly Res. 217 A(III).
44. Sieghart, 1983:53-54.
45. United Nations, 1980.
46. Capotorti, 1979. The clash would be minimized by an understanding of what "equality" and "discrimination" mean, such that Indians can demand special measures of protection. McKean, 1970.
47. Sieghart, 1983:381-384.
48. Supra, note 6.
49. Capotorti, 1979:66-68.
50. (R. 6/24) HRC 36, 166.
51. While Canada moved to protect the rights of women under the Covenant it ignored the Article 27 right of Indians, Inuit and Metis Peoples in general to enjoy their own cultures. Surely some balance could have been struck. For example, see, note 46.
52. See, Elberg, in this volume (Canada); Case, 1983 (United States); Hennesy, 1983.
53. National Lawyers Guild Committee on Native American Struggles, 1982:15-26, 89-95; Barsh, 1982.
54. See, Berkhofer, 1979.
55. "In the main it is impossible to look to the Indian tradition for help because many of the kinds of relationship which need regulation did not exist in pre-reservation Indian society; they were brought into the Indian life by the economic and social system of the non-Indians. Although Indian law applies, there is for the most part no discoverable law created by legislative action of

the tribe." *Wippert v Burlington Northern, Inc.,* 397 F. Supp. 73, at 75 (D. Mont. 1975).

56. See, *White Eagle v One Feather,* 478 F. 2d 1311, at 1312 (C.A. 8, 1973); *Yellow Bird v Oglala Sioux Tribe,* 380 F. Supp. 438, at 440 (D.S.D. 1974); *Janis v Wilson.,* 385 F. Supp. 1143, at 1150-1151, 1155 (D.S.D. 1974); and *Martinez v Santa Clara Pueblo,* 402 F. Supp. 5, at 17-18 (D.N.M. 1975).
57. Green, 1975.
58. See, note 9, *supra*.
59. The same judge who could not find Blackfeet traditional law (note 56, *supra*) took judicial notice "that many tribal members with small fractions of Indian blood have moved from the reservations and into the mainstream of Montana life," and invalidated a statute giving Indians a preference for Federal contracts. *Montana Contractors' Assn. v Secretary of Commerce,* 35 St. Rep. 1823, 460 F. Supp. 1174, at 1178 (D. Montana, 1978). The judge noted the style of clothing, skin color and lack of feathers of the Indian litigants and simply decided Indians had assimilated.
60. See, note 9, *supra*.
61. An author writing in the late 19th Century uses the term, "ethnological jurisprudence." Post, 1915. Nader, 1965:17, uses the term "ethnography of law". Bohannan, 1980:55-56, likes the term, "jural ethnography". "Ethnojurisprudence" implies in a better way that each People can have a systematic law, a jurisprudence.
62. For enjoyment as well as scholarship read, Cushman, 1953. (which Vine Deloria says is the most accurate account of reservation life written); Baylor, 1980; Schwartz, 1976 and any of the Indian tales of W.P. Kinsella, including Kinsella 1977, 1981 and 1984.
63. Vine Deloria's *Custer Died for Your Sins* should be required reading.
64. Anthropologist Laura Nader suggests that research into alternative dispute resolution has gotten off the track because it does not address the moral question of "access to justice for the masses, for the many," and does not speak to moral decay. These are the sort of policy questions which are suggested. National Institute for Dispute Resolution, 1985.

References

BARSH, R.L. (1982)
"Indian Land Claims Policy in the United States," 58 North Dakota Law Review 7.

BAYLOR, B. (1980)
Yes is Better than No.

BELL, D. and P. DITTON (1980)
Law: The Old and the New. Canberra: Aboriginal History.

BENEDICT, Ruth (1959)
Patterns of Culture.

BENTZON, A.W. and H. BRONDSTED (1983)
"Recognition, repression and transformation of customary law in Greenland during the last forty years of transition to capitalism." Papers of the Symposia of Folk Law and Legal Pluralism, XIth International Congress of Anthropological and Ethnological Sciences. Vancouver: Canada, (Unpublished, August 1983) 598. (Hereinafter cited as "Papers").

BERKHOFER, R.F., Jr. (1979)
The White Man's Indian. New York: Alfred A. Knoff.

BLACKSTONE, Sir W. (no date) Commentaries on the Laws of England.

BLOOMFIELD, L. (1934)
Plains Cree Texts. New York: G.M. Steehert & Co.

BOHANNAN, Paul (1980)
"The Differing Realms of the Law," in P. Bohannan (ed.), Law & Warfare. Austin: University of Texas Press. CAPOTORTI, F. (1979)
Study on the Rights of Persons Belonging to Ethnic, Religious and Linguistic Minorities. 66-67 (UN Doc. E/CN.4/Sub. 2/384/Rev. 1, 1979).

CASE, D. (1983)
"Alaska Native Sovereignty, The Final Claim." Papers 622.

CUSHMAN, D. (1953)
Stay Away Joe. New York: Viking Press.

DAVIES, M. (1985)
"Aspects of Aboriginal Rights in International Law," in B.W. Morse (ed.), Aboriginal Peoples and the Law: Indian, Metis and Inuit Rights in Canada. Ottawa: Carleton University Press.

FARRER, C.R. (1985)
Review, 10 Parabola 121 (August).

FRANK, J. (1963)
Law and the Modern Mind. Garden City, N.Y.: Doubleday & Co.

GOVERNMENT OF CANADA, Government of Saskatchewan, Federation of Saskatchewan Indian Nations (1985)
Joint Studies: Reflecting Indian Concerns and Values in the Justice System.

GREEN, L.C. (1975)
" 'Civilized' Law and 'Primitive' Peoples," 13 Osgoode Hall Law Journal 233.

HAILE, B. (1981a)
Women Versus Men: A Conflict of Navajo Emergence.

---------- (1981b)
Upward Moving and Emergence Way.

HALE, Sir M. (1794)
The History of the Common Law. (5th ed.). London.

HARDING, A. (1966)
A Social History of English Law. Baltimore: Penguin Books.

HENNESSEY, P.K. (1983)
"Extracts from Relevant Australian Legislation." Papers 1143.

HOEBEL, E.A. (1954)
The Law of Primitive Man. Cambridge, Mass.: Harvard University Press.

KINSELLA, W.P. (1977)
Dance Me Outside. Ottawa: Oberon Press.

---------- (1981)
Born Indian.

---------- (1984)
The Moccasin Telegraph and other Stories.

LLEWELLYN, K.N. and E.A. HOEBEL (1983)
The Cheyenne Way. Norman, Okla.: University of Oklahoma Press.

LOCKE, R.F. (1976)
Book of the Navajo. Los Angeles: Mankind Pub. Co.

LOPEZ, L. (1984)
"Taking Care of Their Own: Navajos Dispense Traditional Justice to Retain Harmony," The Arizona Republic, August 6, 1984, A1-A2.

LYNAUGH, T.J. (1977)
"Developing Theories of State Jurisdiction Over Indians: The Dominance of the Preemption Analysis," 38 Montana Law Review 63.

McKEAN, W.A. (1970)
"The Meaning of Discrimination in International and Municipal Law," 44 British Year Book of International Law 177.

NADER, L. (1965)
"The Anthropological Study of Law," in The Ethnography of Law. 67 American Anthropologist, No. 6, Pt. 2 (Special Publication) 3.

NATIONAL INSTITUTE FOR DISPUTE RESOLUTION (1985)
Dispute Resolution Forum.

NATIONAL LAWYERS GUILD COMMITTEE ON NATIVE AMERICAN STRUGGLE (1982)
Rethinking Indian Law. New York, N.Y.

NAVAJO REPORTER (1984-85) Vols 3 & 4.

OPEKOKEW, D. (1982)
The First Nations: Indian Governments in the Community of Man. Saskatoon, Sask.: Federation of Saskatchewan Indians.

PATTERSON, E.W. (1953)
Jurisprudence: Men and Ideas of the Law. Brooklyn: The Foundation Press.

POST, A.H. (1915)

"Ethnological Jurisprudence," in A. Kocurek and J.H. Wigmore (eds.), Primitive and Ancient Legal Institutions. Vol II of Evolution of Law: Select Readings on the Origin and Development of Legal Institutions. Boston: Little, Brown and Co.

RYAN, Kenneth (1985)
"Transition of Give-Away Ceremonies: Is it More Expensive to be an Indian Today?" 12th Annual Montana History Conference, Helena, Montana, November 8.

ST. GERMAINE (1974)
Doctor and Student, 91 Selden Society.

SCHWARZ, H.T. (1976)
Tales from the Smokehouse.

SIEGHART, P. (1983)
The International Law of Human Rights. Oxford: Clarendon Press.

UNITED NATIONS (1980)
"Status of International Conventions in the field of human rights in respect of which the Secretary-General performs depository functions." UN Doc. A/35/389.

WATERS, F. (1963)
Book of the Hopi. New York: Viking Press.

YABSLEY, G.R. (1984)
"Nunavut and Inuit Customary Law." Unpublished.

ZION J. (1984)
"Harmony Among the People: Torts and Indian Courts," 45 Montana Law Review 265.

---------- (1985)
"The Navajo Peacemaker Court: Deference to the Old and Accommodation to the New," 11 *American Indian Law Review* 89.

ZOLBROD, P.G. (1984)
Dine bahane: The Navajo Creation Story. Albuquerque: University of New Mexico Press.

Part II

General Relations Between Indigenous Law and The State: Analyses

Persistence of folk law in India with particular reference to the tribal communities

B.K. Roy Burman

I. The context of the problem

A. General considerations about typology

Folk law in the context of the nation-state is an ensemble of behavioural norms whose persistence depends on the acceptance of rights and duties among the members of primary groups or between primary groups, this acceptance being essentially an act of conformity to moral obligation, rather than of submission to the coercive power of the state.

Folk law may exist as complementary to state law, or as an alternative frame of behaviour in indifference to or even in defiance of state law. But, as will be indicated later, folk law may exist not only in the context of the functioning of the nation-state. In areas where customary laws have not been codified, the same exist as parallel to behavioural norms prescribed by a non-state establishment in respect of basic institutions like the family and property.

Another dimension of folk law requires to be noted at the outset. Folk law of today may be a reincarnation of state law of yesterday; it may be in the process of becoming state law of tomorrow; it may symbolize a dialectical relationship between the state and the society; and it may cover behavioural realms not covered by state law. It may also be a vanishing trail of the past.

All these types of situations exist in India. Before discussing them, the historical, political-economic and cultural aspects of the presence of folk law will be briefly touched upon with particular reference to the tribal communities.

B. Historical Context

In the ancient Maurya Empire, in the third century BC, there was a separate minister in the imperial cabinet called *Ant Mahamatya* to look after the relations of the state with the forest dwellers. The Maurya emperor Asok, in one of his famous rock edicts, assured the hill dwellers of his commiseration for them. By and large this represents even today the national ethos of India in respect of the tribal population, at the ideological plane. But it does not mean that state policy in respect of the tribals has always been guided by humane considerations.

In the pre-British period, when India was divided into several kingdoms, the relations of the kingdoms with the forest dwellers were often determined by the pattern of relationships among adjoining kingdoms. Frequently the forest dwelling people served as bridge or buffer communities between the kingdoms (Burman 1966). While the bridge role tended to promote egalitarian social structures along with incomplete segmentation, the buffer role tended to create, within a vaguely identifiable socio-political orbit, several segmental structures which, in their turn, were internally stratified. On a closer analysis, it became obvious that the persistence of tribal communities as distinct entities, without forming themselves into organized states, was a necessity for the contact kingdoms. But at the same time, some form of regulation was needed to ensure the flow of commodities, movement of traders, and march of armies through the bridge and buffer zones. As a result, what has been described by Weber as regulated anarchies prevailed among the forest dwellers (Harsch 1978). Empirical evidence of such regulated anarchies, involving politico-social integration of the tribals and surrounding civilizations in the peripheries of organized states, is furnished by Burton Stein with reference to what he calls 'nuclear areas' in South India and by Hermann Kulke in respect of the tribal areas of Eastern India (Stein 1969; Kulke 1978).

To enable the regulated anarchies of Chotanagpur in the central tribal belt of India to perform their bridge role, the tribal communities constituted what may be described as 'kings without kingdoms' in the early middle ages. In an UNESCO publication of 1979 the author suggested that kingship was a borrowed cultural form for a functionary whose role was no more than that of coordination of the response of the self-governing local communities to the requirements of external contact (Burman 1979). Partial confirmation that kingship was a symbolic representation of an inter-ethnic situation rather than a political institution, has also been provided by Marine Carrine Bouez (1978).

With the establishment of colonial domination during the late 18th and early 19th centuries and the extension of road and rail communication, the bridge and buffer roles of tribal communities became dysfunctional except on the international borders. The British adopted a policy of commercial exploitation of the forest resources which led to a series of violent uprisings and revolts.

In 1874 the Scheduled Districts Act was promulgated. It enabled the Government to determine by notification which laws were to be enforced in the Scheduled Districts. A step towards simplification was taken in 1880, when the Frontier Tracts Regulation was promulgated. This provided for the exclusion from operation of laws which were unsuitable in border areas. For instance the Criminal Procedure Code was considered to belong to this category and until now it has not been enforced in the hill areas of North-East India.

In 1919 a limited transfer of power to Indians in selected subjects took place under the Government of India Act. Under this Act the Governor-General in Council was authorized to declare any territory in India a backward tract, to which Acts passed by the Central Assembly were not to apply without authorization by the Governor-General. These were mostly tribal areas, distributed in five provinces and covering a population of more than ten million. The Governor-General could also empower the provincial governors to make similar declarations regarding Acts passed by local legislatures.

The new Government of India Act 1935 was mainly based on the recommendations of the Simon Commission on Statutory Reforms. Under this Act most of the tribal areas were declared to be Excluded or Partially Excluded Areas. Both these categories were excluded from the competence of the provincial and federal legislatures. The rationale for these provisions was given as follows by the Simon Commission: 'The stage of development reached by the inhabitants of these areas prevents the possibility of applying to them the methods of representation adopted elsewhere. They do not ask for self-determination but for security of land tenure in the pursuit of their traditional methods of livelihood and the reasonable exercise of their ancestral customs'.

The provision in respect of Excluded and Partially Excluded Areas caused considerable misgiving in nationalist circles. But while the Constitution of Independent India of 1950 does away with Excluded and Partially Excluded Areas, it includes Scheduled Areas and Tribal Areas in their stead. The constitutional provisions have considerable bearing on the persistence of the customary laws of the tribal communities. But this should be viewed against the backdrop of the basic socio-cultural processes and political economy of the country.

C. Socio-cultural and political-economic context

'The main feature of Indian society seen at its strongest in the rural part, is caste: this means the division of society into many groups which live side by side, but often do not seem to live together. Members of different castes cannot intermarry by religion, though law now permits complete freedom in this respect'. (Kosambi 1978). In theory there are only four castes: Brahman (priest), Kshatriya (warrior), Vaisya (trader and husbandman) and Sudra (corresponding in general to the working class). In practice, the number of caste groups goes into thousands. Morton Class presents an account of the units of the caste system (Sharma 1983). Sub-castes or marriage circles exist as 'corporate groups' within which a person must marry. These groups maintain certain rules of behaviour, on such matters as the choice of marriage-partners and of occupation and enforce these rules by sanctions which include expulsion. They are interconnected mainly through the exchange of economic services. In contrast to the sub-castes or marriage circles, the caste or jati is, according to Class, simply a conglomeration of sub-castes and has no corporate existence of its own. Sharma (1983) however argues that Class is wrong. In the historical (pre-British) caste-feudal society, there existed two institutions for enforcing caste-prescribed behaviour. One was indeed the sub-caste, but the other was the feudal state which gave reality to the principal castes. The present author is inclined to agree with the view of Sharma, that, while the socio-cultural process, particularly in Hindu society, enjoyed considerable autonomy, it was not completely free from the intervention of state power. The supremacy of the Brahman in Hinduism actually meant supremacy of the priest-warrior power syndrome. At the same time he considers that it would not be correct to ignore the ethos of internal self-management of castes in the Hindu society, symbolized in the aphorism 'Unity in diversity'.

An essential difference between tribal communities and the caste entities in medieval India was that, even where the tribes had political links with the organised states, the ideology of the relationship did not provide any scope for state intervention in the socio-cultural processes of the tribes. In fact the bridge and buffer roles of the tribal communities would have made such intervention self-defeating. In this context the cultural ethos of unity in diversity would fully legitimize the persistence of distinct behavioural norms and the self-generating enforcing mechanism of the tribal communities.

The regionally diversified history and political economy of the country also provide contextual setting for the persistence of folk laws. Four categories of area need consideration. First, the bulk of the area of the country, starting from the north to the south (but leaving out large portions mainly in the North-East), was under common political domain, at various periods of history, before the subcontinent came under colonial domination. Secondly, the North-East has been part of some political systems in India and shares many cultural traits with the rest of the country, but has also been part of the political systems of South-East Asia, and shares cultural traits with the people of those countries. Different areas in the North-East have distinctive features in their ethnic processes, including internal social control mechanisms. Thirdly, in many areas there are enclaves of tribal concentration, which came under common political control and effective administrative system during colonial rule. Lastly, there are areas in the North-East which came under colonial suzerainty but to which regular civil administration was extended only after Independence.

In the first areas the feudal mode of production prevailed in the pre-colonial period. During the colonial period an alliance of feudal and capitalist forces took place. In the post-independence period, while vestiges of the feudal mode of production continue, the capitalist mode is rapidly taking over. The predominant social organization in these areas is caste. The tribal populations live in small enclaves in the midst of the caste-groups. They have imbibed caste ideas to a considerable extent, and for some time a process of their integration in the caste system has been going on, together with an erosion of their customary law. This process has coincided with the progressive eviction of the tribal communities from their traditional resources, such as the forests. Currently, with the spread of education and political communication, there is a reversal of the earlier trend and in some areas attempts are being made, through social mobility movements supplemented by political mobilisation, to revive or set up autogenous social control mechanisms.

In the second class of areas the feudal mode of production co-existed with an archaic peasant mode of production during the pre-colonial period. The caste system penetrated here in an incomplete manner. During the colonial period state-sponsored capitalist enterprises arose while indigenous entrepreneurship lagged behind. In the post-Independence period, state capitalistic enterprizes have arisen haltingly. As the centripetal pull of caste was never strong in these areas, micro-regional social formations retained many of their autogenous control mechanisms. Hence the customary laws of the tribals retained many of their former features, though changes occurred in the nature of the sanctions.

In the areas of the third and fourth categories, the mode of production was patriarchal during the pre-colonial and colonial periods. The economy was predominantly non-monetized. While in some areas of the third category caste-like structures came into existence, the caste-system as such did not penetrate significantly in most areas of these two categories. In the post-Independence period productive activities in these areas have been mainly oriented to the needs of the national market, imparting great urgency to the adaptive processes of the ethnic groups including the tribal communities. These processes take various forms, among which two are of particular relevance for the persistence of the customary laws.

When the settlements of primitive peoples in outlying areas begin to come under the sway of market forces and the people find that the channels for circulation of goods and services through social relations of reciprocity cannot cope with the new situation, almost as a reflex action they try to respond jointly to the challenge. The old differences among the groups are minimized and by a process of synchretism new unities are perceived. The old myths are restructured and a kinship is established among different groups. In a paper published in the mid 1960s this process was termed by the author 'infra-nationalism'. In the phase of infra-nationalism the process of identity expansion is promoted by the traditional elite who adapt the traditional communication network to serve modern needs. But there is also a phase when the motive-force and direction of identity expansion may be provided by the educated elite, who form a modern type of formal association: this may be termed proto-nationalism (Burman 1971).

While both infra- and proto-national movements are directed towards the expansion of identity, there is an important difference between the two, apart from differences in the nature of the elite and the medium of communication. The motivators of infra-national mobilization are concerned not only to protect their traditional control over the resources associated with them, but also to retain the traditional pattern of use of those resources. They are essentially moral proponents. They are aware of the functioning of the nation-state power, but their response to it is in moral terms. On the other hand, proto-national motivators not only strive to retain their traditional resource base, but also demand a share of the services and resources developed by the Welfare State. Without striving for independent power, they expect a share of state power. The pre-eminent common concern of both infra-nationalism and proto-nationalism as movements within tribal populations, however, relates to the common land and forest resources. In 1982, a committee set up by the Government of India on Forests and Tribals reported not only the persistence of common property resources within tribal communities but also the autogenous regulation of the use of such resources (Government of India 1982).

It is in this socio-cultural and political economic context that the relevant constitutional provisions need to be noted.

D. Relevant constitutional provisions

In the Constitution of India the Fifth and Sixth Schedules are specially concerned with the tribal areas. The Fifth Schedule applies to most of the predominantly tribal areas throughout India. The Sixth Schedule specifically applies to the States of Assam and Meghalaya and the Union Territory of Mizoram.

In areas designated under the Fifth Schedule, laws enacted by the legislature come into force unless the Governor directs otherwise. In addition, the Governor is empowered to make regulations for the peace and good government of such areas. The Constitution provides further that Fifth Schedule Areas shall have Tribal Advisory Councils, three-fourths of whose members shall belong to the tribal communities. The Sixth Schedule provides for the constitution of autonomous districts and for regional councils in respect of the areas so designated. Powers of regulation on a fairly large number of subjects are reserved to these councils under the overall control of the Governor acting in consultation with the ministers. These include the protection of the people's land, the management of forests (except reserve forests), the use of canals and water courses, the regulation of shifting cultivation, the establishment of village councils, the appointment or succession of chiefs or headmen, the inheritance of property, and marriage laws and social customs.

In addition to special provisions in respect of tribal areas several other provisions in the Constitution sustain a congenial climate for the persistence of certain aspects of customary law. For instance, there are constitutional provisions for the protection of certain rights regarding freedom of speech, of conscience, of the professions, and for the propagation of religion; the promotion of educational and economic interests of the weaker sections; and the reservation of seats in legislatures, and the recognition of special claims to services and posts.

II. Evidence of persistence of folk law

The foregoing rapid appraisal of the political history, socio-cultural processes and political economy of India has aimed to delineate the external environment for the persistence of folk laws. Some of the empirical evidence of such persistence will be furnished now.

A. Folk law complementary to state law

Basic institutions like marriage, succession and adoption among the communities statutorily recognized as tribals in India are guided by their customary laws. In 1971 about 40 million persons were enumerated as belonging to the scheduled tribe communities. The bulk of them claimed to be Hindus. A small number professed Christianity; much smaller numbers returned Buddhism and Islam as their religions.

The Hindu Marriage Act, Hindu Inheritance Act and Hindu Adoption Act which apply to Hindus and Buddhists do not ordinarily apply even to those tribals who claim Hinduism as their religion. The Hinduised tribals can be brought within the purview of these Acts only through the issue of a public notification by the competent authority. No such notification has yet been issued in respect of any tribal community.

Indian Christians are guided in the matter of inheritance by the Indian Succession Act, 1927. This provides for the exemption from the Act of Christians belonging to aboriginal communities by the issue of notifications. A large number of communities were thus exempted before India attained its independence from foreign rule, and no exemption has yet been rescinded for any aboriginal community.

The Muslims of L.M.A. Islands, who have been included in the list of the scheduled tribes, are guided by Muslim personal law in respect of self-acquired property, but by the customary laws of the various islands in respect of family property, which is acquired by succession (Burman 1961a).

There is frequently uncertainty and variability in the administration of customary law. Provisions in various statutes require the courts to be guided in deciding cases by evidence as to the custom of the population concerned. About three decades ago the author examined the administration in parts of Eastern India of such provisions in the Agra Oudh Judicial Act, 1885. He found that in the course of five years the same court had given three different versions of the customary laws of the same tribe, residing in the same area.

In other areas also he found that the customary laws were in flux, and that there were different versions of customs. But there was almost unanimity on one matter, namely, that customary laws should not be interfered with. It seemed that people looked upon the unstructured status of customary laws as a symbol of their partial independence from the apparatus of the state (Burman 1961b). In another context, the author found much later that cognitive differences over customary laws were sometimes essentially functional. The issues on which differences were expressed by vocal sections of tribal communities were not really of great importance. The differences had instrumental value, representing differences over the strategy for preserving from the long arm of the State commonly cherished basic structures. This will be further discussed later.

Institutional arrangements for the recognition of customary law as complementary to state law exist in their fullest form in parts of the Sixth Schedule areas of North-East India. Some of the Autonomous District Councils and Regional Councils have set up their own courts to try cases according to the customary laws of their communities. Some Autonomous District Councils also enacted legislation codifying customary laws in matters connected with marriage, inheritance, chiefship, community land and so on. But these have not met with much success. For instance, among the matrilineal Khasis, where property is inherited in the female line, codification recognizing the custom gave rise to a number of disputes. Empirical evidence was produced to show that within the broad framework of the custom there existed diverse practices, mostly designed to ensure some continuity in productive activities based on a sex-wise division of labour. A number of amendments were made to take account of the newly perceived needs, but it seems that considerable confusion still prevails. Intervention by the District Council, which in some contexts tends to assume the role of a supra-tribal entity, has not been of much help.

An adaptation of folk law as complementary to state law, directed to a planned change of land use patterns, has been reported from Nagaland. Here Village Development Boards have been constituted by the traditional Village Councils. While composition of the village council conforms to the prevailing custom of the village, members of the Board may be from outside. The Board is a legal person, capable of receiving a bank loan with state guarantee. It is the Village Council which allots land to the Board out of the village common land for the development of horticulture, coffee plantations and so on. The income generated pertains to the village as a whole and is spent as such. A number of new issues have arisen out of this development, but it is not proposed to discuss them here.

B. Folk law indifferent to the administrative-legal framework of the state

Before the extension of colonial administration to the tribal belt of East, Central and South India, among many forest-dwelling communities resources, particularly in land and forests, were held in common by various politico-legal groups. Land survey and settlement operations in the pre- and post-independence periods have frequently ignored these communal systems. Thus in respect of the Gonds, Fuchs reports that, in spite of the conferment of proprietary rights on individuals by survey and settlement operations, fellow villagers recognize such rights only to the extent that is compatible with customary law. If the allottee of land wants to sell it, fellow villagers generally refuse to buy (Fuchs 1960). Ethnographic studies also show that side by side with the state system a parallel system of rights in respect of the land and forest prevails among tribal communities over large parts of the country. Irrespective of their status in state law, the forest dwellers generally recognize the jurisdiction of specific communities over specific hill ranges, water-ways and so on. Persons of other villages or communities can have access to such resources only on some payment which at the conceptual level is a mix of economic category and political category. The payment is more frequently categorized as tribute or symbol of alliance than as rent or price.

C. Folk law in opposition to state law

When the British brought practically the whole of India under a single political system, some of the communities, like sections of Mina, which played peripheral roles in the military establishments of the middle ages, suffered a loss of role. Some, like the Lodha of West Bengal, found themselves divested of their access to traditional sources of livelihood. The resulting protest took the form of violence against life and the appropriation of property. The British declared them to be criminal tribes, under the provisions of a law specially enacted for the purpose. But to them crime was not so much an anti-social activity as a form of guerrilla warfare against the barbarism perpetrated by "civilization". Many of these communities developed their own norms for carrying out these activities. For instance, if some community had the exclusive right of committing burglary with an iron rod, some other community had the exclusive right of highway robbery. Deviations from the norms were reported to invoke negative sanctions from the respective communities. After Independence the Criminal Tribes Act was revoked, and a number of rehabilitation measures were adopted. But the social organization and reward system sustaining crime had become too deep-rooted to be eradicated rapidly.

D. Folk law parallel to behaviour norms prescribed by non-state establishments

In Brahministic Hinduism, the killing of a cow is one of the greatest of sins. In the middle ages in Hindu kingdoms cow slaughter was a crime. The Directive Principles of state policy, which form an integral part of the Constitution of India, now require the state to endeavour to stop cow slaughter, though the religious ground has been veiled by other grounds.

The Totos of West Bengal, a small tribe, perform an annual festival involving the sacrifice of nine cows, but claim to be Hindus. When some Nepali migrants tried to stop the practice, the Totos complained of interference with their religion. Again, beef-eating, though now rapidly disappearing, was a fairly common practice among many tribes in the Central and Southern tribal belt of the country. They also called themselves Hindus, but exhibited a parallel system of beliefs and practices.

E. Persistence of folk law through metamorphosis of the state law of the past

An interesting example is provided by the Totos, just mentioned (Burman 1969). They are a small tribe living in a single village, Totopara, on the border of North Bengal and Bhutan. Before the Bhutan War of the 1860s Totopara was a part of Bhutan. Every year a Bhutanese official used to come to Totopara to collect tribute due to the King of Bhutan. When the change of regime took place without the Totos being actively involved, a metamorphosis occurred in their relations with the King. Earlier, when the officials of Bhutan had exercised power over the Totos the king had been the source of legitimation of that power. With the passing of control of Totopara to the British, the Bhutan officials ceased to exercise power, but in their ignorance of the intricacies of inter-state relations, the Totos did not dislodge the king of Bhutan from his position in their minds as the ultimate authority. As his position was no longer manifested in secular form, it was transformed into sacred authority. Until a few decades ago an official of Bhutan used to come to the border of Totopara every year to receive offerings. The Totos used to collect rice, poultry, pigs, and several species of local plants, and after performing a ritual the Toto priest used to hand over these to the official. Thus the secular tribute was turned into sacred offering.

A metamorphosis of different order has been reported in the relations of the mountain-dweller Sherdukpens of the sub-Himalayan region in North-East India, and the Kacharis, a tribal community living in the plains. Before the effective extension of administration to the region, the Sherdukpens used to raid the Kachari villages, and frequently extort payments. Since Independence the Sherdukpen area has been fully integrated into the regular administration. But even now the Sherdukpens come to the Kachari villages and there are exchanges of gifts, to a certain extent to the advantage of the Sherdukpens. But whereas in the past such exchange symbolized forcible exaction, now it symbolizes the continuity of an old relationship, with a new meaning.

F. Folk law as potential state law of tomorrow

With growing concern for environmental management folk laws are assuming a new dimension. Many tribal communities have traditional taboos, beliefs and customs for regulating the use of natural resources.

For instance, the Rongmeis of Manipur maintain tree rings around their village to protect them against the fire hazard of slash and burn cultivation. Anybody doing damage to the tree ring is required by the traditional village council to pay a fine. The Angamis have a custom that when a particular plant is removed by somebody, for any purpose, he has to plant two replacements (so that at least one may survive). Such folk laws, which belong to the realm of ethno-ecology, were almost completely ignored by bureaucrats and technocrats, and even by anthropologists. Recently they have received some attention, and it seems that some of them will provide the basis for more imaginative state laws relating to the environment.

G. Folk law as a dimension of the dialectical relationship between state and society

The Autonomous District Council of a certain District in North-East India appointed a committee to examine various issues of codification of the customary laws with the present author as Chairman. Memoranda were submitted to the committee by mutually opposed groups. One group, headed by a minister of the state, submitted that chiefship in the tribe was elective. Another group, headed by the Ex-President of an opposition party, submitted that chiefship was hereditary. Both contentions were endorsed by a large number of chiefs and genealogical evidence was produced in favour of each. A detailed enquiry, however, revealed that both had the same aim of avoiding the take-over of all communal lands by the state. One group thought that if the hereditary principle of chiefship was recognized, the chief could be presented to the state as the owner of communal land, and at the same time through internal political action be prevented from acting in an arbitrary manner in his personal interest. The other group thought that the recognition of the elective principle would be more acceptable in the context of India's political ethos of democratic decentralisation. Both feared that, given the corrupt character of the bureaucracy, it would be difficult to prevent the fragmentation of common property resources over a length of time if they were brought under state control. Thus both groups tried to take advantage of some ambiguity in the relevant folk law so as to protect the common resources.

H. Pragmatic aspects of folk law

The foregoing narration shows that folk laws are not steel frames for social action. They are quite frequently flexible in operation and pragmatic in orientation.

In the Union Territory of Arunachal situated in East Himalaya, the Gallong tribe practices fraternal polyandry. During the post-Independence period education has spread more rapidly among them than any other tribes in the region, and they are also flourishing in business. In the early 70s the educated young men convened a conference to abolish polyandry. The elders also attended. The latter argued that polyandry had enabled the common fathers to provide higher education for those lads who showed promise, or to help them enter trade and commerce. Abolition of polyandry, they argued, would prevent the accumulation of capital in their techno-cultural milieu and the community would stagnate. This put off decisive action by the young men.

An example of a different type is from Ladakh in Jammu and Kashmir. Rizvi has provided a number of case studies of marriage between Buddhists and Muslims where the spouses and children have exercised their choice as to which of these two faiths they would profess. He has also indicated how sometimes mundane interests have become linked with such marriages and the choice of faith.

I. Long-term implications of the persistence of folk law

In India, Gandhi considered the state as the source of evil. His position was that of philosophical anarchism. Marxists speak of the withering away of the state. Sol Tax, the doyen of the anthropologists, in his Planning the Utopias, has also presented a vision of stateless, interlinked localities (Sol Tax 1982). The moot question is, if ever a stateless society comes into existence, what will be the nature of the non-state regulatory process? Perhaps a detailed investigation of the persistence of folk laws in diverse ecological and historical contexts will provide more understanding of the problem.

References

BOUEZ, M.C. (1978)
"Acculturation and/or dialectics," in Moser and Gautam.

BURMAN, B.K. Roy (1961a)
"Chetlat - an island: L.M.A. group of islands," Village Survey Monograph, Census of India.

---------- (1961b)
"Demographic and socio-cultural profile of North-East India," Census of India.

---------- (1966)
"Structure of bridge and buffer communities," Man in India.

---------- (1969)
Hundred Years in a Tribal Village: Totopara. Trends of Socio-Economic Change in India 1871-1961. Simla: Institute of Advanced Studies.

---------- (1971)
"National movements among the tribes," Social Democracy 4.

---------- (1979)
"Post-primitives of Chotanagpur: identity dilemmas and ethnic relations," in Trends in Ethnic Group Relations, UNESCO.

FUCHS, S. (1960)
The Gond and Bhumia of Eastern Mandla, Bombay.

GOVERNMENT OF INDIA (1982)
Report of the Committee on Forest and Tribes, Ministry of Home Affairs.

HARSCH, H.G. (1978)
"From regulated anarchy to proto-nationalism," in Moser and Gautam.

KOSAMBI, D.D. (1978)
Culture and Civilization of Ancient India. Delhi: Vikas Publishing House.

KULKE, H. (1978)
"Early state formation and royal legitimation in tribal areas of eastern India," in Moser and Gautam.

MOSER, R.R. and M.K. GAUTAM (eds.) (1978)
Aspects of Tribal Life in South Asia. Bonn: University of Bonn.

SHARMA, S.P. (1983)
"Origin and continuity of caste system in south Asia," The Eastern Anthropologist 36 (1).

STEIN, B. (1969)
"Integration of the agrarian system of south India," in R.E. Frykenberg (ed.), Land Control and Social Structure in Indian History. Madison, Milwaukee and London: University of Wisconsin Press.

TAX, Sol (1982)
"Planning utopias," Cultural Futures Research 7.

Comprehensive claims, culture and customary law: the case of the Labrador Inuit

Nathan Elberg

I. Introduction

There are approximately two thousand Inuit and Native Settlers occupying northern Labrador, along Canada's eastern seaboard. The Labrador Inuit are related to east Baffin Island Inuit, according to archaeological and other evidence (Fitzhugh, 1977:30). The Native Settlers, making up around one quarter of the population, are white people mainly of British and Scandinavian ancestry, whose families have been long-term residents of Labrador, living alongside the Inuit, but maintaining a distinct culture.

---

*) The author wishes to thank the following people for their comments and suggestions for the paper: Dermot Collis, Veryan Haysom, Amos Maggo, Robert Schneider, George Wenzel, and Fran Williams. Thanks are also given to Edmund Carpenter for permission to quote his material. The views expressed in this paper are those of the author.

The support, financial and otherwise, of the Cultural and Linguistic Section of the Department of Indian and Northern Affairs, Government of Canada, for the Labrador Inuit Associations's Customary Law Research Project is acknowledged. The author thanks particularly John MacDonald and Sam Metcalf of the Cultural and Linguistic Section of D.I.N.A.

Thanks are due, as well, to Chesley Andersen, Land Claims Director of the Labrador Inuit Association, and to Alice Gutkind, former Librarian of the Library of the Centre for Northern Studies and Research, McGill University, for her assistance with reference material.

The Labrador Inuit are among the least popularly known of the Inuit populations of the world. There have been no famous expeditions to them, and they have not been romanticized in any novels. The Government of the Province of Newfoundland, which has jurisdiction over Labrador, has only recently acknowledged the presence of native peoples within its borders (though it has long recognized Labrador's resource value). To many Canadians, Labrador is just a breed of dog. To others, it is the "land that God gave Cain," as Jacques Cartier so picturesquely described what to him was a forbidding and barren land.

A. Brief history

It was to the people of this forbidding and hostile-seeming land that the Moravian Church (a pre-Reformation Protestant sect) sent missionaries in the latter part of the eighteenth century. The initial reception given to the missionaries by the Inuit was as unfriendly as the land appeared to be. A party of missionaries disappeared, forcing other missionaries working with them to return to England.

A second attempt was made shortly thereafter, using a missionary who had learned the Greenlandic dialect of Inuktitut, and was thus able to communicate with the Labrador Inuit in their own language. A foothold was successfully established, and it was expanded over the two centuries that followed. Today all of the Labrador Inuit are Moravians, identifying with the church, its beliefs and institutions.

The missionaries, for their part, sought over the centuries to protect and isolate the Labrador Inuit from all possible corrupting influences, such as outside traders (the Moravians had a trade monopoly until early in this century), Newfoundlanders fishing off the Labrador coast, and other Inuit who had not yet been brought into the fold of the Church. In order for the Church to isolate Christian Inuit from their "heathen" brothers, it was necessary to transform the economic as well as the religious base of the people to one that facilitated their sedentarization around the mission stations. The Moravians saw their job as a complete remodelling and restructuring of Labrador Inuit life.

I will not discuss whether the transformation was as radical or complete as the Moravian Church believed. The restructuring brought a host of problems. Besides social and cultural upheaval, the more visible ones included massive epidemics resulting from sedentarization, hunger, and a not highly profitable trade to support the mission stations. In this century, the problems have resulted in the consolidation and integration of communities (against the will of the residents), the loss of trade, and continued social and cultural disruption.

Matters that were previously in the hands of the people, the Church, or Church-controlled institutions, are now in the hands of the state; these include social welfare, child welfare, education, community administration, and social control. The Church still plays a major role in the life of the people of northern Labrador, but the trend toward secularization has brought the Labrador Inuit closer to the mainstream of Canadian life.

B. The current situation

At present, the Inuit and Settler population is centred in five communities. Nain, the northernmost, is the largest. Others are Hopedale, Makkovik, Postville, and Rigolet. As well, there is an Inuit population in Happy Valley/Goose Bay, a service centre for Labrador, with a population of several thousand.

The economies of the northern Labrador communities are based primarily on commercial fishing, transfer payments, trapping and hunting, as well as some wage employment (not necessarily in that order). Economic problems include problems with the fishery, difficulties in obtaining, or low rates of transfer payments, the high costs and uncertainties of hunting (including government restrictions on activities), a lessening knowledge of hunting techniques among the population, scarce employment, the high cost of store-bought food and supplies, and so on.

There are other major problems facing the people of northern Labrador, many of which can be viewed as symptoms or causes of further problems. Certainly they are not unrelated, and dealing with various issues in isolation from their context would be and has been unsuccessful. These issues include (besides the economic ones listed above) a decline in the ability of Inuit youths to speak their language, the stated inability by parents to control children, alcoholism, vandalism, a high crime rate (reputed in Nain to be equivalent to that of New York City), declining family stability, a decline in the effectiveness of the Inuit sharing ethic, and many more too numerous to mention.

To the Labrador Inuit, things have gotten out of hand. More specifically, things have gotten out of their hands. Their communities, the institutions, and the authorities that make important decisions regarding their lives are alien, or are run according to principles that are alien to their culture. The people of northern Labrador are presented with sets of alternatives for dealing with their problems that involve only modifications or adjustments to those alien institutions or authorities. They are offered degrees of independence or self-control only insofar as they are willing to accept external standards and goals, and to act in the same manner as the aliens they are supposedly replacing. In other words, to achieve some measure of self-control they are expected to become like those who are now in control.

In the schools, Inuit are hired as "teachers' aides" and convey to their students a role model of subservience. When the court comes to town, an Inuk courtworker acts as translator, ostensibly in terms of both language and culture. He assists in seeking the "facts" of the case so that the accused, if guilty, can be given the appropriate punishment. Fisheries and wildlife officers supervise and enforce regulations and laws designed to protect fish and game. Even when such persons are Inuit, they act according to the science of biology, which carries a quantitative, reductionist, empirical, logical and mechanistic approach to nature, reflecting the influences of Aristotle, Galileo, Descartes, and Newton (Capra, 1982). When an Inuk steps into the shoes of "wildlife officer" or "fisheries officer," he steps into a paradigm that belongs to and was developed by a particular cultural history.

The task that Labrador Inuit have taken upon themselves is to find an alternative course of action that will enable them to take control of their own lives and institutions in a manner that truly reflects their culture, and yet is acceptable to those presently holding power and authority. The means selected for achieving some form of control is through negotiation of a comprehensive claims agreement (popularly known as "land claims") with the Governments of Canada and Newfoundland. The form of control that is being sought in these negotiations will be determined through the customary law of the people of northern Labrador.

C. Comprehensive claims

In 1973, the federal Minister of Indian and Northern Affairs made a commitment to negotiate settlements with native groups in those areas of Canada where native rights based on traditional use and occupancy of the land had not been extinguished by treaty or superseded by law. Due to the broad spectrum of subjects included in the discussions, such as land, money, resources (renewable and non-renewable), education and other institutions, the negotiations are designated "comprehensive claims".

There are numerous native groups wishing to negotiate such claims. The federal government has established a priority list of six groups, with whom negotiations are actively taking place (the "short list"). There is, as well, a second priority list ("medium list"), and a "long list", for lowest-priority claims. Urgency is to be determined by the threat of developments in the region under consideration, or by territorial overlapping of claims between priority and non-priority native groups. The Labrador Inuit were placed on the short list in

December of 1984, following the successful conclusion of an agreement with a western Artic Inuit group (Inuvialuit).

The government has established certain criteria for settlement of the claims. The basic principle is the extinguishment of native title in exchange for monetary and other considerations (although alternatives to this are being sought).

The quintessential claims settlement, the James Bay and Northern Quebec Agreement, was achieved in 1975, the parties being the Cree of Quebec, the Inuit of Quebec, and the Governments of Quebec and Canada. This Agreement established the precedent of extinguishment of title in exchange for specified rights and benefits. Although the Agreement was denounced by many native leaders, it was hailed by the federal government as a precedent, which it has indeed proved to be. Other Agreements currently being negotiated, though containing many variations, are sticking to these basic principles.

In examining the Agreement, La Rusic (1979) states that the Cree Indians achieved only administrative, rather than political control of their lives and their institutions, and thus transferred their dependency from government to their own bureaucrats. These bureaucrats, in turn, found their actions to be restricted or determined by the nature of the bureaucracy of which they were part. La Rusic points out that the various provisions of the James Bay and Northern Quebec Agreement were reached by non-Cree negotiators hired by the Cree, who worked with the government technical representatives. The very process of negotiation seriously damaged the possibilities for achieving an Agreement that truly reflected Cree culture.

I. Customary law

The Labrador Inuit see a comprehensive claim that will enable them to take control of their lives and institutions in a manner that truly reflects their culture as being possible through an Agreement reflecting the principles of Labrador Inuit customary law.

A. Definitions and implications

"Customary law" does not refer to the old law books of the Inuit of northern Labrador. Nor does it refer exclusively to the community "by-laws" that the Village or Church Elders used in the past to govern or regulate the communities. It is, in fact, easier to make a list of things that customary law is not than to say what in fact it is, for it is not a concept which is inherent to or a regular part of Labrador Inuit culture. In the northern Labrador dialect of Inuttut, the terms generally used to refer to customary law are either "ways of following" or "ways of trying" (loosely translated). Thus, customary law is best defined as those phenomena in Labrador Inuit culture which deal with matters that, in Euro-Canadian society, are touched upon by law.

This definition is widely inclusive. As Stanley Diamond states, "We live in a law-ridden society .... " (1974:257). However, as these laws are spawned by the cultures of Euro-Canadian society, they do not conflict excessively with the customs of Euro-Canadian cultures, which guide everyday life in that society. In Euro-Canadian society, "law" is equated with "order", especially among members of the political right. In a society, however, where the laws are spawned by an alien culture, the guidance given by law will conflict with the guidance given by custom. Law thus becomes a source of disorder, and touches upon an even wider spectrum of phenomena.

A basic example with regard to custom and law deals with property. "Property" is one of the most essential principles of our legal system. Diamond (1974:259) cites Jeremy Bentham that "property and law are born together and die together". Property rights almost became part of the Canadian Constitution, and may still do so. Hegel and Marx take property as the departure point for the philosophy of law (Hegel, 1967:449; Marx, 1970:207). Marx, however, points out that in many tribal societies there are possessions, but not property (ibid.). According to Gluckman (1965:46), "Property law in tribal societies defines not so much rights of persons over things, as obligations owed between persons in respect of things." In other words, material transfers are symbolic of relations between people. It is the *relation*, rather than the item, that is of primary significance.

Dermot Collis, in ethnolinguistic research on Labrador Inuit customary law, has noted that there is no term in their own language that encompasses the whole notion of property among the Labrador Inuit (cf. Dorais, 1984). There are degrees of possession according to the degrees of importance attached to items. Traditionally, only a very small number of items were accorded the highest form of possession, "namminkaa, it is my own", wherein there were tight limitations on others using the item.

If an item with a lesser degree of possession was borrowed without permission, the person from whom the item was taken would make known his dissatisfaction, and the person who took the item could say that he had intended to ask permission later, or that he really needed the item, and thus had the right to borrow it. The borrower would repay the item by returning it, by giving its equivalent, or in some other manner. The incident would be an event in an ongoing relation, and would be dealt with in that context. If the two parties could not resolve the matter to their mutual satisfaction, the Elders would be asked to mediate. Their aim would be to restore social harmony, to see the relationship continue in a manner that would not have ongoing pejorative implications.

Collis has noted that at the present time, if someone complains of an inappropriate act that, according to Euro-Canadian law, can be classified as theft of property, and brings the matter to the police for action, the long-term result can be a disruption of relations between individuals, or even vendettas between families. This weakens the social networks and relationships that serve to maintain order in the communities. The net result of law would then be disorder.

B. Kinship

The quintessential flexible social organization of the Inuit is one which enables people to adapt to various and changing situations, and emphasizes interpersonal dyadic ties (Wilmott, 1960). Ben-Dor (1966:58-91) presents a detailed analysis of Labrador Inuit social organization in Makkovik, including an account of how it has adapted to the centralization of populations in communities. For purposes of this essay, let it suffice to say that the system of reckoning relations is significantly different from the Euro-Canadian one.

Euro-Canadian customs give certain prerogatives, and place certain expectations and obligations on the "family" in areas such as child support, child rearing, inheritance, and so on. Many of these prerogatives, expectations, and obligations have been translated into laws. These laws, however, do not reflect the customs of the Labrador Inuit regarding "family", nor do they reflect the Labrador Inuit concepts inherent in their notion of "family". While legal authorities in recent years have tended to be understanding of the cross-cultural settings, their flexibility is limited by the basic paradigms and assumptions that form the basis of the Euro-Canadian world-view. It is also limited by the actual laws they are responsible for enforcing.

Ben-Dor (1966:68) gives an interesting example of how the enforcement of the perspectives of one culture upon another created a problem, and then caused difficulties with its resolution. According to Ben-Dor, illegitimacy is a recent phenomenon in Labrador. Traditionally, girls were married as soon as they reached puberty, precluding illegitimate children. The Moravian Mission established and gradually became successful in enforcing a minimum age for marriage. However, they were not as successful in changing the sexual mores of the people.

The Labrador Inuit were able to deal with this phenomenon through adoption: illegitimate children were almost always adopted by the mothers' parents. However, as the Newfoundland government increasingly applied its jurisdiction in northern Labrador, the adoptions had to go through the legal machinery of the child welfare system, with checks on the competence of the potential adopters and increased bureaucratic interference. According to informants, only in the last five years has the ratification of these adoption procedures been resimplified.

Lee Guemple (1979, p. 81) makes an interesting comment on Ben-Dor's material regarding the concept of illegitimacy: "Among the Labrador Inuit too the concept remains one which is important to the superordinate white community. It continues to mean little to the Inuit themselves except as it affects their standing with the white community."

C. Environment

S.K. Hutton, in his warm depiction of the Labrador Inuit (1912), ascribes to them a certain fatalism, summed up by the phrase "ajornarmat", meaning "it cannot be helped". Other authors have remarked upon this fatalism and this phrase among various Inuit groups. This "fatalism", however, must be carefully interpreted. The Inuit are not the helpless victims of the inexorable laws of nature. Carpenter (1983:6) points out that although "... they accepted life on its own terms, they did more than accept: they took upon themselves the responsibility for the fact that life was the way it was."

The Inuit relation with nature is an interactive one. This is not simply in terms of harvesting the animals that nature provides. The actions of the Inuit affect their relation with nature. Hawkes (1916:124) cites an early account given to Moravian missionaries about an old couple who control the animals of the land and the animals of the sea. When properly appeased, they will always assist the Inuit in their hunting by sending out the animals. An elaborate system of taboos for the Labrador Inuit avoided offending the controllers, helping to assure the supply of animals. Various practices, such as giving a piece of one's first catch to the midwife who delivered one (in pre-nursing station times), or slitting the eyes of the seals and whales one has caught, helped to ensure future hunting success (Hawkes, 1916; Hutton, 1912).

These examples show that the Labrador Inuit, though possessing the barest of implements in what Euro-Canadians consider the harshest of conditions, actively dealt with and affected the conditions of their lives. The details of contemporary practices are secondary to the cultural paradigm established over the centuries and described here. It must be remembered that these contemporary practices have evolved from, rather than replaced, previous practices, although they might now be described as "conservation practices" or "Elders' by-laws". The shift in terminological context from sacred to secular should not be confused with cultural discontinuity.

The Inuit paradigm of interaction can be contrasted with the Euro-Canadian one, deriving from western cultural history. As mentioned earlier, the science of biology takes a quantitative, reductionist, empirical, logical, and mechanistic approach to nature. Marcuse explains the western approach to nature (1964:146):

> The quantification of nature, which led to its explication in terms of mathematical structures, separated reality from all inherent ends and, consequently, separated the true from the good, science from ethics .... And no matter how constitutive may be the role of the subject as point of observation, measurement, and calculation, this subject cannot play its scientific role as ethical or aesthetic or political agent.

Western man established an alienated relation with his environment. The "laws of nature" (laws imposed on nature by his cultural paradigm) enabled him to objectify and remove himself from nature. It is such an alienated approach which allows a government to encourage the building of an open-pit mine in an important breeding ground of a caribou herd, while at the same time restricting the hunting of the animals by Inuit in order to protect the herd.

The Inuit approach is ecological, interactive, holistic, and aesthetic. It requires one to work with nature and the environment, rather than studying and objectifying it. Labrador Inuit mythology tells of the shaman "... who felt it his duty to find out for the people the place where the caribou went when they pass in great numbers into the interior" (Hawkes, 1916:154). However, once he found the place he refrained from telling the people the location for fear that they would kill too many animals. There is a desire for understanding reflected in this myth, which plays against an approach that it is wrong to have certain knowledge. Among Baffin Island Inuit, this reticence toward "studying" the animals is expressed in the attitude that it is offensive to animals to count them (Wenzel, 1983). This attitude is held even though the Baffin Regional Inuit Association conducts a "harvest study" to count the animals killed by the Baffin Inuit.

In Labrador, a reticence toward counting may have been a factor in the rejection of a proposed harvest study by delegates to the 1982 Labrador Inuit Association's Annual General Meeting, in spite of recommendations in favour of the harvest study by some of the Association's advisors. In 1985, the Labrador Inuit are reconsidering the harvest study, but they insist that it be only one part of an overall study which includes more direct evaluation of their harvesting activities, enabling the study to include their own paradigms. According to research by Amos Maggo, control of hunting by the Labrador Inuit was fairly straightforward, relying on people's own knowledge of nature and the environment, which came not through formal study but through cultural knowledge, apprenticeship to hunters, and personal experience.

The Inuit approach is holistic. The Inuit know that action "A" will affect situation "B", whether "A" is the taboo regarding the distinction between sea animals and land animals and "B" is future hunting success, or whether "A" is building a mine in a caribou breeding ground and "B" is future caribou hunts.

The Inuit approach to nature is aesthetic. An Inuk from Iglulik, in the Northwest Territories commented (Rasmussen, 1929:56):

> All the creatures that we have to kill and eat, all those that we have to strike down and destroy to make clothes for ourselves, have souls, like we have, souls that do not perish with the body, and which must therefore be propitiated lest they should revenge themselves on us for taking away their bodies.

Poems and songs relate to the hunt by describing the actions of people and the actions of nature. These songs and poems are not restricted to professional poets and singers, but are the prerogative of all people. Carvings depict the dynamism, the sense of action in the animals (Hawkes, 1916:101). Carpenter (1973:42) states:

> The Eskimo seem to be saying that nature is there, but man alone can free it from its dormant state; that it requires a creative human act before the world explored becomes a world revealed; that the universe acquires form, "existence", only through man the revealer: he who releases life inherent in nature and guides its expression into beautiful forms.

The relation between environment and man is perhaps best expressed through the Inuit concept of "sila". At once it refers to thought, a person's nature or character, and the outside. "Silami" means outdoors; "silatunerk" refers to strong character. Carpenter states (1973:44):

> Thought, to the Eskimo, isn't a product of mind, but the forces outside man. Yet, thought can't exist without man. True, the universe must speak first, make itself known to man, affect him, move him. But he alone can release it from its chaotic state.

When nature moves man, when he feels emotion welling up within him,

> then he knows the feeling of being alive, of existing in relation to the universe, and at this moment he gives expression to these feelings.
>
> Here, then, is a world of chaos and change, a meaningless whirl of cold and white; man alone can give it meaning - its form does not come ready-made.

II. Conclusions

Although this paper is about the customary law of the Labrador Inuit, it has refrained from attempting a statement of the content of that law. Rather, it has attempted to outline the nature of the problems and some of the basic issues involved in delineating this customary law. E.A. Hoebel (1954), a founder of the field of the "ethnography of law" within American anthropology, has argued that in order to get at the laws of a people properly, it is necessary to understand the basic postulates of the culture of that people. Customary law is, after all, an expression of culture, and it cannot be isolated from the cultural context. This paper, by outlining some aspects of the culture and history of the Labrador Inuit, provides a framework for understanding their customary law.

The Labrador Inuit Association's research on customary law includes many parts. Amos Maggo, an Inuk from Nain, Labrador, has gathered descriptions and discussions of customary law from the communities of northern Labrador. Data gathered include kinship information, accounts of incidents and events wherein customary law has come into play, narratives, Church accounts and more.

Dermot Collis and Louis-Jacques Dorais, of Université Laval, have conducted ethnolinguistic research (including field research in Nain) on the expression of concepts of customary law through language. This includes the compilation of a lexicon of terminology related to the law used by Labrador Inuit.

The Labrador Inuit Association includes among its membership "qallunangajuit" (literally "not white people") or "Native Settlers". These are people of European-mixed extraction, whose families have been long-term residents of northern Labrador. Eric Loring, a student at Hampshire College, working with Drs. Barbara Yngvesson, Debra Martin, and George Wenzel, conducted research in a qallunangajuit community (Postville) on wildlife use and customary law.

Although the work is laborious, it is hoped that the approach to customary law used herein, emphasizing the cultural context, will facilitate the achievement of a land claims agreement for the Labrador Inuit that truly reflects Labrador Inuit culture. The land claims negotiations are underway between the Labrador Inuit, the Governments of Canada, Newfoundland and Quebec, and other interested

Native parties. The use of the customary law approach, a novel one for such an endeavour, was conceived and demanded by the people of northern Labrador. It is finding favour and is being considered by other native groups in the Northwest Territories, Quebec, and British Columbia. In view of the realization by many natives that they are indeed capable of running their own lives according to their own ways, and government realization of the feasibility of native self-government, customary law is an approach whose time has come. The only qualification is that, in order to be appropriate, customary law must be determined through careful and detailed ethnographic research.

References

BEN-DOR, Shmuel (1966)
Makkovik: Eskimos and Settlers in a Labrador Community. St. John's: Institute of Social and Economic Research, Memorial University of Newfoundland.

CAPRA, Fritjof (1982)
The Turning Point: Science, Society, and the Rising Culture. Toronto: Bantam Books.

CARPENTER, Edmund (1973)
Eskimo Realities. New York: Holt, Rinehart and Winston.

---------- (1983)
Introduction to Stephen Guion Williams, In the Middle: The Eskimo Today. Boston: David R. Godine.

DIAMOND, Stanley (1974)
In Search of the Primitive: A Critique of Civilization. New Brunswick, New Jersey: Transaction Books.

DORAIS, Louis Jacques (1984)
"An Ethnolinguistic Study of the Labrador Inuit Customary Law Concepts." Presentation to 4th Inuit Studies Conference, Montreal, Nov. 15-18.

FITZHUGH, William W. (1977)
"Indian and Eskimo/Inuit Settlement History in Labrador: An Archaeological View," in Carol Brice-Bennett (ed.), Our Footprints are Everywhere - Inuit

Land Use and Occupancy in Labrador. Nain, Labrador: Labrador Inuit Association.

GLUCKMAN, Max (1965)
Politics, Law and Ritual in Tribal Society. Chicago: Aldine.

GUEMPLE, Lee (1979)
Inuit Adoption. Canadian Ethnology Service Paper No. 47. National Museum of Man, Mercury Series. Ottawa: National Museum of Canada.

HAWKES, E.W. (1916)
The Labrador Eskimo. Canada Department of Mines, Geological Survey, Memoir 91. Anthropological Series No. 14. Ottawa: Government Printing Bureau.

HEGEL, G.W.F. (1967)
The Phenomenology of Mind. Translated, with an introduction and notes by J.B. Baillie. New York: Harper and Row.

HOEBEL, E.A. (1954)
The Law of Primitive Man. Cambridge, Mass.: Harvard University Press.

HUTTON, S.K. (1912)
Among the Eskimos of Labrador. London, England: Seeley, Service and Co.

LA RUSIC, Ignatius E. (1979)
Negotiating a Way of Life: Initial Cree experience with the administrative structure arising from the James Bay Agreement. Montreal: ssDcc Inc.

MARCUSE, Herbert (1964)
One-Dimensional Man - Studies in the Ideology of Advanced Industrial Society. Boston: Beacon Press.

MARX, Karl (1970)
A Contribution to the Critique of Political Economy. New York: International Publishers.

RASMUSSEN, Knud (1929)
Intellectual Culture of the Iglulik Eskimos. Report of the Fifth Thule Expedition 1921-24, Vol VII, No. 1, Copenhagen: Gyldendalske Boghandel, Nordisk Forlag. Reprinted 1976, New York: AMS Press.

WENZEL, George (1983)
Personal Communication. Montreal: Centre for Northern Studies and Research, McGill University.

WILMOTT, W.E. (1960)
"The Flexibility of Eskimo Social Organization," 1 Anthropologica 48-59.

How state courts create customary law in Ghana and Nigeria

Gordon R. Woodman

I. Introduction: the scope of the inquiry

The modern state is rarely contradicted with success. Therefore, when state institutions act upon relationships which have previously been the concern of folk law, the effect on folk law is likely to be terminal. It might seem that a possibility of survival lies in an injunction by state law requiring state institutions to preserve or enforce portions of folk law. Hereby, it might appear, folk law will be perpetuated and even fortified by the authority of the state. The conclusion is false. State institutions, when instructed to apply folk law, in practice do not. They rather are apt to create a new body of law, which they misleadingly call folk or customary law.

Most of the papers in this volume suggest expressly or impliedly that it would be desirable for certain states' laws to begin to preserve certain folk laws, or to do so to a greater degree than hitherto. The present paper surveys two legal systems in which state courts have for a century been required to "apply" folk law. While not questioning the desirability of the objective, the paper will argue, in the light of that experience, that it cannot be so simply achieved.

The state institutions used as illustrative are the legal systems of Ghana and Nigeria. "Legal system" here refers to the personnel who operate the state courts when performing their official roles. These persons are principally the judges and secondarily the other members of the legal profession who present cases before judges, but they include all who participate in the functioning of the courts. The judges have long been required to apply "customary law" (formerly "native law and custom") in deciding certain categories of cases. In complying, they have frequently declared norms to be customary law when those norms did not have general social recognition. These declarations constitute authoritative statements of law, which are followed in subsequent cases. Thus lawyers' customary law has diverged from sociologists' customary law or folk law. I have argued elsewhere that this divergence is not a result only of lawyers' misconceptions about the content of existing social norms, but is entailed by the nature of the state legal system. The state courts' remedies and procedures are such that they cannot reproduce the circumstances in which social norms operate and by which they are enforced, and consequently they cannot simply "apply" those norms. The legal systems of necessity exercise a creative function: when they appear to apply customary law, they in reality create a new type of "customary law". An alternative formulation is to say that customary law is institutionalized by the state legal system. However, "institutionalization" should not be taken to imply that the product is not substantially new. (Woodman 1985).

Recognition of this reality raises further issues for inquiry. In particular it calls for the analysis of the process of creation or institutionalization. This paper seeks, through an examination of the process in Ghana and Nigeria, to account for the content of lawyers' customary law in those states. Thus it examines the birth of a type of state law and aims, by placing the emergence of this law within a plausible historical account, to contribute to discussion of more general issues concerning law and the state.

Some characteristics of the Ghanaian and Nigerian cases need mention. The legal systems are themselves recent constructs, dating for practical purposes from 1876 or later, within the recently created nation-state structures. The courts are not claimed to be lineal descendants from or adaptations of dispute-settlement institutions of other political units. The application of "customary law" may therefore entail a more obvious and extensive creative function than might be required if the courts were continuations of the previously independent "native courts", over which the state had assumed control. (Cf. Gluckman 1955; Bohannan 1957; F. von Benda-Beckmann 1979.) The social norms supposedly applied were not designed to be readily applicable in state courts, as were the norms of some, more general systems such as Islamic law.[1] The litigation to be discussed consists entirely of civil cases concerning land and family relations. Customary law is excluded from criminal cases, so that there is no possibility of simple "enforcement" by state-imposed penal sanctions for breaches of "customary-law" imperatives. The institutionalization of civil customary law in state courts is a relatively complex process, involving state compulsion in relation to the social concepts and norms of property, kinship and marriage.

The discussion will rely upon the records of state courts during roughly the past one hundred years. There is a sufficient volume of material, for the courts have heard very many cases governed by customary law, and a substantial portion has been made readily accessible in published law reports.[2] Using this material we may consider the process whereby members of the legal systems take the information on sociologists' customary law available to them, and use it to reach decisions which expressly or impliedly declare norms of lawyers' customary law. Thus the discussion will look on state courts as participants in social administration rather than in their aspect of dispute-settlement institutions: as producers not so much of adjudications as of norms. While the adjudicative procedures need examination, their significance lies in their production of state legal norms.

In any litigation which turns on norms of customary law, the court needs information on the content of that law. Sometimes the judge has information available, particularly in the law reports, of the authoritatively declared content of lawyers' customary law. In these cases the judge normally follows the authorities. Frequently, however, there is only information on the content of sociologists' customary law, and then the judge needs to determine on the basis of that information what is the content of lawyers' customary law. The information may be of various types, ranging from the judge's own childhood socialization to the evidence in court of expert witnesses. I have argued elsewhere that there is a strong possibility of the information being misleading (Woodman 1969a). My objective there was merely to demonstrate that there was a body of legal rules, referred to by the state courts as "customary law", which differed in content from that customary law which held more general social recognition. The clearest means of demonstrating this was, as it still is, to show (a) that the courts relied on forms of evidence which were likely to be unreliable, and (b) that they followed a system of precedent. From those practices it followed that, assuming the courts to be willing and able to apply sociologists' customary law, they would nevertheless, as a result of misinformation about that law, establish a lawyers' customary law which was different. Today, when we have for Ghana and Nigeria a fuller knowledge of the rules of lawyers' customary law, it is possible to advance to an examination of the differences.

The paper is concerned primarily with the process of reasoning subsequent to the acquisition of information about sociologists' customary law. It aims to show that, even assuming (without accepting) the courts to receive entirely reliable information about sociologists' customary law, they will not and cannot apply it as lawyers' customary law. Ultimately a full analysis of the development of lawyers' customary law will need to take account both of the deficiencies of state courts' sources of information and of the impossibility of enforcing sociologists' customary law in state courts. I am now inclined to believe that consideration of the latter is likely to provide the more important perceptions about the development of the states in question.

Although this paper is not, therefore, generally concerned with the accuracy of the courts' sources of information, it is necessary to notice one factor which bears on that issue. The more formal modes of presenting information, and especially expert evidence, are likely to be biased by the existence of established processes of reasoning. For example, if it is known that certain types of social norms are systematically excluded by judges from consideration, it is likely that in time members of the legal system will cease to present to judges information about such norms. The presentation of information by formal modes is conducted by members of the legal system. The expert witness, for example, gives evidence in the form of answers to questions by parties, who usually act through professional counsel. The questions are designed to elicit answers which can be incorporated into the established processes of reasoning. When this happens the process of creating lawyers' customary law starts some time before the judge receives the information. It would be misleading to consider only the process which begins when the judge hears the evidence. It is for this reason that I refer to the legal system, not to judges, as using the various types of information and misinformation to create lawyers' customary law.

II. How customary law is "applied" in state courts without explicit modification

The great majority of cases in which state courts have ostensibly "applied" customary law fall into the category discussed in this section, since the express modification of socially recognized norms has been relatively rare. Although the judgments suggest that the application of customary law is unproblematic, further consideration of particular cases shows that it is not. Parts of the judicial process will be used to illustrate the manner in which sociologists' customary law as known to the personnel of the legal system is transformed before emerging as the lawyers' customary law of the state courts.

A. Forms of claims, remedies, and modes of enforcement

The procedures of state courts, as distinct from the substantive laws which they apply, do not claim to be "customary". Certain aspects of these procedures affect the substantive norms of customary law. By restricting the forms in which claims may be presented, the types of remedies which may be awarded, and the modes of enforcing those remedies, the courts have debarred themselves from recognizing substantive rights which cannot be asserted and enforced through the permitted processes. Such rights, existing in sociologists' customary law, are not rights in lawyers' customary law.

The courts have required claims, remedies and enforcement to be expressed in the categories of the common law, or, for this purpose, English law. Even in the days when "native courts" recognized by the state were entitled to hear claims instituted by customary procedures, they were required to fit these processes into the common law categories, a requirement which was enforced through a general right of appeal to the non-"native" courts.[3] The requirement is so clear that these cases almost fall within the subject-matter of the next section, as explicit modifications of social norms. They are discussed here because the replacement of the socially recognized processes, and the resultant modification of substantive norms have never been expressly stated nor based upon legal authority. The entire personnel of the legal systems have tacitly accepted that common-law notions must govern these matters.

(a) Forms of Claims It is a characteristic of all the forms of claims recognized by state courts that they can be brought only when a dispute has reached an advanced stage of conflict. A case in a state court can, therefore, arise only when the social norms have failed to resolve the conflict, and have in a sense been exhausted. The state court process then adds something new, and for this reason also cannot be a reproduction of an existing, socially-recognized process.

The forms of claims are: the action for trespass to land; the action for a declaratory judgment (which is always brought against a defendant who disputes the right of which a declaration is sought, and who has infringed it or threatened to do so the remedy is thus not normally available to determine the correctness of initial steps towards a transaction, nor even necessarily the validity of a completed transaction); the claim for partition or sale of family property; the claim for a debt or other certain sum of money due; the claim to custody of a minor; the claim to maintenance for a minor or a wife; and the claims for slander, adultery and seduction of a ward. A claim expressed in one form may raise an issue which could have been raised more directly in a different claim. Thus the validity of a marriage may be put in issue by a claim to a declaration of title to land after the death of the landholder, or in a claim for slander. Although claims in the inferior state courts are not required to be expressed in precise or technical language, the informal claims made are translated into categories of English law when they reach lawyers, that is, at the latest when appeals are brought. However, the restriction of prospective claimants to a limited number of forms of claim normally takes effect before court proceedings are initiated. People do not come as far as the courts advancing claims which cannot be framed in forms acceptable to the courts.

The result is that a number of norms which are socially recognized cannot be the subject-matter of claims in state courts except after breaches have occurred, and have produced serious consequences. It may, for example, be socially wrong for a man to fail to make particular presentations prior to his marriage; or to consent to a sale of family land in particular circumstances; or to sell land without demarcating it. But there is no means of presenting these acts as justiciable wrongs immediately after their commission. Infringements of these rules can be made issues in state courts only by questioning subsequently the validity of the marriage or sale. The state courts, if they then decide to "apply" these norms, can do so only by holding the marriage or sale void, a sanction which they may find excessively severe, and which in any case is not in accord with sociologists' customary law.

(b) Remedies The term "remedies" is used here in the narrow sense of the orders which courts may issue at the conclusion of cases for the purpose of enforcing those legal duties which they find to exist. The principal relevant remedies of English law are: monetary damages; the order for payment of a debt or other sum of money due; the declaration of a right; the injunction; the order for recovery of possession of land; the order to render an account; the order for sale or partition of property; and the order for custody of a minor. In some jurisdictions the courts have been given power to grant divorces, but that is a change produced explicitly by legislative enactment. By adhering to the English law of remedies, even when customary-law duties are to be enforced, the state courts generally limit the possible results of cases. We may take two examples.

The limitation is particularly apparent in the case of damages. In the applied English law a successful complainant is for some wrongs (but not all) entitled to at least nominal damages. With rare exceptions, the complainant may not receive more than nominal damages unless loss, of a type regarded by the common law as measurable in money, is proved, in which case the award must be of a sum equal to the loss. Generally there is no room to share a loss, for example by awarding damages equivalent to a proportion only of the loss suffered. Nor may a court substitute some other recompense, such as a public apology, prestations of objects of symbolic or practical value, or the satisfaction of having a wrongdoer publicly rebuked, although such remedies may be socially recognized (e.g. Date-Bah 1973: 137-143).

The order for accounts requires a strict, detailed statement of income and expenditure in respect of the subject-matter of litigation, such as a farm which has been administered by the defendant on behalf of the plaintiff. The statement is required to be in money terms, and when the account is received the precise balance found due is ordered to be paid. There has long been controversy among lawyers as to whether an order to account should ever be issued against a head of family or chief at the instance of members in respect of property vested in the family or community as a corporation. It was eventually decided in Ghana that this should in some circumstances occur, and legislation was enacted to this effect in the *Head of Family (Accountability) Law,* 1985 (P.N.D.C.L. 114). The result is to confer on specified sections of the group a right to receive accounts in the approved form, and (presumably) to be paid precisely any sum shown to be due. It seems on the whole unlikely that this, or any other such development, will effectuate norms of sociologists' customary law, and most of those who have advocated the development have recognized this (Bentsi-Enchill 1964: 95-108; Nwabueze 1972: 163-168; James 1973: 81-85; Asante 1975: 109-121; Woodman 1976).

The divergence is again accentuated by the fact that these remedies, like the forms of claims, are generally suitable for award only at a late stage in a conflict. Damages, for example, can be awarded only when a wrong has been committed and a loss suffered.

(c) Modes of Enforcement The declaratory judgment is not imperative. If its implications are disregarded, the plaintiff has to bring a fresh action for one of the other remedies.

The award of damages and the order for payment of a sum due are enforced typically by the process of sale in execution. On application by the party entitled to the payment, which after the award constitutes a judgment-debt, court officials take control of property rights held by the judgment-debtor, and sell them by public auction. The purchaser receives a guarantee from the state that he acquires the "right, title and interest" in the property of the judgment-debtor, while the sale price is allotted to the payment of the expenses of the process, then to the satisfaction of the judgment-debt, with any balance left thereafter being paid to the judgment-debtor. The process was an early innovation by the state,[4] said to be introduced as an alternative to indigenous modes of enforcing payment, which had been suppressed.[5] State officials' objections to the other modes were, it appears, that they threatened the liberty of the individual, were liable to provoke breaches of public order, and were not exercised under the supervision of the state. No legal authority was advanced for the development, although statute subsequently endorsed it in Nigeria.[6]

This device enables the property rights affected to be sold for money without restriction as to possible purchasers. Its effectiveness would be limited if any substantial category of property rights were excluded from its scope, and none have been. In a number of different instances, courts have upheld sales in execution at dates when it was doubtful whether they would have upheld voluntary sales of those interests to those purchasers.[7] Once the legal systems had accepted that a right might be subject to this process, it became less likely that they would accept rules placing limits on voluntary sales. Thus the process may have contributed to establishing a general principle that interests in land are freely alienable.

The process requires not only that property rights be alienable, but also that they be clearly defined and allotted, so that a prospective purchaser knows with certainty what he will acquire. In determining cases arising out of sales in execution the courts have been required to determine issues which might otherwise have been left unanswered, and perhaps settled at later dates according to different norms. Most notably there have been series of cases in which it was necessary to distinguish strictly between property of a family, which might be validly sold in execution only for a liability of the family as a legal person, and property of an individual member, which might be validly sold in execution only for a liability of that member as an individual. The significance of this distinction in lawyers' customary law will be mentioned again below.

The other remedies are enforced typically by imprisoning a recalcitrant party until he or she obeys. The winning party can thus at will ensure that the state power compels compliance, subject only to impossibility of obedience, or successful rebellion against the state. This mode of enforcement is by definition different from those of sociologists' customary law. It is arguable that the outcome actual compliance with the substantive norms in those cases where the successful party insists is no different from those of sociologists' customary law, which is enforced by other means. However, state courts apply no rules which might induce a successful party to show leniency or to compromise. It is likely that in some cases this has the result of making the substantive norms more absolute in practice than they would otherwise be.

B. The selection of norms as legal

There is available to the state legal system information on a large body of socially recognized norms. Not all of these can, if the established practices of the state legal system are followed, be recognized as legal. Therefore the personnel of the system select some, which they designate customary law, relegating the others, usually tacitly, to the category of customary morality. This does not reflect a socially recognized distinction. The resultant body of lawyers' customary law is not simply sociologists' customary law with gaps. The gaps are so important that what emerges as legal is, taken as a whole, a newly created body of norms.

To establish this argument by an exhaustive survey of sociologists' and lawyers' customary laws would require excessive space. I shall therefore summarize two examples which I believe to be typical. They are taken from property law, and especially land law, because that is the area in which most of the state judicial experience lies.

The first example concerns sales of land, that is, of the allodial title in, or ownership of land. Land is considered to belong primarily or invariably to communities or families, so that these corporations need to be considered as the possible vendors. However, the issue in question is the rules governing the alienability of this interest in land as a set of rights, the rules being applicable to the interest as such, irrespective of the character of the holder.

It appears to be generally believed that sales of land have for a long time been possible, although in earlier periods they were as a matter of fact rare, and perhaps in some areas unknown. The evidence suggests that a landowning body will sell land only when circumstances justify it. It is justified, for example, to sell land to another community which migrates to the area and is a potential ally; or when it is necessary to raise money to pay off a community debt which may otherwise be enforced in damaging ways, such as by a sale in execution of other community property. It is preferable if possible to grant a licence to use the communal land, so that title is not lost, or to pledge it, so that it may be redeemed. When it is sold out of necessity, it is considered that the purchaser has an obligation to negotiate a resale on reasonable terms if at a later date the vendor's fortunes recover. There have been changes in the practice. It is commonly said that sales are more frequent today than they were a century ago. There is, however, evidence that the grant of licences in preference to sales is now more marked than 30 or 40 years ago. There is no reason to suppose that the basic rules have changed.[8]

There have been attempts to recognize various aspects of these practices as rules of law. It has been suggested by lawyers that land can be validly sold only to another community (Ollennu 1985: 76-79), and that it can be validly sold only to pay off a pressing communal debt.[9] While there is still some controversy, the conclusion appears now to have been reached in favour of the simple rule that land may be sold by the holder at will.[10] The rules as to the circumstances in which a sale is permissible have not become rules of lawyers' customary law.

Secondly, we take the example of the control of individually owned property. Although much property is held by families and other corporate persons, it is not uncommon for substantial property interests to be vested in individuals. Such property-holding has become more common during the past century. The importance of family membership in the individual's social and economic life raises questions as to how far individual ownership entails individual powers of control and disposition.

It seems that social norms do not draw a clear distinction between individual and family property. The information available to the legal systems shows that social norms display a policy of maintaining family solidarity. A family ought to nurture and assist its members. In practice many individuals' education, training and advancement is financed either by their families as such or by relatives who consider it their duty to assume this family obligation. Such individuals can thus be regarded as owing reciprocal obligations to their families, both because of what they have received and because of the benefits they expect for the future, and so they ought to use a substantial portion of their abilities and assets to benefit the family and other members. Thus a member should as far as possible assist in meeting family liabilities, such as debts for which family property has been pledged, or which have been incurred for family purposes. A member should give financial and other assistance to other members who are sick, in financial difficulty, in need of education or jobs or legal help, or who simply wish to be accommodated in that member's house.

A member ought not to allow substantial individual property to pass away from the family, either during his or her lifetime or on death. Consequently, on the member's death the family succeeds to most of the assets, rights, obligations and liabilities of the deceased. It may be reasonable for the individual to indicate by will how the family is to administer the estate. It is only in special circumstances that the individual can justify disposing of property outside the family by will, and the family may for good reason disregard such a will. (Writers who discuss the effect of wills show some uncertainty as to the extent to which they are binding on inheriting families: e.g. Sarbah 1904: 95-100.) Thus even when property is designated individual property, the holder has only limited control over it, the extent of that control varying with the circumstances, and in cases where the member's control is greatly attenuated the status of the property merges into that of family property. There appear to be many points on this spectrum, and it is quite possible that the position of a particular property may change over time as circumstances change. If, for example, members of the individual owner's family ask for and are given possession of a house or a farm, that property moves towards the category of family property acquired for the family by the individual. That category, although referred to above as family property *simpliciter*, has been distinguished from "full family property with all the incidents of family property" (Ollennu 1985: 39-41), because the individual acquirer enjoys special influence in its control.[11]

This is an area in which changes in social practices over the past century are indicated by the evidence. Nevertheless, the legal system's response to these issues seems to indicate clearly a selection of a limited number of social norms from a larger number existing at any time. A relatively rigid distinction is drawn between individual and family property, subject only to the possible variation in types of family property whereby a person playing a predominant role in an acquisition may hold special rights. Rules have been stated to enable the distinction to be drawn in particular cases, largely by reference to the circumstances of acquisition (Woodman 1963; James 1973: 56-64). The principal rule is that property acquired by the use of family resources is itself family property unless those concerned have agreed otherwise. It might seem to follow that all property acquired by individual members was family property, because virtually every individual owes his or her ability to acquire property to family assistance. The courts avoid this conclusion by classifying assistance from a family to a member in training or education as an outright gift.[12] A general rule of inheritance has been stated under which on intestacy an individual's property is inherited by his or her family or a designated part thereof as family property.[13] However, property which is individually owned may be used and disposed of in the holder's unfettered discretion, both during lifetime and by will. A Ghanaian court has explicitly stated that the reciprocal obligation of a member to assist other members is moral, not legal.[14]

The formulation of these rules has accompanied changes in social norms whereby the educated individual has become relatively independent of his or her family. It has become easier to engage without further family assistance in activity remunerated in money, and with these funds to purchase property. It may have been in consequence of these social changes that the courts have weakened, and arguably have abandoned an earlier rule that, in cases of dispute, land was presumed to be family property until the contrary was proved. However, there is no ground for supposing that the developments summarized in the previous paragraph were only reflections of changes in sociologists' customary law. The contrary conclusion is suggested by the fact that much of the information referred to as available to the legal systems is contained in recent writings.

C. The development of new norms to meet new circumstances peculiar to state courts

A number of rules are so directly concerned with the state court processes that they could not exist outside the state court system, but at the same time are so intimately related to the main body of lawyers' customary law that they are referred to as rules of customary law.

Once it was established that certain groups such as families had legal personality, and could be parties to suits in state courts, it became necessary to have rules determining which individuals might act on behalf of such corporate persons in litigation. The courts have determined that the head of the family or other group is the appropriate person to act, but needs the consent of the "principal members" (persons who, like the head, are designated by established rules). There have been some developments towards the determination of rules on who else may act, and in which circumstances (Woodman 1974: 25-26). These rules may be analogous to rules of sociologists' customary law determining authority to act on behalf of corporate groups in other situations such as the performance of ceremonies. Nevertheless it seems clear that social norms operating outside the courts cannot include norms specifying procedures within specifically court processes.

The institution of the sale in execution has resulted in further consideration of the rule that the individual should assist his family when it is in need. It has been held to be a rule of customary law that, if family property is sold in execution for a family debt, and is purchased by a member, that member presumptively intends to reacquire the property for the family, not for himself or herself (Ollennu, 1985: 150; James 1973: 63-64). Again it seems that this rule must be an invention of the legal system.

The courts have laid down a number of other presumptions for cases governed by customary law. These have generally been attempts to state propositions of fact which would normally be true, and when social circumstances have changed the courts have been willing to abandon them. Thus it was held at one time that land was presumed to be held by a family unless proved to be held by an individual; and that property held by a chief was presumed to belong to the office, not to the chief in his or her private capacity. Each of these presumptions has been weakened or abandoned. There is limited but as yet unchallenged authority for the presumptions that: where a head of a group litigates on behalf of the group, he or she has been authorized to do so, but when someone else litigates on its behalf, they are acting without authority; a documentary transfer of group-owned property, if executed by the head and at least one other principal member, purporting to act on behalf of the group, is properly authorized, whereas transfers not so executed are not authorized. While all these rules are classified as rules of customary law, they are directed exclusively to the conduct of cases in state courts.

III. How social norms are explicitly modified for application in state courts

In some classes of cases state courts have spoken as if they could have "applied" sociologists' customary law, but declined to do so on specified grounds, usually based on statutory authority. Some of the instances, in which the legal authority for the modification is not clearly expressed, might justifiably have been placed in Section II. Likewise the two-fold division which follows is largely a matter of convenience.

A. Uses of the "[natural] justice, equity and good conscience" provision

This phrase first appeared in two contexts in the Supreme Court Ordinance, 1876, of the Colony of the Gold Coast and Lagos. (See generally Daniels 1964: Chap. 10.) The first occurred when the original injunction to the courts to apply "native law or custom" was qualified by the words "not repugnant to natural justice, equity and good conscience". This is commonly known as the repugnancy clause. From 1876 until 1960 every superior and inferior court in Ghana and Nigeria had the clause in its constituting statute.[15] In Ghana it was removed in 1960 on the grounds that all "repugnant" norms must by then have been eliminated, and that it would be offensive for statute to suggest otherwise (Bennion 1962: 416). Nigeria has retained it. The second use of the phrase occurred later in the same section. Having provided for the application of customary law and English law respectively to various classes of cases, the section ended with the instruction that "in cases where no express rule is applicable to any matter in controversy, the court shall be governed by the principles of justice [sic], equity and good conscience". This is known as the residual clause. It was not repeated in all courts statutes. It disappeared in Ghana in 1960, and does not apply in all Nigerian courts.

The clauses have been interpreted as applying a single, general criterion of rightness or justice. It would perhaps have been possible to take the constituent phrases separately, and to give technical meanings at least to "natural justice" and "equity". There has been some discussion of the possibility,[16] but the courts never seriously adopted it. There has been some doubt as to what was the appropriate standard of justice. It seems clear that it cannot have been the standard of the societies whose social norms were in question, because a society will not have socially accepted norms which are repugnant to its own social standards. Thus, if the repugnancy clause was to have any effect, the standard was to be external. Perhaps the view was that ideally it should be an absolute, universal standard. In practice the judges were not likely to be free of their own cultural prejudices, so the standard was likely to contain at least strong elements of English ideals.[17] Some decisions can be read to imply that English ideals ought to be applied.[18] On the other hand, the courts have also asserted that exclusively English standards are not to be applied, and have refused to strike down norms as "repugnant" merely because they were un-English.[19]

(a) The Uses of the Repugnancy Clause The clause has been cited by the courts as authority for the following developments.

(i) It was used in 1898 to import the English law of inheritance where a deceased had contracted a Christian marriage, by holding that any other conclusion would be "repugnant".[20] In Ghana this holding has been superseded by statutory provisions,[21] while in Nigeria it has not been followed (Salacuse 1965).

(ii) Slavery and the incidents of slavery have been held illegal on this ground.[22] There were, however, express statutory provisions on slavery, which could have formed the basis for the courts' decisions.[23]

(iii) It has been held in Ghana that the clause would be used if necessary against a rule of local customary law which unfairly "naturalized" a stranger so that he or she became subject to that customary law.[24] However, since the courts statutes expressly defined the classes of persons subject to customary law, it is not certain that customary-law norms of naturalization remained.

(iv) A number of cases have concerned custody of minors. In *Edet v Essien*[25] it was argued that the relevant customary law would confer custody on a man who had given a marriage payment in respect of the minor's mother when she was a child, and who had not been repaid, even though another man had later made a payment and taken her as his wife. This was held repugnant. However, it was also held that no social norm to this effect had been proved to exist. In *Mariyama v Ejo*[26] a native court had held that custody of a child born within ten months following its mother's divorce must be awarded to her former husband, even if he was demonstrably not the genitor. The High Court held this repugnant, but would probably have reached the same result on the basis of a statutory provision that in guardianship cases the child's interest and welfare were to be the paramount consideration.[27] In another Nigerian case, *In re Whyte,*[28] the clause was applied to an alleged norm of Fanti (Ghana) customary law. A Fanti man having died intestate in Nigeria, his Ghanaian successor, representing the family (lineage) to which the deceased had belonged, argued that the family's obligation to maintain a child of the deceased could be made conditional on the custody of the child passing from the mother (resident in Nigeria) to the successor (in Ghana). More recent cases in Ghana do not support such a norm. Finally, as if in retaliation for that decision, in *Loromeke v Nkegho*[29] a Ghanaian court held an Urhobo (Nigeria) norm repugnant. This norm provided that, if a widow refused to accept the new husband offered her by the family of her deceased husband, she was obliged to surrender to them custody of her children by the deceased. These four cases taken together indicate that any social norm which deprives a mother of custody of her child, or tends to induce her to surrender custody, is liable to be regarded as repugnant unless there are good reasons for it. However, of the four cases, it is only in *Mariyama* and *Loromeke* that the alleged social norms appear to have existed, and in *Mariyama* the court may not have relied exclusively on the repugnancy clause. In Nigeria the courts are now generally subject to the statutory provision which may have been referred to in *Mariyama* (Kasunmu and Salacuse 1966: 19-20). This might appear to have ousted the customary law totally, subject only to the qualification that social norms may be relevant factors in a determination of the interest and welfare of a child. However, the courts still tend to presume that they should "apply" the social norms, treating the new provision as another qualification on customary law, co-existing with the repugnancy clause.[30]

(v) In Ghana the norm whereby a family was held liable for all the debts of a deceased member was held repugnant to the extent that the debts exceeded the assets of the member's estate.[31]

(vi) At one period the repugnancy clause was used in Ghana to modify the norm that only a head of family was entitled to sue on behalf of the family, by holding it repugnant not to allow another member to sue if the head had refused to act.[32] Subsequently the courts declared further exceptions to the rule as inherent in customary law,[33] suggesting that this exception would have developed in the same way in the absence of a repugnancy clause.

(vii) In Ghana where a chief wished to sue a majority of his councillors to recover stool (community) property, it was held repugnant to require their consent as a condition for admitting the suit. The court added that customary law quite possibly reached the same conclusion without needing modification.[34]

(viii) In Ghana it has been held that, if Anlo customary law gave a man's children on his death equal shares in his estate, but no right to sue caretakers or the successor for accounts to enforce this, it would be repugnant. However, on appeal it was held that in customary law there was a right to sue for an account in such circumstances.[35] In any case, as suggested above, there is difficulty in any argument contending that social norms include provisions regarding actions for accounts in state courts, and it may be preferable to regard this as a case where the courts had to reach a decision which could be neither an "application" of sociologists' customary law nor a rejection of an otherwise applicable sociologists' customary law.

The repugnancy clause may also have been used in the following instances, although the judgments do not show this conclusively.

(ix) The old social norm in Ghana allowing "panyarring", or the kidnapping of a debtor's relative to compel repayment of the debt, may have been abolished by the repugnancy clause.[36] It could equally have been abolished by the criminal law, and the social norms also probably changed to exclude it.[37]

(x) It has been said that in Ghana the matrilineal system of inheritance was once considered repugnant.[38] The case has not been reported, but it is conceivable that an early colonial judge may have taken such a view. It was not followed.

(xi) In both Ghana and Nigeria the common-law doctrine of acquiescence would appear to have been introduced into the customary law on the authority of the repugnancy clause, although this view is not universally accepted. It will be examined separately below.

(xii) In Nigeria the initial decision introducing acquiescence has been extended. It has been held that, in cases where customary law might otherwise allow a licensee to be ejected, but there has been "acquiescence" by the licensor in the licensee's continued possession over a long period, the courts will prevent his ejectment, but will impose an obligation on the licensee to pay a reasonable rent as a condition of remaining. This appears to have become a distinct doctrine. It is not conditional on all the elements of estoppel by acquiescence, and operates not as an estoppel but to modify the terms of the licence. However, the first case in the development of the doctrine, while it spoke of the court's "equitable jurisdiction", and cited the leading case on acquiescence, also doubted whether customary law would allow ejectment. It gave no ground for imposing a rent except for saying that, as the court was giving protection to the licensee, "the time [had] come" for her to pay rent.[39] The reference to an equitable jurisdiction might have been a reference to the doctrines of technical equity which give relief against forfeiture in common law. Thus it is not certain that customary law was modified by the repugnancy clause here. Subsequent cases did not rely on the clause.[40]

(xiii) In both Ghana and Nigeria the common-law doctrines of estoppel by litigation may have been introduced on the authority of this clause. This, however, is doubtful. The development is discussed below.

(xiv) There is one class of instances in which the clause had some importance, but which has been superseded by legislation. In Nigeria customary criminal law and procedure remained in force until relatively recently for some purposes. The norms were significantly affected by the clause.[41] The customary law of crimes and criminal procedure have now been abolished for the state legal system.[42]

Finally, (xv) the clause has been used in a number of cases as a reinforcing argument. In these the courts have stated, sometimes with doubt and sometimes with certainty, a social norm as the basis of a legal norm; and they have then stated as a subsidiary ground that any different norm would be rejected for repugnancy.[43]

It would seem that in many of these instances the norms applied today would have been applied even if the clause had not existed. In many of them there were adequate alternative grounds for the decisions. I would conclude that the only instances in which the clause has affected the substance of the law today are (iv), (v) and probably (xi). Moreover, even in those the principle, early established as authoritative, that customary law consists of that which is reasonable (below), would probably have enabled the courts to do the same in these cases.

(b) The Uses of the Residual Clause This clause is designed to operate when a court has selected the applicable system of law, but finds a lacuna in that system on the matter in issue. It has been referred to only in the following cases.

(i) In a Ghanaian case the parties had married in a Christian church. It was held that customary law was not applicable to the question of the validity of the marriage, and that there was no common law which could be applied. On the grounds of public policy the court applied the residual clause and recognized the marriage as valid.[44] Presumably the court did not consider itself bound to find and apply a norm of customary law because this would have resulted in the marriage being adjudged void. The case is not relevant because it concerned an alleged lacuna in the common law, not customary law.

(ii) In one case in Ghana an appeal court held that "it would be a very difficult matter to apply either English law or native custom entirely to the facts", because they concerned a transaction or transactions with elements of both. Therefore, the court said, it was sufficient to apply the residual clause, "and to say that this court is absolutely satisfied that justice was done by the Court below."[45] The reasoning is not easy to follow, and the decision has not been followed.

(iii) The clause was cited in a Nigerian case where the court was required to decide who was entitled to letters of administration of the estate of a deceased who had been a Yoruba, born outside wedlock, and had died childless. The applicant represented a daughter of the father of the deceased, born within wedlock. The opposing party represented a uterine brother of the deceased. The court found that it was "futile" to obtain reliable evidence of customary law on the point, and, applying the residual clause, decided to share the estate equally between the claimants.[46] While evidence of the relevant norms may not have been available in that case, it would seem that today customary-law norms could be found to apply.[47]

(iv) In *In re Whyte* (above) it is possible that the residual clause was used to formulate a norm in place of one struck down for repugnancy. As I have suggested, today the social norm which was found to be repugnant might not be held to exist, the situation being governed by other, acceptable legal norms.

(v) It is possible that the doctrines of estoppel to be discussed in the next section were introduced on the authority of this clause. However, the courts never stated that the customary law contained lacunae in these areas, nor that the common-law doctrines were the embodiment of "justice, equity and good conscience". If express statutory authority has to be found, it seems slightly simpler to attribute them to the repugnancy clause.[48]

Thus it does not seem possible to find any clear, lasting effect produced by the residual clause.

(c) The Effects of the Clauses These clauses could have been used by the courts to assert wide powers to create customary law. In practice neither seems to have produced significant demonstrable results. Indeed, the cases where the courts have refused to apply the repugnancy clause are, on a general view of the case-law, at least as important as those where it has been applied.[49] Similarly, the Nigerian provision for guardianship cases, while it could have been taken to abolish customary law, has been treated as little more than an additional repugnancy clause.

If, however, we take the view urged above of the legal system's function regarding customary law, we should not look for instances of these clauses enabling the courts to move beyond "enforcement" of existing customary law to a creative function. If mere "enforcement" has not been the practice, and the creation of lawyers' customary law has been the routine consequence of the institution of customary law as a type of state law, the clauses may have had a different, less tangible effect.

When the courts have appeared to follow the statutory injunction to "enforce" customary law, their creative function has usually been unacknowledged, and possibly unconscious. The instances listed in the previous section illustrate this. When they rely upon rules which expressly confer discretionary powers, they are more likely to act consciously and deliberately, and to create rules with less appearance of similarity to the rules of sociologists' customary law as known to the legal system. A number of rules confer such powers. There is a judge-made rule that customary law coincides with the canons of reasonableness, which was early established and has been repeatedly used as a reinforcing argument.[50] That rule appears to be related to another judge-made rule that totally unreasonable norms will not be enforced by the courts, even if found to be socially accepted.[51] The repugnancy and residual clauses may be added as further supporting a general principle that judges have some discretion deliberately to insert their own notions of justice into the process of determining the rules of customary law. We may conclude that the courts have assumed such a principle, and that its acceptance may have been indirectly assisted by these clauses. However, it seems that the principle would probably have been accepted to much the same degree if the clauses had not existed.[52]

B. The importation of common-law doctrines

Two sets of common-law doctrines have been explicitly imposed on the customary law in Ghana and Nigeria. They both happen to be doctrines of estoppel, although this does not seem particularly significant. Possibly the doctrines of estoppel embody ideas of justice which are especially strongly held by common lawyers, so that it has seemed more imperative to impose them on the customary law. Possibly also it seems a less drastic interference to introduce what is in theory a defence to another's claim, than to give a new right although estoppels in effect do create new rights.

It has been mentioned that the introduction of estoppel by acquiescence might have been based on the repugnancy clause. The earliest cases on the doctrine in each country either cited the clause as authority or made references to "equity", which quite possibly meant the clause.[53] The implication was that the doctrine was introduced by holding that social norms operating contrary to it were "repugnant to natural justice, equity and good conscience". However, a reading of the subsequent cases suggests that the courts have not attached great importance to this authority. They sometimes imply that they introduced this doctrine simply because justice required it. In the case of the doctrines of estoppel by litigation, there was even less an attempt to give authority for the development, and an even more obvious assumption that the need for it was self-evident.[54]

(a) Estoppel by Acquiescence (See Woodman 1971.) This doctrine was introduced to mitigate a problem caused by the social norms, as perceived by the courts at the beginning of the century. They found that, if a person occupied and improved land in the genuine but mistaken belief that he or she had an interest in it, the true interest-holder was entitled to eject the occupier and take the benefit of the improvement, regardless of the length of time which had elapsed, and even if the true interest-holder had known of the true state of affairs and deliberately encouraged the other's mistake. Moreover, it seemed likely that this situation would arise with increasing frequency, because of the growth of a land market combined with the unreliability in new conditions of the existing, non-literate methods of establishing titles.

The doctrine had been developed in the English courts of law and equity, principally in the latter half of the seventeenth and in the eighteenth centuries. It was an instance of the doctrine of estoppel *in pais,* or by representation, which provides that, if a person makes a statement to another intending it to be acted upon, and it is acted upon by that other to their detriment, the representor will be estopped from denying the truth of the statement. Acquiescence is that form of the doctrine in which the representation is implied by conduct, when a person fails to assert a right in a situation where, if they had one, they could reasonably be expected to assert it. The omission to act is construed as an implied representation, confirming a mistaken belief of the other party. By applying the doctrine in the circumstances just described, the Ghanaian and Nigerian courts estopped the true interest-holder from asserting his or her interest against the mistaken party, thus enabling the latter to enjoy the improvements they had made. It has been applied in many cases in both countries.

There are grounds for contending that the courts could have developed a doctrine of lawyers' customary law which would have met the problem they perceived without having recourse to English law. It is possible to trace the germ, and some growth of a doctrine which would have divided the benefit of land between the *bona fide* trespasser who improved it, and the person entitled to possession.[55] Moreover, certain norms of lawyers' customary law are analogous to and consistent with such a norm. For example, it is possible that customary law does not include the rule that things attached to land, or growing upon it, become the property of the landowner; it may regard improvements to land as the objects of different rights from those in the land itself.[56] This example may be of particular significance. Sociologists' customary law probably does not regard fixtures as becoming part of the land (Woodman 1970). In the cases now in question the state courts were committed to the view, deeply embedded in the common law, that buildings, crops and other developments on land were inseparable from the land itself. Thus rights to a land and its fixtures must be vested in a single legal person. This view structured their approach to the problem. It led them to an answer which in a few cases those in which the elements of acquiescence are all present takes land away from the holder without compensation and gives it to the improver, while in most cases it leaves the improved land with the title-holder and allows the improver no compensation (Woodman 1971: 56-57).

(b) Estoppel by Judicial Decision (See Woodman 1969b on the Ghanaian development. The Nigerian has been parallel.) The authority for the application of these doctrines has not been stated by the courts. It has simply been assumed that they must be applied.

The doctrine of *res judicata* provides that a person is estopped from litigating over an issue if a previous valid judicial decision has been reached on the same issue in a case between the same parties or their privies. Secondly, the doctrine of estoppel by standing by during litigation provides that a person is estopped from litigating over an issue if a previous valid judicial decision has been reached in a case which was fought by someone "in the same interest" as the party now estopped, and to his knowledge. Both doctrines have frequently been applied in cases where all the other relevant norms were customary-law.

The principal issue for the legal systems has been the applicability of these doctrines in cases where the previous litigation has been fought by different parties from those subsequently before the court. It has become necessary to elaborate the concepts of a "privy" for the purposes of *res judicata,* and of a case fought "in the same interest" for the purposes of the second doctrine. The customary-law system of land tenure is such that several persons may hold interdependent interests in the same land. Repeatedly it has been necessary to decide whether litigation by one estops another. For example, a community holding an allodial title litigates over its boundary with a neighbouring community. Does this estop a wider community of which the losing party is a part, and with which it shares the allodial title? Further, does it estop members of the community who wish to claim interests derived from the allodial title? Such questions could not have arisen within English law.

The initial development was towards expanding the concept of privity, to enable *res judicata* to be pleaded in such cases. Thus it has been held that in some areas a wide community is a privy of its constituent sub-communities. However, this development was superseded by an extension of the concept of a case fought "in the same interest", which enabled the doctrine of estoppel by standing by during litigation to be applied. In a leading Ghanaian case it was argued on appeal to the Privy Council that it ought not to be extended beyond the classes of cases, those of wills and representative actions, to which it had been applied in England. The court said:

> "Assuming, without deciding, that the English decisions have hitherto been so confined, their Lordships would point out that there is nothing in the principle itself which compels it to be limited to wills and representative actions. The principle ... is founded on justice and common sense."[57]

It appears that today "the same interest" includes any rights which under customary law could not exist in the absence of the rights which were in issue in the previous case.

In summary the courts have added to the body of lawyers' customary law a set of rules, adapted from common law, for determining the effects of litigation about customary-law rights in state courts. Sociologists' customary law contains no rules for this purpose. The general consequence is to make determinations by state courts conclusive of legal rights and duties. But since these are rules of lawyers' customary law, the determinations are conclusive only in subsequent cases in the state courts themselves.

Conclusions

Relatively specific studies are necessary if excessive abstraction and unjustified generalizations about the relationship between folk law and state law are to be avoided. This paper has aimed to describe in summary a particular aspect of state legal activity in two contemporary nation-states. The topic chosen has been the emergence of certain of the state courts' laws. These have been treated as having their existence in the courtroom conduct of judges, which conduct can be investigated primarily through a study of court records (cf. Snyder 1981[58]). I have not been concerned with the effects of these laws on social behaviour outside the courtroom. However, I have not viewed judges as engaged only in the deciding of specific cases. Neither have I viewed them as fashioning rules for deciding disputes only. The rules of customary law which they have created have been expressed primarily as rules of social ordering, which are used incidentally to decide cases.[59] Whether the judges have been right to expect social conduct to be determined by their decisions is a different issue. Here I assert only that the judges' conduct can be best understood by recognizing that they consider themselves to be engaged in social administration.[60]

The choice of topic has been based on reasons largely concerned with my own experience and the accessibility of information, and not exclusively because of the significance of issues raised. However, I do not accept that the study of state laws should be avoided on the ground that it supports an ideology of legal centralism (or "statism"), provided that other aspects of folk law and society are the subject-matter of other studies and are recognized as also having importance.

Subject to these qualifications, it may now be useful to seek, first, the general patterns in the developments recorded, and, secondly, the wider conclusions concerning folk law and the state which appear to be supported, although they cannot be finally proven, by this study.

This process of emergence of a particular part of state law may itself have changed over the period in question. Thus far the account of particular aspects of the process has in the main assumed virtually unchanging consistency in the process. I believe that a plausible general account can be thus developed, suggesting that the changes in the process were relatively unimportant. However, the point will be considered further below.

It has been emphasized that the state legal systems created a new body of rules. They have not "applied" a pre-existent customary law. This conclusion is contrary to customary legal rhetoric. The orthodox view is that the courts follow, or ought to follow, binding rules in deciding issues of customary law. It asserts that, when a party makes a claim based upon an asserted customary-law right, the court hears evidence or consults authority as to the content of the relevant "customary law", discovers by these means the applicable norms, and then applies them, subject only to the repugnancy clause when in force. According to this view there is normally no judicial discretion. Judgments may be criticized as containing wrong decisions, in the sense of being based upon false evidence or departing from truthful evidence, but not as following mistaken policies. The view may, however, accommodate the opinion that in exceptional cases the rules do not lead to a necessary answer, in which case the court must exercise discretion.

It has been argued here that the process is not governed by rules in this way. The examples given show the Ghanaian and Nigerian courts creating individual rules or sets of rules, not adopting rules already in existence. The application of sociologists' customary law would have required radically different rules of application and procedure, if it had been at all possible. Thus the orthodox view is mistaken, both as an account of the actual process and as an account of an attainable ideal against which particular acts of the courts may be criticized. More generally the analysis shows to be untenable a concept of law which views "the elementary instance of law ... [as] a court applying customary norms of behaviour" (Collins 1982: 93; cf. Hunt 1983: 240-241). Furthermore it refutes the critique of customary law by those students of law and development who object that customary law as applied in state courts merely maintains a traditional form of society, whatever that may mean (Seidman 1966). Still more generally, it tends to refute the view that law is always a conservative force, designed to maintain the status quo.

It is surprising that this conclusion has not been more generally recognized, for there is a closely similar aspect of colonial legal history which has been more adequately studied. The British colonial regime introduced in Northern Nigeria and then extended to many other territories the policy of indirect rule (Hailey 1950-54, 1957: 414-417, 452-470, 517-532). This was expressed as a policy whereby customary leaders of communities would continue to exercise their customary functions, but would be authorized to do so, and supported in that exercise, and given some further functions, by the colonial state. The only changes to be imposed by the state would be those necessary to maintain public order between communities, and to induce occasional and minor developments. Economic development was in general to occur spontaneously through local, popular initiatives. This policy also did not operate in practice in the manner asserted in the expressed plans, even in communities where the institutions of chieftaincy already existed and the state was correctly informed as to its nature. The ultimate basis of the chief's authority was of necessity changed, and became the coercive power of the colonial state. In consequence the detailed modes of exercise of authority were changed, and the state did not eventually enforce customary forms of conduct (Busia 1951).[61]

The experience of customary law in state courts is, therefore, not adequately described by designating it institutionalization of sociologists' customary law (Bohannan 1967[62]). However, having emphasized the discontinuity between sociologists' customary law and lawyers' customary law, it is now necessary to rebut the opposite notion, that the courts create lawyers' customary law with unfettered discretion. That which they create bears some relationship to sociologists' customary law. The assertion of continuity, while mistaken, is not a totally empty ideology concealing the creation of laws reflecting only the judges' notions of justice or expediency. The bare account of many a rule or concept of lawyers' customary law frequently describes an element which, if taken out of its context in state law, is similar to an element of sociologists' customary law. For example, it is a rule of both bodies of rules that a head of family must consult the principal members before disposing of family property, although the effect of breach, and so the significance of the rule, differs widely between two systems. Again, a concept of both bodies of rules is that of parentage, although the rights and duties associated with the concept, and even more their enforcement, differ. Thus, in recognizing that courts make law we must immediately recognize also that they make it by a structured process, and that the notion of law as the emanation of an unlimited judicial legislature is a fantasy in this area as elsewhere. (Cf. the more extreme views quoted and criticized in Kantorowicz 1934.)

How then can we explain the content of lawyers' customary law? We may first dispose of some possible explanations which are obvious but of limited significance. It might be argued that the divergence between sociologists' and lawyers' customary law arises from practical factors. Put in its strongest form, this argument says that the basic organization and necessary procedure of these state courts make it impossible for them to enforce sociologists' customary law to any greater extent than they do. This seems erroneous. It is not inconceivable for such institutions to hear claims of different cateogires from those they have previously been accustomed to hear, to grant different remedies, or to enforce their decisions in different ways. There would be no impossibility in their recognizing as legal many rules which they have relegated to the category of morality, for example, by developing legal rules whereby families would be compelled to assist, up to certain limits, those members who needed help. Assuming some freedom of the legal systems to choose between different objectives, nothing in the necessary judicial procedures made such rules impossible.

Put in a weaker form, the argument of practicality suggests that state courts are limited by their resources in the extent of activity they can undertake. It may be argued that for this reason the state cannot bring to bear the types of influences and pressures which would determine the effectiveness of social norms in the absence of the state. State activity is expensive, and so has to be limited in volume (Griffiths 1985). This explains why state courts in general act only when a conflict has arisen and an injury has been done; why they must normally limit themselves to ordering monetary payments; why there have to be narrow limits on the number of duties which can be enforced. However, this argument does not explain factors such as the introduction of the doctrines of estoppel. Nothing shows that the state legal systems have operated up to their maximum capacity (however that can be defined), nor that the refusal to extend their activities has been a result of calculations about their supplies of official working time and coercive authority. There is, indeed, little evidence for the assumption that their policy has been to enforce social norms without change as far as practicable.

A further possible explanation of the content of lawyers' customary law would point to the narrowness of the legal culture to which the legal systems belong. Those educated in the common law, it may be argued, may be unable to conceive of forms of action, remedies or criteria of justice, equity and good conscience other than those known to the common law. This explanation gains support from the absence of explicit discussion within the legal system of many of the developments examined above. The lack of debate suggests that the developments were produced unconsciously and without recognition of the alternatives. However, it is also clear that the legal systems have shown some appreciation of sociologists' customary law. The argument fails to explain the distinction between those elements of sociologists' customary law which are understood and those which are not. It again assumes that the state policy was to enforce sociologists' customary law fully, and seeks only to explain derogations from this.

A more persuasive explanation may be developed from the observed fact of state creation of rules, rather than the fallacious notion of state adoption of social norms. It has been argued above that there is a considerable body of newly created lawyers' customary law. What are the main features of this?

Lawyers' customary law in Ghana and Nigeria seems to envisage a society in which the individual, although developing within a family, will by his or her own individual exertions acquire property. This property-holder receives considerable legal autonomy. Few legal obligations are imposed on an individual in favour of his or her family, and when a family is held entitled to property, the tendency is to define that family as a relatively small group. A man's obligations to his wife and children are defined in economic terms and given legal force. The holder of property is not subjected to legal rules inhibiting the use of that property or restricting the holder's enjoyment of it, while it is fully and effectively protected from legal claims and the slightest physical interference from whatever source. Where the holder is a family, the law contains certain rules supporting the authority of the head, and further rules allowing the property to be removed from the category of family property and replaced by individual properties of members; beyond this, the law abstains from control. All property-holders are generally free to sell, this general legal freedom being apparently designed to facilitate the development of a property market in which all property, and especially interests in land, may be exchanged for money without normative restrictions. All these rules and principles would seem to point towards the general objective of the creation of a law appropriate to market capitalism. (See also Asante 1975. Developments in marriage law not discussed here seem to have displayed the same trend: Adinkrah 1980.) The examples given above, and many others which could be developed, point to the conclusion that this is the main explanation of the content of the new rules of customary law.

This conclusion might be demonstrated in more detail through a full analysis of the current law. Since that cannot be provided here, discussion will be limited to a further brief observation on one of the developments already mentioned. It was suggested that the doctrine of estoppel by acquiescence was introduced to answer a problem resulting from a combination of circumstances which included the rule that things attached to the land became part of the land. This latter rule, it was further suggested, was itself imported from English law. It is perhaps significant that the rule is commonly stated as if it were a natural fact. It is not, of course; the rule really means that the holder of the land gains the benefit of objects which he or others attach to the land. Its formulation as a natural fact is an ideological device which benefits the landholder by maintaining and adding to his wealth, at the expense of those whose wealth takes other forms. By applying it in West Africa, the legal systems have tended to maintain the inviolability of land-holders' rights, and to increase their wealth. Thus rights to land as a form of wealth with a secure market value have been assisted. The rule is generally followed except in the narrowly and precisely defined class of cases where the elements of estoppel by acquiescence can be proved essentially those where a landholder has fraudulently sought to take advantage of another's error. It is just in this class of cases that the rule on fixtures threatens the operation of a land market, because it can lead to the loss of investments and so to the disappointment of economic expectations. Here the legal systems explicitly overrode what they had stated to be the customary law.

Given this explanation for the content of lawyers' customary law, we must view differently those rules which appear designed to conserve social norms continuing from earlier economic orderings. The explanations referred to above as obvious, and dismissed, take the notion of state adoption of social norms as central, and look for special reasons to explain the departures from that process. Since I have argued that state adoption of social norms does not occur, I have taken the creation of new law as the central characteristic of the state legal process. But it does not follow that every reference by lawyers' customary law to sociologists' customary law must be regarded as in need of its own peculiar explanation. Neither need every such instance be viewed as a concealment of reality (Diamond 1973).

If the bodies of legal rules were designed to foster an economy of the market capitalist type, it would certainly not have followed that rules modelled in every respect directly on contemporary English law, or the law of any other capitalist society, would have been appropriate in the historical circumstances of these states. Assuming a policy of movement towards a form of capitalism, that development would be assisted by effecting continuing change from the basis of existing social relations, rather than attempting immediately to destroy all those relations. Thus it would not have been rational planning totally to abolish all family property in the early colonial period by refusing to recognize family titles. This would not only have produced a degree of social disorder which would have weakened the power of the state. It would also have denied the basic tenet of capitalist law that established rights should not be changed against the will of the holders, which tenet having been shaken would have been difficult to re-establish. Change in the desired direction was more likely to be induced if the courts simply held all family property to be alienable at the will of a limited number of members according to defined rules, or to be partitioned by a court in specified circumstances provisions which might have been expected to result in the total disappearance of family property in due course.

Thus the legal systems did not adopt sociologists' customary law according to a process determined by a body of binding rules, nor did they exercise unfettered discretion to create such law as they thought fit. The rules which they created form such a pattern as to manifest the consistent pursuit of a policy, worked out in a body of legal principles determining the process to be followed. (See Dworkin 1977.) By way of illustration, there appear to be principles that interests in land may be bought and sold, that contractual terms voluntarily agreed should be enforced between the parties, and that people should not lose as a result of reasonable reliance on apparent rights. It is also a legal principle that statutes ought to be followed, and thus the statutory injunction to "enforce" customary law, although it cannot be a rule because of its impossibility, gives rise to a principle. This, it is suggested, is to the effect that forms of conduct enjoined by social norms should be enforced by state courts. The rules of lawyers' customary law were created by working out the implications of these principles in particular cases, a process which included weighing them against each other in the very frequent instances where they pointed to conflicting results. (The process appears closely similar to that described by Dworkin 1977: Chap. 4.)

A full account of the relevant legal principles would need to be based upon a further lengthy analysis of lawyers' customary law, which cannot be attempted here. This account would need to consider the changes over time in the weight of the various principles. For example, that principle which requires state courts to enforce socially required conduct has varied in weight, as (to express the fact in terms of traditional, imprecise legal analysis) the attitude of the courts towards customary law has changed. A hundred years ago some judges (at least) were willing to give little weight to the principle, regarding sociologists' customary law as a system of doubtful justice which would disappear with social change. This attitude was already changing at the turn of the century, although there are still instances in the early decades of the twentieth century of the weakness of this principle.[63] The trend has in some respects continued in recent decades, with an increasing willingness to contemplate a customary law of torts, and to apply the customary law of inheritance to the estates of foreigners. However, there appears also to have been a recent trend towards overt, conscious creation of new norms by the courts, which have been giving increasing weight to other competing principles.[64]

This analysis is inconsistent with an account of history which asserts a policy of conservation of "traditional" modes of production and their accompanying laws. In Ghana and Nigeria the evidence of the state legal systems does not support the view that the colonial states sought to maintain pre-capitalist formations and direct them to functions which would subserve the developing capitalist mode of production.[65] (Cf. the account in Fitzpatrick 1980; also the general discussion of Fitzpatrick 1983.) The conservation thesis is perhaps more tenable for societies which have developed into or to include labour reserves, a category to which Ghana and Nigeria do not in the main belong (Amin 1972).[66] The analysis suggested here is also inconsistent with an interpretation of lawyers' customary law as being at any particular moment a weapon of an older generation seeking to recover authority (Chanock 1978).

Some practical application of a study such as this may perhaps be found in legal policies for ethnic minorities within modern states. The experience of Ghana and Nigeria suggests that the social relations of a community will not be preserved by the adoption of its social norms as state law, and that rules which have previously operated independently of a modern state cannot be "enforced" by the state. However, the creation of state power over a community necessarily changes social relations within it. The state cannot insulate a community from its own power, any more than from economic relations with other communities. There is, therefore, no immediately feasible policy. Advice to "respect" the norms of the ethnic minority may be useful as an antidote to ethnocentrism and racism, but do not provide a programme. The foregoing discussion suggests that the state will exercise its power through a body of rules which, whatever the intention, will be different from those which have been socially accepted previously. Policymakers (who may be mostly members of the minority communities) should therefore decide what type of desired social relations are feasible, and deliberately design state laws to promote them. If it is decided that existing social relations should in general be preserved, state laws will need to be carefully and consciously designed to do this. It may well emerge that this programme will entail making relatively few state laws (Bayly 1985). It follows from the present argument that a law "adopting" existing social norms may produce far more undesired changes than more specific laws made with more understanding. Moreover, if the experience of indirect rule in West Africa is indeed analogous to that of customary law, as I have conjectured, it follows that state enforcement of established social authority, including state enforcement of decisions by established dispute-settlement processes, will equally not leave society unchanged.

Other conclusions, extending even further from the specific case of Ghana and Nigeria, need to be put very tentatively. It may, however, be worth noticing that this study, having started by examining the expression of separate norms, has concluded by emphasizing the importance of the emergence and development of the state. It may be more fruitful to study the history and nature of a state than to concentrate on distinctions between types of norms in terms of their expression or immediate functions for example, on distinctions such as those between norms for decision and norms of conduct, between norms to assist agreement and norms to assist judgment, or on issues such as the interactions between different categories of norms. Moreover, in using the evidence of norms as a means of studying the state, it may be mistaken to rely upon the assumptions expressed in norms. It may, for example, be erroneous to build a theory on the view that state laws conserve pre-state customary rules, in reliance on statutes requiring state courts to enforce native law and custom. A study of history subsequent to these enactments may well show that in some states such conservation follows, but is likely to show that in others talk of enforcement, preservation or maintenance of customary law is a sham. The emergence of the state may have such a profound effect that little in the previous social orderings can be conserved.

Notes

1. Although in Ghana and Nigeria Islamic law is officially classified for most purposes as a type of customary law, it is not discussed in this paper, because as a body of rules it is not derived from, nor does it purport to obtain its authority from social observance. Islamic jurisprudence distinguishes between rules of law and of morality, the former being framed for direct enforcement by state governments. See e.g. Schacht 1964.
2. In Woodman 1986 the table of cases contains approximately 1,000 references. The total volume of accessible cases from Nigeria is approximately the same, but is growing more rapidly.
3. *Barima v Bechemhene* (1952) D.C. (Land) '52-'55, 78.
4. It was in operation by 1871: *Parker v Mensah* (1871) Sar. F.C.L. 204.
5. *Lokko v Konklofi* (1907) Ren. 450.
6. Sheriffs and Civil Process Act, Cap. 189, *Laws of the Federation of Nigeria and Lagos* (1958). The courts' rules of procedure regulated the process, but these were made by delegated authority which did not include power to alter rights under customary law.

7. E.g. *Addo v Togbor;* Akyem (1945) D.C. (Land) '38-'47, 161 (sale of usufruct to stranger). The sale in execution has, moreover, developed as a means for a pledgee of land to exercise a right of sale: Allott 1954: 407, 429-430; *Kwansa v Brahima,* 1967 (3) ALR Comm. 226; *Attah v Aidoo,* 1968 (2) ALR Comm. 184.
8. The evidence relied upon is principally that referred to in the writings cited in the next paragraph. On the right to re-purchase, see Woodman 1967: 8-9.
9. *Kokomlemle Consolidated Cases* (1951) D.C. (Land) '48-'51, 312.
10. See the authorities cited, Woodman 1964: 23-24; James 1973: 177-179.
11. For evidence, see the works cited in the next paragraph, and Hill 1963: 82, 114, 125-129, 180.
12. *Larbi v Cato* [1960] G.L.R. 146.
13. I add the words "or a designated part thereof" so as to include the cases where property is inherited by the sons and daughters of the deceased, and there is some question as to whether that group is properly called a "family". Whatever the answer to that question, it seems that the inheriting group is regulated, as to its administration of the property, by the rules governing family property.
14. *Larbi v Cato* [1960] G.L.R. 146, 151-152.
15. There were some variations, of no practical importance. Thus the Native Courts Ordinance, Cap. 142, *Laws of Nigeria* (1948), s. 10(1), used the phrase "repugnant to justice".
16. See e.g. Daniels 1964: 267-271. See also the discussion of the origins of the clauses in Derrett 1963, and *Lewis v Bankole* (1909) 1 N.L.R. 82: 84-85, where the court said that it was not sure of the meaning of "natural justice" or "good conscience", but understood "equity" in a technical sense. It seems clear, however, that equity in this sense was not generally considered applicable to customary law.
17. There have been express suggestions to this effect in other jurisdictions. See e.g. Abrahams 1948.
18. E.g. *Ogiamien v Ogiamien* [1967] 1 All N.L.R.

191.

19. E.g. *Andoh v Franklin* (1952) D.C. (Land) '52-'55, 24; *Dawodu v Danmole* [1962] 1 All N.L.R. 702, [1962] 1 W.L.R. 1053.
20. *Cole v Cole* (1898) 1 N.L.R. 15 (Supreme Court of the Gold Coast Colony and Lagos). See also *Ashon v Eduah* (1908) Ren. 480.
21. Marriage Ordinance, Cap. 127, *Laws of the Gold Coast* (1951), s. 48.
22. *Kodieh v Affram* (1930) 1 W.A.C.A. 12.
23. E.g. British Slavery Abolition Act 1883, applicable to all colonies and referred to in *Kodieh v Affram,* above.
24. *Brown v Miller* (1921) F.C. '20-'21, 48.

25. (1932) 11 N.L.R. 47.
26. 1961 N.R.N.L.R. 81.
27. The provision applies throughout Nigeria. The relevant enactment in that case would have been the Northern Region Native Courts Law, 1956 (No. 6), s. 23. The court used words which suggest that it had this in mind, but did not cite it.
28. (1946) 18 N.L.R. 70.
29. (1957) 3 W.A.L.R. 306.
30. E.g. *Mariyama v Ejo,* above; *Diri v Nyikwa,* H.C. (Kano) 25th Oct. 1965; *Ayegba v Ayegba* (1979) 3 L.R.N. 232.
31. *Asiedu v Ofori* D.C. (Accra) 6th Dec. 1932.
32. *Mahmudu v Zenuah* (1934) 2 W.A.C.A. 172.
33. See e.g. *Kwan v Nyieni* [1959] G.L.R. 67.
34. *Quansah v Yankum II* (1949) 12 W.A.C.A. 435.
35. *Tamakloe v Attipoe* (1951) D.C. (Land) '48-'51, 378; W.A.C.A. 22nd June 1953.
36. So suggested Bennion 1962: 410. See also *Lokko v Konklofi* (1907) Ren. 450.
37. Cf. Rattray 1923: 234, stating that it was abolished in Ashanti by legislation before the colonial period.
38. *Andoh v Franklin* (1952) D.C. (Land) '52-'55, 24.
39. *Eyamba v Holmes* (1924) 5 N.L.R. 83.
40. E.g. *Bassey v Eteta* (1938) 4 W.A.C.A. 153, which recognizes that customary law has been modified but gives no authority.
41. See e.g. *Jalo Guri v Hadejia N.A.,* 1959 N.R.N.L.R. 98.
42. Nigeria (Constitution) Order-in-Council, 1960 (L.N. 159), s. 21(10); Keay and Richardson 1966: Chap. 13.
43. See e.g. *Serwah v Kesse* (1959), reported Ollennu 1962: 201, 205; *Commissioner for Lands and Housing, Western State v Fagebo* (1978) 3 L.R.N. 15 (holding that, even if a tenant could be dispossessed at will by the landlord which was not the case such a rule would not be upheld).
44. *Des Bordes v Des Bordes* (1884) Sar. F.C.L. 267.
45. *Boodoo v Bissa* (1910) Ren. 585.
46. *Andre v Agbebi* (1931) 10 N.L.R. 79.
47. The difficulty arose partly from the court's concern about "illegitimacy", that is, birth outside wedlock. Today this is irrelevant in this type of case, and the person patrilineally related to the deceased would have a better claim.
48. So suggested Bennion 1962: 445-446.
49. See also Lloyd 1962: 25, stating that the clause was not used by administrative officers hearing appeals from native courts.
50. This was first expressed in *Yerenchi v Akuffo* (1905) Ren. 366, 367. See Woodman 1969a: 134-135. As illustrative cases, see: *Vanderpuye v Botchway*

(1951) 13 W.A.C.A. 164; *De-Vine v Mould* (1951) D.C. (Land) '48-51, 368; *Tamakloe v Attipoe* (1951) D.C. (Land) '48-51, 378; *Akakpo v Afafa* (1952) D.C. (Land) 116.

51. See e.g. *Akrofi v Akrofi*, next note.
52. A further illustration may be taken from the judgment in *Akrofi v Akrofi* [1965] G.L.R. 13, given in Ghana five years after the repugnancy and residual clauses had ceased to be parts of the law. After recounting evidence of customary law by expert witnesses which, the court considered, was contradictory and illogical, the court continued:
"I am of the view that if there be such a custom, and I do not find, whereby a person is discriminated against solely upon the ground of sex, that custom has out-lived its usefulness and is at present not in conformity with public policy. Our customs if they are to survive the test of time must change with the times."

Here, as often, the argument for express modification of the customary law is a reinforcing argument only. It is said that the socially accepted norm ("the custom") is not as claimed, but it is then added that, even if it were, it would not be acceptable. It may be observed that the reference to public policy is not to any specific legal rule, and therefore asserts an inherent judicial power to modify customary law. See also *Atomo v Tekpetey*, H.C. 26th Oct. 1979, digested [1980] G.L.R.D. 78, holding that a custom was "repugnant to natural justice, equity and good conscience" more than 19 years after the repeal of the repugnancy clause.
53. Bokitsi Concession Inquiry (1903) Ren. 242, Sar. F.L.R. 148; *Lewis v Bankole* (1909-10) 1 N.L.R. 82, 84-85, 87; *Awo v Gam* (1913) 2 N.L.R. 100. Cf. Bennion 1962: 446; Daniels 1964: 280-281; James and Kasunmu 1966: 67-70.
54. The application of both sets of doctrines was confirmed by statute in Ghana in 1960: Courts Act, 1960 (C.A. 9), s. 66(3); today the Courts Act, 1971 (Act 372), s. 49(2).
55. *Tetteh v Tetteh* (1947) D.C. (Land) '38-'47, 344, varied on appeal, W.A.C.A. 11th Jan. 1949. The Land Court upheld generally the judgment of the native court, which had given such a decision, and referred to the repugnancy clause for support. The West African Court of Appeal set aside, without comment, those parts of the Land Court's judgment which had refused to give the original owner possession of the land on which the trespasser had erected a building, and which ordered the value of the land to be paid instead.
56. *Kofi Adu v Sarkodee Adoo*, C.A. 31st Mar. 1969 (1969) C.C. 59. There has also been some talk in Ghana of a customary-law doctrine of acquiescence, which is said to be identical with the common-law doctrine: *Thompson v Mensah*

(1957) 3 W.A.L.R. 240; Ollennu 1985: 73-75. However, the language of the earlier courts suggested clearly that they considered themselves to be applying a common-law doctrine.

57. *Ofori Atta II v Abu Bonsra II* (1957) 3 W.A.L.R. 171, 175, [1958] A.C. 95, 101-102.
58. Snyder's notion of customary law, as of "legal form" generally, is of a somewhat broad and undifferentiated social phenomenon. His impressive and fascinating study would have been of even greater interest to this reader had he found it possible to distinguish further between the various social groupings which contributed to the legal changes he describes, since their motives and roles appear to have varied. Cf. Snyder 1982: 117-119, a reference to two distinct groupings.
59. Cf. Ehrlich 1936: 24. Ehrlich's distinctions are helpful to thought, but I do not here employ his categories according to his meanings.
60. It does not seem helpful in the present study to distinguish between rules as bases for agreement and rules as bases for judgments. All the rules in question seem to belong to bodies of rules designed to form social behaviour both through internalization by members and through coercion.
61. See also the study by Goldschmidt 1981, arguing that the "indigenous constitutional structure of government", even if it had existed as one distinct system, could not have been used as the basis for constructing a modern state constitution.
62. Bohannan was concerned with the institutionalization of norm into custom, and of custom into law (Woodman 1985). The type of law with which he was concerned was not necessarily the law of modern states, although it might seem attractive to extend his notion of institutionalization to the process now under discussion. The principal criticism of his argument, whether extended or not, is that it fails to take account of the difference in content of "institutionalized" norms, and by the use of the term institutionalization avoids an analysis of the process such as that attempted here.
63. Instances of propositions originally accepted by courts and later not followed are: that a social norm was not legally enforceable unless, like a "custom" in English law, it had existed since 1189 *(Welbeck v Brown,* Sar. F.C.L. 185); that a person died "intestate" for the purposes of statute-law if he made a customary-law will *(In re Anaman* 1985) Sar. F.C.L. 221); that if writing was used as evidence of a transaction, customary law was inapplicable *(Amarquaye v Broenner* (1898) Ren. 145); that family property was a "dying institution" *(Lewis v Bankole* (1909) 1 N.L.R. 82); that customary law need not be applied if a case concerned "elements foreign to native life, habit and custom" *(Boodo v Bissa* (1910) Ren. 585; cf. *Henodji v Sallah* (1936) D.C. '31-'37, 158); and

that customary-law sales of interests in land were, "except in the bush", rare and becoming rarer, and the legislature had deemed it wiser to pay no heed to them *(Concession Enquiries 1016 and 1035 (Sekondi)* (1911) Ren. 592).

64. E.g. *Akrofi v Akrofi* [1965] G.L.R. 13; *In re Kofi Antubam (Decd.)* [1965] G.L.R. 138.
65. West African legal history appears to be rather of the form referred to by Luckham 1978. Luckham bases his conclusions primarily on a study of the modes in which private law practice has been organized. However, some of the examples already given of rules created by the legal system could be used in close parallel to his to examine what he calls the "historic mission of lawyers and the courts in restructuring pre-colonial social formations and property relations to assist commercial production in rural areas".
66. There is some evidence that areas within Ghana and Nigeria, such as parts of northern Ghana, have served as labour reserves, and have been subjected to policies designed to exclude "modernising" influences and so to conserve pre-capitalist orderings.

References

(Cases and legislation are cited in the standard legal forms. They are not listed here.)

ABRAHAMS, S. (1948)
"The Colonial Legal Service and the Administration of Justice in the Colonial Dependencies," 30 Journal of Comparative Legislation and International Law, 3rd ser. 1.

ADINKRAH, K.O. (1980)
"Ghana's Marriage Ordinance: an Inquiry into a Legal Transplant for Social Change," 18 African Law Studies 1-42.

ALLOTT, A.N. (1954)
Akan Law of Property, Ph.D. thesis, University of London.

ALLOTT, A. and G.R. WOODMAN (eds.) (1985)
People's Law and State Law: the Bellagio Papers. Dordrecht: Foris.

AMIN, S. (1972)
"Underdevelopment and Dependence in Black Africa Origins and Contemporary Forms," 10 Journal of Modern African Studies 1.

ASANTE, S.K.B. (1975)
Property Law and Social Goals in Ghana, 1844-1966. Ghana Universities Press: Ghana.

BAYLY, J.U. (1985)
"Toward the Development of a Northwest Territories Law Reform Capability to Enable the Development of Proposals for New Legislation to Meet the Special Needs and Circumstances of Northern Peoples," in Allott and Woodman (eds.) 285-97.

BENDA-BECKMANN, F. von (1979)
Property in Social Continuity: Continuity and Change in the Maintenance of Property Relationships Through Time In Minangkabau, West Sumatra. Martinus Nijhoff: The Hague.

BENNION, F.A.R. (1962)
The Constitutional Law of Ghana, London: Butterworths.

BENTSI-ENCHILL, K. (1964)
Ghana Land Law. London: Sweet & Maxwell.

BOHANNAN, P. (1957)
Justice and Judgment Among the Tiv. London: International African Institute.

---------- (1967)
"The Differing Realms of the Law," in P. Bohannan (ed.), Law and Warfare 43-56.

BUSIA, K.A. (1951)
The Position of the Chief in the Modern Political System of Ashanti. London: O.U.P.

CHANOCK, M. (1978)
"Neo-traditionalism and the Customary law in Malawi," 16 African Law Studies 80-91.

COLLINS, H. (1982)
Marxism and Law. Oxford: Clarendon Press.

DANIELS, W.C.E. (1964)
The Common Law in West Africa. London: Butterworths.

DATE-BAH, S.K. (1973)
"Reflections on the Law of Defamation in Ghana," 10 University of Ghana Law Journal 129-148.

DERRETT, J.D.M. (1963)
"Justice, Equity and Good Conscience," in J.N.D. Anderson (ed.), Changing Law in Developing Countries.

DIAMOND, S. (1973)
"The Rule of Law versus the Order of Custom," in D. Black and M. Mileski (eds.), The Social Organisation of Law.

DWORKIN, R. (1977)
Taking Rights Seriously. London: Duckworth.

EHRLICH, E. (1936)
Fundamental Principles of the Sociology of Law (trans. Moll), Cambridge: Harvard University Press.

FITZPATRICK, P. (1980)
Law and State in Papua New Guinea. London and New York: Academic Press.

---------- (1983)
"Law, Plurality and Underdevelopment," in D. Sugarman (ed.), Legality, Ideology and the State. London and New York: Academic Press.

GOLDSCHMIDT, J.E. (1981)
National and Indigenous Constitutional Law in Ghana. Doctoral thesis, University of Leiden.

GLUCKMAN, J. (1955)
The Judicial Process Among the Barotse of Northern Rhodesia. Manchester U.P.

GRIFFITHS, J. (1985)
"Four Laws of Interaction in Circumstances of Legal Pluralism: First Steps Towards an Explanatory Theory," in A. Allott and G.R. Woodman (eds.) 217-27.

HAILEY, W.M. (1950-54) Native Administration in the British African Territories. Colonial and Commonwealth Relations Offices: London.

---------- (1957)
An African Survey Revised. Oxford University Press.

HILL, P. (1963)
The Migrant Cocoa-Farmers of Southern Ghana: a Study in Rural Capitalism. Cambridge: Cambridge University Press.

HUNT, A. (1983)
review of Collins 1982, 46 Modern Law Review 236-243.

JAMES, R.W. (1973)
Modern Land Law of Nigeria. Ile-Ife (Nigeria): University of Ife Press.

JAMES, R.W. and A.B. KASUNMU (1966)
Alienation of Family Property in Southern Nigeria. Ibadan University Press.

KANTOROWICZ, H. (1934)
"Some Rationalism About Realism," 43 Yale Law Journal 1240.

KASUNMU, A.B. and J.W. SALACUSE (1966)
Nigerian Family Law. London: Butterworths.

KEAY, E.A. and S.S. RICHARDSON (1966)
The Native and Customary Courts of Nigeria. London: Sweet & Maxwell.

LLOYD, P.C. (1962)
Yoruba and Land Law. London.

LUCKHAM, R. (1978)
"Imperialism, Law and Structural Dependence: The Ghana Legal Profession," 9 Development and Change 201-243.

NWABUEZE, B.O. (1972)
Nigerian Land Law. Enugu (Nigeria): Nwamife Publishers.

OLLENNU, N.A. (1962)
Principles of Customary Land Law in Ghana. (1st ed.) London: Sweet & Maxwell.

---------- (1985)
Principles of Customary Land Law in Ghana. (2nd ed.) Birmingham: CAL Press.

RATTRAY, R.S. (1923)
Ashanti. London: O.U.P.

SALACUSE, J.W. (1965)
"Birth, Death and the Marriage Act: Some Problems in Conflict of Laws," 1 Nigerian Law Journal 59-72.

SARBAH, J.M. (1904)
Fanti Customary Laws. (2nd ed.) London (reprinted, 1968, London: Frank Cass).

SCHACHT, J. (1964)
An Introduction to Islamic Law. Oxford: Clarendon Press.

SEIDMAN, R.B. (1966)
"Law and Economic Development in Independent, English-Speaking, Sub-Saharan Africa," Wisconsin Law Review 999.

SNYDER, F.G. (1981)
Capitalism and Legal Change: an African Transformation. New York: Academic Press.

---------- (1982)
"Colonialism and Legal Form: the Creation of 'Customary Law' in Senegal," in C. Sumner (ed.), Crime, Justice and Underdevelopment. London: Heinemann (also published in a slightly shorter form in 19 Journal of Legal Pluralism 49-90, 1981).

WOODMAN, G.R. (1963)
"The Acquisition of Family Land in Ghana," 7 Journal of African Law 136-151.

---------- (1964)
"The Alienation of Family Land in Ghana," 1 University of Ghana Law Journal 23-41.

---------- (1967)
"The Formalities and Incidents of Conveyances in Ghana," 4 University of Ghana Law Journal 1-27.

---------- (1969a)
"Some Realism About Customary Law the West African Experience," Wisconsin Law Review 128-152.

---------- (1969b)
"Estoppel by Judicial Decision in Ghana," 13 Journal of African Law 80-97.

---------- (1970)
"Rights to Fixtures in Customary Law," 7 University of Ghana Law Journal 70-76.

---------- (1971)
"Acquiescence in English Law and the Customary Land Law of Ghana and Nigeria," 15 Journal of African Law 41-59.

---------- (1974)
"The Family as a Corporation in Ghanaian and Nigerian Law," 11 African Law Studies 1-35.

---------- (1976)
"Rationale of the Head of Family's Immunity to Actions for Accounts," 8 Review of Ghana Law 147-152.

---------- (1985)
"Customary Law, Modern Courts, and the Notion of Institutionalization of Norms in Ghana and Nigeria," in A. Allott and G.R. Woodman (eds.) 143-63.

---------- (1987)
Customary Land Law in the Ghanaian Courts. Birmingham and Legon: CAL Press and University of Ghana, forthcoming.

Part III

Constitutional Arrangements

Entering Canadian confederation the Dene experiment

John U. Bayly

In Canada's Northwest Territories the aboriginal peoples are currently negotiating over their aboriginal rights with the Government of Canada. These rights are based on lands which the aboriginal peoples claim to have used and occupied since time immemorial. Several groups are in the process of exchanging their aboriginal title to land (which has never been successfully defined in law) for rights and benefits which are more easily understood by the Euro-Canadian legal system. Part of this exchange involves the granting of lands to the aboriginal peoples either in fee simple or to be held for them in trust by a government or a corporation. Other rights in land are also under discussion. These include subsurface rights to oil, gas and minerals and the rights to preferential or special uses of renewable resources such as game, fish and timber.

Among the negotiating groups are the Dene of the Mackenzie Basin, a region of more than 450,000 square miles of boreal forest, great freshwater lakes and a major river system. The Dene differ from the other aboriginal peoples of Canada's north in one important respect. So far they have not expressed a wish to give up their aboriginal lands following the pattern of land settlements they have seen in James Bay (northern Quebec), in Alaska and across continental North America. Instead, they are seeking land control by negotiating a new system of public government for all northerners regardless of race. This would entail a government based on the Dene's own traditions rather than on those of Britain which have supplied the model for the rest of Canada.

The Dene began the process of negotiating such political and constitutional change at the aboriginal rights negotiating table. They were persuaded by the Government of Canada to take the debate to other northern residents who would be affected but who were not present or represented at that table. A Western Constitutional Forum was created to provide a venue for all to carry on the debate the Dene had helped to initiate.

Who are the Dene? Michael Asch says:

> Anthropologists know them as the Northern Athapascan-speaking peoples of the Mackenzie River Valley who live in what is now called the Northwest Territories in Canada's western sub-Arctic. They are usually referred to in our literature by their regional or 'tribal' designations such as Slaveys, Dogribs, Chipewayans, and Hare.[1]

What brought the Dene, at this point in Canadian history, to their unique position? To answer this we need to look briefly at their relations over the years with the Government of Canada.

I. Negotiations Between the Dene and the Government of Canada

Unlike the other aboriginal peoples of the Northwest Territories, the Dene signed treaties with the Government of Canada. Treaty Number 8, covering the area south of Great Slave Lake, was signed in 1899 and Treaty Number 11, covering the Mackenzie River and its environs, was signed in 1921. By these treaties the Dene surrendered their title to much of their traditional land. In return for this title they received treaty benefits, goods and cash payments which continue to be made to this day. The Dene have always interpreted these as peace treaties rather than treaties which took away their lands. As one of the preconditions to signing, many of the chiefs insisted on assurances that the Dene would be permitted to use and occupy their lands indefinitely. These assurances were given. However, unlike most treaties, the terms of these set aside no lands as reserves for the Dene. Subsequent efforts to set aside reserve lands have been resisted by the Dene and their descendants. With the exception of a small tract of land on Vale Island in the mouth of the Hay River, there are no reserves in the Northwest Territories.

In the early 1970s, acting on their belief that title to their lands had never been surrendered, the Dene chiefs, led by Francois Paulette of Forth Smith, sought to file a caveat[2] in the Northwest Territories Land Titles (Registry) Office to warn all land holders of the unsurrendered Dene interest in the area covered by the treaties. The Registrar of Land Titles refused to accept the caveat and the matter was dealt with in the courts. Mr. Justice Morrow of the Territorial (now Supreme) Court of the Northwest Territories travelled through the lands covered by Treaties 8 and 11 and heard evidence from witnesses, signatories and interpreters who had been present when the treaties were signed. He concluded that aboriginal title to the lands had not been surrendered as the treaties indicated, and he permitted the caveat to be filed. This decision was overturned on appeal. The case went to the Supreme Court of Canada which held that the caveat could not be filed because most of the lands described in it were 'unpatented', in other words, not within the land titles system recently set up under federal legislation in the Northwest Territories. The Supreme Court decision did not deal with the issue of whether the Dene had surrendered title to their aboriginal lands.

Buoyed by the recognition Mr. Justice Morrow had given to their assertion that their title had not been surrendered, the Dene declared themselves to be a nation within Canada and began to talk, not about giving up lands, but about recognition of their nationhood and limited sovereignty over Dene lands. In 1976 the Dene presented a paper to the Government of Canada styled an 'Agreement in Principle'. In it they stated their interpretation of the treaties:

> For our forefathers, the treaties were an agreement with the non-Dene whereby we would live in peace and mutual respect, whereby our right to continued self-determination would be guaranteed.[3]

However, they presented a view of the history of the treaties which many, even after reading the evidence before the Territorial Court in the Paulette case, would regard as revisionist. Among other things they stated:

> In 1899 and 1921 our forefathers saw fit to enter into Treaties 8 and 11 with the Dominion of Canada. We did so in an effort to protect our interests from the continuing invasion of non-Dene. Our forefathers saw a need to obtain assurance from the non-Dene government, whom they felt was responsible for the actions of non-Dene on Dene lands, that the security of our way of life would not be undermined, that our right to continue to lead our chosen way of life and govern our own affairs would not be challenged.[4]

It can be argued from the historical record that the Dene were eager for a treaty because they also felt it would bring twine for nets, ammunition, medical attention and government aid in times of deprivation and need.

However, whether or not the Dene's historical interpretation is accurate need not be of concern in this discussion. What was apparent by 1976 was a clearly stated Dene goal of self-government. In fact, the seventh principle they sought unsuccessfully to have the Government of Canada accept was:

> There will, therefore, be within Confederation, a Dene government with jurisdiction over a geographical area and over subject matters now within the jurisdiction of either the Government of Canada or the Government of the Northwest Territories.[5]

The Dene were concerned that in any government structure which might be proposed the non-Dene in their midst would overwhelm them. The solution in their 1976 Proposal was for separate institutions for Dene and non-Dene. This was stiffly resisted by the Government of Canada and alienated many of those who might otherwise have supported them. It was clearly a political concept with no prospect of implementation and the Government of Canada turned its back, not only on the so-called Agreement in Principle, but also on the Dene.

It was four years before the Dene reappeared politically. By 1981 they had reassessed their political objectives and published a discussion paper, *Denendeh, Public Government for the People of the North*. According to the paper, the Dene no longer seek separate institutions for themselves. Instead, they are saying:

> As in the past, we still make decisions today according to our own rules of order and conduct, with maximum involvement and participation of people, with respect for rights of the individual and the community and by consensus. Our proposal builds on these traditions to create a modern democratic political structure suitable to the needs of the Dene and other Canadians.[6]

The Proposal provides that after a 10-year residence in Denendeh, the Dene province-like jurisdiction, and two years in a particular community, any resident who is a Canadian citizen shall have the right to vote and run for office. The Dene have stated in discussions that the 10-year residence requirement is negotiable and have remained in the discussions when three to five years have been suggested. They ask for exclusive representation only in the Denendeh Senate, the functions of which would be limited to review and veto of legislation which would prejudice aboriginal rights.

The Dene have obviously made major concessions in this proposal. And yet it is obvious that it represents but another approach to the central goal of their legal and political struggle, namely to maintain control over their traditional lands. Land is the central issue because to the Dene, the man-land relationship is fundamental. It is fundamental because the Dene rely on the land for their basic protein sources, meat and fish. It is fundamental because the trapping economy still provides a stable source of community income and something to fall back on when other things fail. It is fundamental because the Dene define themselves, and see themselves, as a land-based people.

II. Dene Man-land Relationships

Let us examine the Dene man-land relationships, past and present, and compare what we find with what is contained in the Denendeh Proposal. Such a comparison ought to indicate whether the Dene are really attempting to incorporate their land-based folk law traditions into this constitutional experiment.

Uncovering the past traditions is not easy. Much of the Dene traditional man-land relationship has disappeared or been altered in post-contact times. As June Helm MacNeish, recognized authority on Dene customs, observes:

> Of the truly aboriginal condition of the Northeastern Athabascans, there is, of course, no direct knowledge. In even the earliest reports it is evident that the contact situation had already wrought changes in the aboriginal way of life. Indeed, if Hearne is correct, the smallpox epidemic circa 1781 so destroyed the population (90 per cent of the Chipewyans by Hearne's estimate) that Northeastern Athabascan society must have been shaken to its foundations. ... Another indirect effect of the European world upon Dene society that preceded the first explorer was the stimulation given to the gun-bearing Crees to raid and plunder the defenseless Mackenzie River Dene for their furs. Whole populations fled their home territories in consequence. ... That these factors affected the socio-political organization may be well surmized, but the facts are unknown.[7]

As she points out elsewhere, the fur trade economy, technological changes, and government regulations further altered the evolving Dene pre-contact, man-land relationship:

> ... Such evidence as can be gathered from informants concerning earlier times indicates that the more aboriginal condition of settlement for the Indian was deeper into the bush, centring around "fish lakes", which provided food when land game failed. Today, the Indian bush communities have moved to the river for easy access to the fort. Also, they have become much more stabilized. Log cabins, in other words

> permanent dwellings, are now built. People either live in them most of the year round or work out from them as bases for their trap-line activities. The factors in this increased 'sederunty' (Honigmann) are several. For one thing, the increase in material possessions makes their continual moving about less feasible. And of course when furs can be traded for food, the mobility demanded by the old-time food quest is obviated. The government's actions have been the decisive factor in the settling of the Indian at a permanent base. For many decades there was the trap-line allotment which, by allowing a man to trap only along a certain route in the bush, made a fully mobile camp life pointless. ... The trap-line system has recently been superseded in most sections of the Mackenzie region by the band-area allotment system. ... They may set their trap-lines as they wish within the area, observing other persons' priorities, but they may not go outside that area to trap without government consent.[8]

The mobility stimulated and demanded by the 'old-time food quest' is well demonstrated in the accounts of the early European explorers who travelled through the Dene lands. For example, Samuel Hearne set out in December of 1770 from Fort Prince of Wales, now Churchill, Manitoba, with the Chipewayan chief, Matonabbee, who was from that area. Matonabbee had agreed to take Hearne to the Coppermine River. Six months into their overland walking trip, probably near what is now Point Lake, their party encountered a group of Copper Indians. Hearne says: 'Having arrived on the North side of this river, we found that Matonabbee, and several others in our company, were personally acquainted with most of the Copper Indians whom we found there.'[9] Throughout the journey Matonabbee evidently knew exactly where he was, where to obtain bark for canoes where birch trees were scarce, where caribou were likely to be encountered and when fish were plentiful enough to sustain his party of several dozen. And one must keep in mind that the round trip took some 18 months to complete.

The Dene understanding of country and sense of direction was highly sophisticated as well. Sir John Franklin describes the knowledge of geography and land use of his guide-to-be Akaitcho and his band of Yellowknife Indians.

> As the water was unusually high this season, the Indian guides recommended our going by a shorter route to the Copper-Mine River than that they had first proposed to Mr. Wentzel, and they assigned as a reason for the change, that the rein-deer would be sooner found upon

> this track. They then drew a chart of the proposed route on the floor with charcoal, exhibiting a chain of twenty-five small lakes extending towards the north, about one half of them connected by a river which flows into Slave Lake, near Fort Providence. One of the guides, named Keskarrah, drew the Copper-Mine River, running through the Upper Lake in a westerly direction towards the Great Bear Lake, and then northerly to the sea. The other guide drew the river in a straight line to the sea from the above-mentioned place, but, after some dispute, admitted the correctness of the first delineation.[10]

Akaitcho went on to recommend the establishment of a winter fort at the headwaters of the Snare River. This site indeed affords the only adequate building timber for scores of miles and the last opportunity to build winter quarters before reaching the barrens, which are a mere half dozen miles to the north. Having travelled the Akaitcho route myself by canoe in 1970 with the aid of aerial photographs, detailed maps and space age gear, I was humbled by the knowledge of the country that the Dene had in the early 1820s.

And what of the Dene of recent times? It is evident that land is important to them economically and spiritually, but have the man-land relationship and related customs altered since the time of Helm's observations in the early 1950s? Do the Dene have a land tenure system either surviving from earlier times or one of more recent origin which has been influenced by contact with Europeans?

Although they find the exclusive ownership and the buying and selling of property in our agricultural and urban man-land relationships strange and alienating, the Dene have a strong sense of territoriality. They have not been shy about expressing their feelings about the land and their relationship to it and have done so in public hearings and in the press. For example, speaking to Mr. Justice Berger at the Mackenzie Valley Pipeline Inquiry in Aklavik, Mary Husky said:

> We don't want to give up our land. We are stingy of our lands, and when we were first given a Treaty, no one spoke of taking our land from us ... Now they are trying to take our land from us and we are very stingy of it, and we live off the land, and don't eat white man's food, especially the older people live off the land. And besides, it is our land they are going to build the pipeline on, and we are very much against it, very much so.[11]

Not only are they stingy in the sense that they will resist the encroachment of outsiders on their lands, but they are territorially competitive amongst themselves.

If the Dene are a nation, as they profess to be, then they are a nation of tribal peoples. They speak five languages. According to their most recent definition of themselves in their aboriginal claims negotiations, they include the Cree, Chipewayan, Slavey, Dogrib and Loucheux peoples. If lands are to be exclusively Dene lands, can we assume that they are in the first instance exclusively Dogrib, or Slavey, or Loucheux? In the past, raiding between tribes was not uncommon, and open warfare was a phenomenon of even post-contact times. Dene stories and legends are full of accounts of the treachery of other Dene tribal peoples and the boldness and cunning of the storyteller's own.

Today the Dene sense of ownership is said to be collective. Nevertheless, they have a sense of exclusivity which appears to have been sharpened by generations of conflict and competiton - much of it amongst the tribes which make up the present Dene Nation. In recent times conflicts within the core of a tribal area are largely sorted out by the politics of band and family. Permission must be sought by a newcomer, whatever his tribal origins, to use lands for hunting, fishing and trapping. On the periphery the disputes may remain unresolved, particularly as between tribal groups. For example, although both Slavey and Dogrib people use the Horn Plateau country, each tribe thinks of the other as something of an intruder. Although there are no hostilities, it is easy to detect resentment. But it is not only from competition and conflict that the Dene derive their traditional views of land. It is also from their patterns of land use. The observations of Helm (supra) indicate that the patterns have been changing, particularly in post-contact times. Have the changes resulted in the erosion of the system or in its evolution? The evidence is scanty and confusing. However, there appear to be some surviving features from earlier times. Of the earlier man-land relationship, Asch reports:

> The evidence suggests the existence of a tenure system in which the ownership of land as a means of production was vested in a collective larger than the local band. In practice, this unit was probably the Dene who lived in a particular marriage isolate.[12]

There remain vestiges of that tenure system to this day. A Dogrib woman told me of the 'inheritance' of her grandmother's trapping area. A Loucheux chief informed me that he sends his sons down river to trap and fish from the camp he built. I observed a 101 year old woman from Fort MacPherson who sat in the middle of her family, of about two dozen people of five generations, as they split and dried fish at a camp on the Peel River. Although she was not overseeing or organizing the work, she was evidently the titular head of the family group and great deference was paid to her knowledge of bush lore.[13]

In spite of these examples it is clear that there are many factors which may have modified the earlier tenure system. For example, the airplane provides access to country and to game which might otherwise remain unhunted. Therefore, it is unnecessary to travel through another person's area to reach it. Forest fires destroy or alter habitat forcing people off traditional lands and into country occupied by others. Winter roads into mining properties provide access to game for native and non-native people. Motor toboggans (skidoos) provide not only access to a greater area of land, but the option to hunt and trap part time (for the wage earning native person).

These are perhaps indicators of change, but do they affect the values which underlie the traditions? As Chief Justice deWeerdt of the Supreme Court of the Northwest Territories said in a recent judgment:

> Today, the traditional pursuits and methods of the indigenous peoples of the Northwest Territories have been modified by reliance upon firearms, powered vehicles and vessels, and other artifacts of industrial society. Tradition, viewed in that light, is a living, evolving and still developing reality. It must not be understood in a narrow or technical sense, if the purpose of Section 22 of the Northwest Fishery Regulations enacted pursuant to the *Fisheries Act* of Canada is to be fulfilled. As defined by Walker in the *Oxford Companion to Law*, at page 1230;
>
> *Tradition*. The aggregate of beliefs, customs, habits and practice which develop in a particular culture and, by being continued, give it continuity.[14]

One important change is that the Dene can no longer be said to live in particular marriage isolates. Arranged marriages are now a relic of the past. The Dene have been drawn into towns, hamlets and villages from a wide area. Their children have attended residential schools. They have intermarried between bands, tribes and beyond, and have moved about. Native people from other parts of Canada have settled in the Dene communities. The Dene have begun to identify with the settlements, hamlets and towns of their permanent residences. They spend considerably more time at home than on the land. Politically it is the community, through its Band Council, Community Council or Hunters and Trappers Association, which deals with land-related problems. Lands are identified as community lands. Where a single community is not influential enough, communities will try to co-operate on a regional basis. The regions are, for the most part, the tribal groupings. In one case among the Loucheux communities, a Mackenzie Delta Regional Dene Council has been formed to deal mainly with the problems associated with oil and gas development on the lands of the Loucheux and with the competing, or overlapping, land interests of the Inuvialuit or Western Arctic Eskimo. The Dogribs and the Slaveys are looking at both the regional Dene councils and regional governments set up under Territorial legislation.

Sometimes the communities or regions will call upon the Dene Nation and Metis Association, which they call national organizations, for assistance. But the land problems are expressed for the most part in community terms, band terms or tribal areas of interest and use.

III. The 1981 Proposals on Land Tenure

With their far from static relationships between man and land, what are the Dene proposing be their new constitutional relationship to their land? The Dene Proposal of 1981[15] proposes that land and its resources should be owned and managed in three categories. First, 'Exclusive Dene Land' would form a large proportion of the total. Its management would be the sole responsibility of the Dene, acting through such agencies and institutions as they collectively determined, and complying as far as possible with the resource development decisions of the Government of Denendeh. Secondly, the remaining land and resources other than private property would be 'Land and Resources Controlled by the Government of Denendeh'. In these the aboriginal rights of the Dene to hunt, fish and trap would take precedence over all other uses. The Government of Denendeh would manage them according to the Charter of founding Principles. Decisions on the development of non-renewable resources would be subject to the following conditions:

(a) The resource is surplus to Denendeh's own needs, determined on a reasonable basis of present and future consumption.

(b) The southern Canadian need is determined on the basis of 'a conserver society' level of usage and a firm commitment to renewables.

(c) Exploration, development and transportation will not create undue social dislocation in Denendeh or any of the communities most directly affected.

(d) Preparation, construction and operation of the facilities will not damage the environment of Denendeh or any of the communities most directly affected.

(e) The project is judged to be technically sound.

(f) The project has been determined to be financially feasible and economic benefits will accrue to the Government of Denendeh.

(g) The project is consistent with the economic development plans of the Government of Denendeh.

(h) Ten percent of all resource revenues collected by governments will be paid into an Aboriginal Trust Fund (a Dene Heritage Fund) controlled by the Dene.

(i) The remaining resource revenue accruing to the Government of Denendeh from the sale of non-renewable resources will be distributed in the following way:

.. first to cover the costs of government in Denendeh at both the community and 'provincial' levels;

.. in the event that revenues in any given year are less than the costs of government, the Government of Canada will make up the difference;

.. in the event that revenues exceed the costs of government in Denendeh, the excess money will be first used to pay the Government of Canada for direct federal assistance going into Denendeh, such as unemployment insurance benefits, children's allowances, etc.;

... in the event that there is enough revenue to provide for the above, the rest will be divided 50% to the Government of Denendeh and 50% to the Government of Canada.[16]

Thirdly, 'Private Property' in the form of present titles of ownership would be honoured, but future grants would be limited to long leases with occupancy rights, while a native collective or the Government of Denendeh retained ownership. Within a community, certain lands would be designated as available for leasing in this category on terms set by the community. Outside the communities, terms would be negotiated with the owning collective or government.

Is there very much new to non-Dene in this part of the Proposal, or would Denendeh really be a province in which the Dene held a large area of land as (collective) private owners and their provincial (Denendeh) government owned the Crown land? The main difference appears to be that private ownership, except insofar as it includes ownership by the Dene collectively, will be the exception, not the rule.

What may be of more significance is that the Dene have sought a formula for determination of the worth of resource developing projects. Furthermore, they have proposed that the wealth derived from oil and gas and mineral extraction be distributed in ways which appear similar to the way game and fish are divided in their small communities. It is their traditions and practices of sharing what the land produces that they have suggested be the basis of the new man-land relationship which they have proposed.

Let us examine the proposal that land will be owned by the Government of Denendeh or a native collective and that only lands within community boundaries will be under the control of community governments. This appears to run contrary to the developing trend amongst the Dene to identify lands well beyond community boundaries with the community and its native residents. For example, the Community Council of Fort Good Hope, the first settlement to experiment with a combination of Dene band and municipal government, is seeking an expanded boundary to gain control of the hinterland surrounding the settlement, and in that particular case, the adjacent community of Colville Lake, some 80 miles east.

From a native perspective there is nothing novel in this. The Alaskan natives organized themselves into boroughs to include lands within village government control and the Inuvialuit, through their Committee for Original Peoples' Entitlement (COPE), are pursuing a Western Arctic Regional Municipality in their land claims negotiations and elsewhere.

A regional municipality could hardly be said to be a Dene folk organization. Unfortunately, the Dene have not expanded on or explained what they mean by a 'native collective' as the expression is used in their land tenure proposal. Is it intentional that it is expressed in the singular? If so, it departs from any traditions we can trace save the general tradition of collectivity. If they mean 'native collectives' in the more local sense, folk traditions may be incorporated. Perhaps it will emerge as a tribal council or even the existing Chief and Band Council. Both these options have been discussed and their functioning in this way would be consistent with the Dene traditions of land control, although neither would exactly satisfy Asch's definition.

If land is held by the Government of Denendeh, have the Dene proposed no more than the transfer of the root of title from the Crown in Right of Canada (the federal authority) to the Crown in Right of Denendeh (the provincial authority)? If they have, the Proposal again runs contrary to their traditions as they appear to have evolved.

The Proposal is clear that authority will not be granted to community governments beyond their boundaries. And in the exercise of that authority which is granted within those boundaries, community governments will be far less autonomous than municipalities are under current Territorial legislation.[17] Although I have suggested that the Denendeh Proposal is reflective of Dene traditions and values in the sharing of resources extracted from the land, it is apparent that local self-determination would be restricted to community boundaries and by guiding principles. Have the Dene consciously traded off the stronger local and regional authority which appears consistent with their evolving values and traditions for a strong central government which may be better able to withstand the outside world on their behalf? I would be better able to advance that theory had I seen this problem discussed and debated amongst the Dene themselves. In their assemblies and leadership meetings, there has been little discussion of the Proposal and none that I am aware of on this point.

Strangely enough, the Dene in their communities have not reacted in public to the limitations proposed on their local self-determination. There has not been a whimper about the failure to include or even acknowledge the long-standing regional and corresponding tribal unities and initiatives. Perhaps the lengthy list of 'heads of jurisdiction' has impressed the Dene leaders at the community level so that the corresponding lack of powers has gone unnoticed. Perhaps they are just biding their time until the division of powers is discussed, when they will remind their national leaders of the Dene traditions which must underlie any constitutional relationship made in their image. Or perhaps strong central authority reaches back to the traditions of their great chiefs who roamed freely across the country and they are content. Perhaps they are even reassured by it, particularly if they can retain numerical majority at the polls and remove large tracts of land for their exclusive use into the bargain.

I have found that there is very little public debate in the Dene communities about the Denendeh Proposal. Nor does there seem to be a grass roots movement to achieve the Denendeh community objectives. I have detected a reticence to be critical of the Proposal and the 'collective' support is largely delivered in the form of silence. There is some evidence that it is not well understood. The document is not available in any of the Dene languages although parts of it have been discussed at leadership meetings and tape recordings of portions of the document in translation have been distributed by the Dene Nation office.

But the Dene have continued to stress that the Denendeh document is first and foremost a proposal, a working document. It has been presented to the people of Northern Canada for discussion. It is being taken apart, modified and reassembled by a variety of people, governments and interest groups. Regional governments, tribal councils and altered community government structures have, among other things, been proposed. The debate continues on a semi-formal basis at the Western Constitutional Forum where the major interests have been actively represented. The Dene Nation and Metis Association of the Northwest Territories have been involved, but increasingly, the detail is being discussed by constitutional experts and work is being contracted out to consultants from Southern Canada. It is too early to tell whether the Dene will want to, or be forced to, agree to a man-land relationship which departs from and, in the worst case, undermines their own traditional concepts of land law.

For a time the Dene and Metis appeared to have withdrawn from the debate. Although their political leaders still attended meetings of the Western Constitutional Forum, fewer and fewer of the ideas expressed used the Denendeh document as their touchstone. Instead, there was an increasing reaction to (and sometimes against) the more aggressive and clearer position of the Inuit and the Nunavut territory immediately to the north and east of the Denendeh region.

There was some indication that Dene and Metis regretted their failure to oppose division of the Northwest Territories. They remained increasingly concerned that if they did not achieve their objectives for self-government modelled on their approach prior to the division of the Northwest Territories, they might be unable to do so afterwards when they could very well be the minority of the population in the Denendeh region.

During 1984 it appeared to many observers as though a stalemate had been reached on both the division of the Northwest Territories and political and constitutional development in Denendeh. Early in January of 1985, however, the Western and Nunavut Constitutional Forums met together and emerged from two days of meetings with a tentative boundary to recommend to both their peoples. They certainly used the work of constitutional experts and consultants from other parts of Canada, but in the political negotiations that took place, it was the Dene, Metis and Inuit political ideas that were debated. In that meeting, they reconfirmed their shared belief that political government structures with special aboriginal rights provisions represent the best prospects for the exercise of sufficient and extensive political jurisdiction in the present Northwest Territories. They reaffirmed their belief that failure to achieve such structures would lead to fragmentation of the political system and a variety of small units ethnically defined and limited in political strength. Interestingly, the dividing line places the Dene and Metis with the Inuvialuit, a small but aggressive group of Western Arctic Eskimos who have just recently settled their land claims with the Government of Canada. They are seeking their own political self-determination through a Western Arctic Regional Municipality in which they would have many provincial powers. The Inuvialuit may, by their presence and influence in the Denendeh territory, strengthen the Dene and Metis positions and arguments for responsible self-government in their own image. They may also, because their ways and traditions and goals differ, frustrate the Dene and Metis aspirations.

It is too early to tell what this very recent change will do. There is no doubt that it will reinvigorate the debate and bring very much closer the creation of two separate territories, each with its own province-like government. The Minister of Indian and Northern Affairs for the Government of Canada is of that view. In opening the Legislative Assembly of the Northwest Territories in early February 1985, he committed Canada to division of the Territories by 1987 and urged northern peoples to incorporate aboriginal customs and traditions into the democratic forms of self-government which Canadian northern peoples design.

Notes

1. Asch, 1982:347.
2. A caveat is a document which can be registered against land advising or warning present and subsequent owners and encumbrancers that the caveator has or claims to have an interest in the land.
3. Dene Nation, 1976:1.
4. Ibid.:3.
5. Ibid.:3.
6. Dene Nation, 1981:5.
7. MacNeish, 1956:131-32.
8. Helm, 1961:9-10.
9. Hearne, 1958:77.
10. Franklin, 1969:204
11. *Transcript of Proceedings at the Mackenzie Valley Pipeline Inquiry,* Community Hearings Volume I, p. 31.
12. Asch, 1982:347.
13. Personal observation, August, 1981.
14. *The Queen v Rocher,* [1983] Northwest Territories Reports 123, 138.
15. Dene Nation,1981.
16. Ibid.
17. Ibid.:13.

References

ASCH, Michael (1982)
"Dene Self-Determination and the Study of Hunter Gatherors in the Modern World," in Eleanor Leacock and Richard Lee (eds.), Politics and History in Band Societies. Cambridge University Press: Cambridge, England.

DENE NATION (1976)
Agreement in Principle between the Dene Nation and Her Majesty the Queen in Right of Canada. Yellowknife.

---------- (1981)
Denedeh. Public Government for the People of the North. Yellowknife.

FRANKLIN, John (1969)
Narrative of a Journey to the Shores of the Polar Sea in the Years 1819, 20, 21 and 22. Hurtig.

HEARNE, Samuel (1958)
A Journey to the Northern Ocean, 1769-72, Richard Glover (ed.). MacMillan.

HELM, June (1961)
The Lynx Point People: The Dynamics of a Northern Athabaskan Band. National Museum of Canada, Bulletin No. 176.

MacNEISH, June Helm (1956)
"Leadership among the Northeastern Athabascan," Anthropologica II, Ottawa.

The Inuit and customary law: constitutional perspectives

Jeff Richstone

I. Introduction

The process of constitutional reform in Canada has been marked by ideological conflict, political theatre, historical accident and judicial drama, set against a serious and often bitter power struggle between federal and provincial authorities. That the aboriginal peoples of Canada forced themselves upon the arena of national reform in the late 1970s, and by and large succeeded in being recognized as major political actors, is less a reflection of the solicitude with which governments viewed their concerns, as it is a testimony to their political skills and the rapidity with which they learned the crucial lessons of national politics.[1]

On March 15-16, 1983, the First Ministers of the ten provinces attended a conference convened by the then Prime Minister of Canada Pierre Trudeau, in fulfillment of the terms of Part IV, section 37 of the *Constitution Act,* 1982.[2] To cite the words of subsection 37(2), the conference was to discuss "constitutional matters that directly affect the aboriginal peoples of Canada, including the identification and definition of the rights of those peoples to be included in the Constitution of Canada". For the first time in Canadian history representatives of the four national aboriginal organizations -- the Inuit Committee on National Issues (ICNI), the Assembly of First Nations (AFN), the Native Council of Canada (NCC) and the Metis National Council (MNC) -- directly participated along with Canada's highest ranking non-native politicians in a constitutional conference.[3] The governments of the two territories, the Northwest Territories and the Yukon, were also invited.[4]

At the close of the conference, all parties, with the exception of Quebec, whose participation was limited as a result of its opposition to the patriation process,[5] signed the *1983 Constitutional Accord on Aboriginal Rights.*[6] Despite its lofty title, the Accord had little to say about the content of aboriginal rights, but it did call for passage of a Resolution in Parliament and in the provincial legislatures to make several critical amendments to the *Constitution Act, 1982.* One amendment established an ongoing process of constitutional discussions: there were to be three further First Ministers Conferences, in 1984, 1985 and 1987.[7]

The agenda for this series of conferences was embodied in the Accord. It had formed the agenda for the 1983 Conference, but, running to 19 separate items, could not possibly be covered in a two-day affair. One item that figures within the Accord, headed 'Statement of the Particular Rights of Aboriginal Peoples', alone comprises a number of discrete rights and freedoms that aboriginal peoples had argued should be subsumed under aboriginal rights. All this was left for future conferences to settle.

The next two Conferences were dominated by the issues of self-government and sexual equality. That of 1984, convened on March 8-9, was undermined at the outset by a Prime Minister who had earlier announced his resignation and by an impending federal election which the opposition party looked likely to win. Consequently the government's proposal regarding self-government made without warning in Trudeau's opening speech won no acceptance.[8] A last-hour proposal dealing with sexual equality rights was also rejected and the Conference ended in failure.

The 1985 Conference was also dominated by the issue of self-government--clearly the most important item on the constitutional agenda for the aboriginal peoples. The federal government tabled a proposal for an accord; it contained a suggested constitutional amendment which would have set out a right of self-government for the aboriginal peoples, subject to a process of negotiation with the appropriate federal and provincial authorities.[9] It was unclear on the first day whether this proposal would have the acceptance of the necessary number of provinces required for a constitutional amendment. On the second day of the meeting a compromise version was tabled, which gained the support of the needed number of provinces and, moreover, two of the four aboriginal associations. The Inuit delegation asked for, and were granted, a two-month delay to further study the proposal. At a later meeting of ministers held in June 1985, ICNI rejected the proposal and the 1984-85 reform process ended in stalemate.[10]

As of the present writing, the agenda for the 1987 Conference has not yet been set; it is evident that the issue of self-government will again predominate unless consensus forms in the near future on a compromise proposal. This may well occur should the parties decide on a conference in 1986. In any case, the agenda that figures in the 1983 Accord is still the operative legal text dealing with the constitutional reform process. Its outline of the major issues confronting aboriginal peoples will be as relevant in 1987 as it was in 1983. The topic of this paper is the right of the aboriginal peoples to practise their customs and traditions. The next section will examine in some detail the discussions at the various meetings just referred to in so far as they dealt with this topic. The final section will consider the constitutional options and arguments regarding the topic. It is possible that it will not be discussed or resolved by the last constitutionally mandated conference. It is certain, however, that the questions raised by this subject, because of its importance to Canada's aboriginal peoples, must some day be discussed and finally settled in the constitutional forum.

II. Review of the constitutional discussions relating to Aboriginal customary law 1982-85

The deal that was struck in January of 1981[11] between the federal government and aboriginal political leaders survived patriation in somewhat tarnished form and became legal reality on April 17, 1982, when the Queen proclaimed the *Constitution Act, 1982*.[12] The section 37 process dealing with aboriginal constitutional matters was thus set in motion.

The process was initiated in late fall of 1982 and a series of preparatory meetings were held at the official and ministerial level throughout the winter and spring of 1982-3. Customary law was placed under the heading of 'family law'. Aboriginal speakers, particularly Inuit, called for entrenchment of customary law in the Constitution. Inuit representatives stressed the persistent conflict between provincial law dealing with civil matters[13] and the Inuit 'lex loci'.[14] A frequently cited example was drawn from adoption practices: most provincial laws do not allow for disclosure of the identity of the natural parent as a matter of course without consent. Inuit custom, however, insists on the beneficial consequences gained from open acknowledgement of the adopted child's biological parents.[15]

Government response was predictably cautious. Some officials recognized the strains between aboriginal customs and provincial laws in family matters. That recognition of traditional practices should be constitutionally expressed was not rejected out of hand. Concerns were voiced regarding the practical consequences of recognition once elevated to a constitutional rule -- would existing provincial rules relating to marriage and adoption be immediately replaced by aboriginal law? would aboriginal customs that ran counter to non-aboriginal values be constitutionally impregnable? Unfortunately, subsequent discussions did little to clarify or settle these questions. In the remaining months prior to the 1983 First Ministers Conference, delegations became more interested in focussing on the areas that seemed likely to be addressed and resolved by First Ministers.

By the time the conference was convened, all the aboriginal associations had made public their positions on the amendments they wished to see included in the Constitution. Customs and traditions figured as specific rights for all organizations. The ICNI position was that an open-ended definitional section should be placed in Part II of the 1982 *Constitution Act* entitled 'Rights of the Aboriginal Peoples of Canada'; in its relevant portions, the proposed clause read as follows:

> The aboriginal rights of the aboriginal peoples of Canada constitute both collective and individual rights and include:
>
> (b) the right to practise their customs and traditions ...[16]

The AFN also submitted draft amendments which contained a non-exhaustive list of rights including the practice of customs and traditions. The proposals of the other two associations contained similar wording.

Although these proposals were never addressed, the federal government indicated that discussions during the preparatory sessions had produced some shift in thinking. Prime Minister Trudeau, in his opening statement to the conference, declared:

> Language, religion and custom form another set of issues which inevitably will appear on our agenda for the future. We have been successful in establishing constitutional provisions safeguarding our two official languages and assuring all ethnic groups within our society the enjoyment of their own cultural heritage. Clearly our aboriginal peoples each occupied a special place in history. To my way of thinking, this entitles them to special recognition in the Constitution and to their own place in Canadian society, distinct from each other and distinct from other groups who, together with them, comprise the Canadian citizenry. The Government of Canada is prepared to examine with the other participants in this phase of constitutional renewal ways and means of preserving through the Constitution the languages, religions and customs of the several aboriginal peoples.[17]

The federal delegation circulated a draft resolution outlining amendments for acceptance at the conference. It proposed adding a new part to the Constitution providing for an ongoing process, prefaced with a preamble of some seventy-five lines of purplish prose.[18] Its very length and belated revelation at the onset of the meeting (to say little of its content) precluded its being agreed to. The last two recitals of the preamble are directly relevant to this discussion:

> And whereas it is fitting, in the process of constitutional renewal, to identify the distinct place that the aboriginal peoples occupy in Canadian society, having regard to the cultural differences between those peoples, and to define their rights as aboriginal peoples for entrenchment in the Constitution as a charter of rights of the aboriginal peoples;
>
> And whereas it is fitting for the conferences provided for in this Part to consider the following for inclusion in that charter of rights of the aboriginal peoples:
>
> ... the preservation and enhancement of the use by the aboriginal peoples of their own cultures, customs, traditions, religions and languages including the education of their children within their own languages, as well as within one of the official languages of Canada, in order that their children may be equipped to live in the cultural milieu of their choice ...

The clause does not inform us in what manner aboriginal customs are to be constitutionally preserved and enhanced. For reasons unknown, the official languages policy of the former federal government was explicitly linked with recognition of customary law. What the one had to do with the other in a specific charter of rights of the aboriginal peoples is something which has not to this day been explained.

As indicated above, the 1984 and 1985 Conferences never addressed these questions. The subject, however, was not forgotten and the notion of aboriginal cultural rights surfaced in federal drafts. The Proposed 1984 Constitutional Accord called for a new Part to the Constitution entitled "Commitments relating to Aboriginal Peoples of Canada".[19] Commitments relating to aboriginal culture read as follows:

> 35.2 Without altering the legislative authority of Parliament or of the provincial legislatures, or the rights of any of them with respect to the exercise of their legislative authority,
>
> (a) Parliament and the legislatures, together with the government of Canada and the provincial governments, are committed to
>
> (i) preserving and enhancing the cultural heritage of the aboriginal peoples of Canada, and,

> (ii) respecting the freedom of the aboriginal peoples of Canada to live within their heritage and to educate their children in their own languages, as well as in either or both of the official languages of Canada ...

The *Proposed 1985 Accord* steered clear of constitutional amendments respecting cultural rights. The opening recital of the preamble to the Accord contained a reference to cultural rights in the following terms:[20]

> WHEREAS the aboriginal peoples of Canada, being descendants of the first inhabitants of Canada, are unique peoples in Canada enjoying the rights that flow from their status as aboriginal peoples, from treaties and from land claim settlements, as well as rights flowing from Canadian citizenship, and it is fitting that:
>
> (a) there be protection of rights of aboriginal peoples in the Constitution of Canada,
>
> (b) they have the opportunity to have self-government arrangements to meet their special circumstances as well as the opportunity to exercise their full rights as citizens of Canada and residents of the provinces and territories, and
>
> (c) they have the freedom to live in accordance with their own cultural heritage and to use and maintain their distinct languages ...

As mentioned above, the cultural elements of these drafts were not dealt with because of the priority given by the aboriginal associations to self-government. It is nevertheless clear that until this issue receives a thorough debate, culture, language and customary law will continue to occupy a special place on the constitutional agenda. It is appropriate, therefore, to consider several matters related to the recognition and enforcement of customary law.

III. Entrenching Aboriginal customary law

The aboriginal organizations have proposed constitutional recognition and enforcement of their customs and traditions. This raises two points: the terminology to be employed and the nature of the enforcement sought.

It may be questioned whether the terms 'custom' and 'tradition' ought to be preferred to 'customary law', the latter employed notably by the Papua New Guinea and Australian Law Reform Commissions.[21] Selection of any term is of course fraught with danger: "the mischief done by the word 'custom' in anthropology, where it reduced thought to habit, is perhaps only exceeded by that which it has done in legal history, where it reduced thought to practice."[22] In discussions concerning the differences between European and non-European conceptions of law, it is a commonplace to emphasize that distinctions habitually found in the one are often not found in the other. Along with certain other aboriginal peoples, Inuit, for example, do not make distinctions between on the one hand, standards of behaviour or moral norms, and on the other, binding rules which are regularly visited with sanctions or strictly regulated. Customary law exists in a socio-cultural matrix in which legal norms evolve and from which they draw their force. Jurists trained in the English common law or French civil law should not expect to discover formalized and identifiable rules in terms fashioned by those legal traditions. Notwithstanding this, Inuit throughout the circumpolar north do possess systems of law.[23]

If it is wrongheaded to question whether Inuit, or any other aboriginal people for that matter, have 'law', it is also conceptually misleading to distinguish between 'custom' and 'customary law'. These issues turn too easily on definitions which themselves are matters of theoretical policy and rhetorical preference. The reality is that any term must encompass the entire cultural life of a people, from kinship systems to quasi-penal sanctions. It was for this reason that the more compendious terms, 'custom' and 'tradition' were adopted in the constitutional drafts.

The next point to consider is legal recognition. If customs and traditions are to be legally enforceable, the question that arises is in which forum will these matters be addressed. No proposal of the aboriginal associations has called for a completely autonomous court system and the diversity of Canada's aboriginal peoples would render such an idea impractical. Moreover, many aboriginal people (particularly Metis and 'non-status' Indians) do not presently live on an exclusive land base and would not benefit from separate judicial systems set up to administer law on aboriginal-controlled lands.

Accordingly customary law would be dealt with, at least in part, by the ordinary court system. This in itself raises a great many questions. The first concerns how the aboriginal custom is treated by the state court forum. When a court is invited to select which rules of customary law to apply, and in which circumstances, the legal situation has been described as an 'internal conflict of laws'.[24] Under private international law rules, foreign law must be pleaded and proved as a matter of fact; likewise the aboriginal law must be adduced and proved by evidence. In ascertaining the existence of this law, the domestic court will incorporate it into its own body of laws; in other words the law becomes cognizable and enforceable under the laws of the forum.[25]

This is hardly an innovative or radical idea. One need merely point to African, Asian or Pacific experience to find numerous examples of the co-existence of indigenous law with colonial European-derived law.[26] The Australian Law Reform Commission has undertaken a comprehensive investigation of aboriginal customary law and the several areas in which recognition may best be sought.[27] Comparative international treatment of the interaction between indigenous and European law will undoubtedly provide a major source of information and a precedent for participants in the Canadian constitutional reform process. Despite marked differences between the Canadian situation and African, Asian or Pacific experience, a similar goal is at stake - the need to provide for the preservation and development of distinct indigenous cultures, by conferring legal status on their norms of behaviour.

Since these norms are destined to be applied and interpreted in the ordinary courts, the question of compatibility with other rules of the forum becomes crucial. In countries under former British colonial rule, the courts were directed not to apply a customary law where it conflicted with laws of general application or was repugnant. The repugnancy clause was found in the statutes and ordinances of a number of African jurisdictions and provided that customary law was applicable insofar as it was not repugnant to natural justice, morality or equity and good conscience. After independence, many countries dropped this rule but retained the test based on incompatibility with national legislation: a custom was valid if it was not inconsistent or incompatible with any statutory prescription.[28]

A practice measuring the viability of a customary rule of law by a non-aboriginal criterion runs into serious difficulties. The most obvious is, by which values are such judgments to be made? The problem becomes particularly acute when violations of human rights standards contained in constitutional charters of rights or international covenants are involved.[29] Resort to a repugnancy test involves a morally weighted discourse. This exercise is clearly question-begging: the choice of the set of values to be adopted determines the answer given. Once a non-indigenous standard is accepted to determine the validity of aboriginal norms, a conceptual trap has been set. It is sprung once a court refuses to sanction a custom on the ground of repugnancy to a Euro-Canadian sense of morality or justice.

The intractable nature of the issue is not attenuated by articulating a standard of incompatibility to law, federal or provincial. Very little protection would then be afforded to aboriginal customs and the fortunes of indigenous law would be at the mercy of legislative majorities. This would not take one much beyond the present state of affairs and indeed, with entrenchment of "existing" aboriginal rights in the Constitution, can only be seen as a regressive step.

This is not to say that the judiciary will refrain from exercising discretion in its selection of customary norms and rules to enforce. In the post-colonial era, the courts of many countries in Africa, Asia and the Pacific continued to follow colonial directives and to subject indigenous customs to judicial notions of propriety.[30] In this regard Canadian experience is similar to overseas jurisprudence - one only need cite the decisions of some of the more sympathetic of Canada's judiciary to discover how pervasive and rooted this attitude is.

In a pair of decisions on adoption and marriage practice among the Inuit, Mr. Justice Sissons of the N.W.T. Supreme Court held that Inuit customs were cognizable under the common law of the Territories only because they complied with the requirements of English law.[31] For example, in *Re Noah's Estate,* the validity of an Inuit customary marriage was questioned in deciding the distribution of the intestate's estate. Sissons J. upheld the customary marriage since it was "the kind of marriage which the English Law recognizes" and no statute or ordinance had expressly abrogated the rights of Inuit to practise such customs.[32]

In the famous *Calder* case, Mr. Justice Hall characterized the system of land tenure of the B.C. Nishga tribe in these terms:

> What emerges from the ... evidence is the following: the Nishgas in fact are and were from time immemorial a distinctive cultural entity with concepts of ownership indigenous to their culture and *capable of articulation under the common law* having, in the word of Dr. Duff [an expert witness] 'developed their cultures to higher peaks in many respects than in any other part of the continent north of Mexico'.[33] (emphasis added)

In effect Hall J. is stating that the aboriginal 'lex loci' was cognizable because it complied with Anglo-Canadian criteria and would therefore fit into common law categories. His reasoning proceeds on precisely the same lines as that of Blackburn J. in the notorious Australian Gove lands case, where the judge accepted that aboriginal customs of the plaintiff clans constituted a system of law, but paradoxically ruled that they could not fit into common law property terms.[34] All three judges tacitly accept the premise that for a particular custom to be valid, it is necessary to show that it conforms to English common law notions. The question whether the particular custom is valid under the aboriginal system of law never enters the discussion.[35]

Such ethnocentrism on the part of some of the more well-meaning of Her Majesty's judges is not accidental. Experience in other jurisdictions (some in fact having overwhelmingly indigenous majorities) has shown that, despite indigenization of the judiciary, training in the European legal tradition tends to cause custom to be interpreted through non-aboriginal filters. Indeed, this process inheres in the very structure of judicial decision-making. Woodman has argued that there are in fact divergent varieties of customary law - one for use in the courts ("lawyer's customary law") and the other socially recognized outside ("sociologist's customary law").[36] This distinction is for him, "not a consequence of unfortunate, remediable defects in the process of establishing lawyers' customary law, but ... a necessary, irremovable phenomenon in the enforcement of customary law by state courts."[37]

If aboriginal custom is inevitably modified to suit the preconceptions of the bench, this does not mean that indigenous law should not receive some sort of constitutional protection. The true answer to the issue of recognition, I would argue, lies in the creation of mechanisms of judicial control placed in the hands of the aboriginal peoples, who best are able to determine and shape their own law. Enforcement of customary law by the ordinary courts may ensure that aboriginal law will be adhered to in individual cases, but it does not guarantee the continued survival and enhancement of indigenous law on the collective level. This can only be assured by the creation of another system of justice.

Canada is a country founded on legal pluralism. Since the *Quebec Act* of 1774, two systems of law have coexisted, one based on the civil law derived from French provincial custom and the Napoleonic Code, the other on the English common law.[38] Cultural diversity is further recognized in the *Canadian Charter of Rights and Freedoms:* section 27 provides that:

> 27. This Charter shall be interpreted in a manner consistent with the preservation and enhancement of the multicultural heritage of Canadians.

Other sections of the Charter underline cultural pluralism in Canada. Section 2 of the Charter, dealing with fundamental freedoms, guarantees freedom of religion.

The question whether this right covers the cultural and religious practices of aboriginal peoples may soon be raised. Recently the issue was argued in a case in which two members of the Tsarlip tribe of Saanich were charged with hunting deer out of season contrary to the B.C. *Wildlife Act.*[39] They contended that the deer were to be used in a religious ceremony practised by the coast Salish people, the essence of the ceremony being the burning of deer to provide food for their dead ancestors. The B.C. Court of Appeal in a split decision found against the defendants, holding that religious freedom did not confer immunity from the general law. The dissenting judge argued that where there was no legitimate state interest in overriding the custom, a practice "that has been followed by the Coast Salish people for 20,000 years" should be preserved.[40] The Supreme Court dismissed the appeal. The Court noted that the charges were laid prior to the coming into force of the Charter; therefore, there was no constitutional (or even statutory) basis to the right of religious worship pleaded by the defendants. The Court went on to note that no evidence had been adduced that the killing of the deer was related to the religious ceremony, or that the ceremony required the use of fresh meat. Moreover, the alleged religious belief was related to "motive" and as such, was irrelevant to liability.[41] We must consequently await future litigation for a decision on an argument more securely based on section 2 of the Charter.

Section 35 itself, by recognizing and affirming "existing aboriginal rights", may arguably be said to entrench aboriginal customary laws. A superior court decision in the Northwest Territories has held that Inuit customary adoption should be considered to be an aboriginal right.[42] Although this is to date the sole case on this point, it can be argued that at common law, aboriginal customs have been recognized on the same theoretical principles as were rights to land and to hunt wildlife.[43] This common law position can be said to have been entrenched by section 35(1).

If legal pluralism, particularly with respect to aboriginal peoples, is both legally recognized and politically accepted, the issue turns to the form such pluralism should take. The answer is bound up with and indistinguishable from, the principle of self-determination. Expression of the distinctiveness of Canada's aboriginal peoples in the realm of customs and traditions is only one aspect of the wider proposition that aboriginal peoples are self-determining within the Canadian federation. For justice to function in aboriginal societies, it is not enough that a court may hear and occasionally enforce a cultural practice; the real question is how best to attain justice for and within those societies.

At the heart of the constitutional proposals of all aboriginal organizations is the demand for self-government, for control over the institutions that shape law and social development within native communities. The forms that such government may take vary widely as do the situations of the aboriginal peoples themselves. On the first day of the 1985 First Ministers Conference, the federal government tabled a proposal which, in many features, was based on a proposal formulated by the ICNI. It called for (1) recognition of the right of self-government for aboriginal peoples, subject to (2) a commitment by the federal government and where concerned, the provincial governments, to negotiate the precise institutional, financial and jurisdictional arrangements involved, and (3) the resulting agreements to be constitutionally protected.[44] On the second day, a compromise proposal was submitted with point (2) above excised from the schedule of constitutional amendments and relegated to the political accord. As mentioned earlier, it was the Inuit principally who caused this compromise proposal to fail.[45] It seems clear, however, that the earlier, three-point proposal for a self-government amendment has the potential to meet fully the wide diversity of needs and interests of the several aboriginal peoples in Canada.

Mechanisms to implement aboriginal law could be elaborated within the body of the self-government agreements. This would allow the parties to spell out the intricate interrelationship between the ordinary courts and the aboriginal courts. Some communities, bands or tribes may seek a village-based court system, others may look to regional councils; the variations are enormous and crucial.

Conclusion

The above considerations raise fundamental issues regarding the future of aboriginal peoples, their cultures and traditions within Canada. The present system of administration of justice has created a sense of frustration, hostility and despair among aboriginal peoples. There is open and widespread acknowledgement that the legal system has radically failed to overcome the serious conflicts between aboriginal methods of social regulation and Euro-Canadian models of control.[46] Indeed, for a jurist writing about conditions in Northern Quebec, the conflict between traditional values and the imposed justice system is such that Inuit social control mechanisms are gradually disappearing. For him, the legal apparatus in the North is structurally biased towards assimilating Inuit into the dominant society, despite official intentions and discourse to the contrary.[47] A lawyer with extensive practice in the Northwest Territories writes that:

> [I]t is amazing that a system which is foreign to this territory; which is run by individuals from outside the territory; and which has not won the hearts and minds of the majority of the people who come before it, could persist without challenge in a democratic society.[48]

The challenge posed by these issues will be faced by the ongoing constitutional reform process. The discussions will be shaped by the willingness of the participants to face the serious problems caused by the imposition of 'outside' values on aboriginal communities. Any resolution of the divisions that exist in Canadian society between aboriginal peoples and the established institutions of government can only come about by a frank acknowledgement that important structural change is imperative.

No one doubts that the Canadian justice system has failed to gain the respect and adherence of the aboriginal peoples. Conflicts between distinct social orders and perceptions of justice have produced a virtual breakdown in the effective administration of justice in aboriginal societies. When aboriginal peoples play a greater part in determining the course of justice within their communities, this disastrous situation will begin to be redressed. In a pluralist society such as ours, it is reasonable to assume that the aboriginal peoples, with their manifestly different cultures, have a right to determine their own pace and set their own terms of survival into the future. Once this assumption is made, a great deal will follow.

Notes

1. Since 1982, there has been an outpouring of studies on patriation; see especially Romanow and ors., 1984; for a journalistic treatment, Sheppard and Valpy, 1982. The aboriginal side to the story is well served by: Jull, 1981; Zlotkin, 1983; Sanders, 1983.
2. Schedule B to the Canada Act, 1982, c. 11 (U.K.).
3. The ICNI was created in 1979 by its parent organization, Inuit Tapirisat of Canada, to represent Inuit on constitutional issues. The AFN represents status Indians; the NCC represents non-status Indians and Metis. Disagreements within the NCC led in 1983 to a split in which the three prairie associations in Manitoba, Saskatchewan and Alberta formed the MNC, to represent western Metis.
4. Pursuant to section 37(3) of the Constitution Act, 1982.
5. The story of Quebec's role in the November 1981 First Ministers Conference is well recounted in Sheppard and Valpy, 1982.
6. The accord has been reprinted in Lyon, 1985.
7. The Schedule to the 1983 Accord was proclaimed on June 21, 1984 as the *Constitution Amendment Proclamation, 1983,* SI/84-102. It inserted Part IV.1 in the 1982 *Constitution Act* to continue the ongoing process and added sections 35(3) on land claim agreements and 35(4) on sexual equality.
8. For an excellent discussion on the background negotiations leading up to the 1983 and 1984 Conferences, and for other matters surrounding the process generally, see Schwartz, 1985.
9. Document 800-20/013, Canadian Intergovernmental Conference Secretariat (C.I.C.S.), tabled April 2, 1985.
10. See Hawkes, 1985:36.
11. The deal made in early 1981 included agreement to: (1) insert a new part to the Patriation Resolution (as the *Canada Act,* 1982 was then called) entitled "Rights of the Aboriginal Peoples of Canada" containing one clause -- sec. 34

(renumbered 35 after November 1981); (2) revise section 25 of the Canadian Charter of Rights and Freedoms; and (3) insert Part IV which provided for two First Ministers Conferences on aboriginal rights in which aboriginal leaders would have direct participation. More details will be found in the articles cited in note 1, *supra.*

12. *Canada Gazette,* Pt. III, 33 (September 21, 1982).
13. Pursuant to section 92(14), the property and civil rights clause, of the *Constitution Act,* 1867, c. 3 (U.K.).
14. This term, derived from private international law, has been used to characterize the local laws and customs of a particular aboriginal people; see Lester, 1981.
15. For an excellent study on the subject see, Guemple, 1979.
16. Document 800-17/016 (C.I.C.S.).
17. *Opening Speech,* March 15, 1983, Doc. 800-17/012 (C.I.C.S.).
18. Doc. 800-17/027 (C.I.C.S.).
19. Doc. 800-18/023 (C.I.C.S.).
20. Doc. 800-20/013, revised /041 note 9, *supra,* reprinted in Boldt and Long, 1985: Appendix I, 371.
21. See Papua New Guinea Law Reform Commission, 1977: especially at 74; Australian Law Reform Commission, 1986: especially at Part II.
22. Geertz, 1983:208.
23. For two recent studies on Inuit customary forms of dispute settlement see: Rouland, 1979; Rasing, 1984.
24. The term was first coined by Antony Allott in Allot, 1960:154.
25. See for example, Castel, 1978: Chap. 2. Allott has argued that the private international law analogy is misleading because there is no territorial separation in the two laws involved: see Allott, 1970:115-119.
26. See Allott, 1970:141-44 and 180 ff; Weisbrot and ors., 1982; Weisbrot 1983:90-95; Enwright, 1984-1985.
27. See Australian Law Reform Commission, 1986 and the background referred to therein.
28. See Allott, 1960, 1970; Kludze, 1983, 1985.
29. For example, the Australian Law Reform Commission, 1980, was of the opinion that traditional punishments such as spearing would constitute "cruel, inhuman or degrading treatment or punishment" under Article 7 of the International Covenant on Civil and Political Rights, para. 89-99, at 51-6. Six years later, the Commission reversed itself and acknowledged that a court could take such punishments into account at sentencing: 1986: vol. I, para. 492 ff.
30. For further information on Papua New Guinea see, Weisbrot and ors., 1982;

for Africa see for example, Kludze, 1983, 1985; Sawyerr, 1978, 1979; for Malaysia see Green, 1970.

31. *Re Adoption of Katie* (1961), 32 D.L.R. (2d) 686 (N.W.T.S.C.); *Re Noah Estate* (1961), 32 D.L.R. (2d) 185 (N.W.T.S.C.); generally see Morse, 1980.
32. *Re Noah,* ibid., at 197-198.
33. *Calder v Attorney-General of British Columbia,* [1973] S.C.R. 313 at 375 (S.C.C.).
34. *Millirpum v Nabalco Pty. Ltd.* (1971), 17 F.L.R. 141 (N.T.S.C.) at 181-3 and 270.
35. It may be argued that this reasoning runs counter to Privy Council authority. In *Amodu Tijani v Secretary,* Southern Nigeria, [1921] 2 A.C. 399 (J.C.P.C.), at 402-3, Lord Haldane warned against construing native title in terms solely appropriate to common law systems.
36. Woodman, 1985, and in this volume.
37. Ibid.
38. *Quebec Act* 1774, c. 83 (U.K.), reprinted in R.S.C. 1970, App. No. 2.
39. *R v Jack and Charlie* (1983), 139 D.L.R. (3d) 25 (B.C.C.A.).
40. Ibid., per Hutcheon J.A., at 42.
41. [1985] 4 C.N.L.R. 88; (1986), 21 D.L.R. (4th) 641 (S.C.C.).
42. Re Tagornak Adoption Petition, [1984] 1 C.N.L.R. 185 (N.W.T.S.C.).
43. See Morse, 1980.
44. See note 20, *supra.* The precise wording of the federal proposal caused some difficulties with the Inuit and the other national associations, but this was not fully discussed on the second day of the Conference.
45. Under the *Constitution Act, 1982,* Parliament and at least seven provincial legislatures (of which must be included Ontario or Quebec at the present time, due to population distribution in Canada) have to agree to an amendment to the provisions dealing with aboriginal peoples across Canada: s. 38(1).
46. See, inter alia, Harold Finkler, 1980; Federal-Provincial Conference, 1975; Sanders, 1983.
47. Rouland, 1983: Part I at 179, Part II at 313.
48. Crawford, 1985:20.

References

ALLOTT, Antony (1960)
Essays in African Law. London: Butterworths.

AUSTRALIAN LAW REFORM COMMISSION (1980)
Discussion Paper, "Aboriginal Customary Law - Recognition?"

---------- (1986)
Report No. 31. The Recognition of Aboriginal Customary Laws (2 vols.). Canberra: Australian Government Publishing Service.

CANADA GAZETTE (1982)
Part III (September 21) 33.

CANADIAN INTERGOVERNMENTAL CONFERENCE SECRETARIAT (1983)
Document 800-17/012.

---------- (1985)
Document 800-20/013.

---------- (no date)
Document 800-17/016.

---------- (no date)
Document 800-17/027.

---------- (no date)
Document 800-18/023.

CASTEL, J.G. (1978)
Conflict of Laws (4th ed.). Toronto: Butterworths.

CRAWFORD, Anne (1985)
"Outside Law and Traditional Communities in the Northwest Territories," Unpublished paper delivered at a meeting of the Western Regional Science Association. San Diego, California.

ENWRIGHT, W.G. (1984-85)
"Customary Law in Zimbabwe: traditional mechanisms and colonial control," 49 Saskatchewan Law Review 37.

FINKLER, Harold (1980)
Les Inuit et l'administration de la justice. Lassalle, Quebec: Hurtubise.

GEERTZ, Clifford (1983)
"Local Knowledge: Fact and Law in Comparative Perspective," in Local Knowledge. Further Essays in Interpretative Anthropology. New York: Basic Books.

GREEN, L.C. (1970)
"Native Law and the Common Law: Conflict or harmony," 12 Malaya Law Review 38.

GUEMPLE, Lee (1979)
Inuit Adoption. Ottawa: National Museum of Man.

HAWKS, David C. (1985)
Negotiating Aboriginal Self-government. Developments Surrounding the 1985 First Ministers Conference. Kingston: Institute of Intergovernmental Relations, Queen's University.

JULL, Peter (1981)
"Aboriginal Peoples and Political Change in the North Atlantic," 16 Journal of Canadian Studies 53-68.

KLUDZE, A. Kodzo Paaku (1983)
"The Effects of the Interaction between State Law and Customary Law in Ghana," in Harold Finkler (ed.), Papers of the Symposium on Folk Law and Legal Pluralism. XIth International Congress of Anthropological and Ethnological Sciences, Vancouver, Canada, Vol 1. Ottawa.

---------- (1985)
"Evolution of the Different Regimes of Customary Law in Ghana within the framework of the Principle of Stare Decisis," in Antony Allott and Gordon R. Woodman (eds.), Peoples Law and State Law. The Bellagio Papers, Dordrecht: Foris Publications.

LESTER, Geoffrey S. (1981)
The Territorial Rights of the Inuit of the Canadian Northwest Territories: A Legal Argument. Unpublished doctoral dissertation, York University.

LYON, Noel (1985)
"Constitutional Issues in Native Law," in Bradford W. Morse (ed.), Aboriginal Peoples and the Law: Indian, Metis and Inuit Rights in Canada. Ottawa: Carleton University Press.

MORSE, Bradford W. (1980)
"Indian and Inuit Family Law and the Canadian Legal System," 8 American Indian Law Review 199.

(No Name) (1985)
Menno Boldt and J.A. Lang (eds.), The Quest for Justice: Aboriginal Peoples and Aboriginal Rights. Toronto: University of Toronto Press. Appendix 1.

NATIONAL AND FEDERAL-PROVINCIAL CONFERENCE (1975)
Native Peoples and Justice. Reports on Native Peoples and the Criminal Justice System. Ottawa: Solicitor-General.

PAPUA NEW GUINEA LAW REFORM COMMISSION (1977)
The Role of Customary Law in the Legal System. Report No. 7. Waigani.

RASING, Wim (1984)
On Conflict Management with Nomadic Inuits: An Ethnological Essay. Unpublished doctoral thesis. Catholic University of Nijmegen, Netherlands.

ROMANOW, Roy, John D. WHYTE and Howard LEESON (1984)
Canada ... Notwithstanding. Toronto: Methuen/Carswell.

ROULAND, Norbert (1979)
"Les modes juridiques de solution de conflits chez les Inuit," Etudes Inuit Studies, Vol 3, no. hors-serie.

---------- (1983)
"L'acculturation judiciaire chez les Inuit du Canada," 13 Recherches Amerindiennes du Quebec, Part I and II.

SANDERS, Douglas (1983)
"The Indian Lobby," in Keith Banting and Richard Simeon (eds.), And No One Cheered: Federalism, Democracy and The Constitution Act. Toronto: Methuen.

SAWYERR, A. (1978)
"Customary Law in the High Court of Tanjania," 6 Eastern African Law Review 265.

---------- (1979)
"Application of Law in Tanjania: A Proper Remedy Approach," 7 Eastern African Law Review 233.

SCHWARTZ, Bryan (1985)
First Principles: Constitutional Reform with respect to the Aboriginal Peoples of Canada 1982-1984. Kingston: Institute of Intergovernmental Relations, Queen's University.

SHEPPARD, Robert and Michael VALPY (1982)
The National Deal: The Fight for a Canadian Constitution. Toronto: Fleet Books.

WEISBROT, David, Abdul PALIWALA and Akilagpa SAWYERR (eds.) (1982)
Law and Social Change in Papua New Guinea. Sydney: Butterworths.

WEISBROT, David (1983)
Human Rights for Aboriginal People in the 1980s in Garth Nettheim (ed.). Sydney: Legal Books Pty.

WOODMAN, G.R. (1985a)
"Customary Law, state courts, and the notion of institutionzliation of norms in Ghana and Nigeria," in Antony Allott and G.R. Woodman (eds.), People's Law and State Law: The Bellagio Papers. Dordrecht: Faris Publications.

---------- (1985b)
"How State Courts create customary law in Ghana and Nigeria," in Antony Allott and G.R. Woodman (eds.), People's Law and State Law: The Bellagio Papers. Dordrecht: Foris Publications.

ZLOTKIN, Norman K. (1983)
Unfinished Business: Aboriginal Peoples and the 1983 Constitutional Conference. Kingston: Institute of Intergovernmental Relations, Queen's University.

Recognition of traditional laws in state courts and the formulation of state legislation

Peter R. Grant

I. Introduction

The Gitksan-Wet'suwet'en Tribal Council Association is a society incorporated in 1977 by the seven Indian Bands of the Gitksan and Wet'suwet'en people. These Bands set up the Tribal Council to negotiate land claims with the governments of Canada and British Columbia. The Tribal Council has presented the claim to aboriginal title to their territory of approximately 25,000 square miles in north-central British Columbia to the government of Canada, which accepted that claim in principle in 1977. The government of British Columbia has failed to accept any aboriginal claims within the province.

The Tribal Council recognized that they had to develop a solid research base in order either to negotiate or litigate land claims. As part of this research effort, a "codification project" was launched which would include an analysis of the traditional laws of the Gitksan and Wet'suwet'en peoples. This paper will briefly review the methodology of the codification project and give examples of traditional laws which are based partly on that research.

The Tribal Council has also argued in British Columbia Courts for the acceptance of traditional laws in determining issues that affect their hereditary Gitksan Chiefs and particularly the fishing rights of the Gitksan and Wet'suwet'en peoples. This argument was made because the objective of the Tribal Council is to promote a greater understanding and a recognition of their traditional laws in the Anglo-American Courts. One aspect of this paper is a consideration of the extent to which courts have recognized traditional laws and the effect of that limited recognition on Indian rights.

Finally, the Gitksan-Wet'suwet'en Tribal Council has negotiated with the government of Canada for recognition of traditional laws through legislation. Although this work is being carried out in a number of areas, one of the Council's primary concerns is the recognition of the Indian right to the traditional fishery and the Indian laws which govern the conservation and management of that fishery. These discussions, in which the author has been actively involved, have resulted in the negotiation of fishing by-laws.

This writer will consider the recognition of traditional laws in state courts and the use of traditional laws to develop legislative schemes which could be utilized by aboriginal peoples in their drive for self-government.

II. Gitksan and Wet'suwet'en codification project

The Gitksan-Wet'suwet'en Tribal Council Association hired Gitksan and Wet'suwet'en people to undertake primary research and interviewing of hereditary Chiefs in 1981. In preparation for the fieldwork, the researchers took part in a two week workshop to review basic concepts of "traditional law" and the general meaning of "law". There was an extensive discussion of certain aspects of the basic concepts of law raised by Hoebel.[1] After reviewing English and American definitions, the researchers (who were already familiar with the traditional Gitksan and Wet'suwet'en legal systems) and the lawyer (whose background was in the Anglo-Canadian legal tradition) adopted a modified form of Hoebel's definition of law as follows:

> A social norm is legal if its neglect or infraction is regularly met, in threat or in fact, by the application of physical force, ostracism or shame by an individual or group possessing a socially recognized privilege of so acting.

The discussions had led to the conclusion that "physical force" as a mode of penalty was not the only one used in Gitksan and Wet'suwet'en tradition, and that ostracism and shame were at least equally powerful. This departs from Hoebel's definition which suggests that the application of physical force without fear of reprisal is the definitive criterion for determining whether a "social norm" is legal. The consensus was that Hoebel's definition does not sufficiently take into account the spiritual and societal forms of coercion. In the northwest coast society, ostracism or exile appear to have been severe forms of punishment and, in Gitksan society at least, exile was much more serious than any application of physical force. A Gitksan person had to be a member of a House, and a failure to have a name and a place in a House was tantamount to denial of one's existence. Similarly, the spiritual powers of the Shamans were taken very seriously as a form of punishment. For example, a Gitksan did not throw away the entrails of a fish, but put them back in the river so that the fish would return the following year. This respect for the non-human resources of the territory was based on a very strong spiritual belief and respect for all creation. Starvation was the inevitable penalty for not complying with this rule.

In the preparatory workshop, the researchers also discussed the methodology of data collection. As the project developed, both researchers and supervisors placed more and more emphasis on the case method approach. This approach calls for the interviewer to raise a particular subject, such as access of non-House members to the fishing sites owned by the House Chief, and to encourage the informant to give examples of circumstances in which the rules had been violated and the consequences of such violations.

In the early stages of the research many advisors made only general comments unsupported by case histories. Although the general comments can be taken to express the accepted view when repeated by several different advisors in different situations, case approach examples in which the laws are demonstrated clearly explain the principles of Wet'suwet'en and Gitksan laws. The case approach is extremely valuable in Anglo-Canadian courts because the use of examples is a powerful means of demonstrating the continued existence of traditional laws. Furthermore, the importance of the case method in the Anglo-Canadian legal system makes state courts receptive to this method of explaining Gitksan and Wet'suwet'en laws.

The next phase of the researchers' training was to discuss particular areas of law. The Tribal Council's objective was to deal with those areas affecting Gitksan and Wet'suwet'en property laws. To determine what had to be established to demonstrate their property system the following components of a property system, as set out by Professor J.C. Smith, were considered:

1. a community
2. a quantity of limited or scarce resources
3. a set of rules regulating the acquisition, access to and use of those resources ...
4. a set of possessive pronouns ...
5. a set of rules protecting the property relation by ... providing sanctions when it is wrongfully interfered with.[2]

The third and fifth components were most important for an investigation of traditional laws. Over the course of the project, other similar discussions focussed on areas of traditional law such as adoption, management rules relating to the fishery resource, succession, settlement feasts, and war and peace.

Interviewing in the later phase included followup interviews of particularly knowledgeable Chiefs and elders with a view to clearing up ambiguities. This process has continued as the draft of traditional laws is formulated and reviewed by the hereditary Chiefs.

The second phase of the codification, the analysis of the interviews and the development of summaries of the traditional laws in each major area is presently under way. A significant component of this phase is the use of secondary sources, such as the Barbeau-Beynon papers.[3] Drafts of territorial laws have now been developed and a detailed analysis of the Barbeau-Beynon papers is being carried out to determine consistency with the contemporary oral tradition of Gitksan and Wet'suwet'en laws. After detailed summaries of each major area of traditional law have been prepared, they will be discussed with the hereditary Chiefs and modifications made based on their comments.

III. Results of Gitksan-wet'suwet'en codification

The project is now well into the record phase, involving analysis and draft summaries. The following example relating to Gitksan adoption is subject to review by the hereditary Chiefs and a possible modification in the light of further interviews. This example is intended only to show the format of the final codification. It is important to recognize that "codification" is probably a misnomer. The best way of setting out the laws would be through a description of examples of their application in different circumstances, a method similar to the development of the common law system.

The Gitksan have a number of rules concerning adoption. One is that:

A person who, for whatever reason, is exiled from his village may be adopted by a house which is of the same clan as he originally belonged to in another village.

The highest Chief of Kitsequecla is Wii Gyat, who arrived at Kitsequecla from another village from which he had been exiled. Two high Chiefs of Kitsequecla, Gwis Gyen and Guxsan of the Giskaast clan, adopted the man and his sister into their clan and made a space for him between them at their feast table. Even now, Gwis Gyen and Guxsan sit on either side of Wii Gyat during feasts.

Another rule may be stated as follows:

When a house or clan is in danger of extinction because there are no

> *females, the house chief may adopt a woman from another clan to carry on their house.*

The father of a present hereditary Chief of Kispiox was a member of the Lax Seel (Frog) clan. As this clan was dying out they adopted his daughter, who according to the prevailing system of matrilineal descent was a member of the Wolf clan, so that her father's house would carry on.

> *The children of a woman adopted under the rules set out above are considered members of the house and clan into which she has been adopted.*

> *To recognize traditional adoptions a number of adoption feast ceremonies, each having their own name, are held by the adopting clan.*

An important consequence of Gitksan adoption is the adopted child's right of access to the territories of his adoptive as well as his natural parents. A major area of interest to the researchers is the rights of access of persons, including adopted children, with different relationships to the House. The evidence suggests that adopted children have rights to their adopted parents' territory on the same basis as natural children have rights to their natural parents' territories. For example, a natural child has rights of access during his father's life to his father's territory. At the time of his father's death, these may be extended by the person who inherits his father's traditional name. The adopted child may have corresponding rights of access to his adopted father's territory.

The example of rights of access demonstrates the importance and complexity of the adoption system as part of the traditional law of the Gitksan people. The utility of recognizing such laws is now considered.

IV. Use of traditional laws in state courts

Since the time of first contact between European fur traders and North American Indian peoples, the Anglo-Canadian courts have on occasion been required to consider the effect and enforceability of traditional laws. Over the last one hundred years, however, the consideration of traditional laws and their effect on Anglo-Canadian law declined until recently. In the last few years courts have increasingly considered the applicability of traditional laws to fishing regulations, hunting laws, Indian status, and even awards to hereditary Chiefs in personal injury cases.

Contemporary State Court decisions in Australia as well as North America have taken account of traditional laws. For example, In *Napaluma v Baker,*[4] the South Australia Supreme Court awarded $10,000 to an aboriginal for his loss of position in the aboriginal community as a result of the injuries he has suffered. In *Gawa v Horton & Watson,*[5] Judge Hutchinson considered similar circumstances. Ten days of evidence was called, much of it related to the role of the Plaintiff as a hereditary Chief within the Gitksan community. Hit by a car while walking home one evening, the plaintiff sustained a serious head injury resulting in permanent partial disability.

Evidence was led that Mrs. Gawa had been one of the few female Chiefs in her House. In that capacity, she was responsible for training the younger women who would rise to chieftainship within her House. Her loss was, therefore, also a loss to the members of her House.

Both hereditary Gitksan Chiefs and anthropologists gave evidence with respect to Gitksan traditions and the role of hereditary Chiefs. One hereditary Chief spoke of a particular type of feast, the name of which could be translated as "wiping away the blood". This feast was held by a hereditary Chief whose blood had been spilled in public to wipe away the humiliation of the incident. Another Gitksan gave evidence that such a feast had taken place in the 1950s. According to Gitksan law, a blow to the head of a hereditary Chief was a particularly humiliating injury and unless the Chief held a feast to "wipe away the blood", his status within the community would be greatly reduced.

The second effect of the injury was that the plaintiff became forgetful and an object of pity. Anthropological evidence led at the trial demonstrated how, in Gitksan tradition, a person who was pitied was considered subordinate, weak and unable to live up to their obligations or to display the characteristics of chieftainship including qualities of leadership, counsel and knowledge of Gitksan laws, language and custom. With respect to compensation for her loss of status, the Judge concluded that he could "... take into account the plaintiff's loss of status in the community, her inability to perform the ceremonial functions as chief that she used to perform, and her social ostracism ..."[6]

Although the court did not give a specific award for the cost of a feast to "wipe away the blood", the court took that element into account as well in making a global award for the Plaintiff's injuries and their effect on her lifestyle.

This case underlines the importance of presenting evidence of traditional laws where rights and customary laws are relevant to issues before Anglo-Canadian courts.

A second Canadian example involved a section of the regulations under the *Fisheries Act*[7] which allowed an Indian person to fish for the purpose of "obtaining food for himself and his family".

In *R v Bolton*,[8] Ron Nyce, a status Indian, had obtained a special fishing license as required by the legislation and, as was his habit, had given his catch to his brother-in-law, Andrew Bolton. Not only was Bolton, the accused, married to Nyce's sister, but Nyce was married to Bolton's sister. The evidence was that Bolton had no boat or fish net and that it was very difficult to fish in the Skeena River without assistance from family members. On appeal from conviction, Bolton argued that it was not appropriate to apply a concept of family contrary to the Indian understanding of the term. The court stated:

> In interpreting a statute, it is preferable, when considering the intention of Parliament, to examine the etymology to decide on its meaning, rather than delve into anthropology to decide what it means to the Indian. For here is an example of the difficulties that can result from an anthropological approach. Robert Nyce and his sister are of the Kitselas Band of the Tsimpshean Tribe from Terrace. Andrew Bolton, the Respondent is of the Haisla Tribe, from Kitimaat. Moreover, the evidence shows that Robert Nyce and his sister are of the Black Fish Clan, while the Respondent is of the Eagle Clan. There was no expert testimony adduced to link these disparate groups more closely. The connection claimed was by marriage and by Robert Nyce's assertion that as he has no brothers, that he has adopted his wife's brothers as his family, including Andrew Bolton.
>
> As the claim to "family" is based on marriage and is no closer than a unity connected by that affinity, I can see no basis for adopting the anthropological approach. Even if it were supported by evidence it could lead to uncertainty and inconsistency in interpretation: every House, Clan, Tribe or Nation could have a different concept of who belongs to their "family", according to the customs or history. I reject that argument.[9]

The salient point here is the comment that no expert testimony had been led to link the disparate groups more closely. Furthermore, it is interesting to note this decision was authored by the same Judge who had accepted evidence by non-Indian experts as well as by Indian people with regard to the loss of status of a traditional Gitksan Chief in *Gawa v Horton & Watson*.[10]

Clearly, both in establishing traditional laws and in using them to interpret Canadian statutes, "uncertainty and inconsistency in interpretation" must be avoided by adducing appropriate evidence. It is suggested that this is a major reason why a clarification of traditional rules is important. If those rules are clearly established and understood, parties relying upon them will be able to argue that they are certain and consistent.

V. Use of traditional laws in legislative schemes

A major objective of the Gitksan-Wet'suwet'en Tribal Council in codifying traditional laws has been to utilize their traditional laws in legislative schemes for the advancement of Indian self-government.

The Council has encouraged its seven Indian Band constituents to pass a comprehensive Indian Fishery by-law. This by-law includes a regulation authorizing the hereditary Chiefs of the traditional clans of the Gitksan and Wet'suwet'en to form an advisory body. The Chiefs can make recommendations with respect to management plan which will incorporate traditional fishing practices in regulations in the traditional Wet'suwet'en and Gitksan fisheries. The Council hopes that the government of Canada will allow them to develop a fishery management plan which will incorporate traditional fishing practices in regulations so that there can be Indian control over the Indian fishery within the upper Skeena territory.

The by-law is clearly a first effort at reinstating the hereditary Chiefs in their rightful position of management and control of the resources of the Gitksan and Wet'suwet'en people. Unfortunately, the by-law is hemmed in by the constraints of the *Indian Act,* which only recognizes Band Councils created by statute as a legitimate form of government. This is one of the reasons why the government has been reluctant to negotiate over the by-law to the present date. If it were validated, the hereditary Chiefs by making recommendations, would have a strong moral influence on the decisions of the Band Councils and the fishery officers' enforcement of the law. For example, the hereditary Chiefs might see that certain elders in the community were not getting a fair share of the fish and might insist that the fishermen distribute a portion to those elders who appeared to be in need. Similarly, they might be concerned about shortages of certain species of fish and might recommend that the river be closed so that those fish could be returned to their spawning ground.

Negotiations on the traditional fishery by-law appear to be coming to a close after almost a year and a half. Although certain officials within the Department have expressed concern at the Gitksan and Wet'suwet'en people's desire to reinstate traditional laws and to involve themselves in the management of the fishery resource, there have been recommendations that the by-law be approved. If the by-law is approved, as it could be in the near future, it will be one of the first occasions in Canada on which there has been realized a potential for incorporation of traditional laws through state legislation.

Conclusion

This paper has presented a brief overview of research methodology in traditional laws and their potential use. The utilization of traditional laws in arguments in contemporary court cases has barely been touched upon, but there is no doubt that as knowledge of the traditional laws of Canadian Indian natives grows, more such arguments will be presented.

Recently the media have drawn attention to the Somby case involving a Sami who was adopted traditionally by a west coast Indian nation. The government of Canada has refused to recognize his traditional adoption as a basis for his lawful presence in Canada. Nevertheless, as more Indian nations argue for a recognition of their aboriginal title and a definition of what that title means under Section 35 of the *Constitution Act, 1982,* the courts will increasingly hear arguments based on the demonstration of traditional laws as part of the sovereignty of Indian nations in Canada. It is most important that prior to making assumptions or drawing conclusions, the people presenting those arguments truly understand the traditional laws on which they are based.

Notes

1. Hoebel, 1954.
2. Smith, 1974.
3. Barbeau, and Beynon, 1914-1957.
4. *Napaluma v Baker* 29 S.A.S.R. 192.
5. *Gawa v Horton & Watson* (1981), 37 B.C.L.R. 130.
6. Ibid., at 138.
7. *British Columbia Fishery (General) Regulations,* C.R.C., c. 840 of the *Fisheries Act,* R.S.C. 1970, c. F-14. This has subsequently been repealed and replaced by *British Columbia Fishery (General) Regulations,* SOR/84-248, s. 27 as amended by SOR/85-290 and SOR/85-742.
8. *R. v Bolton,* B.C. County Court (February 12th, 1982), Hutchinson, J., p. 2 (unreported).
9. Ibid., p. 3.
10. See note 6, *supra.*

References

BARBEAU, Marius and William BEYNON (1914-1957)
Unpublished Fieldnotes on Deposit with the National Museum of Man. Ottawa: Ontario.

HOEBEL, E.A. (1954)
The Law of Primitive Man. Cambridge: Harvard University Press.

SMITH, J.C. (1974)
"The Concept of Native Title," 24 University of Toronto Law Journal 2.

Inside Brazilian Indian law: a comparative perspective

Stephen Conn

Indio brabo comigo vai para a cadeia a ainda mando a Policia Federal meter o pau.[1]

President of FUNAI to Chief Manual Apurina, Apurina Indians, as reported to *Estado de Sao Paulo,* October 26, 1982.

I. The Legal Status of Indians in Brazil

Since the turn of the century, Brazilian legal scholars have compared the legal position of the Indian in Brazil[2] with that of the Indian in North America. They have found deep differences (Otavio, 1946:130-132; Ferreira de Souza Pitanga, 1905:42; de Souza, 1889:8-9; Burns, 1970:13 et seq.). The history of Indians in Brazil before the twentieth century displayed a marked contrast between their legal and social status. By law Indians had been granted the rights of citizenship and freed from enslavement (except when taken as prisoners in wars) but in fact, whether slave or free, they formed a source of cheap labour until black slaves provided a more reliable and sturdy substitute (Southey, 1822 (1962, vol. 2:642); Melati, 1970:162). Brazilian scholars have related this to the fact that in South America political arrangements were not struck with the tribes as they were in North America. Competing foreign powers did not need to secure tribal allies or to deny tribal help to adversaries (Mendes Junior, 1912:21-22). In North America national citizenship for Indians came late, giving them, in effect, dual citizenship. Tribal membership was emphasized in North America as a legal device for identifying Indians, because dealing with tribes as groups, treating with tribes, and pushing tribes out of desirable lands onto less desirable lands was found to be an efficient way of dealing with the North American Indian question (Prucha, 1962; Wilkinson, 1982:90).[3] In Brazil Indians were treated as individuals, and thereby exploited as cheap labor and fused into the Brazilian proletariat.

As Brazilian jurists sought to remedy the atrocities of the past and to engage newly discovered tribes on the Brazilian frontier, it therefore seemed logical to focus upon the individual Indian citizen rather than the tribe, and to seek to change the individual's exploited position of citizen into the protected position of both citizen and ward. The essence of the Indian citizen-ward's disability was said to be his primitiveness. To be primitive was to be as one retarded, to be in a near organic condition which left one at the mercy of social predators and of one's tribal culture. To be civilized was to be healthy and capable of undertaking the full responsibilities of citizenship (Otavio, 1946:161). The idea of a scale from sickness to health, from the primitive to the civilized state, was introduced into both the letter and the spirit of Brazilian Indian law and its administration. The treatment of Indians varied according to their place on the ladder of civilization (Sobrinho, 1929:132).

Although wards, Indians remained citizens with some freedom of choice. An Indian's choice of residence served a twofold purpose. It indicated his likely place on the ladder of progress to civilization;[4] and it determined the kind of guardianship he would be afforded. Thus a hierarchy of residential settings was identified so as to locate Indians on the ladder which stretched from the primitive tribe to the folds of the national experience. However, those Indians who as free citizens chose to dwell "in promiscuity" with civilization lost the special protections afforded those who had the good sense to remain in a setting more appropriate to their still primitive state.

This "inner logic" of Brazilian Indian law grew out of the conflicting goals of assisting Brazilian Indians towards a healthy integration into Brazilian society, and avoiding the reintroduction of slavery under the guise of wardship. It has been the basis of Brazilian Indian law throughout the twentieth century, and is especially apparent in the modern application of Brazilian criminal law by the lawyers who represent Indians. Within the law the special guarantees and protections of Indian law conflict with the right to freedom of all citizens and the objective of integrating Indians into "the national communion", the intimate fellowship of national society (The Indian Statute, Law 6001, Art. 1).

Indians' tribal identification is viewed as a kind of cultural enslavement which causes them to behave as abnormal beings and so requires special measures for their protection. However, these measures are viewed as temporary. The process of detribalization is said to make Indians ready for legal emancipation because it constitutes a *cure*, even while it propels them into economic and social oblivion.

Brazilian Indian law seeks to place Indians and their tribes into categories according to their social distance from the bench-mark of full assimilation into Brazilian society (Article 4). It stipulates that loss of the special civil law protections may occur only with the concurrence of the tribe or individual Indian (Articles 9, 10 and 11). The Brazilian military government periodically pressed for the requirement of consent to be replaced by independent criteria to determine who was Indian. Such criteria could then have been used by the federal Indian agency to produce the legal emancipation of persons or groups considered sophisticated enough to take care of themselves. Such persons might have included, for example, the Chavante chief Juruna, a persistent critic of Brazilian Indian policy, who had learned the value of tape-recording his conversations with government officials,[5] and the half dozen Portuguese-speaking Brazilian Indian students from several tribes who were expelled in 1981 from their lodging in Brasilia for issuing a steady stream of criticism of government policy on nationwide television.

The position of the Indian bureaucracy, Fundacao Nacional de Indio (FUNAI) was that Indians were either wards in the private law sense of orphans or incompetents, whose existence and residence should be monitored and controlled, or sophisticated enough to be assimilated and detribalized, and so not entitled to any special protection. The results in particular cases are contradictory and repressive. Thus, the students in Brasilia were told that they would be sent home to their tribes because their heads were being turned by city life. M, a Brazilian student, was said to be unable to become a pilot or employee of FUNAI because, as a ward of the government, he could not be his own guardian. Juruna was said to be too urbane to be considered an Indian, but was also at first denied a passport to testify before an international tribunal on Brazilian Indian policy because he was a ward.[6]

Of particular significance in the administration of Brazilian Indian law is the linking of a cultural qualification with legal protections. This measure of "Indianhood" rarely fails to be applied by a person who appreciates that Indian culture is evolving as much as any living culture. The linking of legal protection and cultural purity suggests that anthropologists have provided legal technicians with an immutable definition of that which is aboriginal.

Despite its absurdity, this view has the practical effect of enabling officials to exclude from Indian groups (or at least to challenge) potential culture brokers, especially leaders - those persons who can hold their own both in the political world of the tribe and in that of the larger society. While the application of the process to emergent leaders has provoked Brazilian press comment, debate, and even effective opposition, a very similar process has occurred largely unnoticed in the more mundane world of criminal law. At this outer and lower edge of Indian legal practice, one may observe the cultural qualification test at work in the hands of FUNAI attorneys in distant outposts.

Brazil is not the only nation to employ either explicitly or implicitly a cultural qualification test to determine who should be afforded the special legal rights of indigenous persons. What other determinant might be employed? In the United States the application of Indian law turns upon abandonment of tribal relations, not acculturation. The territorial jurisdiction of tribes and states is defined ultimately by Congress, drawing upon its plenary authority as arbiter of the political relationship between tribes and the federal government *(Worcester v Georgia,* 1832; Strickland et al, 1982). In American federal law, Indians are defined by their political association and not by their culture *(Cherokee Nation v Georgia,* 1831). On its face this approach is less individualized and more mechanistic (Wachtel, 1982:117-119). One can argue that it conceals cultural projections and cultural sterotyping, employing underlying concepts rooted in theories of civilization. However, in the main it allows Native Americans to adapt to and engage the larger society without fear of exclusion from the protection of Indian law and tribal association. No law on the status of indigenous people can rebut the charge that it incorporates the economic and social imperatives of the dominant society. However, it is valuable to compare different laws if only to make relative improvements.

While each Brazilian Indian is a citizen from birth, his legal status and capacity is limited by the special guardianship defined in the Indian Statute. In all other cases guardianship of minors or incompetents arises from judicial intervention and appointment. The Public Minister monitors the relationship and can call for the guardian's dismissal (Dallari, 1979:78). But the wardship of Indians is a matter of public law. The guardian is the federal organ of assistance to the Indians, designated by the President of the Republic. The content of the relationship is determined by the national Indian policy, irrespective of whether it is beneficial to Indians.

The Indian statute provides for the cessation of guardianship only when the Indian applies to the court for liberation, and shows that he is at least 21, knows Portuguese, is capable of some useful activity in the national community, and, above all, comprehends the uses and customs of other Brazilians (Dallari, 1979:78; Indian Statute, Art. 9). The law also provides that, where a majority of a group request it, and FUNAI vouches for the group's cultural integration, the President may decree its emancipation (Art. 11). No Indian individual or group has applied for emancipation. On the contrary, many have demanded that their guardian secure their legal protections, and especially that their lands be carefully demarcated and protected.

Yet as Indian and non-Indian engage in land disputes and in other ways enter into regular contact with each other, a process of *de facto* emancipation is occurring through the criminal law. Indians may be convicted of all substantive crimes. While cultural difference may in principle exempt a person from criminal liability by excluding the element of intent, the letter of the law suggests that it is only in sentencing practice that levels of acculturation will be regularly taken into consideration (Art. 57).

Since the mid-1970s there have been efforts within the Brazilian government to end the special statutory and constitutional obligations owed to Indians and Indian groups by bringing about their legal emancipation. Such emancipation, somewhat like that under the North American Dawes Act, would force individuals and groups into the Brazilian underclass as an inducement to their ultimate "civilization." (Compare: Prucha, 1981:229). These moves have been steadily countered by groups such as the Pro-Indian Commissions of Sao Paulo and Rio, the Indigenist Missionary Council (CIMI) and, increasingly, those Indian groups and leaders who have learned how to wage media and political warfare within the limited democratic channels available under Brazilian authoritarianism.

II. Special Protection of Indians in Brazilian and U.S. Law

Sao Paulo law professor and human rights activist, Dalmo de Abreu Dallari, observes that in the North American system the Indian enjoys a special legal situation in that he continues to be treated juridically as an Indian, even after having been integrated into the national communion. Provisions maintain the legal effects of Indian status after mixed marriages, even for descendants with 1/64 Indian blood.

> But in Brazilian legislation, the ancient condition of Indian doesn't have any influence. Once integrated into the national communion the Indian becomes an ordinary citizen with the same rights and obligations that befit all Brazilians.
>
> [I]ntegration is possible without the formal process of emancipation ... Brazilian legislation will only give different treatment to the Indian while he is not thought to be integrated into the national communion. (Dallari, 1979:79).

Once that occurs, writes Dallari,

> [H]e is Brazilian like all the rest without his indigenist origin having any influence. Even though he can't alter the characteristics of his origin, it is rigorously certain from the juridical point of view that the Indian stops being an Indian as he is integrated into the Brazilian communion. From that moment he is an ordinary Brazilian citizen without any privilege or without any protection or special restriction. (Id. 79).

De facto emancipation is occurring in Brazil as Indian lands are invaded and violence results, as Indians are detribalized and their groups disintegrated. This flow of events, absent effective intervention by FUNAI, will drive Indians and their tribes into legal invisibility.

The cases illustrate the North American policy. In *U.S. v Holliway* (1865) federal liquor laws were said to be applicable to a yeoman farmer who happened to be an Indian because he had maintained his tribal relations even though he did nôt live on the reservation. Conversely, in another case an Indian was said not to be subject to the Major Crimes Act because the special relationship between his tribe and the federal government had been terminated *(U.S. v Heath,* 1974:19).

Yet the difference between Brazilian and North American law for "integrated" Indians is not extreme. American Indians have enjoyed the benefits of U.S. citizenship since the 1920s, and as state citizens are entitled to state services. Normally they are subject to tribal political obligations only when they reside on tribal land in tribal communities, or at least in dependent Indian communities, jurisdictional realms which are considered "Indian Country."

The principal difference between Brazilian and North American Indian law resides in the concept of guardianship or wardship (*tutela* in Portuguese). In Brazilian law the concept focuses on the individual Indian and historically is derived from private law, in that it classifies Indians with minors, orphans or youth, i.e., persons who are in need of protection. That private law connotation was analytically disentangled for followers of North American Indian law by Felix Cohen, author of the original *Handbook of Indian Law* (1940 (1971):169-73). He contended that guardianship, rather than a source of personal disablement, was the source of protections over and above those legal rights to which all citizens were entitled.

III. Criminal Law and the Brazilian Indian

The Brazilian Indian statute, in setting principles to govern the application of criminal law to Indians, focuses on the consequences of conviction and not on the invocation of the law. It charges the court with assessing the degree of integration of the forest dweller, and urges it to grant the defendant semi-liberty under the custody of the FUNAI personnel nearest to his dwelling (Article 56). Left aside are the prior decisions of police and FUNAI officials and attorneys, which influence the investigation which leads to prosecution. Also left aside are issues which may be relevant to a defense and which are unique to Indians. These matters are often critical to the outcome.

Article 57 of the Indian Statute disallows death sentences imposed under tribal law and other sanctions of a cruel or degrading nature. However, in other respects it supports the imposition of penal or disciplinary sanctions by tribal groups on their members in accordance with their own institutions.[7]

Crimes against Indians by non-Indians are to be prosecuted by the federal government and not the tribes. Special intervention may be decreed by the President to put down fighting between tribal groups (Art. 20, Sec. 1(a)) or to repress disorder or plunder, a provision which does not clearly designate the status or race of the troublemakers (Art. 20, Sec. 1(e)).

Since 1982, there has been a trend toward an increased application of the criminal law. In 1980 a group of Txucarramae set upon and killed eleven peons who had been sent onto tribal lands to clear them for ranchers (Veja, Aug. 1980) and a month later the Garotire clubbed twenty peons. The government took the view that the Indian law protected the Indians from prosecution (Veja, 1980, Sept. 10, 1980). In contrast, two years later the then president of FUNAI threatened a chief with jail and a beating by police when he asked for compensation for land taken by colonists in Boca do Acre, Amazonas (CEDI, 1982:204:3).[8]

This threat offers a rare public glimpse of the option available to practitioners accustomed to dividing defendants into those sufficiently acculturated to be tried and those too primitive to be held criminally responsible. A decision whether to invoke the criminal law is called for when the FUNAI district offices and their contract attorneys deal with conflicts in which at least one party is an Indian. When the case is likely to attract national publicity, especially if it concerns tribal acts with strong political overtones, the decision is made with concern for the reaction of reform groups in Southern cities and a Brazilian urban public that often sympathizes with Indians. When publicity is not likely, the decision turns on the ethnocentric and often racist views of Brazilian practitioners. It is in these latter cases that the flavor and ultimate threat of Brazilian criminal law are apparent.

Attorneys working for FUNAI met in 1981 to discuss their work and the legal position of Indians. They appointed a four-person committee to consider important questions concerning Indian integration (FUNAI Memo 95/PJ-81, 1981). The committee asked whether the administration of FUNAI could *de officio* - and independently of the proceedings specified in the Indian statute for judicial release from guardianship - recognize an Indian individual or community to be integrated on the ground of actual integration into the national communion, thus relieving FUNAI of its duties as guardian. Its unanimous answer was no. Either the judicial inquiry or the presidential decree required by the Act would be necessary, the committee concluded.

On responsibility under the criminal law, the meeting concluded: "The fact of being an Indian, pure and simply, does not render one entirely unpunishable. It is not just the place of origin of the Indian that identifies the Indian for punishment or that frees him from punishment but the actual state of his development in contact with the civilized world." (Id.:5) Reviewing the work of earlier commentators, the meeting concluded that it was both unjust and inappropriate to place the Indian in the category of those who were criminally incompetent by reason of mental deficiency. The clinical concept of incomplete mental development, to the extent that it suggested physical weakness of the organs of thought, was said to be "teratologically inapplicable" to the forest dweller to whom it had been applied to exclude him from criminal prosecution. The group concluded that "the Indian, depending on his actual state of development, in contact with the civilized world, and the level of his integration is criminally responsible, being subject to the application of penal law" (Id. 5).

FUNAI's attorneys informed the president that, within the realm of civil capacity, an Indian could undertake many activities notwithstanding his being under the guardianship of the federal government. This opinion endorsed by implication a Brazilian high court decision which had allowed Juruna to obtain a passport and to travel overseas. It resolved the issue of whether Indians could work in skilled capacities for FUNAI as drivers and pilots without full emancipation.[9]

Yet they also concluded that an Indian's level of acculturation would be decisive when attorneys in the field were considering the application to him of the criminal law. The attorneys reviewed early learned commentaries on the penal statutes which had explained the special status of Indians as one similar to those of other mental incompetents who could not be tried for crimes. The attorneys rejected the view of primitive Indians as mentally deficient. But an Indian's association with a tribe, the race of the victim, the place where the crime occurred - each matters which might have been relevant in other countries - were not viewed as determinants.[10]

IV. The Law as Applied in Boa Vista, a Rural Town

Boa Vista, the first of three localities to be examined in this paper, is the capital of the territory of Roraima and the headquarters of the 10th regional *delegacia*. There are 40,000 whites in the territory and a larger number of Indians, some in contact with other Brazilians, and some in isolation. The latter include the Yanomami and the former the Macuxi and Wapixana. Dr. Raimundo is the attorney in the FUNAI office, being the second to move there in the past 15 months.

In Sao Paulo advocates of Indian rights attach the utmost significance to the legal position of the 17,000 Yanomami, the protection of their land, their well-being, and especially the danger posed by infection from prospectors trespassing on their land. Dr. Raimundo could shed little light on these matters. His primary concern was with Indians of the Macuxi and Wapixana tribes who were in regular contact with non-Indians.

Signs warning that the sale of liquor to Indians was a crime subject to imprisonment had been posted at the FUNAI office, in places frequented by businessmen, and near villages. A major concern of Dr. Raimundo, almost to the point of a fixation, was alcohol abuse. Indians who came to his office were closely questioned about the use of alcohol and its source. He had learned that Indians were selling *caxiri* (made of manioc root) mixed with *cachacha,* Brazilian sugar cane liquor, purchased from whites. He had learned that whites were selling *cachacha* to Indians on credit and that when the Indians accumulated debts of American $300 or more, the creditors would make them work "as if they were slaves." But despite his extensive knowledge of the alcohol trade, he had received not one case that he could pursue. He said that Indians protected their sources from officials.

Dr. Raimundo generally made every effort to refer problems back to tribal chiefs. He suggested that professionally a lawyer was "a kind of chief among chiefs." In explaining his decisions whether to take cases forward to the tribunals, Raimundo distinguished between cases that involved Indians alone and cases that involved whites as well as Indians. He further distinguished cases that involved what he termed semi-acculturated Indians from those he termed primitive Indians. Thus he categorized the Macuxi and Wapixana as semi-acculturated. "They speak Portuguese. If they move from the village to the town, they can live relatively tranquilly." On the other hand, he termed the Yanomami as completely incapable of making that transition. Speaking of the latter, he stated that virtually everything done between Indians was left to the Indians themselves to deal with.

This applied even to the most serious act because "for them to kill is the most natural thing in the world." However, he speculated that if he learnt of a particularly brutal crime "that contravened the laws of man," he might take it forward to the tribunal.

In practice Dr. Raimundo very rarely takes cases between Indians forward. Unless there is a homocide, he tries to resolve the problem peacably.[11] In cases of assault, he suggested, his action would depend on the degree of acculturation of the Indian: "The Indians don't have the same reasoning process. Quite often when a crime occurs, they will say it was the spirits which made them do it." He said that the Indians were usually peaceful unless they drank. In fact, despite his theoretical division of cases, the only criminal case he had taken to the court was that of a mestico or mixed blood accused of murder. The man had been brought to his office by a chief, along with the victim's mother and four witnesses, and left there to be dealt with by him.

Raimundo justified his approach in terms of his reading of the Indian Statute, especially Article 56, which as shown above is concerned with sentencing. He suggested that the general application of substantive criminal law to his clients would be unrealistic. Like other field attorneys interviewed, he considered that he applied the Indian Statute *the way it should be applied,* which is to say in accordance with his perception of his clients. Violence on the part of the Indian was "part of his makeup," and consequently an Indian was legally nonresponsible. His practice of referral back to the chiefs was beneficial since it strengthened their role in maintaining social order. He would tell potential clients to return to him if their problems were not resolved by the chiefs. He rarely hears from them again, but does not follow up to see what action, if any, has been taken.

The type of problems brought to Dr. Raimundo by individual clients may be illustrated by a few examples. Three Indians, aged 16, 18 and 28 came to town and got drunk. An enemy, also an Indian, attacked the eldest, as a result of which the two younger Indians killed him with a stick. When the police arrested them Raimundo had the sixteen year-old released as a juvenile and the other two out on bond.

Raimundo has dealt with several cases of sex between parents and children. His view is that for them "sex is the most natural thing in the world. They don't see it as bad. It's as if they were animals." The cases were handled out of court except when non-Indians were involved.

An Indian woman complained that her non-Indian consort had been living with her thirteen year-old child. He dealt with this by putting the child under the protection of the mother and initiating a criminal inquiry against the perpetrator. He expected that the defendant would initiate habeas corpus proceedings and flee the territory before being brought to trial. He said that, if the defendant had been an Indian, he would have brought in a social worker for counselling.

An Indian male complained that a neighboring rancher had failed to compensate him for the destruction caused to his garden by the man's cattle. Dr. Raimundo questioned the man closely about alcohol sales and his own drinking. The Indian named two sellers. Dr. Raimundo sent him back to his village with a letter to the chief, asking him to help both in putting down alcohol use and in collecting the compensation.

In letters to the lawyer and to his superior, the regional delegate, Indian leaders sought FUNAI's intervention in a variety of conflicts involving Indians and non-Indians. Thus a chief's letter to the regional delegate in July, 1982 complained that whites were selling *cachacha* in such amounts that his community was not willing to work. The chief named the vendors. He stressed that he had no objection to the sale of other goods, only *cachacha*.

A rancher complained that Indians were raising a fence in an area where he had farmed for sixty years. However, as will be seen, conflicts of this sort involving allegations of trespass by Indians or by farmers tend to be recorded but not resolved.

From the Indian leaders' viewpoint land disputes and the opportunities for violence which they present are the principal source of problems. The chiefs of various villages in Roraima - Malcheta, Canoani, Tabua, Lascada and Pium - met in the Maloca of Manaua at the end of April, 1979. The report of their meeting in *Porantim* well summarizes the plight of the Indians in contact with white farmers. The problems concern trespassing cattle, ranchers, land conflicts and *cachacha* (*Porantim*, Vol. 2, No. 10 (August) 1979:5).

> "We are surrounded by *fazendeiros*," said one chief. "One has only to look to see. Many times we talk about clearing an area for raising pigs. We even clear the wood, but the fazendeiro says that he is going to set fire to it if we build a [place] so we stop ... The map made by FUNAI for demarcation of our area is all wrong. The farms and the waterways are not located correctly. I speak to FUNAI to come here, I even leave almost fighting. They said that they would come to study what is going on but they never return." (Id.)

Conflicts over land use give rise to acts of criminal violence. Yet it is difficult for Indians to secure action when their rights are threatened. On file in the lawyers' office are complaints about unauthorized fences from both Indians and ranchers. One village complained that a rancher had allowed his cattle to graze over their land. The petition was signed by 28 residents. Another letter asked for an inquiry into an assault against an Indian. Another asked for assistance for collection of a debt of seven sacks of corn.

The violent consequences of land disputes are illustrated by the events leading to the declaration of June 30, 1983, in which the Indigenist Missionary Council denounced the arrest of three Wapixana Indians of Roraima. They had been accused of having attempted to kill the rancher Epitacio Lucena, son of the then federal judge for the territory, Hitler Lucena. According to CIMI, the alleged victim was invading Indian lands. "The Indians didn't want to kill anyone, only to set up a fence to impede new invasions [of their land]" (Aconteceu: 228, 7). However, FUNAI did not act to protect the arrested persons, and seems generally reluctant to act. Chief, now state congressman, Juruna delivered a document to the Minister of Justice a day later complaining about FUNAI's failure to support six Indians arrested illegally in various parts of the country (CEDI, 1982-83: 228, 7).

Land is at the heart of most disputes which eventually result in criminal complaints, according to the evidence which I reviewed in Dr. Raimundo's office. FUNAI's functions include activities designed to prevent land disputes. The Indian Statute requires FUNAI to identify, delimit and demarcate land occupied by Indians within five years of its coming into effect. However, as in other parts of the country, FUNAI had not completed the process. My inquiries were made ten years after the Statute took effect.

Dr. Raimundo explained that in Roraima from 1966-67 onwards, when Indians instituted actions for maintenance of possession of land under the Civil Code, territorial judges frequently took provisional possession of the land and gave it to ranchers pending settlement. Though this approached bad faith on the part of the court, according to Raimundo it laid a basis for ranchers to claim at least some payment for the improvements they made during a process which could take as long as four years in a federal court.

Catholic Fathers in the Boa Vista mission confirmed that the Wapiana and Macuxi had not had their land demarcated, and further, that FUNAI had warned them not to put up fences until this had been accomplished. At the time of my visit an administrative edict had just been issued which *delimited* an area of 2,550 hectares within the municipio (county) of Boa Vista and granted permanent possession thereof to these tribes (FUNAI Portaria No. 12/8/C/82). This meant that the boundaries had been set by actual observation and by use of cultural, economic and social indicators. The Portaria prohibited non-Indians (except for persons granted permission by FUNAI) from entering the land (Id. clause four). It further provided that the General Department of Indigenous Patrimony should map and demarcate the land.[12]

The Wapixana arrests of 1983 flowed directly from the unresolved conflict over land rights about which Dr. Raimundo had spoken in 1982. The story emerges from the legal papers pertaining to the episode and full accounts in *Porantim*. According to the Lucena couple, in 1961 they paid one hundred cruzeiros to Jose Lourenco for a shack that was the last dwelling within the 700 hectare territory of the Wapixana. Ten years later they began to fence in the land appurtenant to it. The Indians complained to the chief of FUNAI who stopped the fencing. Subsequently the Indians complained again that the farmers' cattle continued to invade their gardens as the farms were expanded. In July, 1979, the Indians decided to send their ex-chief, a 70 year-old man, to live in the area with his family. He built a small fence and began to plant a garden. The Lucena couple were parents of Hitler Lucena, then public prosecutor. He joined them in an action to expel the old man. The judge in Roraima heard their witnesses and evicted the chief. FUNAI later appealed (*Porantim* 1979-80: Vol. 2, No. 13: 4).

The authors of the story contended that the local judicial action had overlooked the rights possessed by the Indians as established in the Brazilian constitution and the Indian Statute. The judge had a different version of the affair. In the January/February edition of *Porantim* (Vol. 2, No. 15:12), Dr. Eustaqui Nunes Silveira argued that the action was not one for ultimate title to the land, and further, that the defendant's FUNAI attorney had not proven that the territory was Indian territory to establish that the Union had an interest in the case.

Three years later the matter spilled over into violence.[13] Encounters between trespassers, temporary or permanent, and Indians have generated and will continue to generate violence likely to result in the arrest of Indians.

The Indian Statute denies indemnification to persons who invade and build upon Indian land (Art. 18, 22). However, in extended conversations with a solicitor high in FUNAI's legal offices, I learned that a policy of mediation was applied in such cases. In other words, throughout Brazil, the Indian's guardian assumes the role of Solomon rather than acting as the Indian's advocate. Local judges and officials side with local farmers and ranchers. All exploit FUNAI's failure to demarcate the land.

In general terms it may be concluded that in Boa Vista the protections of Indian persons and property guaranteed under the guardianship doctrine are not effectively provided. Civil problems turn into criminal problems as violence escalates. The attorney seeks to avoid the formal process by referring matters to the Indian villages, even when the Indians desire him to act directly to prevent violence. The FUNAI attorney can only blunt the criminal law process to the extent that he himself initiates it. Other territorial and federal officials have little hesitation in using the law against Indians.

V. The Manaus Attorney - View From the City

Dr. B handles both criminal and civil matters in the vast domain west and north of Manaus. Most of his cases, however, involve Indians living in the city. He explained that, in cases in which all parties were Indians, he had to take action over homicide. However, in all other cases occurring in the interior as opposed to the capital, matters were most effectively handled at the Municipio (or rural county) level. He did not even come to hear of rural cases unless an Indian had fallen out with local officials or had crossed someone influential and been sent to town.

For cases arising in the capital, his working assumption was that the Indians there were already incorporated, in that "70 percent of the population was a member of some weak ethnic group." "I am against sending them back to the tribe," he said. "Some already have a secondary school education." Dr. B considered the Indian Statute's special provisions for Indians in such cases to be racially discriminatory.

When Dr. B did go out to the interior, the trip might take four to five days. He said matters there were best handled by the police and the post personnel whom he advised, without judge or prosecutor.

Dr. B's impression that Indians in the city are integrated in all but their legal status is consonant with the perception of other citizens of Manaus who view the estimated 10,000 to 30,000 detribalized Indians living there as mere "*caboclos*," part of the estimated 29 percent of the population who work as street vendors, domestics, prostitutes, and in other small jobs common to members of the Brazilian underclass.[14] Although the archdiocese of Manaus has developed a pastoral plan for urban Indians, FUNAI personnel and Brazilians generally appear to be little concerned with them. According to Indian supporters, police contact with Indians in this and other cities is frequent, with FUNAI intervention limited to a few highly publicized cases.

Indians residing in the 300 thousand square kilometers of the Rio Negro valley in Amazonas are drawn into Manaus and other *municipios* not only because they are attracted to city life but also, according to informed reporters, because missionaries actively detribalize them (Luppi, 1980:8). Collective detribalization occurs when the missionaries impose a new tribal structure, change the natural chiefs, and use indoctrinated students as their agents. Some Indians flee to Colombia. Others are sent to work as domestics, abused sexually by family members and left ultimately to street prostitution in one of the zones. Those who attempt to return to their tribe thereafter are rejected (Id.). Individual detribalization is illustrated by the case of the Yanomami Indian who in accordance with tribal custom returned his wife to her mother after the latter had maltreated him. When he took up with another woman, this constituted a violation of church law. He was forced by the mission to leave his tribe, and those Indians who were Christians shunned him (Id.). According to the press account, he was removed by missionaries to Tirios in Para, 2500 kilometers from his home (Id.). Missionaries constitute a separate legal system in far-flung Indian communities. FUNAI lacks the resources to replace them with federal officers.

VI. Dr. R. of Belem

The most experienced of the three attorneys interviewed was Dr. R. He demonstrated that a competent attorney could counter expeditiously many of the acts committed against Indians and their property, and thus avoid violent reprisal. He had brought many successful actions against invasions of Indian property during his career. In one case, he had gone to the federal court of appeals and retrieved one kilo 324 grams of gold taken by prospectors from Indian land in Macupa.

He had used the defense of incapacity to free an Indian who had been sentenced to 14 years imprisonment for a homicide committed in the city with a rock when drunk. He employed a writ of habeas corpus to have the case reopened. His client spoke and looked Portuguese but (he argued) was still in the legal state of semi-acculturation. Dr. R had argued that for him, when drunk, the murder had been "little more than killing a dog." As a result of Dr. R's representations he was sent to an Indian post in the interior under conditions of semi-liberty.

Dr. R held that a good attorney could take the steps necessary to protect Indian land and property. He saw the problems elsewhere as arising from the lack of experience of the attorneys involved and the failure of FUNAI personnel to bring in attorneys when they were needed.

VII. Recent Developments in the Application of Criminal Law

There continues to be confusion among FUNAI personnel as to the applicability of Brazilian penal law to offenses committed by Indians against Indians in the villages.

In July, 1982 a report reached Brasilia that Valdomiro, a 24 year-old Maxacali, had been knifed to death by fellow tribesmen for practising withcraft in a 436 person settlement 688 kilometers from Belo Horizonte (Estato de Minas, July 10, 1982). He was said to have caused a death by shamanism a year before. A second account from local church personnel stated that Valdomiro had been killed by a rancher (Estado de Minas, July 23, 1982:15). The regional delegate was sent to investigate.

Nonetheless, the press secretary of FUNAI, Odil Teles, emphasized that the mission of the delegate would be only to calm down the Indian factions then in conflict since, he said, the laws applicable to whites did not apply to Indians, and the Indian Statute prohibited interference in internal tribal matters: "We can't deal with the merits of the question since that is the exclusive province of the members of the Maxacalis tribe itself." The press aide cited another case to illustrate the autonomy of Indians in such matters inherent to their own culture.

> When an Indian discovers that his wife has committed adultery, he has the right to beat her as much as he thinks necessary, without having anyone interfere, not even the chief of the FUNAI post who usually lives near them. The chief can, at most, only attempt to return things to peace. But he can't stop the punishment" (Estado de Minas, July 20, 1982).

The suggestion that crimes based on customary beliefs are always left to the tribes cannot be taken at face value. FUNAI interpretations are selective when Indians are seeking to protect their customary land base. On May 1, 1980 federal police intervened to disarm the Chavante of Pimental Barbos who were marking their lands without FUNAI's authorization (CEDI, 1981:19). In October, a special assistant to the President of FUNAI threatened the Chavante with prison should any of them leave their villages, attack ranchers, or fight among themselves.

Land control in Indian settlements is highly situational, as it has been since the early days of the old Indian Protection Service, now replaced by FUNAI. There are reports of the removal of tribal members by Indian personnel to special farms (called prisons by FUNAI's detractors),[15] as well as the exile of trouble-makers to large cities. There are also reports of Indian police in some areas who keep order under the direction of the chiefs of post.[16]

This realm of legal activity and the actual division of authority between FUNAI personnel, missionaries and Indian leaders remains a closed book to the outside investigator, be he American or Brazilian. Lawyers charged with the judicial protection of Indians remain in the cities and towns (as do delegates) at a great distance from rurally based Indians.

On January 28, 1983 the president of FUNAI announced that it had rejected the possibility of modifying the regime of tutela over Indian populations or reactivating initiatives to emancipate Indians (CEDI, 1983:208, 6). It appears from my observations that such steps would have been otiose.

Threats of arrests of Indians have become explicit as violence among dispossessed Indian groups and direct action against government personnel have increased. In late June, FUNAI's handpicked chief Ediso, a supporter of a planned demarcation of a small land base for the Bahian Pataxo tribe, was murdered. FUNAI accused the Indian Higino together with an activist group, Indigenist Missionary Council. Juruna in turn accused FUNAI of creating intertribal conflict. Shortly before this another Indian leader, Nailton, had met with officials in Brasilia and complained, "I am afraid that they will kidnap and make me disappear ... They [Federal police] are saying that [I] am not an Indian because I have a professional card. I have the document because [the old Indian protection service] did away with our lands. I was forced to leave and earn a living. I was obligated to have a document." Nailton was arrested with Higino on the day of the murder although he had not been present when the murder occurred (CEDI, 1982-83: 226:7; 227:7).

Another chief, Severino Fernandes da Silva, was arrested in June after members of the Potiguara tribe had knocked down electricity supply posts erected on their land, according to the Folha de Sao Paulo (CEDI, 1982-83: 226:7).

Other forms of direct action have also led to arrests of political leaders. On June 7 the FUNAI personnel of the 8th delegacia called in federal police to remove twenty Indians who had occupied a health post in protest at the dismissal of a doctor who was to be replaced (CEDI, 1982-83: 225:11). FUNAI's Brazilian headquarters was occupied for three hours by Chavantes on June 23, 1983. The president of FUNAI flew 160 Indians into the capital to defend FUNAI against the Chavante (CEDI, 1982-83: 227:6).

As Indian groups are torn apart by an externally imposed policy and embark upon activist political activity, it becomes likely that the old immunities will fall away and criminal law prosecutions will follow. These will deprive them of leaders because these leaders are now held to be sufficiently "integrated" to be punished like white men. Both the inner logic of Brazilian Indian law and the inevitable contact of Indians with non-Indians merge to guarantee this result.

Footnotes

1. "An Indian who acts fierce to me will go to jail and I will order the Federal Police to beat him with a stick." For the context of this comment see text accompanying footnote 8.

2. Bradford Burns estimates that there were a million Indians in Brazil at the beginning of the 16th century (Burns, 1970:13). The Counselho Indigenista Missionario (CIMI), currently estimates the number at 210,360, divided as follows:

Acre-Rondonia-Labrea-Humaita	12,582
Poraima-Amazona (part of the state)	60,842
Para-Amapa	10,452
Maranhao-North of Goias	9,228
Mato Grosso do Norte	11,388
Mato Grosso do Sul	21,090
East-Northeast	26,278
South	13,500
Total	165,360
Wandering Groups	15,000
Detribalized	30,000
Grand total	210,360

(Source: *Porantim* 2, No. 11 (Sept) 1979:7)

3. At around the same time the *effective* United States Indian policy was the mirror image of the Brazilian. Compare Prucha (1962:186-187):

> The federal government was sincerely interested in preventing settlement on Indian lands only up to a point, and it readily acquiesced in illegal settlements when they had gone so far as to be irremediable. The basic policy of the United States intended that white settlement should advance and the Indians withdraw. Its interest was primarily that this process should be as free of disorder and injustice as possible. The government meant to restrain and govern the advance of the white, not to prevent it forever. It supported Indian claims as far as it could out of justice and humanity to the Indians and above all as far as it was necessary to keep a semblance of peace and to maintain Indian goodwill so that continuing cessions of land could be evoked from the tribes.

4. See Article 6 of Decree No. 5.464 of June 27, 1928.

Indians were classified into categories of residence by Article 2, Decree No. 5.464 of June 27, 1928, *to wit* as (1) Nomadic, (2) Village Indians, (3) Settlement Indians, and (4) Indians who lived in Agricultural Centers or who lived in promiscuity with the civilized. Regardless of the category, Indians who are not entirely adapted remain under the guardianship of the state exercised through inspectors of the Service for the Protection of the Indians and Localization of National Workers. The inspectors are authorized to petition for or nominate an attorney according to the level of adaptation.

Article 3 of the same provided that Indians of the first three categories were to be granted the right to organize and distribute their property among their heirs, perhaps in disagreement with tribal law, with intervention by the Indian Protection Service only to pacify the spirits.

Article 4 provides that Indians in the fourth category will be assisted in pursuit of legal relief before courts and authorities.

Article 5 specifies that Indians will endure the restrictions on their civil law capacity while they are not incorporated into civilized society.

Under the 1928 decree law 5.464, when an Indian committed a penal infraction his penalty depended on his residence and the length of that residence. A nomad, village dweller or a resident of a settlement for less than five years would be placed under the care of an inspector and conveyed to a correctional colony or industrial establishment for a period not to exceed five years. An Indian who had resided for more than five years in a settlement would be punished with half the usual penalty but disciplined in an industrial institution instead of in a cell. Indians who had come to reside in agricultural centers or in promiscuity with the civilized world would be treated as ordinary citizens (Sobrinho, 1929:133).

5. Juruna was elected a federal deputy from Rio de Janeiro. Since then he has called for a Congressional committee on Indian Affairs. He donated his famous tape recorder to the Indian Museum of Campo Grande (Jornal do Brasil, August 12, 1982).
6. There was not a monolithic position within the Brazilian government on those "wards" who were thought too sophisticated to be Indians. In fact, a Brazilian high court finally allowed Juruna to travel.
7. Tribes are a cluster of Indian families or communities living either in a state of complete isolation from other sectors of the national community, or in intermittent or permanent contact therewith, but not integrated therein (Art. 3, Sec. 2.).
8. See quotation in Portuguese at beginning of the paper.
9. However, two weeks later, FUNAI transferred the Indian pilot back to his tribe (CEDI, 1982:78-79).

10. Professor Dallari's opinions regarding the civil guardianship of Indians, the requirements necessary for its cessation, and the responsibility of the Indian under penal statutes were not only published in pro-Indian commission literature but circulated as official documents throughout the FUNAI bureaucracy.

A memo drafted by Dallari on the questions (1) Can a judge in a criminal action decree the cessation of wardship of an Indian accused? and (2) What other points stand out as to the penal responsibility of the Indian? was circulated in February 1982 to the delegates in outlying FUNAI offices.

Dallari stressed in this document (after stating the prerequisites for emancipation as set forth in the Indian statute) that "the liberation of wardship or emancipation should only be conceded by means of a process whose initiative flows from the Indian himself" (Dallari, 1982:2).

Dallari further stressed that even in such a case of a petition apparently initiated by an Indian, the Constitution and Statute of the Indian indicated that the organ of assistance to the Indian and public minister should lend assistance to make sure that the Indian was not being induced to ask for emancipation in order to prejudice himself. The Union had an interest in the case not only arising from its duty as guardian but also because the Indian, in principle, had a possessory interest in federal land.

This said, Dallari emphasized that "The penal responsibility of the Indian does not depend upon his civil capacity. If an Indian practices an act defined as a crime, the precepts of the law relative to incompetency ought to be applied (Id. 3)."

Dallari then directed the attorneys to Article 22 of the penal code that provides for exemption from punishment for those who demonstrate that by incomplete mental development or retardation a person is incapable of understanding the criminal character of action or knowing that he was committing a crime.

He cited Brasilueu Garica who had commented that the article was directed not only to those suffering from mental illness but also at persons such as Indians who might commit a crime in consequence of his incomplete or retarded mental development, even though he would not be considered ill.

"The offenses that he comes to practice can be explained frequently by the deficit (emphasized) in his mental development, in the sense that as he fails to understand the criminal character of the event or understand in conformity with his understanding how the nebulous event occurred" (Dallari quoting Int. de Criminal Law, Vol. I, Work I, p. 330).

Drawing upon this and other commentaries to the penal code, Dallari sought to persuade his readers that "in an imperfect way" the Penal Code left open the possibility of considering an Indian to be either responsible or not responsible when he committed a criminal act depending upon whether he possessed a standard of acceptance or rejections of criminal responsibility uniform with that of Brazilian law.

"It is necessary," said he, "to define responsibility, in each concrete case taking into account the characteristics of the agent, without losing the view that in the case of the Indian it is not enough to consider the biological aspect, it being indispensable to evaluate the cultural integration" (Id. 3).

Although the Indian may be within the non-Indian society, the forest dweller, emphasizes Dallari, has a cultural inheritance that might influence his behavior.

Dallari's commentary (to which I have given only the most superficial appraisal) sought to remind legal advocates in the field that states of mind which might give rise to defenses on grounds of incompetence could include that of the forest dweller whose behavior was guided by differing cultural precepts.

Finally, he reminded the advocates that not only Article 56 of the Indian statute (supra) but the Convention 107 of the International Labor Organization, adopted in Brazil in 1966, provided that in the application of penal sanctions to Indians, preference should be given to methods aimed at recuperation over methods of reclusion.

11. The lawyer for the 10th delegacia in Boa Vista wrote the attorney general of FUNAI in February 1982 concerning steps that should be taken in the case of Indians when beatings occurred between couples or in the case when fathers deflowered their own daughters (Fonseca e Silva, 1982).

He recommended a form of punishment which would punish the author of the crime "without forgetting his condition as ward, in spite of his advancing state of acculturation."

He first determined that FUNAI was authorized to exercise police power in the reserved areas and, within its responsibility as guardian, had the responsibility to intercede whether the Indian was threatened by the surrounding society or by another aborigine.

He referred to Art. 27, Sec. 2 of the Indian statute and its provision that the police measures necessary to keep order (in) the Indian reserve must be taken with the use of persuasive means and in accordance with the interests of the Indians there. This also meant, he said, that Article 6 should be followed and that tribal customs should be respected as described there.

From this, he said, that to receive the stamp of approval of the community in which victim and offender reside, these persons should be taken to their own institutions for punishment so long as the punishment is not of a cruel or degrading character with death prohibited in all cases (quoting Art. 57 of the Indian statute)

"For this reason," he concluded, "we counsel against the use of whatever display of police (be they armed forces, auxiliary or federal police), especially since the collaboration of these entities is more adapted to protection of the lands" (Id:2).

Finally, he suggested that lawyers enter into some understanding with the leaders of the communities in order or discover a way within their institutions to respond to the penal offense. And in the case of the daughter violated by her father, instead of applying the penal sanction, "he ought to listen to the Social Workers regarding the family organization and the causes of the destabilization between the father and daughter" (Id. 3).

This concern with turning cases back to community leaders figures in descriptions of some cases described and observed during my field trip to lawyer's offices in outlying Brazilian cities and towns despite the now accepted interpretation that Brazilian Indians are subject to Brazilian criminal law. As will be seen, to return a case to the village does not always mean that tribal law or rights will be supported.

12. Reports from Brazil indicate that in March, 1983, Decree 88.118 transferred the responsibility for defining indigenous areas to be demarcated to an interministerial work group (CEDI, 1982 220:5). Whether this had delayed demarcations or not, the report of violence occurred ten months later.
13. The Catholic Fathers of Boa Vista reported seeing prospectors within Yanomami territory, but charged that FUNAI denied their presence.
14. See, "Quen e Indio no Amazonas?" *Porantim,* Vol. 2, N. 9 (July) 1979, pp. 12-13).
15. In September, 1979, CIMI charged that FUNAI kept 74 Indians imprisoned on the Guarani Agricultural Farm, known as the Krenak prison. Then president of FUNAI Adhenar Ribeiro admitted that "in the past, actually those Indians who committed offenses in their villages were transferred to Krenak and held as prisoners, guarded by the military police." Eighty-eight Indians of various tribes lived on Fazenda Guarani. These Indians, he said, left their villages of their own volition usually because of problems of adaptation within their own tribal group, but he denied that they suffered any restriction whatsoever (*Porantim*, 1979-80: 2:12, 15, quoting from national press accounts).

The Fazenda Guarani, though no longer a penal colony, continued, according to the president, to be used to "shelter" Indians who had committed offenses in their villages and who could no longer live within their communities. However, he stressed that "there is no person who doesn't want to stay." (Jornal do Brasil, May 9, 1979).

Problems of persons who committed an offense within their own group would only be resolved, he said, by "efficient programs of education."

These accounts leave unclear (1) who decides to send an Indian away from his tribe; (2) whether the Indian's offense is based on federal law, tribal law or religious precept; and (3) where a detribalized Indian might go if he left the Fazenda Guarani.

16. The president of FUNAI stated that the Rural Native Guard, Indian Police, in Fazenda Krenak, the former penal colony, was deactivated at the beginning of 1979. However, some Indians who had been part of the police force (organized by the Military police) continued receiving salaries from the state governor (Jornal do Brasil, May 9, 1979).

References

BURNS, E. Bradford (1970)
A History of Brazil. New York and London: Columbia University Press.

CENTRO ECUMENICO DE DOCUMENTACAO E INFORMACAO (CEDI) (1981)
Aconteceu: Povos Indigenas no Brasil/1980. Sao Paulo: Editoria Prensa Ltda.

---------- (1982)
Aconteceu: Povos Indigenas no Brasil/1981. Sao Paulo: Editoria Prensa Ltda.

---------- (1982-83)
Aconteceu: Factos Destacados da Imprensa. Various Issues. Sao Paulo.

COHEN, Felix S. (1940) (1971)
Handbook of Federal Indian Law. Republished. Albuquerque: University of New Mexico Press.

DALLARI, Dalmo De Abreu (1979)
"O Indio, sua Capacidade Juridica e suas Terras," in Cardernos da Commissao Pro-Indio No. 1, A Questao da Emancipacao. Sao Paulo: Global Editora.

---------- (1982)
Memo 107/GAB. Circular from Chefe do Gabinente, Fundacao Nacional do Indio, February 2, 1982. Unpublished

DA SOUZA, Dr. Inglez (1889)
O Selvagem Perante o Direito. O Direito Vol 112:1-19.

FERREIRA DE SOUZA PITANGA, Antonio (1905)
Selvagem Perante O Direito, O Direito Vol 109:42-43.

FONSECA E SILVA, Geraldo (1982)
Informacao No. 33/PJ/82 a Procuradura Geral, Fundacao Nacional do Indio, February 9, 1982. Unpublished.

LUPPI, Carlos Alberto (1980)
Indios do Rio Negro, no Rumo da Marginalizacao. Folha de Sao Paulo. October 12, 1980.

MELALTI, Julio Cezar (1970)
Indio de Brasil. Brasilia: Coordena-Editora de Brasilia.

MENDES JUNIOR, Joao (1912)
Os Indigenas do Brasil ... Seus Direitos ... Individuaes e Politicos. Sao Paulo: Hennies Iramaos.

OTAVIO, Rodrigo (1946)
Os Selvagens Americanos Perante O Dereito. Brasiliana, Vol 254. Sao Paulo: Companhea Editoria Nacional.

PORANTIM (1979-80)
Vols. 2-3 1979-80, various issues. Manaus.

PRUCHA, Francis Paul (1962)
American Indian Policy in the Formative Years, The Trade and Intercourse Acts 1790-1834. Cambridge: Harvard University Press.

---------- (1981)
Indian Policy in the United States. Lincoln and London: University of Nebraska Press.

SOBRINHO, Oliveira (1929)
O Selvicolos Brasileiros Da Legislacao Patria - O Decreto Legislativo N. 5, 484 de 1928, in Pandectas Brasileiras Vol 6. Rio de Janeiro: Case Graphica.

SOUTHEY, Robert (1822) (1962)
History of Brazil. New York: Greenwood Press.

STRICKLAND, Renard et al (1982)
Felix S. Cohen's Handbook of Federal Indian Law, 1982 Edition. Charlottesville: Michie, Bobbs-Merrill.

WACHTEL, David (1982)
"Indian Law Enforcement," in Laurence French (ed.), Indians and Criminal Justice. Ottawa, New Jersey: Allanheld, Osmun and Co.

WILKINSON, Charles F. (1982)
"Basic Doctrines of American Indian Law," in Laurence French (ed.), Indians and Criminal Justice. Ottawa, New Jersey: Allanheld, Osmun and Co.

Part IV

Questions of Status: Women; Child Placement

Aboriginal women and the recognition of customary law in Australia

Diane Bell

Introduction

We're living in our father's country ... we had a crook man here once. We got him on the road. He shouldn't be in that land. I had a go at that man. I stopped the truck and went to talk to him. Nelson and Murphy, my brothers, were saying, "We're going to fight." But I said, "Listen. I'll soft-talk them and I'll kick them out." Everyone was turning their face. I said, "I'm sorry, but you can't come here. This is my land. You just go straight to the bitumen [Stuart Highway] and to town [Tennant Creek] and we'll see you there today, this afternoon." Poor buggers, they went. We never saw them again. Every time they see our truck in town, they go.

(Myrtle Napanangka Kennedy)[1]

My father was *kurdungurlu* for that place. It was his to look after. He looked after the two places, Waake and Wakulpu, and then I lost him; he passed away. Now it's up to me looking after my country, Jarra Jarra and also Waake and Wakulpu. As my father could not go on to that country, so from when I was a young girl I kept on doing the *yawulyu* [women's ceremonies], looking after the country ... my sisters, Mona and Nancy, they were looking after that country too ... we do that *yawulyu* for Wakulpu all the time ... for fruit ... so it will grow up well so that we can make it green, so that we can hold the Law for ever. My father instructed me to hold it always this way so I go on holding *yawulyu* for that country. Sometimes we dance, man and woman together. For Wakulpu. So we can "catch him up", and "hold him up".

(Mollie Nungarrayi giving evidence in the Kaytej, Warlpiri and Warlmanpa land claim)[2]

When women such as Molly and Myrtle speak, others listen: their authority on matters of land and law is recognized by men and women alike. Yet until recently, the many fact-finding missions which regularly visited Aboriginal communities in search of data on which to base programmes, policies, and projected estimates, rarely consulted women on matters concerning their life choices. The attitudes and preferences of women regarding the basics of life - health, housing, education, community development - were neither known nor sought.

The ramifications of such ignorance and neglect have been all too apparent in the areas of land rights and law reform. In the preparation of the first land claim heard under the *Aboriginal Land Rights (Northern Territory) Act* 1976, women were not included as claimants; and in the first meeting which the Australian Law Reform Commission (A.L.R.C.) held in Central Australia, women were effectively excluded.[3] A discussion of why this should be so and the growing awareness of the importance of consulting women on a wide range of matters affecting their status as individuals, as members of a family and community, and as citizens of Australia, provide the context for an analysis of specific problems which the A.L.R.C. reference on the recognition of Customary Law raises for Aboriginal women in Northern Australia.

I. Aboriginal women's role re-examined

Before beginning fieldwork in Central Australia in 1976, I made a study of the available anthropological and historical literature on the region and was struck by the image of male-female relations it presented. Aboriginal women were portrayed as dominated and exploited, as pawns in the game of the male gerontocracy.[4] This characterization of Aboriginal woman's traditional role was given as a legitimation of her secondary position in the emerging political order of Northern Australia. Even when several anthropologists had written of women as independent members of their society, the focus of their research had been on women within Aboriginal society or on the changes which had occurred within that society. Rarely was there any discussion of the position of Aboriginal women within the wider society of white Australia.[5]

In the course of my research into the changing role and status of Aboriginal women in Northern Australia, my children and I lived for 18 months in a desert community in Central Australia. During that time I worked with women who moved confidently through their country, who related to me stories of their importance as women within their society, who celebrated their relationship to the land in complex ceremonies. Many spoke of their past and present role in maintaining law and order. Although they allowed that this role was changing and that they were finding it increasingly difficult to make their opinions known and to remain informed, they were attempting to make sense of their new situation, and to understand the impact which colonization of their land had had on their lives.

Their attempts to make their opinions known were thwarted at many turns. Firstly, the sex-segregated nature of Aboriginal society makes it quite inappropriate and often dangerous for male researchers to attempt to consult with Aboriginal women. In Central Australia, until very recently, most field officers and community advisers were male. Even where this problem was well understood, no firm policy calling for parallel structures of consultation existed. Too often it seemed the problem was recognized only to be dismissed.[6]

Secondly, deeply entrenched preconceptions of the role of women as secondary in Aboriginal society have constrained research and policy as surely as has the predominance of men in the field. This bias is, although pervasive, somewhat more elusive, and thus more difficult to recognize and overcome. Where the dominant and enduring image of Aboriginal woman is that of a second-class citizen who is excluded from all-important activities, it is not surprising that officials fail to inquire about her role in customary law, or to establish bodies on which she is represented. To challenge this image appears to fly in the face of reason and to deny the existence of obvious facts. White male officials often commented to me that women's failure to attend meetings is a clear indication that they have nothing to say and have no right to speak. Moreover, even when these officials admitted that it might be inappropriate for Aboriginal women to attend these meetings, they still dismissed the idea of holding separate meetings for women. They remained unshaken in their view that women had nothing to contribute to important discussions concerning their community.[7]

In seeking a way to explain Aboriginal women's image of themselves as autonomous and independent members of their society, I found it necessary to explore the nature of the changes in the lives of women who, in a lifetime, had gone from a hunter-gatherer mode of subsistence to a sedentary lifestyle on missions, reserves, cattle stations and in the towns. While many of their reminiscences of life in the bush may be romantic reconstructions of a bygone era, much can be substantiated from early reports.[8] I have argued elsewhere that it is necessary to consider the nature of social change and sexual politics if one is to come to an understanding of the way in which the ethnographic portrait of

Aboriginal women and the theoretical understanding of women's role and status in desert society are related.[9] I have suggested that it is in the dynamic interweaving of these two critically important factors (social change and sexual politics) that we find a means of reconciling women's claims to independence and autonomy with the models that characterize women as dominated and oppressed.

In the past, male-female relations were flexible and subject to change: each sex had room to manoeuvre; each had a power base. But today the roles have become increasingly rigid, the give-and-take a fiction, the checks and balances skewed. Aboriginal men have found a more accommodating niche in the emerging male-dominated colonial society of Northern Australia. It is their power base which has been deemed a negotiating forum, not women's. Men may continue to manipulate the system, for they are the politicians in the eyes of many white Australians. Women have limited access to the world of decision-making. To mark their status as independent and autonomous persons, women are turning more and more to exclusively women's activities (such as certain land-based ceremonies) to give expression to their rights and responsibilities in land and the maintenance of their society. Ironically, in the process, they restrict their access to important institutions *within* the emerging political order.[10]

II. Women's authority

Women's authority is intimately related to the religious sphere. In ritual women emphasize their role as nurturers of people, land and relationships. It is their responsibility to maintain harmoniously this complex of relationships between the living and the land which is manifest in the intertwining of the ritual foci of health and emotional management. Through their *yawulyu* they nurture land, through their health and curing rituals they resolve conflict and restore social harmony, and through their *yilpinji* (love rituals) they manage emotions. In *yilpinji*, as in their health-oriented *yawulyu*, women seek to resolve and to explore the conflicts and tensions which beset their communities. Now that Aborigines live in populous centres, jealous fights, accusations of infidelity and illicit affairs occur on a scale impossible a century ago when people lived in small, mobile bands. The result is that woman's role in the domain of emotional management is, like her role in the maintenance of health and harmony, truly awe-inspiring.

Religious rituals to sustain an harmonious relation of people to land rely on access to the land and the right to use and maintain it as did the ancestors. The intrustion of white settlers, miners, pastoralists and explorers into Central Australia has affected men and women differently. While Aboriginal men complain that whites do not understand their need to protect their country from the ravages of cattle, bush fires and trespassers, women protest the loss of the land over which they foraged as the loss of the basis of their economic independence. Money and rations have proved a poor substitute. "Money", as one woman said, "is not our way, we don't understand about money." It brings with it new sets of relationships over which women have no control.

Women have also lost their autonomy in those ritual domains in which they asserted their status as adult, responsible members of their society. In the past, men and women staged sex-specific rituals through which they were enhanced as members of their society. A delicate balance between male assertions of authority and the solidarity and independence enjoyed by women was worked out in the separate ritual worlds of each. This equilibrium has been fundamentally disturbed by the loss of land and the operation of the new law.

III. Customary law and land

Women in Central Australia (with particular reference to Warlpiri) have the same two sets of rights and responsibilities in land as men. The first is as *kirda* and the second is as *kurdungurlu*. A woman is *kirda* for the country of her father and she shares this responsibility with her brothers, sisters, father, father's brothers and sisters, i.e. with the members of her patriline. She holds certain sacred objects which validate her rights and responsibilities in the country for which she is *kirda*, and she performs certain rituals for the maintenance of that country. Other rituals which focus on emotional management (the so-called "love magic" ceremonies) and health and curing, are also known through her relation to the dreaming of her father's country.

A woman is *kurdungurlu* for the country of her mother, along with her brothers and sisters, her mother's father's sisters' children and her mother's sisters' children. As *kurdungurlu* she is responsible for the safety and correct performance of ceremonies, for the singing and painting of the participants. She guards the knowledge of the dreaming and keeps the *kirda* "straight". Performances of important land-maintaining rituals cannot occur without the presence of *kurdungurlu* who must watch and correct the *kirda* if necessary. *Kurdungurlu* must also be present during visits to important sites. Thus, the relation between *kirda* and *kurdungurlu* is one of interdependence and complementarity.

In the past, a women often lived in the country of either her mother or father while young and learnt something of its religious significance. At marriage, she sometimes moved into the country of her husband, or frequently, the husband lived in the country of her parents for a period. The country of the husband was often the country for which she was *kurdungurlu* and thus she was able to advance her position in the rituals of that country. With subsequent marriages, women moved back to the country for which they were *kirda*. By settling women in an area, say that of a government reserve, where they may not have the rights of *kirda* or *kurdungurlu*, women (and men also) are deprived of their power base, access to knowledge and relationships which are the stamp of authority in old age.[11]

IV. Social security

It is also necessary to explore the changes in the productive lives of women. By virtue of their role as hunters and gatherers in the desert they produced up to 80% of the reliable diet and were thus critical to survival. Further, because they hunted separately from men, they were potentially economically independent. Men caught the prized portion of the diet, the large game, but did not contribute to the daily food intake and relied upon women for staples such as yams, edible seeds, grubs and small game. Although women were expected to feed their male kin, they only did so after they had satisfied their own needs. It is generally assumed that men use food, such as meat, to establish political alliances. But it is well to note that older women, who lived in single women's camps, had few male relatives dependent upon them and could establish alliances as well with their surplus food. Such women were skilled hunters and knowledgeable in the ways of the country and its bounty. The introduction of flour relieved women of the burden of food-getting but also led to a diminution of their importance as producers.

The above sketch shows that loss of land had implications for women in both the economic and religious domains. Their new dependence on social security payments has further undermined their position as independent members of their society. Most payments, such as unemployment benefits, are made to household heads who are assumed to be male. However, as each sex is still responsible for its own needs, the situation today is confused. Women are expected to cope on the money (child allowances) they receive and men are free to spend their money (unemployment benefits) on their needs. It is little wonder women frequently mentioned welfare and social security payments in connection with the breakdown of their law. It is an issue on which both men and women have strong views, but they are not always in accord. Aspects of the payment of benefits impinge on men and women differently, threatening different values. Men and women have separate economic roles which cannot be easily subsumed in categories established by social security departments primarily concerned with the problems facing nuclear families in white Australia.

Some change has marked this field in the last few years. The Department of Social Security is now prepared to pay split cheques. If a woman wishes to receive her entitlement separately, she may apply for the splitting of unemployment benefit cheques. For some time this process was difficult to administer, but now that the Northern Territory Department of Social Security has access to the National computer, more cheques are being processed in this way.

Thus, in the shift from a hunter-gatherer to a sedentary lifestyle, it is evident that women have lost more than access merely to their foraging grounds. They have lost access to what was both a spiritual and economic resource. They have moved from a position of independence to one of dependence. They are no longer independent producers but members of households with nominal male heads.

Once the people are deprived of land or restricted in any way, the law diminishes in strength. It is not so much that the law itself breaks down, but rather that the colonizers' different system of land tenure and usage erodes the basis of authority. The process varies, but the result is the same. Thus people living in remote communities who have been forcibly resettled outside their own country are often in a position just as desperate as those living in the towns, under the control of the new law, but still in their country.

V. The customary law reference

On February 9, 1977, the then Attorney-General, Mr. R.J. Ellicott, referred to the A.L.R.C., established under the Law Reform Commission Act 1973, matters concerning the practice and administration of European law and Aboriginal customary law. He wrote of the right of Aborigines to retain their racial identity and traditional lifestyle, to adopt wholly or partly a European lifestyle where they so desired, and of the need to ensure the enjoyment of basic human rights. Underlying this reference was the principle that no persons or groups should be discriminated against and that all should be able to enjoy their chosen lifestyle to the fullest. The situation of Aboriginal women, therefore, required careful consideration both to determine their attitude to law and to overcome the twin disadvantages of being both black and female.

A central concern of the reference was the problems Aborigines experienced with the Australian criminal justice system. There was, of course, scope for an examination of other issues and indeed the A.L.R.C. has given much consideration to matters such as customary marriage, adoption, custody and community justice.

However, it is the disproportionate number of Aboriginal people in gaol which has captured the imagination of many lawyers and law-enforcement agencies.

Working with women on this reference has convinced me that, while interested in recommendations concerning adjustment of the criminal justice system to take account of customary law, women were more concerned about the way in which violence rebounded on themselves and their female kin. They were also intent on making plain the distress they experienced when separated from sons, husbands, brothers and in-laws who were gaoled for lengthy periods. They pointed out that the imposition of fines on unemployed persons often meant that their pensions were used to keep young offenders out of gaol. Not only had women something to say, they had a fundamental point to make - one which only makes sense in terms of the role of women in traditional society and the nature of the changes in their lives outlined above.

My interest in the role of Aboriginal women in the maintenance of customary legal systems crystallized one afternoon in 1977 during the first round of meetings held by the A.L.R.C. in Alice Springs. Pam Ditton, of Central Australian Aboriginal Legal Aid Service, and I attended the meeting whose purpose was to discuss the reference with people in Central Australia. The dialogue was between men and often referred to matters classified as 'men's business'. Pam and I, on the basis of our experience in the area, knew well that women had secrets which it would be impossible for them to discuss at these large public meetings or in front of men, Aboriginal or white. At the conclusion of the Alice Springs meeting, we talked to those women who had come into the area with the intention of speaking, if at all possible. They impressed upon us the importance of recording their views on matters relating to land and law, and expressed dismay at the male assumption that only Aboriginal men needed to be consulted.

Two years of bullying and haranguing were required before funding for three months' research on the issue could be obtained. The Commission had already noted that "Women have a unique point of view, which is probably only communicable to a woman interrogator".[12] In a field report of that first visit to Central Australia, the Commission's male field officer commented: "The views of women on important matters have not been obtained. This is a question which must be given very serious attention on other field research."[13] Aboriginal women in Central Australia had begun to complain that they were not being consulted.[14] The Land Claim hearings under the Land Rights Act were demonstrating women's importance in the preparation and running of claims. The problems associated with taking evidence from women were being overcome in imaginative and innovative ways, but the Law Reform Commission persisted with the all-male consultations.

Then, in 1979, on behalf of the Central Australian Aboriginal Legal Aid Service, with the assistance of funding from the Australian Institute of Aboriginal Studies, Pam Ditton and I set out to record Aboriginal women's opinions of their changing role within the wider Central Australian society, and their attitude to the reference on recognition of Customary Law.

On the basis of our experience in Central Australia, we isolated six different types of communities which we felt were representative of problems facing Aboriginal women. We chose to visit, 1) a settlement; 2) an outstation; 3) an Aboriginal-managed cattle station; 4) a European-managed cattle station; 5) a town camp with a lease; and 6) a town camp without a lease (see below, map 2). We spent up to a week in each community and made return visits where possible. We also undertook comparative research and examined data from other communities as a check on our own findings and choice of community.

Although time was limited, we did manage to canvass women's opinions on many issues in many different situations. In the communities chosen, we were well known and had previous work experience. As the Warlpiri are one of the largest language groups in Central Australia, with somewhere in the vicinity of 2,000 speakers, we oriented our study towards them. Although they live in communities which may differ widely, they share a common code. By focusing on one language group, we had a common thread uniting our community profiles.

Initially, we asked open-ended questions such as, what troubles are you having here as women? In this way we allowed the women to define the areas of concern to them. Later, as themes emerged, we discussed specific issues such as the role of the Law Reform Commission and its reference on Customary Law. If one complaint about the interaction of the two laws was constant, it was that, in the past, the voice of women had been heeded whereas today that voice was denied because the forums established for discussion of "Aboriginal matters" were dominated by men, both black and white. The women to whom we spoke were delighted we had come to consult with them. The men displayed no hostility, but rather expressed appreciation that we, as women, had come to speak to women.

Our findings are recorded in our report, *Law: the old and the new,* which provides outline profiles of each of the communities visited, a section devoted to special issues and recommendations for future action. Although we found enormous variations within the region, several conclusions were inescapable. Customary law had to be seen as both a body of rules backed by sanctions and as a set of dispute resolution mechanisms. The rules are both formal and informal. The formal rules are backed by sanctions and are clearly articulated in terms of what one should do and why. At a more informal level they are a series of accepted behaviours which allow daily social life to proceed. These more informal areas of behavioural controls may never be clearly stated, but are the stuff of interpersonal relationships, the self-regulating patterns of interaction, of which Professor Ronald Berndt[15] writes. Such are thrown into relief in periods of rapid change when the very basis of people's existence is threatened.

In the six community profiles of *Law: the old and the new,* it is apparent that women are experiencing and perceiving the impact of the new law on the old in different ways. In the areas where Aboriginal control has some meaning, i.e. on the outstations and Aboriginal-managed cattle stations, women are not seeking access to formally recognized channels through which to express their opinions or to ensure their share of resources. Their authority base is still there in their access to land and the economic and religious power they derive from their relationship to it. It is where women are off the land, or denied access to it, that they feel most acutely the need for safeguards. Because of the male bias in the political and legal institutions of the new law, Aboriginal women recognize that unless they have formal recognition within that system, they will be ignored and further disenfranchised.

Finally, we urged in our report that law be seen as encompassing more than the legal institutions which were the visible representations of the new law in Aboriginal communities. We argued that men and women played fundamentally different roles in the maintenance of customary legal systems, but that each jointly subscribed to a code which they maintained in a cooperative manner. The basis of women's authority, like that of men, rested on ritual knowledge and expertise, rights in land and seniority. In order to consult with women it was necessary to develop parallel structures at all levels. Such measures would obviously require an injection of funds and a raising of staff ceilings, but they would also entail a recognition that the reference posed unique problems in the gathering of opinions.

However admirable, the appointment of an Aboriginal woman as Consultant to the Law Reform Commission could scarcely be seen as anything other than tokenism. Moreover, although apparently taking seriously a recommendation that women should consult with women, the Law Reform Commission sent a research assistant with no particular training in law or anthropology on their 1981 tour. During this fieldwork, the Commission took evidence in a Court-like setting and managed to alienate most Aboriginal people in Central Australia with whom they came into contact. At the time the Commission was obsessively concerned with tribal punishment and under-age marriage and hardly at all concerned with the maintenance of law and order.

Then, in late 1981, after the appointment of Professor James Crawford as Commissioner, the tide began to turn. The uniqueness of the reference was recognized and appropriate measures taken. New consultants, including Aboriginal women, were appointed; regional meetings were organized; a programme of writing research papers was instigated; the interests of women began to be taken seriously.

The shift in emphasis is clear to anyone who cares to read the early Discussion Papers of the Commission (e.g. No. 17) and compare them with Research Papers Nos. 1-4. The Commission squarely faced the conflict which arose between Australian Law and Aboriginal Customary Law concerning under-age marriage, promised marriage and polygyny, and during 1982 canvassed the concept of functional recognition of customary marriage. In Research Paper 2 they summarize the argument thus:

It appears that the failure of the general law to accord legal status to Aboriginal tribal marriage causes a number of social and legal problems, e.g. in the areas of adoption, social security, compensation and property distribution on death.

As in other areas of Aboriginal Custom, the rules and practices associated with tribal marriage vary from one community to another.[16]

The Commission argued that while particular Aboriginal customs or practices might be unacceptable to the general community, this should not impede the legal recognition of tribal marriage. Adopting a functional approach, they suggested examining the particular consequences of recognizing tribal marriages in each area of the general law which presently causes legal and social problems.

The approach, although not a recognition of tribal marriage "as such", is the least intrusive in that it does not require the codification or enactment of Customary Marriage rules, and thus leaves Aboriginal communities a greater measure of freedom in developing these rules to cope with new situations. It provides recognition, even if indirect, of important aspects of the Aboriginal social fabric and of Customary Law.[17]

The Law Reform Commission also seriously confronted the need to revisit Central Australia; to consult with women; and to seek not only individual opinion but opinion from communities and groups within communities. Thus, it was that an unlikely bunch of lawyers and consulting anthropologists undertook consultations in Central Australia in October 1982. Professor Alice Tay (of Sydney University and part-time Commissioner) and I met with the women in the communities we visited, while Professor James Crawford, Peter Hennessey, and Chris Kirkbright of the A.L.R.C. undertook consultations with the men.[18]

The input from the women was important in a number of ways. For example, in Tennant Creek, a mining town 500 km. north of Alice Springs, we talked to

Warumungu women who were traditional owners for the area. Their views on under-age marriage were illuminating. Some women expressed the view that a girl may only properly "camp" with her husband or promised husband "when her breasts hang down", that is when she is in her late teens. The problem arose when women drew the distinction between "camping with a husband" and "living with a husband". Living in a residential arrangement with a "husband" is different from entering into a full sexual relationship. It was correct, the women stated, for a young girl to begin sleeping in her husband's camp after "breasts appear" (that is, at menarche), but not to enter into a full sexual relationship until "the breasts hang down". Couching the question in terms of chronological age had caused misunderstanding by drawing a distinction which had not been relevant in the past. Moreover, as the age of sexual maturity is falling, answers in terms of age were more likely to mislead than to clarify the situation.

Older women have indicated that marriage is occurring younger today than it did in the past, and that they don't approve of this development. They also argued that because girls are marrying younger, and because they often go to their husband as the first and only wife, they are placed in an unfamiliar situation and are propelled into a sexual relationship from the beginning of the marriage. Younger women were more ambivalent, but all were clear that, when marital disputes arose, the intervention of older women occurred.

Furthermore, the discussions suggested conceptual problems with the use of the term "husband". One's "husband" is known from birth and one's potential spouses are learnt from socialization into the kinship system, but to have a "husband" is not the same as to be married. The situation is further confused by the dysjunction between sexual maturity and social maturity. In the past, when girls did not begin to menstruate until the age of 16 or 17, it could be assumed that, at that age, they were socially prepared to take on the responsibilities of a young wife. However, today, as a result of earlier sexual maturity, the same assumption cannot be made. Furthermore, as girls are spending their early years in schools away from adult female teachers, they are no longer so well prepared for their role as wives.[19]

The meetings of October 1982 also demonstrated that separate consultations with men and women did not preclude the emergence of a community view. At Utopia, a pastoral station approximately 150 km. north-east of Alice Springs, we held a series of meetings over three days. We began with a community meeting with those who had assembled to greet us on our arrival. This was a predominantly male exchange. Afterwards, I went into the family camps located near the homestead and discussed with the women the ways in which they might like to organize meetings over the following few days. The next morning, women assembled in one bough shade while the men sat in another shaded area. The group of women to whom Alice Tay and I spoke comprised members of each of the land-holding groups of the Utopia pastoral station. We outlined the range of issues which the Commission was considering. When we broke for lunch the women moved off into their family camps, as did the men. Much informal discussion occurred. After lunch we resumed the meetings, the women discussing matters which the men had broached in the morning, and vice-versa. During this session the women stressed emphatically the interrelation of law and land, and the importance of strengthening Aboriginal customary law. A representative of each of the land-holding groups advanced the women's viewpoint on land and law.

The following day the procedure was repeated and, as the meetings began to wind up, the men requested that Alice and I report to them on the women's meetings, while the women heard from James Crawford about what had occurred in the men's meeting. This exchange of information over, we were instructed to speak to each other in order to confirm that a consensus had been achieved, as indeed it had.

VI. Consequences for consultation

Most persons working in Aboriginal Affairs recognize that important matters must be broached with important persons. One does not ask an uninitiated man about ritual matters, nor should one ask a young woman to answer questions on important issues in her community, although it is often very convenient to consult with such women as they are literate and have some experience of white culture. However, younger women, like younger men, do not know the content of the secret law and it is quite inappropriate for them to answer questions on these matters. Older women, like older men, prefer to stay one step removed from the public gaze at meetings organized or required by the new law. Often they are content to allow younger, literate women to deal with the problems of stocktaking in stores, the running of banking agencies and the like. But on matters of law, it is the older women who speak.

Our inquiries into the old law were answered by women with status. Younger women had more to say about the new law. Both old and young had opinions on the interface between the two laws. We were indeed fortunate to obtain the authoritative opinions of older women, as this is not always possible. Care must be exercised to allow interviewees time to discuss issues with the appropriate persons and visitors cannot expect same-day answers to many questions.

Some consultations need to occur in family camps, some at the community level and some with individuals. Very often the question-answer format is inappropriate. In the context of land claims, women often prefer to provide a ceremonial display in answer to questions concerning their relationship to land. Similarly, both men and women often prefer to demonstrate the way in which the law is played out rather than expressing it in words.

The issues raised by the customary law reference are complex. Skilled interpreters are needed to find ways in which the concepts may be explained to people whose primary contact with the Australian legal system is through police, courts and gaols. The preparation of materials in different languages and the use of interpreters in various communities have provided further insights into the conceptual issues raised by recognition of customary law. For example, the notion that recognition may mean the incorporation of Aboriginal law into the law of White Australia is repugnant to most Aboriginal people. The notion of the two laws existing side by side and taking account of each other is more agreeable to them.

Although, since 1977, progress has been made in finding ways to hear and record the opinions of women, there is still a long way to go. No women are employed permanently on the reference to deal with matters concerning women. Aboriginal women in southern Australia are still not satisfied that the consultation has been adequate. At a regional meeting of consultants in December 1982 and at a Special Issues conference in May 1983, these women voiced their discontent. In May 1983 at the Regional Consultants' meeting held in Perth, Western Australia, Dr. Catherine Berndt asked what attention was being paid to women in the consultations in Western Australia. The answer was reminiscent of that of 1977. Due to a lack of resources, no women from the Commission would visit the Eastern Goldfields area (W.A.), with the result that the Commission anticipated difficulties in consulting Aboriginal women there. The Commission did, however, express the hope that because the meetings were being held in a country town environment, the problems of consulting with Aboriginal women would not be as great as in more remote communities.

A Coda

Lest it be imagined that I, as a white feminist, am imposing women's liberationist ideals on Aboriginal women, let me recount a favourite observation of an Aboriginal friend of mine. We had been discussing child rearing and she had pointed out to me that children were shared by a number of members of one's family camp, thus lightening the burden of child-rearing for mothers. White women, however, she observed, were locked inside all day just like prisoners. To escape, they sought the right of equal opportunity in employment and education. To achieve liberation, they attempted to break down sex role stereotyping. In her view, the recognition of women's rights came not through the infiltration of men's domains and a minimizing of the differences between male and female roles, but rather in a recognition of their distinctive contribution to their society. It was not a role wherein she was dependent or dominated. It was a role of independence, responsibility and authority wherein she was enhanced as a woman.

Much recent feminist literature on women and crime has focused on woman as victim and the double-standard in laws such as those which seek to regulate prostitution and to apportion blame in rape cases. Here, I have been arguing that women are victims but in a different sense. Not only has their land been taken, but their role in the maintenance of harmonious relations between people and land has been considered virtually non-existent. It has not only been a matter of not listening, it has also been a matter of not thinking it was worth the trouble to ask the questions in the first place.

Notes

1. Bell and Ditton, 1980:1.
2. Bell, 1983:132.
3. For a discussion of the involvement of women in land claiming see Bell, 1979; Rowell, 1983:256-267. See *infra* for a discussion of the A.L.R.C. meetings in Alice Springs. See also Australian Law Reform Commission, 1977.
4. See Meggitt, 1962; Munn, 1973; and the more generalized portrait in Maddock, 1972.
5. For references to sympathetic and informed analyses of women's position in Aboriginal society, see, note 2, supra; Berndt, 1950; Goodale, 1971; Hamilton, 1979.
6. See Bell and Ditton, 1980:7.
7. Ibid.
8. Bell, 1983:94-106.
9. Ibid.:247-250.
10. Ibid.
11. For more information, see, Bell, 1983.
12. Australian Law Reform Commission, 1977:6.
13. Gunter, 1978.
14. Thornton, 1980.
15. Berndt, 1965.
16. Australian Law Reform Commission, 1982a:iii.
17. Ibid.:iv.
18. See Australian Law Reform Commission, 1982b.

19. Bell, 1983:152.

References

AUSTRALIAN LAW REFORM COMMISSION (1977)
'Report on a visit to the Northern Territory of Australia.' Reference on Aboriginal Customary Law.

---------- (1982a)
Recognition of Aboriginal Customary or Tribal Marriage: General Principles. Research Paper 2.

---------- (1982b)
Central Australian Field Report No. 7, October.

BELL, D. and P. DITTON (1980)
Law: the old and the new. Canberra: Aboriginal History.

BELL, D. (1979)
Women and the Land, *Identity*, 3(11).

---------- (1983)
Daughters of the dreaming. Melbourne/Sydney: McPhee Gribble/Allen & Unwin.

BERNDT, C.H. (1950)
"Women's changing ceremonies in Northern Australia," 1 L'Homme 1-87.

BERNDT, R.M. (1965)
"Law and order in Aboriginal Australia," in R.M. Berndt and C.H. Berndt (eds.), Aboriginal Man in Australia. Sydney: Angus and Robertson, 167-206.

GOODALE, J. (1971)
Tiwi Wives. Seattle: University of Washington Press.

GUNTER, D. (1978)
"Aboriginal customary law: the pitjantjatjarra." Field Report No. 1, Australian Law Reform Commission.

HAMILTON, A. (1979)
Timeless Transformation. Unpublished Ph.D. Thesis, University of Sydney.

MADDOCK, Kenneth (1972)
The Australian Aborigines. London: Allen Lane.

MEGGITT, M.J. (1962)
Desert People. Chicago: University of Chicago Press.

MUNN, Nancy D. (1973)
Walbiri Iconography. London: Cornell University Press.

ROWELL, M. (1983)
"Women and Land Claims," in N. Peterson and M. Langton (eds.), Aborigines, Land and Land Rights. Canberra, Australian Institute of Aboriginal Studies.

THORTON, F. (1980)
"Situation report: Aboriginal communities in Alice Springs and fringe camps," in Bell and Ditton: Appendix 1.

Towards an aboriginal child placement principle: a view from New South Wales

Richard Chisholm

I. Introduction

If there were a prize for the people most oppressed in a wealthy country, Australian Aborigines would have a good chance of winning it. They are to be found firmly located at the bottom of all indicators of well-being: health, housing, income, access to resources, involvement with the criminal justice system, and the rest.[1] They are there because of the extreme injustices inflicted on them by the Europeans who invaded their country, rationalizing what they did as the "settlement" or even "discovery" of Australia, notions that have long been embedded in schoolbooks throughout Australia and are only now giving way to a more realistic and less ethnocentric portrayal of what happened.[2] Aboriginal people were shot and poisoned, and were infected with diseases to which they had little resistance. The invaders destroyed much of the fauna and flora on which Aboriginal life depended.

Most fundamentally, they took Aboriginal land, all of it. There were no treaties, no payments of compensation. Nothing was as profoundly destructive to Aboriginal civilization, for an intimate relationship between the people and the land lay at the heart of Aboriginal identity and law. The Anglo-Australian system of law and land title that was imposed, and still exists, is based on a lie, a legal fiction so gross that it is hard to believe: that when the white man came, Australia was *uninhabited*.[3] In many parts of Australia, there is little left of traditional Aboriginal knowledge: language, laws, and ancestry have become partly lost in the decimation of Aboriginal people and their allocation to "reserves", in which the remnants of different tribal groupings were combined in a way that undermined what was left of traditional patterns of authority, and sowed the seeds of the considerable friction evident within some Aboriginal communities today.

One key to the early history, perhaps, is that Aboriginal civilization was largely *invisible* to the white invaders. There was no obvious organization, there were no towns or villages, no evident laws or leaders. The newcomers did not understand traditional societies having an oral tradition and a social and legal structure based on complex and subtle connections between land and kinship. They thought Aborigines were the most primitive and savage people on earth, and never came to terms with the need to accord them rights as a people, or worked out how to negotiate or deal with them.

A different kind of invisibility remains a problem today. Everybody knows that Aborigines largely live in poverty. But many Australians attribute this to what they assume are individual characteristics of Aborigines: they must be lazy, or stupid, if they remain at the bottom of the heap in a society in which, it is assumed, there are always opportunities for advancement for those who are willing to make the effort. For Australians who think like this, the causes of Aboriginal conditions today are as invisible as Aboriginal civilization was to the first invaders. The long-term devastating effects of dispossession, of the perpetual undercurrents of discrimination, and of the endless celebration of material wealth and individual achievement that is alien to the ways of Aboriginal people, remain invisible to many Australians. Their image of Aboriginal people is the result of selective learning at school and vicious or ignorant stereotypes conveyed in cartoons, pub gossip, media stories, and in countless other ways.

Still, recent years have seen some initiatives, and many promises, that do appear to hold out some hope. In the 1970s the Aboriginal Legal Service developed and within a few years had spread throughout Australia; it is now a very important network of organizations which has done a great deal to give Aboriginal people some sense of power and some hope that their rights can be safeguarded.[4] Aboriginal organizations other than the Legal Services have developed and done effective and heartening work. The Aboriginal Medical Service is a conspicuous example, but there are also a variety of other organizations, some relating to specific activities such as theatre, dance, or sport, others constituting a general meeting point and centre of activities for particular communities. More recently, there has been legislation "giving" land rights to Aboriginal communities, especially in the central and northern parts of Australia, where Aboriginal people retain more of their traditional culture than in the more developed areas on the eastern coast.[5] In some areas, where Aboriginal land is threatened by mining companies, Aboriginal organizations have bargained effectively on behalf of their communities.

For decades, there have been various government policies seeking to deal with the "Aboriginal problem".[6] The variations in policy over time, however, were less important than the common aspects of all policies. They all shared two assumptions: (1) that it was up to the white man to determine the answer, and (2) that Aboriginal people had no rights to land. These assumptions were so basic that it was not necessary to state them. The talk was about "protection", "integration", "assimilation", and the like. In the early decades, policies of "protection" sought to protect Aborigines against slaughter and exploitation of the invaders, and often involved the placing of Aborigines on "reserves" or "missions". Later, especially from around the 1930s, there was talk of "integration" or "assimilation".

The positive side of these policies was the sense that Aboriginal people should not be prevented from participating in the non-Aboriginal community: they should have the same rights as everyone else. The negative side, much better understood now than formerly, was that such policies made no provision for Aborigines to live an authentic *Aboriginal* life. And indeed, some versions of these policies involved little more than the hope (and expectation) that Aboriginal people would be bred out of existence. Such policies, once seen as liberal because they seemed to give equality to Aboriginal people, are now widely seen as fundamentally wrong and, in a subtle way, racist, since they give no recognition to the right of Aboriginal people to retain their own identity; they implicitly identify the good life with life in the non-Aboriginal community. Although assimilationist policies are still practised in Queensland, which has an appalling record in this area, they are generally giving way to a different approach.

The different approach is usually referred to as "self-determination".[7] It seeks to give Aboriginal people the right to choose whether to live in the non-Aboriginal way, or to live in a distinctively Aboriginal way. It recognizes that for those who choose the latter, resources will be required, especially land. Thus land rights recognition reflects not only the notion that Aborigines should be *compensated* for the wrongful taking of their land, but that land is a *necessary resource* if they are to exercise their right to retain, consolidate and develop a distinctively Aboriginal identity. The policy of self-determination further emphasizes the importance of creating or strengthening legal, administrative and economic structures that might enable Aboriginal people and communities to exercise real power in their own affairs.

In 1983 a federal Labor government was installed, committed to the policy of self-determination for Aboriginal people. There are Labor governments, too, in most of the states in the mid-1980s: Victoria, New South Wales, Western Australia and South Australia. While in general committed to self-determination, these governments embrace it with varying degrees of commitment. In particular, New South Wales has passed land rights legislation which is seen by Aboriginal people and most commentators as much less than a real commitment to self-determination would imply.[8] The federal government initially made some tough statements, indicating that if the states did not implement policies of self-determination it would take action to impose such policies. It has the power to do so as a result of an amendment to the Constitution in 1967 under which the federal parliament may make laws for the "people of any race"; and recent decisions of the Australian High Court indicate that this power will be generously interpreted. On the other hand, the draft of preferred options for a national land rights bill published by the federal government in 1985 was rejected by Aboriginal spokespeople as falling short of the government's stated principles for Aboriginal land rights.[9] More significantly, federal legislation on Aboriginal land rights was opposed by the states, both because it entailed a diminution of state autonomy and because it was resisted by powerful vested interests, notably the large mining companies. In 1986, the federal government effectively abandoned the project, leaving land rights in the hands of the states, and leaving a profound sense of anger and disillusionment among Aboriginal people, many of whom felt that the whole exercise represented yet another episode in the continuing story of broken promises by governments and white indifference to Aboriginal claims.

Recent years have nevertheless seen considerable progress in Aboriginal child welfare law, policy and practice. These changes should not be seen in isolation. They are, in the author's view, one outcome of the current efforts to change many welfare and other programmes and laws so that they embody, not the assimilationist policies of the past, but the developing policy of self-determination for Aboriginal people. Such a policy is based on the premise that justice for Aboriginal people requires measures that give them a real opportunity, should they wish to take it, of consolidating and adapting their laws and culture in ways they find appropriate for their times and those of their children. It is fundamentally opposed to the view, still held by many Australians, that the only future that Aboriginal people can or should have is as ordinary members of the Australian community, with exactly the same legal rights and responsibilities. In the eyes of many Aboriginal people this approach is merely the modern form of decades of oppression: they call it "cultural genocide".

II. Aboriginal child welfare in New South Wales

A. Taking the children

In her autobiography *If Everyone Cared,*[10] the late Margaret Tucker tells how, at the age of about 13, she was taken from her family by "the gang of men representing the Aborigines Protection Board". She describes the arrival of the men, the curiosity of the school children at the motor car, the crying children, and the Aboriginal adults looking helplessly on:

> There were forty or fifty of our people standing silently grieving for us. Theyknew something treacherous was going on, something to break our way of life.

Margaret's mother was horrified to learn that the policeman was going to take her baby, who was at the hospital, as well as the older child. However the child was not at the hospital and the policeman decided to leave her. The mother's reaction is a vivid statement of human tragedy, of power and powerlessness: she kissed the policeman's hand in gratitude at having one child left to her. The story ends with the daughter being taken away to a life of exploitation and cruelty, and the mother wandering in dismay into the bush, to be found later moaning "like an animal in pain," half demented and ill. Later she was unable to let the baby out of her sight, and

> for months after, at the sight of a policeman's white helmet coming round the bend of the river, she would grab her little girl and escape into the bush, as did all the Aboriginal people who had children ...

Margaret Tucker's story is important because it is typical of the experiences of many Aboriginal families, and because it was the practical result of the deliberate policies of the white authorities given control over Aborigines in New South Wales. These policies have now been the subject of detailed analysis,[11] and it is only necessary here to cite some quotations from the Board's own reports:

> ... it is desirable that the Octoroon and Quadroon children throughout the State should be under the control of the State Children's Relief Department with a view as early as possible of having all such children absorbed into the general population of the State.[12]

In the Aborigines Protection Board Report of 1914 it was stated that:

> Several ... were handed over to the State Children's Relief Department as neglected children. These will not be allowed to return to their former associations, but will be merged into the white population.

> To allow these children to remain on the Reserves to grow up in comparative idleness, and in the midst of more or less vicious surroundings, would be to say the least, an injustice to the children themselves, and a positive menace to the State.[13]

And here is a 1950s version, from the Board's magazine DAWN:

> ... in view of the fact that many of the wards in the Board's care are of light caste, efforts were made late in 1955, to secure foster homes for these amongst white people. Furthermore this was regarded as being a positive step in implementing the Board's policy of assimilation.[14]

How many children were taken? There are records from which estimates can be made, although the precise number cannot be certainly known. Peter Read has estimated[15] that the total number of Aboriginal children removed in New South Wales alone is approximately 5,625. The actual population of Aborigines under 15 years was about 2,800 from 1910 to 1920, and had risen to about 4,400 in 1936. Thus the impact of the system, in numerical terms, was considerable. More important, perhaps, is the fact that the system was a constant threat for Aboriginal families. Read's work, and that of Heather Goodall and Carla Hankins, show how lasting is the impact made on Aborigines now living, and how profound has been the effect on Aboriginal attitudes to whites and white authority.

B. A separate system: the legal background

The Aborigines Protection Board (later to become the Aborigines Welfare Board) operated from 1909 to 1969 under a separate legal regime[16] giving it power to intervene into Aboriginal families, power for which it had successfully lobbied. In 1969 the Board was abolished, and since that there there has been no formal discrimination in law between Aboriginal and other children. The older system and its application, however, are of great importance in understanding both the claims Aborigines are now making and the difficulties facing those who would make the laws relating to child welfare more appropriate for Aboriginal people. The main characteristics of the system may be stated as follows:

(i) Power was exclusively in non-Aboriginal hands. It was a system of white welfare for black children. (Exceptionally, an amendment in 1943 provided that two of the eleven members of the Board should be Aborigines, and these should be nominated by Aborigines).[17]

(ii) Throughout the evolution and development of the Board, it seems to have been assumed that being Christian and respectable were sufficient qualifications for those who were interested in making and carrying out policy relating to Aboriginals. There was no sense that any professional qualifications were required, or that the powers might be abused, so long as those white people exercising them were respectable and well-intentioned.

(iii) There appears to have been inadequate recognition of the importance and value of Aboriginal methods of child rearing, and especially the importance of the extended family. Carla Hankins gives a neat example, citing a case where a child was removed because she was declared to be an "orphan". In fact, she had a father, several aunts and uncles and eight brothers and sisters ranging in age from seven to twenty-nine years[18] Indeed, it is clear from the Board's reports and other contemporary materials that removal of children from their communities on the Board's reserves was seen as a positive virtue in that it removed the children from patterns of child care which were assumed to be barbarous and harmful.

(iv) A further feature was the lack of procedural justice. An amendment in 1915 inserted a provision that the Board could, without any court proceedings, "assume full control and custody of the child of any aborigine, if after due inquiry it is satisfied that such a course is in the interest of the moral or physical welfare of the child".[19] This remained the law until an amendment in 1940 required the Board to obtain an order from the children's court giving it control of the child. Although the earlier legislation provided for a right of appeal by the parents, there is no indication in Aboriginal accounts of the system or in official records that any such appeals were actually taken. In the absence of Aboriginal legal services, and in the light of the general powerlessness of Aboriginal people so vividly portrayed by Margaret Tucker in the passage referred to above, few if any parents can have taken advantage of the legal mechanisms available.

(v) Finally, the system was characterized by the fact that intervention in children's lives formed part of a wider policy (or policies) relating to the future of Aborigines generally. Briefly, such policies included the desire of the Board to hasten the "assimilation" of Aborigines by removing children of mixed parentage and lighter colour into white families; to provide cheap labour to white people; and to form a basis for controlling the parents, terrified of losing their children if they made a false move.

C. Pressures for change

In this section I shall describe four main sources of pressure for change: Aboriginal demands, the Australian Labor Party's policy of self-determination, research on the actual operation of child welfare systems on Aboriginal children, and the influence of developments in other jurisdictions.

(i) Aboriginal demands Aboriginal people have experienced the child welfare system largely as victims. They were not passive victims; there is now recognition of the struggles of individuals, families and communities against the threat to their children of the Aborigines Protection Board.[20] In recent times this struggle has continued, and Aboriginal demands are now well documented, notably in the three Australian Conferences on Adoption (1976, 1978 and 1982), in published articles and statements and in the policies and submissions of Aboriginal Child Care Agencies.[21] These materials show that Aboriginal demands focus on two matters: the need to retain Aboriginal children with their families and communities, and the need to redesign the child welfare system so that Aboriginal people have responsibility for attending to the welfare of their children, rather than being subjected to a system designed and administered by non-Aboriginal people. More recently, a third theme has emerged, that these two demands should be implemented not merely by administrative policies, but by law. These demands, and how they might be transformed into law, are the main concern of this paper.

(ii) Labor's Policy of Self-Determination Labor's policy adopts the principle of self-determination for Aboriginal people.[22] A key passage is the following:

Linked with the principle of consultation is the principle of self-determination. From the earliest attempts, Government policies for Aboriginals have failed because they were not based on an understanding of Aboriginal culture and society and because Aboriginals were not involved in their formulation and did not want them. Programmes in which Aboriginals determine their own needs and priorities are not only more equitable, they are more successful and cost-effective.[23]

It is clear that such a policy requires fundamental reconsideration of a legal framework that gives no place to Aboriginal people and organizations.

(iii) Research on the Impact of the Child Welfare System on Aboriginal Children Until quite recently, there had been virtually no research on the impact of either the Protection and Welfare Board's efforts or the present system on

Aboriginal children and their communities. In New South Wales, the breakthrough came with the publication of the study *Aboriginal Children in Substitute Care*, by Chris Milne, as part of the Aboriginal Children's Research Project of the Family and Children's Services Agency.[24] That study revealed that while in 1980 Aboriginal children were about 1.5% of the population, 15% of all children in substitute care were Aboriginal, and the vast majority of them were in some form of non-Aboriginal placement. Moreover, 18% of children in corrective institutions (training schools) were Aboriginal. There is also recent evidence of the over-representation of Aboriginal children in child welfare systems elsewhere in Australia.[25]

(iv) Developments in Other Jurisdictions Thinking in New South Wales has of course been influenced by developments elsewhere, in international law, in overseas countries, especially North America, and elsewhere in Australia.

International law has been slow to recognize the rights of indigenous peoples, although it appears to be moving in this direction.[26] It does however embody a reasonably coherent set of human rights. The Australian Law Reform Commission has convincingly argued that such international standards, especially those relating to non-discrimination, are consistent with laws embodying the kinds of demands being made by Aboriginal people in Australia in relation to child welfare.[27] It is arguable that some of these in fact support Aboriginal claims. For example, the provision in the International Covenant on Economic Social and Cultural Rights 1966 (which Australia has ratified) speaking of the right "to take part in cultural life" could be interpreted to support the right of Aboriginal children to have the opportunity to take part in the life of their culture by not being avoidably removed from their families and communities.[28] A similar argument could be based on Article 27 of the Civil and Political Rights Covenant although the scope of this Article is controversial.[29] The rights of indigenous peoples are increasingly being explored in the international arena.

The United States has been perhaps the most influential model. Indeed, Mrs. Mollie Dyer, who was perhaps the leading figure in the development of Aboriginal child care agencies in the 1970s, and was the first Director of the Victorian Aboriginal Child Care Agency, was greatly influenced by a visit to North America and, in particular, by the programme of the Yakima Indina Nation designed by Maxine Robbins. Aboriginal people in Australia have expressed great interest in the Indian Child Welfare Act 1979, because, whatever its limitations in practice, it is an example of a federal law which does implement a form of the Aboriginal children placement principle, to be discussed later, and gives legal recognition to the right of indigenous people to play a responsible part in the child welfare system.

Canada too provides some valuable models in the arrangements for Indian nations to administer their own child welfare schemes either under direct agreements between Indian bands and the federal government, as in the Spallumcheen Child Welfare By-law, or in tri-partite arrangements involving the provinces, as exist for example in Alberta and Manitoba.[30]

For Australian Aboriginal people, whose original sovereign rights to land or self-government have never been legally acknowledged, the agreements and laws in North America have a significance that does not depend on whether their particular provisions are appropriate for Australia.

Finally, the situation in New South Wales has been influenced by recent developments elsewhere in Australia.[31] In the Northern Territory, child welfare legislation of 1983 included a provision giving effect to the Aboriginal child placement principle, by requiring the Minister to arrange placements of Aboriginal children with members of the child's extended family or other Aboriginal people who have "the correct relationship with the child in accordance with Aboriginal customary law", and requiring consultation with appropriate Aboriginal persons.[32] Legislation along similar lines has been introduced in Victoria in connection with adoption.[33] In Queensland, recent draft legislation refers to the desirability of maintaining children's links with their ethnic or cultural identity, without however singling out Aboriginal children for special attention.[34] Australian developments in policy, as distinct from law, are considered in the next section.

D. A national policy?

In 1980, the federal Department of Aboriginal Affairs published a document entitled "Aboriginal Fostering and Adoption - Policy Guidelines" in an effort to bring about acceptable and uniform approaches throughout Australia.[35] It is difficult to determine how influential this document has been. While it was not formally adopted by the states, it appears to have influenced Victoria in publishing its own guidelines, and may have influenced practice elsewhere. In 1983 the state welfare Administrators published the recommendations of a working party on the same subject.[36] These recommendations pursued the goals of Aboriginal placement for Aboriginal children and consultation with appropriate Aboriginal persons in connection with Aboriginal placements. They did not however systematically consider how far the policies should be implemented in law, and they rejected the idea of any federal law, whether or not along the lines of the Indian Child Welfare Act 1978 in the United States. For these reasons, and probably because the recommendations were seen by Aboriginal people to be presented to them on the basis of "take it or leave it", they were not acceptable to the Aboriginal Child Care Agencies which by 1984 had established a national co-ordinating body as well as agencies (in various stages of recent development) throughout the country.[37]

E. Recent developments in New South Wales

In this section, I shall note briefly some of the many recent developments that indicate the beginnings of new directions in Aboriginal child welfare law and policy.

(i) Placement of Aboriginal children There is considerable evidence that to a large extent the Aboriginal child placement principle is now accepted as good practice in state welfare departments. Departmental officers in New South Wales have frequently said that they seek Aboriginal placements where possible; efforts are being made, especially through Aboriginal officers employed by the Department, to recruit Aboriginal foster parents; an examination of the files of one district office showed considerable efforts to maintain contact between Aboriginal wards and their families and communities; a study showed that only 22 Aboriginal children were made wards in 1981-82, and departmental correspondence indicated considerable efforts to place these children with Aboriginal families.[38] There is less evidence available on how far the principle is understood and accepted at field officer level, and whether Aboriginal children are still being unnecessarily placed away from their communities and people in breach of the principle (i.e. where there are suitable placements with Aboriginal people).

Certainly, Aboriginal children are still being separated from their people in various ways. The major force separating children now seems to be the juvenile justice system, under which young offenders are frequently placed on remand or in training schools away from their communities and their people. There may also be some Aboriginal children still being adopted to white families where they could have gone to Aboriginal families, and it is likely that under the health system Aboriginal children are placed for significant periods away from their people in circumstances where, if health services were differently arranged, they might have received treatment in their own community. It is not easy to put numbers on these instances, since available statistical data seldom identify Aboriginal children, and hardly ever identify Aboriginal *placements*.[39]

(ii) Aboriginal Participation in Child Welfare Recent years have seen the emergence of three forms of Aboriginal participation. First, there seems to have been a great increase in the willingness and ability of Departmental officers

to consult and co-operate with Aboriginal people and organizations. An example is an incident described elsewhere, in which several Aboriginal representatives were invited to participate in a case conference to determine what action to take in respect of several neglected Aboriginal children.[40] Another is the practice of police officers in Nowra of discussing with the South Coast Aboriginal Children's Service some young Aboriginal offenders - sometimes, these consultations avoid the need for court proceedings. The author's survey of Aboriginal wards, too, showed considerable use of a variety of forms of consultation with Aboriginal people.[41]

A second form of Aboriginal involvement is the employment of Aboriginal individuals in the state welfare department.[42] In recent years, a considerable number of such appointments have been made, first at the field level and more recently at a more senior level, both in the Department's head office and in the regional offices. This initiative appears to be favoured by both federal and state bodies, for the original appointments were made through funding by the federal Department of Aboriginal Affairs, when the employees were called "Aboriginal case workers". They were subsequently called "Aboriginal community workers", but most recently the policy of the state department has been to convert them to the more senior position of "community welfare officer" - the title of the Department's generalist field staff.

A third form of involvement has been through Aboriginal organizations, notably the Aboriginal Child Care Agencies. These bodies have been involved in a range of child welfare activities, and have, through seminars and in other ways, contributed to a greater understanding of the issues and the needs of Aboriginal children.

All these developments appear to be consistent with Aboriginal demands. But important questions arise about their relative importance, and the principles for allocating resources towards promoting the various forms of involvement. If the objective is Aboriginal self-determination, the emphasis should perhaps be on involvement of Aboriginal people through their own organizations, rather than through the employment of individual Aboriginal people in "white" organizations.[43] At a more practical level, it seems that properly supported Aboriginal organizations active in this area are the most effective ways of delivering child welfare services that are sensitive to Aboriginal attitudes and feelings, and are relatively free of the stigma that has been attached to child welfare as a result of the tragic history referred to earlier.

III. Towards an Aboriginal child placement principle and its justifications

Policies and laws of the kind referred to in the last section have come to be known as "the Aboriginal child placement principle". The term is used to describe various attempts to formulate, either as policy or as law, a systematic approach to the placement of Aboriginal children. The chief elements of the approach are a set of placement preferences intended to reduce the risk of Aboriginal children being removed from the care of their parents, relatives and communities, and mechanisms to ensure the involvement of Aboriginal people in the decision-making process.

The best known example of the principle is contained in the Indian Child Welfare Act 1978 (USA)[44] In Australia, the 1980 guidelines on Aboriginal fostering and adoption prepared by the Department of Aboriginal Affairs[45] (mentioned earlier) was the first formal expression of the principle, although the general direction had been set by a meeting of Aboriginal people and their supporters at a national conference on adoption in 1976.[46] Whatever influence these guidelines might have had in practice, they were not formally adopted by state welfare authorities, and it was not until 1984 that the Council of (state) Social Welfare Ministers endorsed a set of recommendations embodying the principle in the following form:

> It is recommended that in the foster placement of an Aboriginal child a preference be given, in the absence of good cause to the contrary, to a placement with:
>
> > a member of the child's extended family
> >
> > other members of the child's Aboriginal community who have the correct relationship with the child in accordance with Aboriginal customary law
> >
> > other Aboriginal families living in close proximity.[47]

In recent years, versions of the placement principle have also appeared in legislation, notably in the Community Welfare Act 1983 (Northern Territory) and the Adoption Act 1984 (Victoria). Other legislation or proposed legislation, in New South Wales and Queensland, contains some recognition of the importance of Aboriginality, but in more equivocal terms.[48]

The most recent formulation of the principle appears in draft legislation recommended by the Australian Law Reform Commission in its massive 1986 report on the recognition of Aboriginal customary law.[49] The draft legislation defines "Aboriginal child" as a child one or both of whose parents is an Aborigine,[50] and applies to all laws which "make provision with respect to adoption or the care, custody, control, placement, wardship, guardianship or protection" of children.[51] It requires that all state laws should substantially conform to the "Aboriginal child placement principles" set out in the Schedule.[52] Those principles may be summarized as follows:

1. An Aboriginal child should remain in the care of his or her parents except in special circumstances.[53]

2. An Aboriginal child who is not to be in the care of at least one of his or her parents should, unless special circumstances exist, be in the care of a "responsible person". This term means

   (a) a person who, in accordance with the customary laws of the Aboriginal community of which the child is a member, has an interest in, or responsibility for, the welfare of the child; or

   (b) in the case of a child who is, under the law of a State or Territory, in the custody of a person who is not a parent of the child or a member of an Aboriginal community - a person who, in accordance with the customary laws of the Aboriginal community of which a parent of the child is a member, has an interest in, or responsibility for, the welfare of the child.[54]

3. Where a child cannot be in the care of a parent or a "responsible person", the choice of placement should be made with regard to

   (a) the desirability of the child being in the care of a person who is a member of an Aboriginal community; and

   (b) the desirability of the child being able to establish and maintain contact with his or her parents, the responsible persons and the Aboriginal community of which the child is or was a member.[55]

4. In assessing the welfare of a child who is or has been a member of an Aboriginal community, undue weight should not be given to

"considerations of material provision". Due regard should be given to the support (spiritual and emotional as well as material) that members of the community might be expected to give; the benefits that may be expected to arise from the child's being brought up with knowledge and experience of the community's customary laws; the difficulties that might arise if the child's contact with members of the community were terminated or restricted; and the standards of child care and child welfare in that community.[56]

5. Before any placement decision is taken there should be appropriate consultation with the parents, the "responsible persons", and (unless the parents or the responsible persons direct otherwise in writing) with an appropriate Aboriginal child welfare body.[57]

Although differences in the wording of the principle raise issues of considerable importance, I wish here to discuss the more fundamental question: what is the rationale or justification of the principle? The fact that the principle has already received a measure of recognition does not make its justification unnecessary. An understanding and acceptance of the reasons for the principle will be vital if it is to be embodied more widely in Australian law, and if it is to be effectively implemented in practice.

It will be submitted that there are three separate bases on which the principle can be justified. First, as a guide to the welfare of Aboriginal children. Second, as an acknowledgement that Aboriginal child welfare problems are ultimately to be seen against the background of past and present oppression of Aboriginal people. Third, as a recognition of the right of Aboriginal people to maintain their identity and pass it on to their children.

A. The placement principle as a guide to the welfare of Aboriginal children

This was the main argument advanced by the Australian Law Reform Commission in recommending the implementation of the child placement principle. The Commission considered that "[t]here can be little dispute that the overriding consideration in all cases of child custody should be the welfare of the child".[58] However, the principle was too vague and needed to be defined more specificially, especially as it would be implemented by non-Aboriginal courts. The Aboriginal placement principle should be adopted as a useful guide to what was likely to be best for Aboriginal children, and to counter any tendency of non-Aboriginal judges and magistrates to undervalue or misunderstand Aboriginal standards of child rearing.[59]

The question whether placement with Aboriginal people would promote the welfare of Aboriginal children is a difficult one, for at least two reasons, namely the lack of systematic evidence and the value-laden nature of judgments about a child's "welfare" or "interests".

There appear to be no controlled studies that enable predictions to be made about the consequences of Aboriginal and non-Aboriginal placements for Aboriginal children: inferences must be drawn from less satisfactory evidence. There is certainly some evidence that many Aboriginal children brought up in non-Aboriginal care encounter serious problems. The Australian Law Reform Commission cited statistics from Victoria and New South Wales showing that of clients seeking assistance from the Aboriginal Legal Service for criminal charges, 90-95% had been in placement - whether fostered, institutionalized or adopted - the vast majority in the care of white families or authorities. The Commission concluded that while a definite link between the placements and the children's subsequent difficulties could not be established, such a link "has often been asserted".[60] In addition, there is abundant evidence of an anecdotal kind that Aboriginal children encounter "identity crises" of a special kind when brought up in non-Aboriginal settings.[61] Clinical evidence overseas suggests that adult disturbances may be traced to such conflicts.[62] Aboriginal and non-Aboriginal welfare workers have pointed to the difficulties that these children may encounter; subject to discrimination of a kind that neither they nor their white carers may be readily able to combat, and perhaps caught in conflicting loyalties to their white foster parents and Aboriginal relatives, it seems undeniable that they are subjected to pressures that they find difficult to survive without damage. Some seek to return to their Aboriginal origins, to find that they have acquired values and expectations that set them apart from their own people: they may feel rejected by the white community, yet unable to fit in with the Aboriginal community.

We do not yet know just what factors will mitigate these problems and the harm they can cause. It seems likely that much will depend on the individual child, the age of placement, the extent to which the child is separated from Aboriginal relatives and Aboriginal people in general, and the way problems are handled by the foster parents or other carers. Some serious identity problems, typically leading at about adolescence to a wish to establish contact with Aboriginal relatives or, at the other extreme, a denial of the child's Aboriginality, seem common. Much less is known about the experience of children growing up in Aboriginal communities, but there seems no reason to doubt the widely-held conviction of Aboriginal workers that these children find in their membership of the extended family and the community, and in the techniques developed to combat discrimination,[63] a sense of identity and support that is invaluable later in life.

In the light of these considerations, it seems reasonably clear that, *other things being equal*, Aboriginal placements for Aboriginal children should be preferred. But when are other things equal? We know that the prevailing standard of living in material terms is very poor in Aboriginal communities: children growing up are likely to be disadvantaged in terms of nutrition, housing, and conventional educational opportunities. Is it right to adopt a preference for Aboriginal placements in these circumstances?

This question leads to the second problem, namely the value-laden nature of such terms as "welfare". In the non-Aboriginal community, placement decisions for children usually occur in the context of generally agreed values. This is less so for Aboriginal children, since there is no doubt that in important ways Aboriginal child-rearing practices and values differ from those of the non-Aboriginal community. It seems that in general Aboriginal child-rearing is characterized by a great reliance on the extended family, by permissiveness and physical closeness, perhaps with a view that the child will become an adult who will fit easily into the Aboriginal community rather than be an individualistic competitor.[64] In custody and related matters, it is well recognized that the court may have to engage in the difficult task of assessing the value to a child, on the one hand of a close relationship with an extended family, and on the other of the material advantages of a non-Aboriginal family. The present point is that apart from all the difficulties of prediction that such cases involve, they also involve a choice of values about what kind of adult the child will ideally become. There seems no generally agreed basis for the court to make such a choice, and not surprisingly courts have been loath to acknowledge that such choices are involved in applying notions such as "welfare".

It should not be assumed that the courts have a clear-cut choice between providing a child on the one hand with a chance to grow up as a recognized member of an Aboriginal community, and on the other a chance to complete schooling, and perhaps go on to further education and a secure and well-paid job. While posing the question in this way highlights the choice of values involved, it should not blind us to the fact that in reality it seems that Aboriginal children brought up in non-Aboriginal settings will not necessarily fit easily into the non-Aboriginal world, although there is no reliable evidence on such a matter. It is of course largely a matter for speculation how far this fact (if it is true) stems from a resistance in Aboriginal children towards the values and characteristics necessary for a "successful" career in the non-Aboriginal world, from their pre-placement experiences, or from discrimination by the non-Aboriginal community in such matters as employment and accommodation.

The courts in Australia have struggled to come to terms with these difficult issues in custody and adoption decisions. Many decisions on appeal show, as the Australian Law Reform Commission put it, "enlightened and sensitive interpretations of the paramount consideration of the best interests of the child".[65] The same cannot be said for all the reported decisions at first instance, however, and this poses a serious problem since the thrust of much recent law is that appellate courts should be slow to overturn a custody decision.[66] The appellate courts have firmly refused to lay down any presumption that Aboriginal children should by preference be placed with other Aboriginal people, on the ground that such a presumption would be inconsistent with the courts' duty to decide what is best for each child on all the evidence.[67]

This concentration on the facts of the case tends to obscure the values that lie behind the decisions. An optimistic reading of the cases suggests that the courts will regard a placement that is "normal" in Aboriginal communities as being equal to one that is "normal" in the non-Aboriginal community, so that the material advantages of most non-Aboriginal litigants will not determine the issue. This reading, however, goes beyond what the appeal courts have been prepared to state. It follows that if a court at first instance preferred a non-Aboriginal placement on the basis of materialistic factors, it would be difficult to upset the decision on appeal.

On the whole, it seems that an Aboriginal placement principle would provide a valuable guide to courts, without preventing them from placing an Aboriginal child in a non-Aboriginal setting where there was demonstrable advantage to the child in such a placement.

The above discussion has considered the Aboriginal child placement in the context of the court's decisions. However, most placement decisions in child welfare are made not by courts but by officers of the state welfare departments or non-government agencies. The decisions are not so much a matter of choosing between two (or more) claimants, as the court has to do, as *finding* a suitable placement. This might involve recruiting foster parents, training them, and providing financial and other forms of support. It will typically be the case that there are many potentially suitable placements, in both the Aboriginal and non-Aboriginal communities, for Aboriginal children. What will be required is energetic and skilled selection of Aboriginal foster parents and caregivers. In this context, the Aboriginal placement principle takes a different form. The difference may be represented as follows:

TWO FORMS OF THE ABORIGINAL PLACEMENT PRINCIPLE

Applied to Courts:

> Assume that generally speaking an Aboriginal child's welfare will be promoted by giving custody to an Aboriginal rather than a non-Aboriginal litigant.

Applied to Welfare Officers:

> As far as possible arrange for the availability of Aboriginal foster parents and other caregivers so that there will be suitable Aboriginal placements available for Aboriginal children.

It is this second context that is most relevant to the justification of the principle on grounds other than the welfare of individual children, to which we now turn.

B. The principle as a recognition of the historical context of Aboriginal child welfare

This argument looks behind the disadvantages of many Aboriginal families, to the profound and continuing damage done to Aboriginal civilization through European conquest. Against this background, the difficulties Aboriginal families have in providing adequately for their children are ultimately attributable to the consequences of the European invasion. It is manifestly unjust for the non-Aboriginal society now to use the consequences of its own crimes against Aboriginal people as the reason for the removal of Aboriginal children. If it is true that Aboriginal children are disadvantaged in Aboriginal communities, then there must be some responsibility on the non-Aboriginal community to provide the support and resources necessary to enable Aboriginal people to look after their children properly. It is wrong, in other words, to separate child welfare from more general aspects of Aboriginal policy. From this point of view the most important part of a rational policy on Aboriginal child welfare would be the just resolution of Aboriginal claims to land and compensation.

The Aboriginal child placement principle can be readily understood in this context. It embodies the idea that the non-Aboriginal community has a responsibility to see that Aboriginal children are not removed from their families and communities when this can be avoided by the provision of financial or other support. Where Aboriginal parents are unable to care for their children adequately, the first inquiry ought to be whether the problem can be cured by financial or other support for the family. If it cannot, the next question is whether the child can be cared for by members of the extended family or other appropriate

Aboriginal families, *with financial or other support.* It is not uncommon for welfare authorities to say that there are no available Aboriginal families to care for a child, in circumstances where the child cannot remain with his or her family. On the present argument, however, it would be wrong to remove the child into a non-Aboriginal placement if, as is commonly the case, the child could be supported by an Aboriginal family given appropriate support. In New South Wales, there seems to be some recognition of the force of this argument, in that foster payments may be made to members of a child's extended family or other Aboriginal people able to look after the child, when the placement is made or approved by the Aboriginal Children's Service.[68] It is important to stress that the basis for the claim to financial support is different here from the basis on which other families claim support. It is an aspect, and a very important aspect, of Aboriginal people's claim to just compensation for their past loss of their land. It is therefore defensible for the government to allocate resources in child welfare to Aboriginal families in circumstances where, on general child welfare grounds, those resources might not be available to other families in similar economic circumstances.

If this argument is accepted, a number of legal changes seem appropriate.

First, the courts could be given power to make orders binding on the state authorities, requiring financial or other support to be provided. While there is no legal objection to such powers, it seems unlikely that Australian legislatures could be persuaded to give courts this kind of power. Allocation of public resources is seen to be a matter for government, not the courts. Investing the courts with such powers would probably be politically unacceptable in Australia, and arguably courts are not equipped to determine such questions.

A second change might be a legislative provision that the court could not make an order placing an Aboriginal child in a non-Aboriginal setting unless it was satisfied that there was no Aboriginal family which could, *if given reasonable financial support*, adequately care for the child.

If it be thought that this is too drastic, the legislation could merely provide that the court could in placing a child with an Aboriginal family *recommend* to the authority that resources be provided. There could be other provisions to ensure that Aboriginal communities and organizations were represented in the proceedings, and could recommend to the court any Aboriginal placement which they considered would be suitable if financial support were available. Although such provisions would not *guarantee* financial support, welfare authorities might come under pressure to follow the court's recommendations, if only because failure to do so might lead to criticism from the court (to which welfare departments and politicians are rather sensitive) and such criticism might be used effectively by Aboriginal organizations lobbying for changes in funding policies.

C. The principle as a recognition of the rights of Aboriginal people

Statements from Aboriginal people relating to child welfare have often stressed that child welfare questions raise fundamental issues of Aboriginal identity:

> The crisis of Aboriginal children is the crisis of the Aboriginal people as a whole. If Aboriginal children are lost forever to their families - as is the current state of affairs - the survival of Aboriginal people as a distinct cultural and social group is put into question.[69]

> Unwarranted and unjust government interference with Aboriginal family life is perhaps the most flagrant infringement of the rights of Aboriginal communities to govern themselves in our time and the most tragic aspect of contemporary Aboriginal life.[70]

The Australian Law Reform Commission commences its discussion with this theme. It quotes Maria Brandl:

> ... it is the role and right of parents everywhere to pass on their beliefs, knowledge, customs, language, law ... to their children. In that way the culture of a group lives on and its distinctiveness, too, and consequently, the pride of the people who own it. The role and the rights of parents and families in this can become endangered when other institutions take over aspects of handing on a heritage.[71]

It might be thought that since child welfare only affects those children singled out for attention, its effect on a population would not be significant. However, the impact of the child welfare system on Australian Aborigines has been so great that it has directly affected a significant proportion of the population. In the extended families and close communities in which most Aboriginal people live, the taking of children has been a constant threat, and a constant reminder that in white eyes Aboriginal people cannot properly bring up their children. As discussed earlier, reports of the N.S.W. Aborigines Protection Board were quite explicit; it was stated in the report of 1921, for example, that "continuation of this policy of dissociating the children from camp life must eventually solve the Aboriginal problem".[72] It is well known that minorities tend to internalize the values of the dominant society: what must these experiences have done to the confidence and self-image of Aboriginal parents?

It is fairly obvious that if a policy of self-determination for Aboriginal people is to be implemented, or even a policy of acknowledging the legitimacy of Aboriginal culture, every effort must be made to prevent the removal of Aboriginal children from their families and communities. This policy is explicit in the wording of the Indian Child Welfare Act 1978 of the United States, which provides:

> There is no resource that is more vital to the continued existence and integrity of Indian tribes than their children ... it is the policy of the Nation to protect that best interests of Indian children and to promote the stability and security of Indian tribes and families by the establishment of minimum Federal standards ....[73]

Such arguments as there are sometimes resisted on the ground that any laws distinguishing between Aborigines and other people in Australia are inherently discriminatory and therefore objectionable. This question has been discussed at length by the Law Reform Commission.[74] This is not the place to enter that large topic, but it may be useful to note that the Commission's general conclusion was that laws recognizing Aboriginal customary law will not be racially discriminatory, or involve a denial of equality before the law if these measures (i) are reasonable responses to the special needs of those Aboriginal people affected by the proposals; (ii) are generally accepted by them; and (iii) do not deprive individual Aborigines of basic human rights, or of access to the general legal system and its institutions.

A second objection, commonly linked with the first but fundamentally different, is that any form of separate laws relating to Aboriginal people will create resentment among non-Aborigines: the "backlash" effect.[75] This point is about politics, not philosophy; about people's reactions, not about what is fair. But it is often combined with the first argument, since people often attribute to others views which they are embarrassed to admit that they themselves hold. There may indeed be difficulty in "selling" such proposals as the child placement principle to the majority of Australians, who do not have a tradition of sophisticated debate about the rights of minorities. When I have put the difficulty to Aboriginal people in the course of my own research, however, it has usually provoked the comment that things are already so bad that fears of a backlash should not deter people from proposing necessary reforms.

A third possible objection, however, is that the argument is inconsistent with the principle that the child's welfare is the "paramount consideration". This principle precludes *any* interest from competing with the child's welfare in placement decisions: thus there is no place for the interests of Aboriginal people as a whole in the law governing the placement of Aboriginal children. To deal with this objection fully would be outside the scope of this paper, but an attempt will be made to indicate the general nature of a possible response.

The paramountcy principle was developed in the context of competing claims, mainly by parents, to bring up a child. It expressed the view that in such cases the proper focus for attention should be the child's welfare rather than the "rights" of the parents. As this principle developed through the cases, the courts became more and more willing to override the fathers rights (which had been dominant in the early law) where they conflicted with the child's welfare. The principle was also applied to custody disputes between parents and others: it required the courts, even here, to disregard parental rights if they conflicted with the child's welfare.[76] In practice, however, this was not as drastic a change as might be thought, since the courts have generally adhered to the presumption that children's welfare is likely to be best served by remaining with a parent: in practice, the third party needs to demonstrate a *clear* advantage to the child to overcome this presumption.

Despite its extension to disputes between parents and non-parents, however, the principle has not been taken to mean that wherever a child is involved a court can always, on anyone's application, act on its own assessment of what the child's welfare requires. Child welfare law is an important example of the general principle that, however wide a court's discretion may be, it cannot exercise its power until it has found the necessary facts on which to justify its exercise of jurisdiction. Under the legislation of Australian states, it is necessary for the state welfare department to establish some threshold fact before it becomes possible for the children's court to make an order. The threshold is expressed as the need to find that the child is "neglected" or "in need of care", or some similar phrase.[77] Indeed, the recent trend is for the thresholds to be made *more* rigorous, on the basis that the rights of both children and parents will be served by preventing intervention except where the child is rather clearly at risk.

There are less familiar examples of limitations to the application of the paramountcy rule. Sometimes people have tried to use the wardship jurisdiction of the Supreme Courts to by-pass some other legal provisions, or legally accepted values. Thus in *Re Mohammed Arif*[78] an application was made for the court to order that a child should remain in England, although the immigration authorities, by virtue of their statutory powers, had determined that the child could not remain. The Court firmly rejected this application, stating that the jurisdiction could not be used to circumvent the proper functioning of the immigration system. In another case, *Re X*,[79] an application was made to prevent the publication of a book which stated true but embarrassing facts about the child's deceased father: the argument was that publication of the book, though not defamatory or in breach of any other civil or criminal rule, would be damaging to the child, who might be subjected to ridicule, and so on. Since the child's welfare was paramount, the court should make the order. This application also failed, the Court of Appeal holding that the community's interest in free speech outweighed any danger to the child.

These examples shed light on the limits of the "paramountcy" principle. They show, I think, that the principle cannot mean that *all* other interests are necessarily to be subordinated to children's interests. Thus the limitations on the jurisdiction of the children's court may be taken to embody, at least in part, political values about the proper relationship between public officials and citizens. And the two cases mentioned show that children's interests may be properly subordinated to the public interest in, respectively, the functioning of the immigration system, and freedom of speech.

On this analysis, it seems that, while in custody and related matters the principle that the child's welfare is paramount requires the court to subordinate parental interests to children's interests, there are situations in which other important public interests may prevail over the interests of individual children.

It is therefore possible to argue that there is a public interest element in Aboriginal child welfare policy that may override the welfare of individual children. It can be argued that indigenous peoples are entitled to have their identity and culture protected, and this requires protection of their rights to bring up their own children. In the Australian context, this position could be reinforced by the argument that, especially in the light of the tragic history of the destruction of Aboriginal family life by white authority, and the fundamental importance of developing Aboriginal responsibility for their own affairs, there are sound reasons, other than the welfare of individual children, for adoption of the Aboriginal child placement principle.

This approach does not involve *ignoring* children's interests. In *Re X,* for example, the Court weighed up the respective seriousness of the danger to the child and the infringements on free speech. It might be assumed that if the evidence had shown that the child would have been more certainly or more seriously damaged by the publication, the decision might well have gone the other way.[80] Similarly, on the present argument, the desirability of Aboriginal self-determination might justify the placement of Aboriginal children with Aboriginal families where it could not be determined whether an Aboriginal or non-Aboriginal placement would be better for the child, and also where there was only a slight or speculative advantage in the non-Aboriginal placement. But in a case where the only available Aboriginal placement posed a real risk to the child's safety or proper development, the child's interests would prevail over the general desirability of Aboriginal placements for Aboriginal children.

Conclusion

This chapter draws mainly on research in New South Wales, but the issues canvassed are relevant to indigenous people in many countries and certainly in North America.

The argument has been that child welfare laws and policies involve not only the welfare of individual Aboriginal children but their destiny as part of the Aboriginal people. In the past, child welfare has generally been either part of the domination and oppression of indigenous peoples, or, in more recent times, characterized by indifference to their children's Aboriginality. Against the emerging recognition by governments of the rights of Aboriginal people to self-determination, child welfare laws and policies are necessarily being revised.

Much of this revision is relatively straightforward, and consists of undoing some of the worst abuses of the past. But if the advances are to endure, and be further developed, they will need to be linked more clearly with underlying policies relating to Aboriginal people and their rights. This has been the objective of this paper. It has been argued that what has become known as the Aboriginal child placement principle, and several associated reforms of law and policy, are consistent both with the welfare of individual children and with rights of Aboriginal people. If these arguments are accepted, they might provide a basis for work on the difficult issues that have yet to be satisfactorily addressed in Australia, and perhaps elsewhere. These include the definition of an "Aboriginal child" in the present context; finding the appropriate balance between using law and policy to implement changes; determining the roles of federal and state or provincial government; and working with Aboriginal people, rather than against them, in moving towards more effective and authentic forms of Aboriginal control in the laws and services intended to safeguard the welfare of Aboriginal children.

Notes

1. A useful recent summary is contained in Department of Aboriginal Affairs, 1984.
2. See Rowley, 1970-71: vol.1; Reynolds, 1982.
3. See generally, Hanks and Keon-Cohen, 1984.

4. Lyons, 1984.
5. Keon-Cohen and Morse, 1984.
6. See Nettheim, 1981: Appendix.
7. For an instructive treatment see, Morse, 1984.
8. Wilkie, 1985.
9. Department of Aboriginal Affairs, 1985.
10. Tucker, 1977:81.
11. See generally, Rowley, 1970-71, and the citations at note 15 below.
12. Minutes of Aborigines Protection Board (NSW), 1912, 4/7121.
13. Aborigines Protection Board, n.d.
14. *Dawn,* November 1956, 18.
15. Read, 1982. See also Goodall, 1982:135; Hankins, 1982..
16. The Board was created in 1883, following the appointment of a "Protector of Aborigines" in 1881. It was established in law by the *Aborigines Protection Act* 1909 under the title "The Board for Protection of Aborigines" (s. 4). Its activities relating to children are discussed by Read, Goodall and Hankins, ibid.
17. *Aborigines Protection Act (Amendment) Act,* 1943, s. 2.
18. Hankins, 1092:2.1.16.
19. *Aborigines Protection Amendment Act,* 1915, s. 4.
20. Goodall, 1982.
21. This material is discussed in Chisholm, 1985:33-54.
22. A discussion of Labor's policy on Aboriginal Affairs may be found in (1983) 7 Aboriginal Law Bulletin.
23. Australian Labor Party,
24. Milne, 1982.
25. See Australian Law Reform Commission, (A.L.R.C.) 1986:vol. 1, 235-237.
26. Nettheim, 1984.
27. A.L.R.C. 1986: vol. 1, chapters 9 and 10.
28. Id., vol. 1, 128.
29. Id., vol. 1, 130-132.
30. Johnston, 1983. See also A.L.R.C. 1986: vol. 1, 246-249, and the references there cited.
31. Described in A.L.R.C. 1986: vol. 1, 249-254.
32. *Community Welfare Act* (N.T.) 1983, s. 69.
33. *Adoption Act 1984* (Vic.), s. 50.
34. *Family and Community Development Welfare Bill* 1984 (Qld).
35. Department of Aboriginal Affairs 1980, reproduced in A.L.R.C., 1982: 51.
36. Working Party of Standing Committee of Social Welfare Administrators, 1983.
37. Chisholm, 1985: 110-111.

38. Id., 55-97.
39. See Milne, 1982.
40. Chisholm, 1982.
41. Chisholm, 1985: 55-56, 89.
42. Id., 91-96.
43. See also Venne, 1985:2.
44. Discussed in A.L.R.C. 1986: vol. 1, 242-246.
45. Department of Aboriginal Affairs, 1980.
46. Picton, 1976.
47. See A.L.R.C. 1986: vol. 1, 241.
48. For a summary and commentary on this legislation, see A.L.R.C. 1986: vol. 1, 249-254.
49. Aboriginal Customary Laws (Recognition) Act 1986, draft legislation set out in A.L.R.C. 1986: vol. 2, 249-273.
50. Schedule, cl. 1.
51. Section 16(1).
52. Section 16(2) and (3).
53. Schedule, cl. 2.
54. Id., cl. 1.
55. Id., cl. 4.
56. Id., cl. 5.
57. Id., cl. 6.
58. A.L.R.C., 1982:17.
59. Id., 14-19, 28-30.
60. Id., 6. See also A.L.R.C. 1986: vol. 1, 236.
61. See generally Chisholm, 1985: especially chapter 2.
62. Westermeyer, 1977.
63. For an interesting account of these in one Aboriginal community, see Eckermann, 1977: especially at 298-301.
64. See Eckermann, 1980:86; and other sources cited in Chisholm, 1985.
65. A.L.R.C., 1982:16. For a more controversial decision, see *Marriage of Gouge* (1984), 9 Fam. L.R. 500, and the comment in (1985) 13 *Aboriginal Law Bulletin* 9.
66. *Gronow v Gronow* (1979), 29 A.L.R. 129 (High Court of Australia).
67. E.g., *Gouge,* note 65, *supra;* and *F v Langshaw* (1983), 8 Fam. L.R. 833.
68. The payments are made under *Child Welfare Act,* 1939, s. 27A. There were over 200 Aboriginal children in foster care with Aboriginal foster parents under this scheme in May 1985: personal communication from Mrs. A. Weldon, Chairperson, Aboriginal Children's Service, Sydney.
69. Jackson, 1979:4.

70. Austin, 1976.
71. Brandl, 1980, cited in A.L.R.C. 1982:1.
72. Cited in Read, 1982:2.
73. Section 2(3) and section 3 (emphasis added).
74. A.L.R.C. 1986: vol. 1, chapter 9.
75. Id., 125.
76. *J v C* [1970] A.C. 668 (House of Lords).
77. E.g., *Child Welfare Act* 1939 (NSW) s. 72 ("neglected" child).
78. [1968] Ch. 643.
79. *Re X,* [1975] Fam. 47.
80. See, e.g., *In Re X (A Minor) (Wardship: Injunction),* [1984] 1 W.L.R. 1422, an English case in which an injunction against publication was given to protect a child, but the judgment shows a concern to limit the restriction to that necessary for the child's welfare.

References

ABORIGINES PROTECTION BOARD (no date)
Annual Report for 1914.

AUSTIN, J. (1976)
"The Destruction of Aboriginal Families," Nunga News (July 2-3).

AUSTRALIAN LABOR PARTY (1983)
Aboriginal Affairs Policy 1983: Labor's Programme for Self-Determination.

AUSTRALIAN LAW REFORM COMMISSION (1982)
Reference on Aboriginal Customary Law, Research Paper No.4, Child Custody, Fostering and Adoption. Canberra.

(Report No. 31) The Recognition of Aboriginal Customary Laws. Vol 1. Canberra: Australian Government Printing Service.

BRANDL, M. (1980)
"The Aboriginal Children and Families Heritage Project," 5 Australian Child and Family Welfare 20-22.

CHISHOLM, R. (1982)
"Aboriginal Self-Determination and Child Welfare: A Case Conference," 17 Australian Journal of Social Issues 258-275.

---------- (1985)
Black Children: White Welfare? Aboriginal Child Welfare Law and Policy in New South Wales. Social Welfare Research Centre, University of New South Wales, Kensington.

DEPARTMENT OF ABORIGINAL AFFAIRS (1980)
Aboriginal Adoption and Fostering Policy Guidelines.

---------- (1984)
Aboriginal Social Indicators. Canberra: Australian Government Publishing Service.

---------- (1985)
"Commonwealth Preferred National Aboriginal band Rights Model," Aboriginal Newsletter, 140 (February). Canberra.

ECKERMANN, A-K (1977)
"Group Organisation and Identity Within an Urban Aboriginal Community," in R.M. Berndt (ed.), Aborigines and Change: Australia in the '70s. Canberra: Australian Institute of Aboriginal Studies.

---------- (1980)
"Aboriginal Children," in R. Brown (ed.), Children Australia. Sydney: Allen & Unwin.

GOODALL, H. (1982)
"A History of Aboriginal Communities in New South Wales." Ph.D. Thesis, University of Sydney.

HANKS, P. and B. KEON-COHEN (1984)
Aborigines and the Law. Sydney: Allen & Unwin.

HANKINS, C. (1982)
"The Missing Links." B.A. Hons. Thesis, School of Sociology, University of New South Wales.

JACKSON, Bill (ed.) (1979)
"The First Aboriginal Child Survival Seminar," Aboriginal Child Care Agency in association with the Office of Child Care. Melbourne and Canberra.

JOHNSTON, P. (1983)
Native Children and the Child Welfare System. Canadian Council on Social Development. Toronto.

KEON-COHEN, B. and B. MORSE (1984)
"Indigenous Land Rights in Australia and Canada," in P. Hanks and B. Keon-Cohen (eds.), Aborigines and the Law. Sydney: Allen & Unwin.

LYONS, G. (1984)
"Aboriginal Legal Services," in P. Hanks and B. Keon-Cohen (eds.), Aborigines and the Law. Sydney: Allen & Unwin.

MILNE, C. (1982)
Aboriginal Children in Substitute Care. Principal Report of the Aboriginal Children's Research Project, Family and Children's Services Agency, Sydney.

MORSE, B. (1984)
Aboriginal Self-Government in Australia and Canada. Kingston, Ontario: Institute of Intergovernmental Relations, Queen's University.

NETTHEIM, G. (1981)
Victims of the Law. Sydney: Allen & Unwin.

---------- (1984)
"The Relevance of International Law," in P. Hanks and B. Keon-Cohen (eds.), Aborigines and the Law. Sydney: Allen & Unwin.

PICTON, C. (ed.) Proceedings of the First Australian Conference on Adoption. Committee of the First Australian Conference on Adoption, Sydney.

READ, P. (1982)
The Stolen Generations. New South Wales Ministry of Aboriginal Affairs.

REYNOLDS, H. (1982)
The Other Side of the Frontier. Ringwood, Victoria: Penguin.

ROWLEY, C.D. (1970-71)
Aboriginal Policy and Practice. 3 vols. Canberra: Australian National University Press.

TUCKER, Margaret (1977)
If Everyone Cared. Sydney: Ure Smith.

VENNE, S. (1985)
"Indigenous Child Care and Self-Determination," a paper delivered to the Second Conference on Provincial Social Welfare Policy, Calgary, Alberta.

WESTERMEYER, J. (1977)
"Cross-Racial Foster Home Placement among Native American Psychiatric Patients," 69 Journal of the National Medical Association 231.

WILKIE, M. (1985)
Aboriginal Land Rights in N.S.W. Chippendale, New South Wales: Alternative Publishing Coop. Ltd., in association with Black Books.

WORKING PARTY OF STANDING COMMITTEE OF SOCIAL WELFARE ADMINISTRATORS (1983)
Aboriginal Fostering and Adoption: Review of State and Territory Principles and Practices.

Aboriginal child placement in the urban context

Basil Sansom and Patricia Baines

This paper deals with guardianship in Aboriginal conceptions and with social processes that determine:
(i) the allocation and distribution of responsibility for the "rearing up" of "kids" amongst individuals and
(ii) the distribution of children among familial groupings that are labile, forming and re-forming over time.

We deal with Aboriginal guardianship in two distinct places and among different populations. In 1975-6, Sansom worked among Aboriginal Countrymen of the fringe camps of Darwin and the associated camps of that city's north Australian hinterland. More recently (1980 to the present) Baines has been conducting research among people who identify themselves as Nyungar. While Nyungar belong generally to the South-West of Western Australia and are also represented in towns and settlements along the part of the western seaboard that extends from Perth to Broome, those whom Baines has worked with reside in metropolitan Perth and the rural towns of Perth's immediate hinterland.

In this essay we compare the ways in which Nyungar and Darwin Countrymen allocate the responsibilities of guardianship and determine the placement of children. We show that Aborigines of these two distant regions bring similar values to bear in different contexts. The contrasts we note originate in differences of social scale.

In and around Darwin, the Aboriginal presence is notable and the proportional representation of Aborigines in the total population is quite high. In contrast, the proportional representation of Nyungars is low in Perth and the South-West. The social consequences of this demographic difference are several. In the first place, Nyungar familial groupings are smaller than those encountered in Darwin.

Secondly, there is a differentiation and separation of small-scale Nyungar groupings while in the Darwin region the groupings made up of Aborigines who have active dealings with one another are large. There is a further difference. The Nyungar featured in this study are generally housed in dwellings rented either from the State Housing Commission or from private landlords. The Darwin Countrymen, on the other hand, are people of town camps and of camps located on pastoral stations in the Darwin hnterland. Furthermore, some of those called Countrymen are associated with Aboriginal settlements in the northern part of the Top End. Having listed these differences, we should note a point of similarity. Both Nyungar and the Darwin Countrymen are increasingly a people without work. Economically they live as dependants of the State. For the most part, they are only able to make sporadic and short-term forays into the labour market. A consequence of the absence of wages is that welfare payments are of particular significance for members of both populations.

Like Nyungar, the Countrymen of Darwin are less people of particular places, more people who have a provenance in regions that they define for themselves and call their own. Patterns of movement between the places that people collectively command are integral to individual lives. In Nyungar country, people (and especially older people) talk about their "runs" and each person's "run" is made up of the set of places to which he or she has potential access. Runs are dotted with the places in which a person legitimately can stay. The Darwin phrase for such sets of places describes accessible camping sites as a collection - "all that place bla Countryman" and "all that place this mob got alabout". In these regions, patterns of movement have everything to do with the composition and recomposition either of Nyungar households or the hearth-groups of the Darwin Countrymen. In both regions, marriages are fragile. Again, the phenomenon of "on-and-off marriage" (a Darwin term) is common to both areas of study. "On and off" is used in reference to marriages that are sporadically realized. Spouses live together for a time, then go their separate ways then, when fortunes change, the couple may be reunited.

Given movement, the fragility of marriage and the continuous recomposition of local groups, issues of guardianship and the placement of children have frequently to be resolved. Nor can any act of child-placement be considered as final - i.e., as an allocation of a child to a domestic context that will continue to be the setting in which the child will stay until maturity. Histories of childhood are generally chaptered renderings of experience in a series of homes in different places. In some shifts between domestic settings, there is a continuity of guardianship. In other moves a child can experience two kinds of discontinuity - a change of home and home place can be accompanied by his or her allocation to a prime guardian who, while a kinsman or kinswoman, is not the prime carer that watched over the child before the move was made. In sum, we have to deal with guardianship in a social order perpetually characterized by both recomposition of domestic groups and frequent alteration of the definition of the terms of relationships that obtain between kin. To elucidate the latter point, a grandmother who is a child's effective guardian for, say, a five month span is not the same social person during a later phase of the child's life when the child's mother has resumed the responsibilities of care. There are three eternal and related questions: (i) in which place (i.e., sited house or hearth group) to locate a child (ii) of which set of people is the house/hearth group to be composed and (iii) which of the set of people in a house/hearth group will be allocated the prime responsibility of guardianship for the child concerned?

I. Consociate experience and true relations

For the Aborigines we know, the essential source of value in social life comes of co-experience with known, named others. Co-experience creates and is regarded as the source of true and worthwhile relationships between people. Emphasizing the significance of co-experience, Aboriginal people invest directly in social relationships with others in ways that have consequences for (i) the establishment of individual identity and (ii) the composition of regional groupings.

Darwin Countrymen explain that they are people who have "bin running together for years and years". Within the total set of Countrymen, there are subsets of people who have had a great deal to do with one another over time. These are people who, for example, have been associated first with one cattle station, a wet season "camping" of 1962, then the Buffalo shooting camps of 1963 and so on. Adult members of such sets can retail histories of on-and-off association with one another over long periods of years to conclude "wefella one mob". With apparent exaggeration they may add: "Wefella one mob. Bin al along together". Though they gloss over gaps of time, such assertions are nonetheless true. The claim is that the people concerned never gave one another away. Their separations were temporary partings, not desertions. To fill gaps of absence, one "worries for" and shows that one "worries for" relevant persons who are not part of one's present company. Each person is thus able to establish relationships that join him or her to those with whom time has often been spent. This grouping of people constitutes those recognized by Nyungar as "close in" and by Darwinites as "close up". The "close up Countrymen" (Darwin) or "close in lations" (Nyungar) constitute for each person the prime set of significant others in life. They, above all, are the people who hold one's identity for they have the power to determine social worth among their membership. After all, they and they alone command the information that is proof of a person's nature, character and social potential.

It has often been written that social relationships in traditional Aboriginal communities are "determined by kinship" (cf Berndt and Berndt 1977). Nyungar and Aborigines of the Darwin region do indeed live in a world in which all significant others are allocated kinship positions whether they are born into the local ambit of kin relations or are adopted into it. This means that each person can use kinship terms of reference and address for the range of consociate others. Most social relationships are thus comprehended by the idiom of kinship. One moves in a world of brothers, sisters, aunties, sister-cousins and so on. This, however, is to deal merely with nominal kinship. We wish, however, to emphasize the difference between such nominal kinship and what we call *effective kinship*. This is to distinguish between two ways of defining relationships. There is, on the one hand, the recognition of genealogical relationships. On the other hand, there is the recognition of people who are not only genealogically related but who are those kin who truly count. In the Darwin region, this yields the local distinction between people who are "jus lations" and people who are not only "lations" but "lations" who can also be counted as "close up". "Close up lations" are kinsmen and kinswomen who (from an individual point of view) have been important to one in the experience of life's progress. In our terms such people are *effective kin* and we write also of *effective kinship*.

In both the regions we consider, the difference between merely nominal and truly effective kinship is most marked in the use of a designation - "father for nothing". A "father for nothing" is a man who acknowledgedly is the begetter of a child but who played little or no part in the business of rearing that child. Nugatory fatherhood is not denied - "Gotta call that ol man 'Dad' but he doan matter: father for nothing really". In such statements, there is a concession of blood relationships together with an immediate denial of effective significance to the relationship; while admitted, the father-child relationship is discounted.

We hold that generally in Aboriginal Australia, guardianship of children is not so much "determined by kinship" as it is a function exercised by allocating and reallocating responsibility for the care and nurture of children within an ambit of a grouping of effective kin. This is to say that guardianship belongs to a set of "close up Countrymen" in and about Darwin or to the set of Nyungar relations reckoned to be "close in".

There is another distinction that is germane to Aboriginal conceptions. The people in their speaking consistently note the difference between the class of relationships which come of experience between adults and the class of relationships that link children to other children and adults. For our purposes, this yields:

(i) Relationships between adults that were begun in adulthood;
(ii) Relationships between children who have (for any significant fraction of juvenile life) been "reared up together"; and
(iii) The relationship between children and those adults who have to any degree participated in their "rearing up".

Any person's "close up" fellows are constituted as a set made up of those who reared one up, those whom one was reared up with, those one has kept company with in adulthood and, finally, those whom one has helped to rear. Of the types and sorts of "close up" people, special significance is attached to those who, as children, kept company with one in childhood dependency, to those whom one served when they were young and dependent, and those to whom one owes recognition as people who participated in one's own upbringing. Of the categories of relationship we have distinguished, three are thus marked. In "reckoning up" those relations who are "close up", a speaker assigns special status to those historically connected to him or her in any relationship in which the dependency of childhood is a factor.

II. The watching brief and worry

The next step in our argument is to register a further fact of commonality. Among Nyungar and in the Darwin region, the business of "watching for" and "worry for all them kid" is the business of groupings of close up people. This is to say that care for kids and the expression of concern for their respective destinies falls with the weight of obligation on a set of people made up not merely of nominal kinsfolk, but of those who are recognized as effective kin. Since the placement of children and the allocation of responsibilities for guardianship ordinarily belong within the ambit of "close up" kinship, special problems are encountered when a grouping of "close up" kin fails to accommodate and care for a child.

Any child born into the close up kin group has, by the fact of his or her birth, the right to proper care. Members of the close up kin group exhibit and prove their care by "worrying for" the child and by actively seeing to his or her welfare. Both orders of action - the expression of concern and actual service to the child - count as aspects of "rearing up". Again, a distinction is made when situations demand that one person be allocated more credit than another. First importance is accorded to those who "always bin gibbin tucker" (Darwin) or who are bosses of the places "where I gotta feed" (Nyungar). Prime guardianship is signalled though day-to-day provisioning.

There is another dimension to "worrying for" a child and, in this aspect, "worry" has the capacity to bridge distance and fill in those gaps of experience of a child's maturing that are occasioned by separation. When at a distance from a child, those close to it in terms of kinship and obligation will express "worry for that kid". This kind of worry is announced to the world by word and gesture. "How that lil Tommy doing? I worry, all the time worry for that kid." Declarations of this sort should evoke a response from those present who thus become witness to one's enunciated worrying. Then there is the retreat of person into contemplative brown study and silence - a withdrawal designed to cause comment:

Q. "What you so quiet? You doan wanna play card?"

A. "Alla time I worry for that kid, lil fella that Maisie bla Nora n Joe".

"Worry for" and "watching for" are Aboriginal notions that we comprehend in our provided terms as *the watching brief* that close up people are in principle obliged to discharge with reference to all children born or adopted into the close up kindred. The watching brief, in short, is a label for an obligation that falls on a collectivity. Members of that collectivity have to see to its discharge by ensuring that the active particularities of caring for any child are allocated to members of a particular household/hearthgroup. Once any such allocation of responsibility has been made, it is the duty of the watchers to see that the prime guardian "feeds up" that child and gives it proper care. The care of a child in a Nyungar household or a child "sitting down" next to a Darwin camp fire is thus monitored by a set of watchers who witness the caring and report their verdicts on the nature and quality of caring to any members of the group who have been away and, in their absence, have been worrying rather than watching for the kid.

We have sought to establish several major general points:

(i) Social value in Aboriginal society derives from the accumulations of co-experience which make persons meaningful to one another.

(ii) People of co-participation who, in the Darwin phrase, have run together for years and years, constitute sets of persons who are reckoned to be "close up".

(iii) Close up people constitute groupings in which the relationships between individuals are the time-proven ties of effective kinship.

(iv) Guardianship and its monitoring ordinarily belong to groupings of effective kinsfolk, sets of people who are prepared and predisposed to accept that arrangements for child care are subject to revision. In any instance of reallocation of guardianship, all those who have previously proven their concern for the child in question can rightfully have a say and so should be consulted.

Things discussed so far can be said equally of Darwin and of the South-West of Western Australia. However, in these two distanced places, the similar values that Aborigines entertain are brought down in distinct social contexts.

III. Of mobs, marriages and kids (Darwin)

Issues of guardianship are brought to the fore when marriages dissolve, or when hearth-holds to which a child has been assigned are radically recomposed. Such events are frequent among Countrymen. The upset of a marriage or the recomposition of a hearth group occur, in the Darwin region, within the sited social context that is a place or "camping" held in possession by a particular "mob". Here all domestic arrangements (and not only the care of kids) are subject to controls exercised by the collectivity of mob-members. As a first step towards describing the system of control that is brought, *inter alia*, to matters of guardianship, we may deal with the siting of mobs. The point at issue is the suitability of a camp and mob as a harbour for kids. Judgments of suitability or unsuitability are to be made after considering mob "style". "Style" comprehends a characteristic and total way of life typical of a named "camping" and its habituees. In this regard, there is an important distinction between places that are "good for kids" and places that are compromised because they are drinking places in which incidents of violence are expected to occur. Places of noise and violence in which people drink a lot are not places in which large numbers of youngsters can safely be accommodated. In the North, the distinction between drinking camps and camps in which drinking is absent or minimized is not one that involves the total exclusion of children from camps of the former sort; rather, it involves capacity. In a drinking camp you "can have too many kid". In such places, an excess of children spells their neglect or, worse, their encountering of danger. We elaborate with reference to the contrast between a major Darwin fringe camp and camps of the pastoral hinterland.

Elsewhere Sansom (1980) has documented regimes for the control of drinking in a Darwin fringe camp (Wallaby Cross) to show how "Masterful Men" of the camping scene "organize for grog". Masterful Men work to minimize risk and danger and to reduce the probability of violence. They also work to ensure that any binge drinkers affiliated to the camp will recover from their bouts and not be robbed.

Masterful Men implement controls by the canny use of space, monitoring the disposition of people over the drinking pitches and recognized camping sites that constitute the local scene. At Wallaby Cross on any day at least one Masterful Man will be at the centre of a grouping in which women and children predominate. In this grouping, rates of drinking are sedulously policed while adults who are drunken in their comportment or otherwise threaten to disturb the regime of moderation (called "drinking slow") are sent away. There is, then, a veritable island of quiet in the midst of a more boisterous world. On the urban fringes, the quietness of a special child-centred camp or drinking place is sustained by work. At Wallaby Cross leaders will from time to time complain: "We gotta problem, too many kid bin coming up". The leaders work within a region in which their authority extends to the management of the dynamics of a political demography in terms of which Countrymen are distributed among the mobs and camps of Darwin and its hinterland. When at Wallaby Cross a leader is moved to register an excess of children, he is remarking upon an imbalance. The ratio of children to potential child-carers is unsatisfactory. This means that too many adults - both women and men - are taking a holiday from domestic responsibilities. There is an insufficiency of helpers willing to adopt a more sober style and maintain the child-centred island of quiet camping. To remedy this situation, some people must be told to leave both for their own good and that of children they have brought with them.

Limited capacities for child-minding at Wallaby Cross contrast with the social amenities available in rural encampments, especially those that are well distanced from any country pub. Such places are always good for kids. On the edge of town, Wallaby Cross exists as a sort of Aboriginal hotel run by a core of permanent residents who provide a safe context for visitors who are country based but come to town to do business or to take time out, living for a while in the state of irresponsibility that is called "holiday". Overall, the stated preference is that "you shouldn be bringing that kid up longa town. This a drinking place".

In and around Darwin, the child-holding capacities of any camp and mob are noted and related to local "styles". "Darwin style", with its adult celebrations that have drink as a focus is one thing, "Station style" or "Mission style" is something else. So a woman declares: "We gonna rearim up this lil one Station style longa Minkelbury". Leaders at Minkelbury allow no fighting and, furthermore, there is a regime to control the importation of grog which comes to the station in small quantity on specified days. Camps that are good for kids are, in sum, places where there is political management dedicated to the maintenance of quiet camping. If a child in any camp "gets accident", the camp leaders stand to share in the blame that will be meted out, especially if it can be shown that one or other of them allowed things to "go out of control".

This leads us on to enunciate a theme. We translate the Aboriginal English "caring for kids" as guardianship. Furthermore, "caring for kids" is, in the first instance, a collective concern for a child-centred camp that must as an entire unit be made a place in which the business of rearing up can go forward. In policing everyday behaviour, one standard reproach is: "What you two fighting. You doan care for kid?"

Among Countrymen, the making and breaking of marriages and control of the comportment of married couples are also matters within a mob's jurisdiction. To sustain a marriage within a mob and camp, a couple must attend to their own provisioning and demonstrate their ability to maintain a "kitchen" of their own. Couples who have children are watched with particular attention. Hearth-holders who have children are immediately attacked if their provisioning fails. If a child goes round the camp snatching food or "crying for tucker", that child's primary guardians will be arraigned at once. If they do not show that they can arrange to "feeding up lil fella", the child will be taken into another grouping - a *de facto* removal that is justified by the child's hunger. The sickness or injury of a child can similarly be a signal for his or her removal from guardians who, by allowing the sickness or injury to happen, seem (prima facie) to have been guilty of neglect. Similarly, a medical diagnosis of malnutrition has profound effects. The word of a nurse or doctor is a declaration of force - no mere allegation, but proof positive of inadequate provision of rations and tucker over a period of months or weeks.

The *de facto* removal of a child from prime guardians is done by people who declare that they "have reason". Their status is, at this juncture, that of persons who have "bin taking kid". The responsibility then devolves on the takers to justify their action and, furthermore, the allocation of future responsibility for the prime guardianship of the child is put at issue. Nor do the takers who jump into the role of self-appointed fosterers always want to assume the responsibilities of primary guardianship. Taking is an act of intervention. Its justification and the ethic that makes it possible lies in Aboriginal assumptions concerning responsibility within the collectivity that is a mob. Key phrases in this regard are "watching out for kid", "checking up", "rearing up" and "worry for".

Every adult in any camp should watch out for all children in the camp. There is, then, a generalized watching brief that is communal. Within the camp, leaders carry special responsibility but they rely on those who are "close up" to hearth-holders to be the most assiduous watchers who "check up" on the "detail" of the day to day domestic routines performed around neighbouring camp fires. Women of proximate hearths will know details about children feeding, about evacuation, about any crying that could signal neglect. Reproof of errant mothers or prime guardians begins with mild intervention in exchanges between proximate hearth-holders. If a prime guardian persists in the neglect of a child, the witnessing close up camper brings the details of alleged neglect to wider attention. From this moment on, the targeted, allegedly neglectful person becomes a focus of mob concern. The guardian's child-minding regime is made a matter for daily assessment by camp members. If a picture of neglect is limned out in detail over the days, an act of taking the child will follow unless the person thus on trial decamps declaring that the child will be better sited and cared for elsewhere. Following a decamping move, those who witnessed neglect do not relinquish responsibility. People who remove go to destinations where news, "the word", about their actions, will pursue them.

Following any act of taking a child, the issue of future prime guardianship remains to be determined. Delinquent guardians may in the end be given "nother chance". This is unlikely, however, if the child has been taken on the grounds of hunger. Delinquent family members will either have to modify spendthrift ways or, if without sufficient money, will have to find new sources of income. After an act of taking there is an interim, a period of uncertainty when the child is in temporary care. This period comes to an end when, with communal approval, the child is "given" to a new prime guardian who is accredited as such by mob members. Such allocations are subject to discussion among the population of Countrymen. Before the act of giving is accomplished in a mob, sufficient time must pass for those of the child's close up kin who are in other mobs to be apprised of the crisis. If interested, they can then attend the camp in which the child's future is to be decided. Recognition of child neglect or abuse thus leads to a series of events that culminate in an approved reassignment of guardianship.

The procedures by which allocations of blame are made, status determined and disputes settled have been discussed in detail in *The Camp at Wallaby Cross.* It is sufficient to note here that these procedures allow bids for guardianship to be made. Applicants have to justify their proposed assumption of caring responsibility. For grounds, they refer to close up kinship statuses, adduce evidence of financial capacity, and also point to their probity and proven records of child-caring. "How many kid you reckon I bin growing up?". Other work has also to be done. The guardian whose alleged wrong actions were the source of crisis has thoroughly to be discredited, declared to be "no bloody good," and a "mother/auntie for nothing". In the business of discreditation, all the detail of neglectful performance that the campers have stored up is paraded. They are collectively "witness for" neglect and tell its details. In the end, when the facts have been established and there are no contending witnesses to "back up" any defensive counter claims that the accused guardian may be disposed to enter, the matter is settled with a formal transfer, the giving over of the child to its new prime guardian. In this moment, and not before, the "no good" guardian's treatment of the child ceases to be a matter for detailed spelling out. It is categorically defined as "abuse": "That Mary bin abusing kid, that lil Johnny, longa Pipeline".

Data drawn from Darwin thus demonstrates the communal context of and for guardianship, which is legitimated with reference to the onus on everyone to "watch out for kids" and participate in the watching brief that is an aspect of the very articles of mob association. To define the watching brief is to specify some of the ground rules of camping associations. We have not yet addressed issues that concern the identity of preferred guardians and the rewards of recognition that go to people who have been active in the business of "rearing up". While Darwin is distinctive in that in the North the Countrymen still move in mobs and so subject guardianship to mob procedures, people of both Darwin and the South-West share similar ideals about the preferred identity of guardians. Given similar allocations of value in these respects, we use Nyungar data to deal with the hierarchy of preferences that specify who, in principle, should be assigned prime caring responsibilities in the business of child-rearing.

IV. Nyungar good places and appropriate placements

In the South-West, the groupings of intimates bound together by their provisioning and protection of a "lot" of children live in houses situated some distance from one another. The distance between places may be between streets, between suburbs, or, at the furthest extent, between different towns. As a consequence, the exercise of oversight must rely not only on direct witnessing but on reporting between adult family members, and on the interpretation of the domestic signs of person and place.

The Nyungar "good place for kids" is a house in which things are arranged to testify to its suitability for and dedication to child care. The "boss of the place" must maintain in her house the socially acknowledged and recognized markers of order and propriety. This is both a daily task of organizing for tidiness and an ongoing maintenance of areas within the living space in a manner which signals the convergence of an intergenerational devotion to continuity and survival. The lounge should be set up with photos of grandparents and grandchildren, with trophies and awards for sporting skill, and with pictures of the country of the South West painted by close in kin. The "boss of the place" should also have a nice garden signalling the well-being and growth of everything in her care. The place's boss must continually manage the combination of persons stopping with her, to retain across departures and arrivals of kin, a company which is able to protect the children in her care and which is committed in interest and in allocations of monies to providing for them.

This ordering and organization of domestic space provide a continual testimony to intention. If the order is abandoned or if an uncontrollable or undedicated company is gathered, then the place has by that selfsame evidence become an unsuitable place for children. The establishment and maintenance of the right conditions for caring for children must, however, be supported by an ongoing commentary among the members of the close in kin that the children in a boss's care are "going good". The signs of bodily well-being are critical. The appropriateness of the placement of a child is immediately called in question if the child becomes sick, or if a child who is able to talk testifies to ill-treatment.

There is, however, another consideration which does not have to do with neglect, abuse or crisis. Attention is accorded to each child's own assertions about desired placement both in terms of whom (s)he wants to be with and where (s)he wants to stop. The extent of this familial attention increases as a child gets older but may also operate in respect of socially precocious but declaratively definitive demands.

Little Clevie, then aged three, was, because of his special and particular attachment to his paternal grandmother, by familial consensus acknowledged to be "Nanny's boy". He was, therefore, supported by his close in kin in his wish to visit and stop frequently with his favourite grandmother. His mother lived in the neighbouring suburb, so in fulfilment of his wishes Little Clevie was taken frequently between the two houses, sleeping the night at one or other of them. His affection for his paternal grandmother was not, however, an indictment of maternal care. This fostering of an early expression of personal attachment and residential desire took a new turn when the now four year old Clevie went to visit his Auntie Alice with his paternal grandmother. Auntie Alice lived in a town a couple of hundred miles from Clevie's mother and paternal grandmother. Little Clevie declared that he wanted to stop with his Auntie Alice, which was allowed. Some weeks later, he was brought south again where the pattern of dual domestic residence was re-established. Although this was curtailed once he started school, it exemplifies the way in which the selection of suitable, and therefore possible, placements is a negotiation among kin, and how this decision making can (as later it must) include the child.

So far the social parameters for such decisions have not been discussed, although the overriding consideration given to the expressed wishes of children has been intimated. The agreements reached between close in kin in the care of their lot of children is guided and constrained by an interrelated set of assumptions about the nature of person. Nyungar (and Aboriginal) child care is not so much an attempt to make the child into a particular sort of adult but an ongoing attempt to discover through the recognition of signs who each person is and is therefore becoming. In other words, the issue of child placement is premised on an understanding of two needs. In the first place, children must be guaranteed the conditions for survival. This is the creation and maintenance of a safe place within which the transformation of being from spirit through an intermediary and incomplete existential form as child to adult can be achieved. Secondly, however, once options exist regarding safe placements, the location for the optimum expression and fostering of the realization of spiritual potential must be selected. As has already been indicated, children are considered to say what they really need. Their words are treated as an immediate and authentic expression of spiritual volition. Children's gradual and increasing verbalization about whom they want to be with and where they want to stay, leads over time to familially supported action.

Johnny had by the time he had ceased to be a "littlie" (around seven years old) and became a "kid", gained the nickname "Nobody's Child". This was not an indication that nobody cared for him but rather a sign of his extraordinary acts of residential relocation. Whenever the place where Johnny was currently stopping was visited by other members of his close kin, he would invariably climb into their departing vehicle with them. Although Johnny demonstrated residential preferences, stopping "mostly" with his mother or one particular maternal Auntie, he was not thwarted in his departures for the other "good places" which were maintained by his close kin. He was "Nobody's Child" because he had demonstrated early that he was "his own boss". The attainment of self management is the goal of child care. As a consequence, the early achievement of having one's say and doing what one "has to" (out of an internal imperative) is encouraged, although always monitored. Johnny would not, for example, have been permitted to stop at the topsy-turvy and volatile drinking place where his maternal Auntie Sally and her man lived in various degrees of inebriation. The familial consensus was that Auntie Sally was "off her head with the grog". The place where she stopped was controlled by threat and muscle. It was therefore a dangerous place and, as a consequence, "no place for kids".

V. The social ordering of placement possibilities

The bond established between children and the members of their close kin who have brought them up and between children brought up together, creates the basis for future claims of closeness. For the recollection of participation in the rearing up of particular children can be reinvoked to dissolve lengthy separations and times of non-involvement in the lives of those who were once close kin. An individual's dedication to the care of particular children (regardless of the actual degree of genealogical closeness) is then a way of marking a stretch of time with a transcendent meaning. No other episodes of consociation are socially denoted in this way in the South West (although in the North putting lads through initiation and being initiated together create a similar constancy of relevance of particular others).

The overriding significance of the guardianship of children, while creating the context for a primacy of attention to childrearing, is not a condition for direct competition among close kin. Rather, there is a socially recognized order of rights which dictates in the first instance who should be caring for a child. It is when there are reported failures to create, manage and maintain the appropriate conditions for a child's well-being that other close kin and also other relations may intervene. A moment of queried guardianship of little Jade exemplifies the talking, watching and eventual intervention which may occur.

I (Baines) met the toddler, Jade, in the arms of twenty-two year old Nadine who said she was looking after the child. Nadine and her man had, they told me, been left in charge of Nadine's mother's place. Nadine's mother had gone to a relation's funeral in another town and was expected to be away for a few days. The state house, with its inscribed door "Home Sweet Home" and garden with recently planted trees and flowers, was at that time accommodating half a dozen children under six and a suitable complement of mothers and aunties to take care of them. All were Nadine's immediate relations. I asked who Jade's parents were and was simply told by Nadine that this was Jade Sullivan. Before I could ask further about Nadine's family providing care for a small child who was not a member of the close kin, Nadine's man came up. Taking Jade and giving her a cuddle, he asked me whether she wasn't "solid". Since I was regarded as "like a sister" to his mother, I could be expected to "check up on" all the littlies in the care of himself and his woman. I confirmed that the child was looking plump and healthy. Nadine declared that the child had not been looking well when she had first taken charge of her (an indictment of the child's previous caretakers).

A couple of days later I was present when another family was discussing the whereabouts of little Jade Sullivan. The oldest woman in the group had initiated the conversation, expressing concern for the child's well-being. I said that I had in fact just seen the toddler. I was asked detailed questions about how the child was looking, who was looking after her and who was stopping at Nadine's mother's place.

I had, I discovered, testified to the mother's side's allocation of an appropriate placement for Jade. The woman questioning me was a senior member of Jade's father's relations. As the daughter of Jade's father's mother's sister, she had as oldest "sister cousin" been acting on Jade's father's behalf in trying to find out about his child. She was, indeed, acting in the place of his mother or one of his mother's sisters, all of whom were sick and therefore unable to carry out the "watching brief" of grandparents. She led me to understand that Jade had ended up in Nadine's care out of a series of acts of negligence.

Jade's mother had, they reported, "taken off" with the baby, leaving her man (their cousin), but had soon tired of the child and left Jade with her maternal grandfather. He had been unable to care for Jade as he was "a sick man" (therefore a wrong placement for the child). He had asked his girlfriend, Nadine's mother, herself a grandmother, to look after the child. The members of the patriline commented to one another that Nadine's mother was "not a well woman". Nadine's mother had handed the child over to her daughter and her man. Nadine's comment about the child not looking well when she first took over her care was also a criticism of the care given to Jade by the mother's side. Indeed, Nadine later commented with a laugh that her own mother "couldn't look after her own children" so that to hand the child over to her was an act of evident wrong placement.

The father's side, Jade's patrilineal kin, expressed their doubts about the present placement. While Nadine's mother's interest in the child was not queried in terms of her not being kin, she was referred to with nods of assent from other family members, as "a rambler". I interjected that she had gone to a relation's funeral (a socially required act). My comment, however, encountered their shared judgment that Nadine's mother was "always rambling, always taking off". This negated the construction of Nadine's mother's place as a safe and suitable place for small children (despite her eight years' tenancy of the house). They set out the preparation made by Jade's father with a view to assuming care of his daughter. He had moved in with his sister who kept a "good place for kids". He had got himself a job so that he could contribute financially to the care of his child.

The situation was one of interpretation and counter-interpretation. The argument had not yet developed to a point which would allow the father to send his sister over to get the child. If I had said the child had been looking sick, this would have provided a basis for action. At the same time, Jade's maternal grandfather had apparently been trying to get word to his daughter to come and fetch the child. The father's side, for their part, had approached the Department of Community Welfare expressing concern for the safety and well-being of the small child. It was asserted that not only had Jade's mother abandoned the child, but she was drinking. The evidence was still largely circumstantial. The mother's side lived mostly in a northern Wheatbelt town. Most of her relations were regarded by the father's side as "boozers". Jade's mother had gone to that town, she was with relatives who drank, therefore she was drinking.

The story of Jade, while involving a unique set of negotiations, nevertheless exemplifies both the cultural constraints and the interactive processes which operate with regard to a child's placement. Nyungar people say "children follow in the mother's line" or "fall on the mother's side". They, therefore, accept that it is the prerogative of the matriline in the first instance to see that a child receives proper care. Should there be enough proof of negligence and neglect, then the father's side are required to intervene. If close kin are unable to provide for the children who are in the first place theirs to care for, then members of the extended kin group, their relations, may offer to accommodate a child for a while. All placements are up to a point temporary arangements, able to be altered so that the child is not deprived of knowledge of and intimacy with other members of his or her close kin. A child is encouraged to get to know his father's and his mother's people as that width of relationships is one dimension of patterns and priorities of association in adulthood. The child who experiences limits or restrictions on intimacy with his kin, will lack those socially highlighted relationships which will offer support and significance to future living.

VI. Placement and Identity

The question of child placement is, for Nyungar people, historically loaded. Older Nyungar people tell stories of their experiences arising from government legislation which divested them of the final allocation of guardianship (e.g. the 1905 Aborigines Act and its various amendments). They tell stories of children having their faces blackened, pale skinned babies being hidden in bushes, and mobile youngsters being instructed to scatter and hide when representatives of the Chief Protector of Natives approached. White law had made him the official and superordinate Pater of all Aboriginal and part-Aboriginal children.

Yet alongside the stories of the forced removal of children, are accounts of Aboriginal guardians deciding to place their children in missions and government institutions. This is not as contradictory as it first appears, although those who once placed small children in White care are obliged to explain to their successors why the group of effective kin were unable to care for them. Such placements arise from doubt about the ability of close kin to accord the infant the kind of care which would ensure its physical survival - a factor which had to be weighed against the spiritual and social deprivations imposed by the decision.

The legislative imposition of a White supervisory paternity was fiercely objected to because, in practice, the legal guardian usually assumed the right to decide on the appropriate placement of the paler skinned children. These were regarded as half-castes by White society but were treated and accepted as Aboriginal by their Nyungar mothers and grandparents. The strength of the still remembered resentment of those forced removals of children must be understood in relation to Nyungar beliefs about the nature of being. Indeed, it is these beliefs which are at the basis of all decisions as to what is a good place for a particular child to live. Children are presumed to have a pre-natal relationship with a particular part of the country and with particular members of their close in kin. They are said to have pre-existed in a place in the land as spirits where they kept company with their ancestors. Nyungar people say that the spirits of those who are to become their children are "found" and "drawn" into mothers by each mother's spirit helped by the child's future grandparents. This means that children can be expected to feel a special attachment to particular places and particular persons. To be deprived of these pre-existential bonds is to be denied a spiritually and spatially grounded identity. The denial or deprivation of contact with those persons and places is one which renders them homeless and heartless; for they have then been separated from the spiritual foundation of their beings.

A decision to hand children over to White people to bring up is, therefore, very hard because children who are brought up by "strangers" may survive physically but will experience social isolation and spiritual impoverishment. Such "loneliness", as it is referred to, may lead to the development of a dangerous adult. A young Nyungar man recently murdered a young White courting couple. He was not exonerated for his act by Nyungar people, who spoke of it as "terrible thing", but they did offer the explanation that he was "brought up too lonely". Children who have been removed from their families and kin or placed in missions or children's homes by their guardians, speak as adults about "missing out", not being "given their identity", and not knowing their "own people". While genealogical knowledge can be given to adults, the lost time of childrearing, as a time of a specially marked consociation, cannot be given back. On the other hand, older Nyungar children may view placement in educational institutions as giving them opportunities for developing their talents which they would not otherwise have had. A life history in which separation is interpreted as a fostering of ability may allow the person to regard the experience as singling her or him out for a future life dedicated not to the welfare of the kin group but to "the good of their people".

Conclusion

In both the Darwin region and in the South-West, the guardianship of children is subject to allocation and reallocation amongst persons over time. Reallocation occurs within the context of the extended family as all adult members of the kin groups are expected to watch over the kids of the new generation and participate in rearing them up. In this paper we have tried to indicate the criteria that are brought to bear in determining child placement and the allocation of primary responsibilities for child-care when guardianship is put at issue.

References

BERNDT, R.M. and C.H. BERNDT (1977)
The World of the First Australians. (Second Edition), Rigby, Melbourne.

SANSOM, B. (1980)
The Camp at Wallaby Cross. Australian Institute of Aboriginal Studies and Humanities Press, Canberra and Atlantic Highlands, N.J.

Part V

Issues in State Criminal Justice Systems

Exercising discretion: sentencing and customary law in the Northern Territory

Diane Bell

I. Introduction

On May 29th, 1981, in a deserted beer garden of the Parap Hotel, Darwin, Jan Draskoveic was beaten to death with a length of iron water pipe. A week later three young Aboriginal women, Pamela Nangala Sampson, Ngaire Nungarrayi Herbert and Rhoda Wurrawilya Gibbs, were brought in for questioning and subsequently charged with murder. They pleaded 'Not Guilty' but were convicted and sentenced to life imprisonment against which verdict they appealed successfully. At the retrial they again pleaded 'Not Guilty', but were once again convicted and sentenced to 12 years each with a non-parole period of five years

---

*) I am grateful to Professor James Crawford of the Australian Law Reform Commission for his assistance while preparing this paper in locating primary source material and comparative studies of situations outside Australia. I am also grateful to Colin MacDonald, Len Hartnett and David Avery, counsel for the defendants in the Parap murder trial. I have also been assisted by the comments of fellow members of the "Gender Workshop" of the Anthropology Department, A.N.U.; Martha McIntyre and Margie Jolly have both been extremely generous; Marcia Langton and Vai Stanton assisted with their invaluable insights into the Darwin scene. I thank also John von Sturmer who listened while I thought out loud; and Pamela Sampson, Ngaire Herbert and Rhoda Wurrawilya for their cooperation. When I last visited the latter in September 1985, they were in good spirits and anxiously awaiting their parole date in February 1989.

and six months. The Crown appealed unsuccessfully against the leniency of the sentence; there was no cross appeal on severity of sentence.

In the Northern Territory murder in most cases attracts an automatic life sentence and indeed this was the sentence imposed by Mr. Justice Gallop, the first trial judge. However, under the legislation in force at the time, there was provision for the exercise of discretion in sentencing Aborigines found guilty of murder. Sections 6(1)(c) and 6A of the *Criminal Law Consolidation Act and Ordinance* read:

> 6(1)(c) Where an aboriginal is convicted of murder, the judge may impose such a penalty as, having regard to all the circumstances of the case, appears to him to be just and proper.
>
> 6A For the purpose of determining the nature and extent of the penalty to be imposed when an aboriginal is convicted of murder, the Court shall receive and consider any evidence which may be tendered as to any relevant native law or custom and its application to the facts of the case and any evidence which may be tendered in mitigation of penalty.

On June 17th, 1983, at the conclusion of submissions on sentencing, Mr. Justice O'Leary, the second trial judge, reserved his decision and stated that whilst he was mindful of the period which the women had spent unsentenced, he wished to give a considered decision in writing.[1)] In his judgment, delivered August 24, 1983, he found that 'a wide and unfettered' discretion was available to him, but that there was no power at common law or under any Northern Territory statute, that allowed him to ante-date the sentence. Thus, the time in custody, two years and three months, was added to the sentence,[2)] and each of the women is exposed to a maximum of just over fourteen years' imprisonment. The case raised questions concerning the nature of sentencing discretion which are central to the Australian Law Reform Commission Reference on Customary Law.

The matter of sentencing in respect of murder has been subject for comment in other States of Australia and elsewhere in the world. The trend appears to be to widen rather than restrict or abolish sentencing discretions. However, in the Northern Territory, where 21% of the total population of 125,000 people are Aboriginal, the government has removed this discretion. Under Clause 167 of the *Criminal Code Bill* 1983, section 6A of the *Criminal Law Consolidation Act and Ordinance* was repealed and replaced by a compulsory life imprisonment provision. The Parap murder trial was the last heard under the old legislation. The Australian Law Reform Commission, legal practitioners in the Northern Territory and various Aboriginal organizations have expressed disquiet and openly criticized the proposed Code, but the Clause remains.[3] Under its Terms of Reference the Commission can only make recommendations in relation to Aborigines, but it would be possible nonetheless to recommend that a general discretion was preferable to a restricted one. The Parap case raised further interesting questions concerning: the taking and relevance of evidence concerning customary law; the role of anthropologists as expert witnesses; the interpretation of the existing provisions; and the possibility that the discretionary provision in respect of Aborigines may have been invalid in terms of the *Racial Discrimination Act*.

II. An anthropological perspective on the defendants' background

Although an anthropologist and not a lawyer, I have worked with lawyers in the preparation and hearing of land claims brought under the Aboriginal Land Rights (Northern Territory) Act 1976; given expert witness evidence in various cases involving Aborigines; acted as consultant to the Honourable Mr. Justice Toohey, the Aboriginal Land Commissioner (1977-1982), and I was a consultant with the Australian Law Reform Commission on the Customary Law Reference. My competence to comment on the issue of sentencing discretion derives from the nature of the issues canvassed in the Parap murder trial. Although my involvement in the matter was confined to submissions on sentencing, I have a more general interest in the case. Since 1976 I have undertaken research in Central and Northern Australia with Aboriginal women. Two of the three women in this case come from communities which are well known to me. In 1979-1980, in conjunction with Pam Ditton, a lawyer of the Central Australian Aboriginal Legal Aid Service, I undertook a project on the role of Aboriginal women in the maintenance of customary legal systems. Violence, alcohol, the introduction of a cash economy, the ramifications of changes in the marriage system, and the problems engendered by the lifestyle of towns, missions, settlements and cattle stations were topics to which women turned their attention during our research. The very problems facing the three women found guilty of murder in the Parap case were those which older women had discussed with Pam and me.[4]

Many pages of transcript have been generated by the two appeals and two trials. When read in conjunction with the records of interview, unsworn statements, pre-sentence reports, and antecedent reports, they provide a wealth of data concerning the urban Aboriginal subcultures of Darwin.[5] At some future date it would be a rewarding and worthwhile task to analyze that body of data systematically. Here reference to this material aims only at providing the context for a discussion of the issues raised in sentencing the three women found guilty of murder.

Pamela Nangala Sampson was born at Yuendumu, a government reserve northwest of Alice Springs. Warlpiri people were moved to Yuendumu in the 1940s when the official government policy was assimilation. On reserves such as Yuendumu, Papunya, Warrabri (Ali-curang) and Hooker Creek (Lajumanu), Aborigines were to be introduced to the "benefits" of the white Australian lifestyle. These benefits have not been apparent and there are few positive features to the settlement lifestyle. Chronic unemployment, ill-health, lack of basic facilities such as housing, water and nutritious food characterize the lives of many people who were forcibly moved to government reserves during this period. Fights, drunkenness and intrigue are rife. Whereas it was possible in the past, when the people lived in small mobile bands, to resolve a dispute by simply removing oneself from the vicinity of trouble, this option is no longer available now that resources are concentrated on reserves.[6)] More recently, with the granting of land rights and the implementation of a policy of self-management, Aborigines who live on what are now ex-government settlements are taking control. Nonetheless, the problems of unemployment, the problem of retaining youth and providing a future for them remain.

Pamela grew up at Yuendumu and received her schooling there. She is described as having been raised in a "traditional Aboriginal environment" but this only has meaning if we are prepared to construe the word "traditional" in a broad sense.[7)] Obviously Pamela has been influenced by aspects of white Australian society. Equally obviously, her lifestyle, values, aspirations and socialization as a woman in no way approximate those of persons of similar socio-economic status in white Australia. In spite of her absence from the community for some time, Pamela was concerned that she had not participated in the funeral of an uncle of hers and felt she must return to the community in order to fulfil her obligations as a niece.[8)]

As a child Pamela was promised to a man some years older than she, who worked in the kitchen at Yuendumu. He was already married to a Pintupi woman from Papunya and there was one child.[9)] When Pamela first went to live with her husband, at the age of 18 or 19, his other wife was not present. When she arrived some time later, brawls broke out between the two of them until, after some two years of fighting, Pamela finally decided to move to Alice Springs to live with her parents. They had moved from Yuendumu when she was about 9 years old and in their absence she had been cared for by her mother's sisters and granny. It was these women who had taken her hunting and taught her the significance of women's ceremonies and affiliation to country.[10)] Life with her parents in the town camp of Alice Springs also proved to be violent and she moved on to a camp north of Tennant Creek.[11] Here she continued to live with close family and participated in further ceremonies.

Over the next year Pamela moved between Tennant Creek, Hooker Creek and Katherine. For a period she lived in Kununurra with a white man who drove a transport truck between Katherine and that Western Australian town. One of her classificatory husbands took her back to Hooker Creek, where she again found herself in trouble with promised husbands. Her father, who had been ill, had received kindly treatment from an older man to whom he had said, "Pamela must go in marriage". At the time she was living in a caravan at Hooker Creek with a white man who was working on a building contract in the community. The man to whom her father had said she should go in marriage was angry when she wouldn't sleep with him and his wives wanted to make her work for them. With the assistance of female kin she managed to get together the fare to fly from Hooker Creek to Darwin. At the airstrip her aggrieved husband-to-be remonstrated with her, swung boomerangs in a menacing fashion and issued all sorts of threats. He was restrained by her aunties and uncles who told him that she was not his promised wife and that he should let her go. In so doing, her relatives were drawing a distinction which is not always made clear when evidence concerning the status of a marriage is taken. The promise entered into at initiation time between the circumciser of the initiate, who undertakes to find a wife for the boy, the women who nominate the potential mothers-in-law for the boy, and the boy's family themselves, constitutes a true "promised" marriage. It is different from marriages which are arranged outside the context of initiation.[12]

On her arrival in Darwin, Pamela stayed with a classificatory brother at Bagot, one of the main town camps. She met other women who had come into Darwin, and formed a circle of drinking mates. She also formed associations with various white men in Darwin, living for a time with one of them at Humpty Doo. However, she became lonely for her family and friends, and drifted back to Bagot where she took up with her drinking mates. She and her friends relied on several white men for shelter and financial support. During her years in Darwin, Pamela was never employed, nor did she receive any Social Security benefits. It is a moot point whether she knew that she could apply for such support.

Her life in Darwin was even more violent than the one she had led at Yuendumu. She was bereft of the support which she had been brought up to expect from close kin, especially the guidance of older female relatives. Although she was oftentimes dependent on a white male for support, Pamela firmly rejected my suggestion that some might accuse her of living the life of a prostitute. Certainly she was exploited, but in her view she was entering into relationships serially rather than living a life of promiscuity.[13] Many of the men with whom

Pamela and the other women associated were in their late forties or fifties and appear to have been drinking partners rather than sexual partners.[14)]

Ngaire Nungarrayi Herbert, the youngest of the three women, was born at Hooker Creek.[15)] The pattern of her life, including her drift into Darwin, was very similar to that of Pamela's. Suffice it to say that she too had extricated herself from a stressful marriage and sought out the "glamorous" life of the bars of Darwin.

Rhoda Wurrawilya Gibbs, in her late twenties and the eldest of these women, had lived in Darwin the longest. Born at Groote Eylandt, she, like the other women, had come into Darwin following problems with men. It was Rhoda who had known the deceased for some years and who had introduced Pamela to him.

III. The incident

On the evening of his murder, Jan Draskoveic had been drinking with Pamela, Ngaire and Rhoda. An argument broke out in the course of which he allegedly called Rhoda "a black bitch" and "a slut".[16)] According to the women, he refused to stop swearing. Rhoda picked up a piece of piping and hit him around the head and shoulders, after which Ngaire and Pamela struck him also. The Crown alleged that the motive of the attack was robbery but the women denied having taken anything. All were drunk at the time and Rhoda described herself as being 'paralytic'.[17)]

It was only some time after the incident that the police questioned Rhoda, and then a further day before Pamela and Ngaire were brought in and records of interview taken. It is interesting to speculate that had the murder been committed by a white, or even a male Aborigine, the police would have had a network of contacts through which to locate suspects. As it was, the police knew little of the world of these three women. Their ignorance is shared by many of Darwin's inhabitants.

To illustrate this point, let me briefly make an aside to the information tabled with the House of Representatives Standing Committee on Aboriginal Affairs in its reference on town campers and fringe dwellers.[18)] They note the problems of definition with reference to town camps and subsequent variations in the statistics produced by the Department of Aboriginal Affairs and the Aboriginal Development Corporation.[19)] The information recorded concerning town camps in Darwin relates to the established and highly visible camps but ignores the many temporary drinking camps and informal camps which shift location according to season and influx of visitors. While to the outsider the scene is chaotic and lacks structure, for those who move in the town camp scene there is a clearly established order. People from certain regions habitually camp with relatives in well-known locations.[20] Even had the police had access to knowledge of the networks of the various camps of Darwin, they still might not have located these women because they also spent time in a number of the hostels and caravan parks where white male contract workers lived.[21]

IV. The legal context

A. The first trial

At the first trial before Mr. Justice Gallop, commencing on October 13th, 1981, the women pleaded 'Not Guilty' to the charge of murder.[22] The defence denied the existence of the relevant intent, and relied on the fact of intoxication. A defence of provocation was left to the jury, who found that it was not established. The trial concluded on the 30th with verdicts of guilty. On November 6th, presenting facts and submission on sentence, Mr. Borchers, Counsel for Rhoda, stated:

> The jury has found this woman guilty of murder and you have heard evidence on which the jury reached that verdict, and consequently, you are aware that there are no native laws applicable to the incident, in that the victim was not an Aboriginal, and the incident had nothing to do with the transgression of traditional customary laws and that what was done was not a matter which was discussed or sanctioned by the prisoner's community.[23]

Mr. Cavit, for the Crown, conceded that "[t]here was not clear evidence that anybody did take any money from the deceased."[24] On November 10th, life imprisonment was imposed on each of the women.

Both conviction and sentence were appealed to the Full Court of the Federal Court of Australia. The appeal was heard on May 26th-28th and July 30th, 1982, in Darwin before Toohey, McGregor and Sheppard JJ.[25] They allowed the appeal (McGregor J. dissenting) on the basis that the issue of intent had not been a question of the capacity or ability to form an intent but whether, on this occasion, the necessary intent had been formed. As that question had not been put to the jury they set aside the conviction and ordered a new trial.[26]

B. The second trial

The second trial was heard before O'Leary J. in the Supreme Court of Darwin in March 1983.[27] The Crown again asserted robbery to be the motive. The jury found the women guilty of murder, rejecting the alcohol factor as sufficient to negative the specific intent necessary to constitute the crime.[28] At the request of both counsel, the issue of provocation had also been left to the jury, who by their verdict indicated that the Crown had discharged the onus of showing that the attack had been unprovoked.[29]

On June 14th, 15th and 17th of 1983 submissions on sentence were presented to the Court.[30] The Crown submitted that the discretion in section 6(1)(c) of the *Criminal Law Consolidation Act* was not absolute or arbitrary, in that it had to be exercised in accordance with sections 6A and 6(1)(c) read together.[31] The *Criminal Law Consolidation Act of 1876* was amended by No. 17 of 1939 which introduced section 6A. Section 6(1)(c), on the other hand, was introduced in 1968 and varied in 1973. According to the Crown, section 6(1)(c) allowed a discretion to impose a just penalty and section 6A governed the exercise of that discretion, otherwise there would have been no reason to include section 6A at all.[32] If this were so, then the Judge would be confined to considering those two matters set out in section 6A in exercising his discretion.

With reference to section 6A, the Crown submitted that evidence of relevant "native law or custom" must be found before "any evidence which may be tendered in mitigation of penalty" could be considered by the Judge. Therefore, if no native law or custom were involved, no evidence tendered in mitigation of penalty could be considered. In summary, the Crown submitted:

> It boils down to this therefore if Your Honour accepts the Crown submission, that Your Honour must find some element of Aboriginality in the offence.[33]

It is worth noting that an element of Aboriginality in an offence is a different conceptual issue from finding the existence of "native law or custom". Unfortunately, this point was not probed further.[34] Had there been greater precision in the use of those terms and the notion of a 'culture' which was not both sexist and racist, the woman may well have had a defence.[35]

The Crown then turned to an examination of the relation of section 6A to the Commonwealth's *Racial Discrimination Act.* It was, they argued, inconsistent with section 9 of that Act. In *Gerhardy v Brown,* a case decided in the South Australian Supreme Court in June 1983, Mr. Justice Millhouse found that section 19 of the South Australian *Pitjantjatjara Land Rights Act* discriminated against any person who was not a Pintjantjatjara.[36] The Commonwealth Act covers the field of racial discrimination and prohibits it. Therefore section 19, which limits entry upon "the lands" of the Pitjantjatjara area without the permission of Pitjantjatjara, was inconsistent with section 9 of the *Racial Discrimination Act*, which prohibits any form of racial discrimination, and thereby was rendered inoperative. The Australian High Court subsequently reversed this decision and Mr. Justice O'Leary was not inclined to accept the argument.[37] If the High Court had done otherwise, then a question would have arisen concerning the validity of other legislation providing specific benefits to Aborigines.[38]

In characterizing the lifestyle of the three women, the Crown suggested that they had chosen to adopt an urban white lifestyle in Darwin. They had been educated, had co-habited with white persons, had frequented predominantly white establishments and, although they had limited access to certain institutions, this was a disability they shared with many Australians.[39]

Counsel for the women submitted that under section 6(1)(c) of the *Criminal Law Consolidation Act* clear sentencing discretion existed.[40] O'Leary J. was concerned that section 6(1)(c) could be read to mean that the mere fact that a person belonged to a particular group was in all cases to be taken into account as a mitigating circumstance. If this were so, the Judge reasoned, then section 6A would be pointless.[41] However, he queried the way in which he could take into account membership in a group without some legislative authority. The comments of Brennan J. in the case of *Neal v The Queen* were not enough:

In imposing sentences courts are bound to take into account in accordance with those principles, all material facts including those facts which exist only by reason of the offender's membership of an ethnic or other group.[42]

This opinion of Brennan J., notwithstanding O'Leary J., suggested that in the absence of some legislative provision he could not take into account native law or custom as a mitigating circumstance.[43] O'Leary J.'s resolution of this problem is discussed below.

Despite these legislative lacunae, Northern Territory judges had previously exercised discretion in sentencing Aborigines and had done so in cases where the issue of the relevance of "native law or custom" had not been advanced. For example, Gallop J., in sentencing Gus Forbes, who was found guilty of rape and murder, took other matters into account in sentencing.[44] Also, in the Huckitta case, Gallop J., having specifically stated that: "[t]his was not a tribal killing nor a payback killing", nonetheless considered all the other aspects of the situation which might go to mitigate the penalty.[45] I can find no other comparative material on sentencing of Aborigines convicted of murder in the Northern

Territory to shed light on the proper construction to be placed upon sections 6A and 6(1)(c).[46] *Jadurin v R* went on appeal to the Federal Court against the severity of sentence imposed following a conviction for manslaughter.[47] It was argued that imprisonment for a term of four years with a minimum non-parole period of twelve months should be reduced to a suspended sentence in order that the appellant undergo traditional tribal punishment.[48] The significance of tribal punishment for sentencing is a difficult matter for the courts. Still, it is worth noting that the Federal Court has been at pains to make clear that an acknowledgement that some form of retribution might be exacted by an offender's own community did not constitute a sanctioning of that retribution by the courts. Moreover, facts such as the likelihood or reality of tribal punishment are material facts which courts are bound to take into account when imposing sentence.[49]

C. Native law or custom?

The interpretation of this phrase proved vexatious. In giving evidence, I suggested that a reference to both native law *and* custom required looking beyond the body of rules which might constitute law to take into account habitual practices which are transmitted from generation to generation and shared by communities.[50] This body of custom, I argued, was not codified in any way - it was adaptable and dynamic. According to the Oxford English Dictionary, custom is "a usual way of behaving or acting, established usage having force of law".[51] The Macquarie Dictionary gives custom as a "habitual practice, the usual way of acting in given circumstances, habits or usage held collectively".[52] Stroud's Legal Dictionary defines custom as "the practice of a particular place, an interrupted practice".[53] When read in conjunction with the words "native law", I suggested, we could construe custom as the beliefs, values and sorts of things that informed people's behaviour.[54] Earlier in the proceedings the judge had commented that the mode of fighting in Aboriginal society could not be considered a relevant custom:

> It seems to me not to rank as a custom at all. It's a way of behaviour, isn't it, really I suppose. I don't know.[55]

Later the judge asked whether the killing could have been considered "sort of ritualistic" and probed the differences between the way in which white women and Aboriginal women fight. He asked: "They react as their culture would almost dictate they react?".[56] These questions and the line of analysis in the Reasons for Sentences (see below) indicate that demonstrating customary law is indeed a threshold problem.

There were, I suggested, several elements of "native law or custom" which impinged upon the incident in the Parap Hotel. In the first place there was the mode of fighting. The women used a pipe similar in shape to the traditional fighting stick: they held it in the same way the traditional item is held; they struck the upper torso and head as is the practice in traditional fights.[57)] On the other hand, women's fights are very carefully stage-managed. Certain categories of kin must be present to ensure that no real damage is inflicted and there must also be persons to bear witness that the fight was fair.[58)] These support and control mechanisms were absent at the critical time.[59)]

That the victim had sworn at one of the women was another element related to "native law or custom".[60)] In Aboriginal society swearing often requires a response from the person sworn at or from those who hear the swearing. Strict rules govern what matters may be broached and what speech styles used in front of what categories of relatives. On Groote Eylandt, Rhoda's home, if a brother hears his sister maligned, then he must respond by punishing her for having brought shame on the family. Similarly for Ngaire and Pamela, if their reputation were to be besmirched, their uncles would respond. Putting aside the issue of provocation, to call Rhoda a "black bitch" and "slut" would have been an insult requiring a response.

A further relevant factor was that the women, especially the two Warlpiri girls from Central Australia, had been socialized to respond to men in ways totally inappropriate for Darwin. Further, their standard of education, while perhaps taking them out of the "traditional" life, had not fitted them to cope with aspects of white society such as applications for Social Security benefits. Having sought the glamour of the drinking places of Darwin and entered into relationships with various white men, the women had brought shame upon themselves. As the men they had befriended had no proper classification within their system, it would be very difficult for them to return to their home communities. In this respect their situation was quite different from that of a poor white girl.[61)]

None of these elements of Aboriginality are as easy to grasp as the notion of a "payback killing". On the other hand, the role of women in the maintenance of customary legal systems is diffuse and is articulated through the kinship system, through customary ways of responding, and through the support which they offer each other as a reference group.[62)]

D. Reasons for Sentences

How then did Mr. Justice O'Leary view the submissions? In his 'Reasons for Sentence' of August 14th, 1983, he rejected the argument that 'native law or custom' could be seen as justifying or contributing, in any way, to the present offence. O'Leary J. stated:

> Whilst I agree that the words "native law or custom" should not be construed too narrowly, they do not, in my opinion, extend to include mere habits or patterns of behaviour that one might expect from an aboriginal person in certain circumstances, as, for example, that she reacted to an insult offered to her by hitting the person concerned over the head in the way an aboriginal woman would do when fighting: see Derham, 1963:500. Apart from anything else, I was told that aboriginal women do not hit to kill; they hit to wound. And they do not hit with heavy iron pipes; they hit with fighting sticks, which are of light wood. Further, fights in traditional aboriginal communities are well-controlled; they are stopped before anyone gets really hurt.[63)]

In this analysis it appears that for behaviour to be accepted as 'customary', it must be 'traditional' in the sense of it being what could occur within a self-contained culture. How then are we to deal with deaths which result from accidents with motor vehicles (non-traditional objects) which deaths are perceived by the actors as the outcome of sorcery and lead to 'pay-back' punishment?

In sentencing the women, O'Leary J. repeated yet again what 'a heinous crime' it had been and emphasized the 'great callousness and brutality' with which it had been committed.[64)] He was less forthright concerning the motive. On the one hand he allowed that there was 'more than a little evidence to suggest robbery', but on the other there was the claim of the women that the attack 'was *precipitated* by the words spoken by the deceased'.[65)] The decision of the jury did not reflect any conclusion they might have reached on the matter of motive as they were not called upon to address the question. There was no necessity for O'Leary J. to endorse either view but he was prepared to state:

> For my part, having regard to the degree of their intoxication, I find it difficult to think there was any clear motive for the killing on the part of any one of them. Rather, for the purpose of sentencing them I prefer to take the view that the attack was precipitated by some offensive words such as I have mentioned spoken by the deceased to Rhoda, aided

> perhaps by the refusal by the deceased of a request for money by them. There is no doubt, however, that whatever passions of anger or resentment were *aroused* in the prisoners, they were *inflamed* by the amount of alcohol that each of them had had to drink (emphasis added).66)

Later in his judgment he went further in concluding that what occurred "seems to have been a natural climax to the kind of life they were living."67)

Yet despite this recognition and the qualifications which the notions of acts 'precipitated', passions 'aroused' and persons 'inflamed' introduce to the judge's analysis of the incident, it was none the less a crime which he believed warranted the 'severest punishment'.68) There is no question that that is what they got.

With respect to the issue of interpretation of the legislation, O'Leary J. found that:

> The discretion there conferred on the sentencing judge is, I think, a wide and unfettered one. It is not, in my opinion, cut down by the provisions of s. 6A. That section clearly refers back to s. 6(1)(c), but in my view, is directory only. It requires the court to receive and consider evidence of any relevant native law or custom, if there be any involved, and its application to the facts of the case, as well as any evidence which may be tendered in mitigation of penalty.69)

He thereby rejected the Crown submission that the sections should be given a restrictive construction and added that he took his approach to be consistent with the practice of other judges. He held:

> It seems clear to me that, whilst fixing the sentence for murder in the Territory as mandatory life imprisonment, the intention of the legislature was that, where it was an aboriginal who was convicted of murder, that penalty should not apply, but rather there should be such a penalty as "having regard to all the circumstances of the case, appears to [the judge] to be just and proper".70)

O'Leary J. gave the submissions based on the expert evidence a sympathetic hearing and devoted eight of the twenty pages of his Reasons for Sentences to a review of the lives of the women. In taking this approach he was able to side step possible conflict with the *Racial Discrimination Act* by showing that he was not taking such evidence into account by virtue of racial considerations but by way of the women being a 'special problem'.71)

In summarizing the women's plight, he remarked on the similarities in their life experiences and depicted their situation thus:

> Their lives revolve mainly around the excessive use of alcohol, and the formation of casual relationships with males to obtain money for the purpose of drinking. They find themselves in a violent and degrading situation where male and female relationships are often a matter of brutality and violence. It is psychologically, and often physically, a brutalising experience for them, giving rise to tension and acute emotional distress. Their plight is a desperate one from which they cannot escape. They have a feeling of helplessness, hopelessness and purposelessness. Their whole sense of themselves becomes so abused that they lose that natural dignity that aboriginal women have. As it was put to me, "they feel they are no longer clean ... they feel dirty and sullied but they are caught [within that situation]".[72)]

In a sense then, it was a concept of culture, rather than race, which informed his analysis. He recognized the shared values and activities of women such as the three being sentenced. However, when he moved from the generalized portrait to the particular case, O'Leary J. relied on an assimilationist typology reminiscent of the 1950-60s rather than reflective of the expert evidence before him. His very obvious appreciation of the many sub-cultures of Darwin, each with its own dynamic, was not pursued with any rigour. Instead, he located the women in Darwin society in terms of disadvantage. They were between worlds, they were in 'limbo'.[73)] As a consequence of this approach, he was able to take account of the evidence of their deprived social background as mitigation. In the process, however, he concluded that they had become cultureless, they belonged 'no-where'.[74)] This was at odds with the Crown submission that, undesirable though it was, many people in Darwin shared their lifestyle.[75)]

While O'Leary J. clearly recognized that their shared experiences and their Aboriginality were central to understanding their situation, there was, he found, no 'relevant' native law or custom involved:

> In those cases, I do not think that the sentencing judge is thereby precluded from considering evidence tendered in mitigation of penalty. In my view, he may, and, in particular, he may consider evidence as to the background and history of the aboriginal concerned, the extent of which he has or has not adopted white ways or manners, the degree to which his aboriginal inheritance predominates and any problem of a trans-cultural nature that he may have experienced. Having considered these

> matters, "(t)he nearer his mode of life and general behaviour approaches that of a white person, the closer should punishment on a native approximate punishment proper to a white person convicted of a similar crime": *R v Anderson* (1954) NTJ 248 at 249. Logically that means that where a native has reached "a state of assimiliation where he may be treated as an ordinary member of the community -", there will be no differential punishment at all: cf. *Namatjira v Roabe* (1958) NTJ 608 at 629. But to decide whether or not a person has reached that state of assimilation, the sentencing judge must consider all the relevant evidence, and he is not precluded from doing so simply because no native law or custom is involved. Furthermore, if the legislation is construed in this way, there is no question of his sentencing someone purely on the basis of colour. On the contrary, it involves sentencing an aboriginal by reference to the special "problems" of aboriginal people as, I think, was intended by the legislature.[76)]

There are a number of forms of analysis which are lurking in O'Leary J.'s Reasons for Sentences. Reconciling them is a difficult task. There is a recognition of the distinctiveness of the women's culture and the consequences of their immersion in such a desperate life style; there is a genuine sympathy for their plight as dislocated and disadvantaged persons; there is the willingness to put their Aboriginality to one side and view them as 'special problems'. These women are shown simultaneously to be in 'limbo', deprived and brutalized, unsuccessfully assimilated, and the perpetrators of a callous, heinous crime which is 'a natural climax' to the life they were living. Had there been greater reliance on expert evidence in the earlier trial, and had it been possible to develop parallels with an earlier case, that of Alwyn Peter, these women could have been shown to be the victims of both racist and sexist treatment.[77)] They had struck back just as Alwyn Peter did. O'Leary J. certainly recognized their victim status, but could not make the leap to the sentencing consequences of such an understanding. Indeed it is only recently that feminist criminologists have developed defences based on self defence, provocation and duress for abused women who themselves become violent.[78)]

E. The second appeal

The Crown was not satisfied with the sentence or the interpretation of the legislation. The case went on appeal and on April 11, 1984, the Full Bench of the Federal Court affirmed most aspects of O'Leary J.'s judgment. They approved his ruling that s. 6(1)(c) conferred a discretion on a judge to impose such penalty as to him appeared proper in the circumstances of the case. They accepted O'Leary J.'s assessment of the women's background and said that the basic task of the trial judge was:

> to balance the gravity of the crime and the need for punishment of the prisoners and the protection of the public with the special considerations applicable to the prisoners both as Aboriginals and as individuals. The task was faithfully undertaken and executed.[79)]

Therefore, the Court dismissed the claim that the sentences were inadequate. Their Honours held that it was for the trial judge to consider what was *just* and *proper* in the circumstances and not be constrained by the life sentence which was mandatory where a non-Aboriginal was involved. O'Leary J. had taken the circumstances of the crime into account and had not erred in his approach.[80)] Unfortunately, they did not express a view concerning whether native law or custom might be said to have justified or in some way contributed to the offence because that was not necessary to dispose of the Crown appeal, and the respondents (i.e. the three women) did not appeal against conviction or sentence. It would be interesting to know how they would have treated an appeal from the women on that issue. What then would have been *just* and *proper*?

There was, once again, a recognition of the plight of the women, but it was matched by a determination to punish. Having reviewed the facts of the case, they stated:

> We hope that we do not underestimate the seriousness of the tragedy which caused three unhappy human beings enmeshed in a life of discomfort and degradation to take the life of another perhaps equally unhappy but entirely innocent human being. Further, we are conscious that it is inappropriate to consider what sentences the prisoners should have received merely by reference to their interests. A severe penalty was essential both by way of punishment to the prisoners and by way of a deterrent for the protection of the public.[81)]

One wonders what sort of a deterrent 14 years in jail for three young women offers to other young women who are in pursuit of the glamorous image of city life. One wonders for what were they being punished so severely: a brutal murder, or their ignorance; the inadequacies of social welfare policies, or their lifestyle; their violent and non-female behaviour which had brought them to the 'climax' of their lives? In the absence of a cross appeal on severity of sentence on behalf of the women, the Federal Court was not called upon to consider such painful issues.

V. Sentencing for murder: practices in Australia and overseas

In the Northern Territory, the term to be served under a life sentence is fixed by the Executive. At present there is no real indication of just how the government will fix sentences: too few persons have been found guilty of murder since the N.T. achieved limited self-government. Thus, in order to gain some feel for the determinant sentence range it is necessary to turn to statistics from elsewhere in Australia. The statistics for South Australia (which include those for the N.T.) from December 1918 to December 1974 show an average life sentence for women of five and a half years. This is considerably less than for men: the New South Wales average for women of 10 years 4 months was the highest, while the Western Australian average of 3 years 1 month was the lowest.[82)] O'Leary J. commented in the instant case, "It makes rather strange reading of life imprisonment, doesn't it? It in fact can mean 3 1/2 years?".[83)] With his sentence of twelve years for each of the women, he gave more than a life sentence for women in Australia. Perhaps the women would have been treated more leniently had they received 'life sentences'. It might well have halved their time in prison.

The *Crimes (Homicide) Amendment Act* 1982 of New South Wales significantly alters two areas of the law relating to unlawful homicide which have come under criticism in recent years.[84)] The Act abandons the mandatory life sentence for murder and allows the judge discretion to impose a lesser sentence in compelling cases. The New South Wales government was, nonetheless, not prepared to go as far as the Lord Kilbrandon proposal which would have abolished the crimes of murder and manslaughter and replaced them by a single category of unlawful homicide.[85)] The discretionary power embodied in the New South Wales legislation is a limited one as it is restricted to cases in which there are mitigating circumstances relating to culpability. It would not therefore allow subsequent developments, such as a defendant's personal circumstances, to be taken into account. In the only reported decision on the amended provision, Cross J. was of the view that upon conviction for murder a life sentence was mandatory unless there was material before the judge that satisfied him of the existence of a mitigating circumstance which sufficiently diminished the prisoner's culpability.[86)] In Cross J.'s view the burden of proof of so persuading a judge was on the balance of probabilities, but the onus did not specifically fall upon the prisoner.[87)]

Woods, Q.C., in reviewing the options available to the New South Wales legislature, considered the Kilbrandon option, the distinction between degrees of murder, an unrestricted discretion and a restricted discretion, the option which was finally selected.[88] At present, New South Wales is the only Australian jurisdiction to permit a judicial discretion in a whole category of murder cases but the Victorian Law Reform Commission has put forward a proposal to this effect.

From the three Western Australian cases cited in the Law Reform Commission's Research Paper No. 6A, it is not possible to draw any conclusions concerning discretion in sentencing Aborigines for murder because in each the conviction was for manslaughter.[89] It is however possible to discern a tendency on the part of the judges to impose a sentence which takes into account the lifestyle of the defendants. More recent decisions in Western Australia indicate that judges continue to take into account the "traditional elements" of crimes while emphasizing that to inflict grievous bodily harm on another will not be condoned by Australian law.[90]

In New Zealand the Maoris' situation is comparable to that of the Aborigines before the advent of Aboriginal Legal Aid services.[91] When unrepresented, Maoris receive disproportionately heavier sentences than do those of European ancestry.[92] It is of course possible to draw various conclusions from this fact. Mugford asks: "Are the different sentences due to factors 'located' in the offender and offence or in the courts that try him?"[93] To answer the question he looks at the sentences for similar offences received by individuals belonging to different racial groups, and concludes that, despite the limitations of his study (a small group) and problems with the methodology, a general trend is discernible: the courts seem to show some bias in their treatment of offenders by race and social class, with social class being the more important factor.[94]

In a different assessment of the New Zealand judiciary's attitude toward sentencing and penal policy, judges were asked to consider whether special provisions and assistance, or more sensitive methods, were needed for the benefit of offenders from different cultural groups.[95] A majority of judges in the District Court, High Court and Court of Appeal, were of the opinion that sentencing alternatives were not necessary. However, several judges did suggest that there should be an attempt to determine the disposition of the community or the peer group atmosphere of the offender.[96]

In an overview of the "Influence of race on sentencing in England", McConville and Baldwin note that "no empirical research has ever been conducted in this country into the relationship between the race of the offender and the severity of the sentence received."[97] This, they comment, is in direct contrast to the experience in the United States where extensive research has been undertaken.

Like the authors of the New Zealand study, they admit to limitations in their approach but conclude confidently that "there is no support for the proposition that black defendants are sentenced more severely than white defendants in the Crown Courts in these cities."[98]

The Papua New Guinea *Criminal Code Amendment Act* 1976 implemented the recommendation of the Papua New Guinea Law Reform Commission on punishment for wilful murder. There now exists a general discretion in sentencing in murder cases. The Commission concluded:

> Criminologists and other people concerned about the sentencing and treatment of offenders have experimented with many different methods of imposing and reviewing sentences. From these experiments they have concluded that the fairest and most just system is for the judge who knows the facts of the case to punish each wilful murderer as he considers appropriate for the offence.[99]

In so doing, they recognized that the term "murder" might comprehend a wide range of crimes. However, Weisbrot has pointed out that the Papua New Guinea judiciary have been rather reluctant to use customary law expressly as a mitigating circumstance.[100] Still, less than life sentences are quite common for murder in Papua New Guinea.

Research Paper No. 6 of the Australian Law Reform Commission examines Report No. 7 of the Papua New Guinea Law Reform Commission on the role of customary law in the legal system.[101] One of the more important changes outlined in the report was the Underlying Law Bill which would have the effect of making customary law the basis of the Underlying Law rather than a subsidiary element of it.[102] A new offence of diminished responsibility killing for certain homicides which would attract a maximum penalty of 3 years' imprisonment was also proposed.[103]

The above discussion of sentencing discretion for murder where the offender is an Aborigine highlights certain aspects of the topic rather than providing a comprehensive overview. One important issue is that of the definition of murder. It is significant that in the 47 cases reported in Research Paper No. 6A, only one was a murder conviction while 24 were for manslaughter.[104] There is already pressure upon the courts to find provocation or similar mitigating circumstances to reduce the offence to manslaughter so that the judge may exercise discretion in sentencing. Moreover, now that Clause 167 of the Criminal Code is law, thereby repealing section 6A, this pressure will intensify. Although recently there has been a reassessment of the crime of murder, in the absence of a discretion in

Aboriginal murder cases, there will be no way in which Aboriginal degrees of culpability may be taken into account.

In all the cases involving violence included in Research Paper No. 6A alcohol was a contributing factor. Important as this is for the question of capacity to form an intent, it also suggests the question of whether a crime committed under the influence of alcohol may be termed "traditional". On the basis of the Northern Territory cases summarized, it appears that judges are prepared to take drunkenness into account but are not prepared to permit it as an excuse.[105] In the Parap murder case not only was alcohol involved but the victim was a white man. Could the crime then be considered within the scope of "native law or custom"?

VI. Women and the law

In much of the recent literature regarding the involvement of the sexes in the criminal justice system women are depicted as victims.[106] When women are the objects of vicious attacks, judges observe that there is a high tolerance of domestic violence in Aboriginal society, yet in the Parap case, the women were the aggressors.[107] In light of this critical fact, the case demonstrates two important points. Firstly, the court is unfamiliar with women taking an active role in the maintenance of customary law: that is, with their role in mediating disputes. Closely allied to this are sexist assumptions concerning the proper role of women. Once they violate the stereotype, they are 'guilty' of a crime against the law and a transgression of an entrenched sexist value.[108] Secondly, and closely related, the concept of "native law or custom" canvassed in the courts has most commonly to do with violent punishments such as paybacks. Courts have no problems in recognizing such spectacular events as falling within the scope of "native law or custom". However, they are less familiar with mechanisms for keeping the peace and the ramifications of violations of important relationships or the non-maintenance of certain obligations.

VII. Expert witnesses

Increasingly judges seek expert evidence in regard to what might constitute customary law. No longer are statements from the bar table sufficient.[109] In the Parap case expert evidence from anthropologists and Aboriginal women was called. The expert evidence of Vai Stanton, an Aboriginal woman of standing in the Darwin community, provided further graphic details of the brutalizing effect which the Darwin pub scene has on the lives of young Aboriginal women. The admissibility of her evidence was not questioned. On the admissibility of Aboriginal evidence relevant to the proof of customary law, the Law Reform Commission's Research Paper No. 14 stated:

> It is not satisfactory that the evidence of traditionally oriented Aborigines about their customary law and tradition should be inadmissible unless it is forced into one of the limited exceptions to the hearsay and opinion evidence rules. It is not satisfactory that such evidence should be admitted in practice only by concession of the court or counsel.[110)]

The Parap hearing also gave rise, as other cases involving Aborigines had done earlier, to the question of seeking the opinion of the women's home communities.[111)] The pre-sentence reports record that consultation had occurred and that the communities were willing, even anxious, that the women be heard. Each of the women stated a desire to leave Darwin and to live in a "dry area". Despite their immersion into the Darwin scene the families of Ngaire and Pamela wished their daughters to return home. Rhoda wished to live in a context free from the fighting and jealousy in marriage she had known.

Concluding Comment

In Research Paper No. 6A the Australian Law Reform Commission noted:

> In making its recommendations on the substantive criminal law, sentencing and community justice mechanisms in the Aboriginal Customary Law Reference, the Commission must first adopt a principled position on the proper role of traditional punishment and of local community action generally, in maintaining order in traditionally-oriented Aboriginal communities ... At the very least, an understanding of the way in which the courts approach the problem under the existing law is necessary. This is necessary both in understanding how often, and in what form, the problem arises, but equally so in forming a basis for the Commission's recommendations.[112)]

In view of this comment, the outcome of the Parap murder case is important to the Reference. It was the last sentence passed under the *Criminal Law Consolidation Act* and indicates the problems which face the Law Reform Commission. In Canberra in December 1982, Mr. Justice Gallop protested to a meeting of the Comission against the idea of lawmakers telling judges what matters to take into account in sentencing discretions.[113)] In his opinion, judges were capable of taking into account all relevant factors whether Aborigines were involved or not. If the judiciary are hostile to guidelines concerning the exercise of discretion, then, given the problems with existing legislation pointed to by the Parap case, one might well ask what form a discretionary power in the Northern Territory with respect to sentencing Aborigines for murder might take. The attitude of the legislature is apparent in the Criminal Code. However, as has been pointed out, the approach there runs counter to that in other Australian States and other countries. A wider discretionary power than that which exists at present would remove the need to make the exercise of discretion dependent upon the finding of "native law or custom" but, given the potential conflict with the Racial Discrimination Act, it may be preferable to consider a general discretion which does not specify race. But then a more sophisticated approach to 'culture' and 'lifestyle' will be demanded.

Notes

1. Transcript of Proceedings, The Supreme Court of the Northern Territory, *R v Ngaire Herbert, Pamela Nangala Sampson, Rhoda Wurrawilya,* Darwin. 17 June 1983, 1113, 1178 (S.C.C. Nos. 269, 270 and 271 of 1981).
2. *R v Herbert et al.,* Darwin, 24th August 1983, Reasons for Sentence, per O'Leary, 20.
3. See for example Australian Law Reform Commission (A.L.R.C.), 1983.
4. See Bell and Ditton, 1980.
5. See for each of the defendants: Record of Interview; Unsworn Statement; Antecedent Report. These documents were exhibits to the original trial before Gallop, J. and are collated in the Appeal Book, Volume No. 7, 1339-48, which was before the Federal Court (see below note 23). See also the Pre Sentence Reports requested by Mr. Justice O'Leary for 12 May 1982 and the Transcript of Proceedings, op. cit., 842-1180 *passim.*
6. The conditions on settlements in Queensland have been subject for comment. See *Neal v R* (1982), 42 A.L.R. 609, 617-20 per Murphy, J. cf. id., 624-5 per Brennan, J.
7. Transcript of Proceedings, op. cit., 6 November 1981, 1378, 1382-3.
8. Mourning ceremonies provide an occasion for the settlement of old disputes, the formation of new alliances and the reaffirmation of relationships. Pamela's absence on such an occasion jeopardizes her position within the family and community.

9. In times past, co-wives were often actual or close classificatory sisters. The bond between them thus pre- and post-dated a marriage - especially when an older husband predeceased the wives. In the case of Pamela, there was no such bond with the Pintupi wife who spoke a different language and came from a different 'country'.
10. See Bell, 1983:110-144 for a discussion of the range of desert women's knowledge.
11. For a description of these town camps, see Bell and Ditton, 1980:68-90.
12. Ibid.:90; Bell, 1983:205-226.
13. See Bell, 1983:98 for a discussion of women's attitude to their sexuality; Bell, 1980:247.
14. These men are known colloquially as 'deros' from derelict. The nature of their relationship with young Aboriginal women is one which raises important moral questions but these were not pursued by counsel.
15. There are always problems establishing the age of Aboriginal people who were born 'in the bush' and therefore not registered. At the time of the second trial, i.e. 1983, Pamela was in her mid-twenties, Ngaire 21 and Rhoda 28.
16. Transcript of Proceedings, op. cit., 882.
17. This self-description was subject for comment in both trials and the appeal. See *Herbert, Sampson and Wurrawilya v R* (1982), 42 A.L.R. 631, 633.
18. House of Representatives Standing Committee on Aboriginal Affairs, 1982.
19. Ibid.: 16.
20. See Bell, 1981.
21. Since Cyclone Tracey devastated Darwin on Christmas Day 1974 there has been a housing shortage.
22. Transcript of Proceedings, op. cit., 6 November, 1981, 1378-1408.
23. Ibid., 1385.
24. Ibid., 1406/7.
25. *Herbert, Sampson and Wurrawilya v R* (1982), 42 A.L.R. 631 (F.C.A.).
26. Ibid., 645.
27. Transcript of Proceedings, op. cit., March, June 1983.
28. Ibid., June 14th, 882.
29. Ibid., 883.
30. Ibid., 842-1180.
31. Ibid., 850-2, 858.
32. Ibid., 852.
33. Ibid., 855.
34. There is a growing corpus of literature on the concept of Aboriginality, see Langton, 1981.

35. Critical criminologists and feminist social scientists have done much to expose the sexist, racist and class biases of the law. See Leonard, 1982, for a review of the literature.
36. *Gerhardy v Brown* (1983), 49 A.L.R. 169 at 179 (S.A.S.C.).
37. *R v Herbert et al.,* op. cit., 858-861; Reasons for Sentences, op. cit., per O'Leary, 7.
38. It is necessary to distinguish between legislation which is discriminatory (a concept which is carefully defined) and legislation which responds to the special needs of a particular group. See A.L.R.C., 1983a:27.
39. *R v Herbert et al., op. cit.,* 878/9.
40. Ibid., 898, 917.
41. Ibid., 1118.
42. Neal v R (1982), 42 A.L.R. 609.
43. Ibid., 1118-1120.
44. *R v Gus Forbes,* unreported, Northern Terrritory Supreme Court; 29 August 1980 (S.C.C. No. 22, 23 of 1980); see also A.L.R.C., 1982a:24.
45. R v Collins (1979), 4 N.T.R. 1.
46. See A.L.R.C, 1982a.
47. *Jadurin v R* (1982), 44 A.L.R. 424 (F.C.A.).
48. Ibid., at 426.
49. Ibid., at 429.
50. *R v Herbert et al.,* op. cit., 963.
51. Concise Oxford Dictionary (new ed.), 252; see Transcript *R v Herbert*, op. cit., 964.
52. Macquarie Dictionary, 461; see Transcript ibid.
53. James, 1971: Vol. 1, 665, "Custom" sub-para. 5.
54. *R v Herbert et al.,* op. cit., 965.
55. *R v Herbert et al.,* 905.
56. Ibid., 998.
57. Ibid., 997.
58. Ibid.
59. Ibid., 999.
60, Ibid., 992-7.
61. Ibid., 999.
62. See Bell, 1983:145-161.
63. *R v Herbert et al,* op. cit., Reasons for Sentences, per O'Leary, 16-17.
64. Ibid., 2, 18.
65. Ibid., 2.
66. Ibid., 3.
67. Ibid., 19.

68. Ibid., 18.
69. Ibid., 5.
70. Ibid.
71. Ibid., 7.
72. Ibid., 15.
73. Ibid., 16.
74. Ibid. See also Gamble, 1984.
75. Transcript of Proceedings, *R v Herbert* et al., op. cit., 878/9.
76. Reasons for Sentences, op. cit., 7.
77. *R v Alwyn William Peter,* S.C. of Queensland, 8-19 September 1981, Dunn J., unreported, see Wilson, 1982, for an analysis of the case.
78. See Schneider, and ors., 1978.
79. *R v Herbert et al.,* Darwin, 11 April (No. NTG 22, 23, 24 of 1983), Foster, Toohey and Fitzgerald JJ., 17.
80. Ibid.
81. Ibid., 10.
82. Ibid., 1076-1082. See also, Freiberg and Biles, 1975.
83. Ibid., 1079.
84. See Sides, 1983:11; Weisbrot, 1982.
85. Woods, 1983.
86. *R v Murray* (1982), 1 N.S.W.L.R. 740, at 745.
87. Ibid.
88. Woods, 1983:161-164.
89. A.L.R.C., 1982a:50-52.
90. Ibid.
91. Mugford and Grönfors, 1978. This refers to surveys undertaken in the early 1970s.
92. Ibid., 58.
93. Ibid., 60.
94. Ibid.
95. New Zealand Judiciary Department of Justice, 1982:151-154.
96. Ibid., 164.
97. McConville and Baldwin, 1982.
98. Ibid., 658.
99. P.N.G. L.R.C., 1975:10.
100. A.L.R.C., 1983(b).
101. A.L.R.C., 1982c:30-32.
102. Ibid., 30.
103. Ibid., 31.
104. A.L.R.C., 1982a:24.

105. Ibid., 5, 9, 15, 27.
106. See Scutt, 1981.
107. A.L.R.C., 1982a:5, 23, see also 33, 36, 39.
108. These issues are explored in greater detail in Bell, "Aboriginal Women and the Recognition of Customary Law in Australia" in this volume.
109. *Mamarika v R* (1982), 42 A.L.R. 94 (F.C.A.).
110. A.L.R.C., 1983c:vii.
111. A.L.R.C., 1982a:29.
112. Ibid., 1.
113. A.L.R.C., 1982b:7, para. 5:11.

References

AUSTRALIAN LAW REFORM COMMISSION (A.L.R.C.) (1982a)
Cases on Traditional Punishments and Sentencing. Reference on Aboriginal Customary Research Paper 6A. Sydney: A.L.R.C.

---------- (1982b)
Consultants meeting. Canberra, December.

---------- (1982c)
Aboriginal Customary Law and the Substantive Criminal Law. Reference on Aboriginal Customary Law Research Paper 6. Sydney: A.L.R.C.

---------- (1983a)
Aboriginal Customary Law: Problems of Evidence and Procedure. Reference on Aboriginal Customary Law Research Paper 13. Sydney: A.L.R.C.

---------- (1983b)
Transcript of Proceeding. Customary Law Seminar, University of New South Wales. Sydney (Ma 7-8).

---------- (1983c)
The Proof of Aboriginal Customary Law. Reference on Aboriginal Customary Law Research Paper 14. Sydney: A.L.R.C.

BELL, D. (1980)
"Desert Politics: Choices in the 'marriage market'," in Eleanor Leacock and

Mona Etienne (eds.), Women and Colonization: Anthropological Perspectives. New York: Praeger.

---------- (1981)
"Sacred Sites and Town Camps." House of Representatives Standing Committee on Aboriginal Affairs, reference Fringe Dwellers. Vol 2 (September 8th).

---------- (1983)
Daughters of the dreaming. Melbourne/Sydney.

BELL, D. and P. DITTON (1980)
Law: the old and the new. Canberra, Aboriginal History for Central Australian Aboriginal Legal Aid Service.

DERHAM, D.P. (1963)
"Law and Custom in the Australian Territory of Papua New Guinea," 30 University of Chicago Law Review 495.

FREIBERG, A. and David BILES (1975)
The Meaning of "Life", A Study of Life Sentences in Australia. Canberra, Australian Institute of Criminology.

GAMBLE, Helen (1984)
"R v Herbert, Sampson and Wurrawilva, Supreme Court, Darwin, O'Leary J.: 24 April 1983," 8 Criminal Law Journal 58-60.

HOUSE OF REPRESENTATIVES STANDING COMMITTEE ON ABORIGINAL AFFAIRS (1982)
Strategies to Help Overcome the Problems of Aboriginal Town Camps.

JAMES, J.S. (1971)
Stroud's Judicial Dictionary (4th ed.). London: Sweet and Maxwell.

LANGTON, M. (1981)
Urbanizing Aborigines: the Social Scientists' great deception," 2 Social Alternatives 16-22.

LEONARD, Eileen (1982)
Crime and Society. New York/London, Longman.

McCONVILLE, M. and J. BALDWIN (1982)
"The Influence of Race on Sentencing in England," Criminal Law Review 652-658.

MUGFORD, S. and M. GRONFORS (1978)
"Racial Class Factors in the Sentencing of First Offenders," 14 A.N.Z.J.S. No. 1, 58-61.

NEW ZEALAND DEPARTMENT OF JUSTICE (1982)
"Attitudinal Assessment of New Zealand Judiciary about Sentencing and Penal Policy, Part 1, Analytical Summary." Survey Link Consultants under contract to Department of Justice.

PAPUA NEW GUINEA LAW REFORM COMMISSION (P.N.G.L.R.C.) (1975)
Report on Punishment for Wilful Murder, No.3.

SCHNEIDER, E.M., S.B. JORDAN and C.C. ARGUEDAS (1978)
"Representation of women who defend themselves in response to physical or sexual assault," 4 Women's Rights Law Reports 149-163.

SCUTT, Jocelynne (1981)
Women and Crime. Sydney: George Allen & Unwin.

SIDES, M. (1983)
"Sentencing", A.L.B.

WEISBROT, D. (1982)
"Homicide Law Reform in New South Wales," 6 Criminal Law Journal 248-268.

WILSON, Paul (1982)
Black Death White Hands. Sydney: Allen & Unwin.

WOODS, G.D. (1983)
"The Sanctity of Murder: Reforming the Homicide Penalty in New South Wales," 57 Australian Law Journal 162.

One community, two laws: aspects of conflict and convergence in a Western Australian Aboriginal settlement

Robert Tonkinson

This paper focuses on three matters - unmarried mothers, vandalism and drinking - that are seen as problematic by the Aboriginal members of a desert community.[1] These problems highlight the tension between the Aborigines' desire for autonomy and their conflicting wish for intervention by outsiders to solve seemingly intractable problems affecting the community. Major factors relevant to an understanding of the present situation are: the residues of a legacy of paternalism; Aboriginal perceptions of some difficulties as 'non-traditional' and therefore not amenable to solution by the application of Aboriginal Law; and the masking effect of European administration during a period of rapid social and economic change.[2] Successful resolution of these problems is defined here as the non-surrender of important decision-making powers to outsiders. It may require nothing less than an altered Aboriginal consciousness concerning the nature of power and the interrelationship of the two systems of law in which they are enmeshed.

I. The setting

Jigalong, which has a population of about 550 Aborigines and 35 Europeans (July 1983), is one of several large Aboriginal communities on the margins of the vast Western Desert.[3] All are relatively isolated, and situated in areas of marginal economic potential. Their Aboriginal inhabitants are immigrants from the desert proper, who over a period of several decades abandoned a fully nomadic, hunter-gatherer existence to settle down along the European frontier. Major aspects of their 'traditional' society and culture have undergone transformation and their dependence on and involvement with the wider Australian society have increased markedly.[4] The people now identifying as members of the 'Jigalong mob' are Manjilyjarra and Gardujarra speakers, more than half of whom have never seen the desert homelands of their elders - migration ceased in the mid-1960s, once the desert was emptied of people. The settlement is on an Aboriginal Reserve (therefore non-Aborigines need permits for entry) and has been, since 1973, an incorporated Aboriginal community, run by an all-Aboriginal council elected by the Aborigines. It employs some whites (advisor, mechanic, bookkeeper, storekeeper, bank agent) and remains dependent on them for a range of expertise. The settlement has an eight-teacher school and a two-nurse clinic, staffed and funded by relevant state government departments, which pay the salaries of local Aboriginal aides, cleaners, etc. The community runs a cattle-raising enterprise and employs about 50 local Aborigines in a variety of jobs, but there is no employment for most adults, and the revenues from cattle-sales, artifacts and the canvas and steel products made in the adult-education training workshop are too small to meet Jigalong's expenses. There is therefore heavy reliance on funding by the Commonwealth government, in the form of annual grants to the community at large, and fortnightly payments of social security benefits to individuals, the latter being the largest single source of income. Despite a decade of government policies aimed at fostering Aboriginal self-management Jigalong remains heavily dependent on both government funding and white personnel for its continued existence. The community is therefore acutely vulnerable to governmental policy changes and personality factors in respect of outside administering bureaucrats, the community's own white employees, and the character of relationships between them.[5]

The Jigalong of today has been shaped by various forces, which have often been in conflict. First are the continuities stemming from the old life, still strongly evident in important facets of everyday Aboriginal values and activities, particularly those pertaining to kinship, social relationships and religion. All these elements are comprehended within 'the Law', the religiously ordained Dreamtime legacy which still underpins settlement life despite the impact of Western culture. Second are the pressures of constant adaptation to radically altered circumstances of life in what was, until relatively recently, an institutionally closed, paternalistic contact situation. Jigalong was a fundamentalist Christian mission station from 1946 until 1969. This period was marked by unstable accommodation between the two groups, conflict-orientation, and unsteady truce. The missionaries laboured (unsuccessfully) to turn the schoolchildren into Christians and the Aborigines strove (successfully) to exclude the missionaries from the community's vital internal concerns. But the missionaries retained uncontested control of all bureaucratic dealings with the wider society, including receipt of all incoming government moneys such as grants and pensions. They never consulted the Aborigines about anything pertaining to the realm of what the latter came to regard as 'whitefella business'. A third force is the Aborigines' variable experience of markedly different categories of whites. Much of their early contact and later work experience was with frontier, white males on cattle and sheep properties. The missionaries, later arrivals, were experienced as a completely different category of white through their behaviours and values evinced in interaction with the Aborigines, although a basic mutual dependence characterized both situations of contact (Tonkinson 1974).

For a long period the Aborigines dealt with the contact situation on both pastoral properties and the mission through strategies which assured their continued subsistence, while protecting their highly valued right to conduct their internal political, social and religious affairs free from overt outside interference by either whites or other Aborigines. But over the last fifteen years, many important changes have disturbed their earlier confidence that the old and new worlds could be kept in balance, and, more significantly for this paper, be kept conceptually separate and related to on the basis of different presuppositions and strategies. The transition to a cash economy in the late 1960s led to alterations in spending patterns and the rise of vehicle ownership, with important consequences for mobility and access to liquor. Since that time, employment opportunities on pastoral properties have steadily declined and are now virtually non-existent, a development which has produced major effects on movement patterns and on the demography of the settlement. The missionaries gave up in 1969, having failed to gain converts or divide the community on generation lines. However, increasing tensions between Jigalong and its northern Aboriginal neighbours led to a split between the two major linguistic groups and the defection of many members of one. This disturbing development was followed by a further escalation of tensions as the northerners endeavoured to usurp Jigalong's status as the strongest centre for 'traditional' Law in the Pilbara district.

In 1973 the new self-determination policies of the federal government came into effect, and Jigalong became an incorporated community with its own council. This entailed a major transformation: the council, and to a lesser extent the community at large, was for the first time forced to make decisions about what had hitherto been strictly 'whitefella business'. The erosion of the previously firm boundary between the arenas of 'camp' and 'settlement', the physical concomitants of 'mardu' (Aboriginal) and 'whitefella', began in earnest. By the mid-1970s some new and disturbing problems were reaching the forefront of community consciousness. The missionaries who might have taken care of some of them had long since gone, while the newcomers held for the most part very different values and attitudes. They abided by the new policy of community autonomy and self-management and so refused to intervene directly in matters which were the business of the council and community at large.

II. Why problem-solving is not easy

Several problems now confronting the Jigalong people need to be viewed in the light of certain salient factors, including those already briefly alluded to above. Chief among these are two closely interrelated aspects of the contact situation: the emphatic conceptual separation of Aboriginal and European concerns and boundaries of jurisdiction; and the strong paternalism of the frontier, whereby whites controlled and mediated Aboriginal relationships with the outside world, particularly those with government agencies concerned with Aboriginal welfare or social security payments to Aborigines. The Aborigines were rarely if ever consulted about such matters, but made little protest since they considered them to be 'whitefella business', not their own. In their view, the settlement area was the whites' domain of power and therefore events occurring there were the legitimate concern of the missionaries. Even if there were incidents involving Aborigines, such as verbal or physical conflict or the punishing of Aboriginal schoolchildren (then living in dormitories in the settlement area), missionary intervention was tolerated, if not always with good grace. However, the 'camp', a few hundred yards away, was an Aboriginal domain and the locus of Aboriginal Law and jurisdiction. There, intervention by whites was usually loudly protested and always deeply resented. For the most part the missionaries accepted this boundary, and the Aborigines felt that they were in control of their own internal affairs and destinies, so minimal was the direct interference of outsiders. They cared relatively little what the whites were up to most of the time, as long as they were left alone to manage themselves according to the tenets of the Law. The Aborigines liked neither the physical punishment of their school-age children in classroom and dormitory nor the tight mission control of social security moneys, but acknowledged the superiority of 'government law' and its precedence in all matters pertaining to 'whitefella business'. Consequently they were woefully ill-prepared to deal with the bureaucracies of the outside world when the council was instituted and self-determination became the ideology of policy towards Aborigines. They were therefore heavily dependent on white advisors.

This problem has been increased by the emergence of new and unprecedented issues for decision. During the mission era changed circumstances had been engendering new sets of conditions that were to become problematic, but the presence and activities of mission staff had obscured their emergence. After the missionaries had left and, unchecked, such problems emerged as matters for

Aborigines to resolve, their dimensions became clear. Since there are no traditional precedents for some of these more recent developments, social control elements inherent in the Law have either been ignored as irrelevant (in keeping with the perception of 'whitefella' things as completely separate from Aboriginal) or considered but dismissed as inappropriate. However, attempts to get white staff to deal with them have failed, as have attempts to ignore them or put them into the 'too hard' basket, since white staff and visiting agents of the government have reminded the community that these are 'problems' that must be dealt with by the council and faced up to by the community at large.

Also very worrying to the Aborigines are threats of intervention by various outside agencies, especially the police. Most adults have now lost their terror of policemen, largely because of the work of the Aboriginal Legal Service, which has made them realize that policemen are not godlike enforcers who can punish at will. There is now a consciousness that police action may be, to a limited extent, contained by Aborigines by recourse to the ALS. In the mission era, when their fear of police was much greater, this did not stop them from clubbing and spearing offenders in the traditional manner, and even then they were perturbed by police interference in what they regarded as internal matters. Moreover, they were perplexed and resentful at inconsistencies in police handling of such matters, which in their eyes resulted sometimes in the removal of lawful punishers, and sometimes in the arrest of the true offenders. Nevertheless, insofar as outside intervention occurred, the long-term effect of police and missionary opposition to any resort to physical means of punishment was to weaken the operation of the Law as a social control mechanism. This has lessened the Aborigines' sense of autonomy in the arena of 'mardu business' and engendered, not a total rejection of police involvement, but decidely ambivalent views about the need for or wisdom of seeking such involvement in attempts to solve local problems. The ambivalence arises partly because many problems span and therefore obfuscate the already eroded boundary between Aboriginal and 'whitefella' concerns. Since whites are at least in part responsible for the emergence of some of these difficulties, the temptation to enlist their aid is ever-present; but the risk of a significant surrender of autonomy must also be part of the Aborigines' calculus of gain and loss.

III. Unmarried mothers

In the desert culture of the pre-European contact era, there could be no 'unmarried mothers' since all girls were given in marriage and living with their spouses well before they were old enough to conceive.[6] The major rights in, and responsibility for, a female were transferred from her parents to her husband and his close kin for the period of the marriage. If she was widowed, her subsequent remarriages were in principle matters for her late husband's senior male kin to decide. Only later in life, after her child-bearing days were over, was a woman usually able to play a significant role in decisions as to her remarriage. But remarry she would, since widowhood was considered to be a temporary phase, never a permanent status. At any age a woman could assert herself through elopement or refusal to stay with a designated spouse, but both strategies entailed the risk of an unsympathetic public reaction and severe penalties.

In the mission era teenage Aboriginal women graduated from the schoolgirls' dormitory into a closely guarded building of their own. They soon learned that the missionaries were strongly opposed to their arranged marriage to much older men, usually as second or third wives. These teenagers were offered sanctuary in the 'whitefella' arena of the 'settlement' as long as they remained dutiful and unpregnant domestics. This protection aroused much anger among Aboriginal adults of both sexes, who saw it as undermining the Law. They feared to intervene actively, however, being intimidated by missionary threats to involve the police and reminders that, under European law, they could be jailed for offences involving minors. Despite strict missionary supervision, the teenage girls found ways to engage in sexual activities with their boyfriends, and in most cases they eventually became pregnant. Their subsequent banishment to camp was part of their fall from grace. Most eventually abided by the Law and married the men to whom they had been betrothed.

The 'unmarried mother' phenomenon emerged in the 1970s, when increasing numbers of young women refused, despite repeated individual and community efforts, to cohabit with their "Law-ful" spouses. All were dormitory graduates who had been indoctrinated by the missionaries with the notion of a right to a free choice of spouse, leading them to reject arranged marriages with men much older than themselves. Moreover, the economic bases for polygyny no longer existed in a settlement economy in which women's gathering activities had become sporadic and irrelevant to subsistence. First wives increasingly, and in many cases with passion and violence, opposed the entry of second wives into their households. When such opposition was encountered or deemed likely by an intended second wife, her reluctance to join the household was understandable. Indeed, in some cases second wives were amenable to the marriage but the first wives made life so difficult for both them and the husbands that the marriages were abandoned. Another important factor was the advent of single mothers' social security benefits, which, when added to child endowment, gave unmarried mothers what they considered to be a comfortable income and economic independence. Welfare recipients were given full control over their cheques even before the mission era ended, so these young mothers, although like everyone else subject to the demands of kinship obligation, could become what they termed 'own bosses' or 'free agents'.

To the community at large this status attaching to sexually active young women was anathema. Since parents could no longer control and supervise them, they needed to have husbands who would take responsibility for their behaviour. Many young women have continued to reject this reasoning, and have not only refused to be married to their *bilyur* (betrothed one) but say they will marry no one, valuing their status as 'free agents' above all else. They are unamenable to physical punishments, attempts at enforced co-habitation, threats or appeals. The optimists in the community say that such women will come to their senses and settle down eventually. Nevertheless, the lack of community control over them is symptomatic of a general decline in the effectiveness of the Law as a means of maintaining old norms. 'Whitefella' law is no help in this matter, either, because the young women are breaking no European law in choosing to remain single, especially if the marriage envisaged is polygynous. The community therefore sees no solution to this problem in appeals for outside intervention, and only hopes that it will correct itself in time. Men are now marrying younger, the institution of infant betrothal is declining in significance, and there is a freer choice of spouses (but still within the limits set by the kinship system) and less attempted coercion of women.

The successful 'emancipation' of those young mothers who have asserted their autonomy can perhaps be seen as part of a general improvement in the socio-economic status of Jigalong women vis-a-vis their menfolk. For several years now there have been elected women members of council, and Jigalong is the first Western Australian Aboriginal community to have elected a woman as Council Chairman.[7] Men's considerable control over women in the desert situation began to falter in the frontier situation on pastoral properties, where frequently women's roles as domestics and sexual partners of white bachelor pastoralists enabled them to act as influential mediators between the white boss and his male Aboriginal workers. In the mission situation many more women than men had jobs at the settlement. Here they had closer contact and better communication with the whites than did their menfolk, who avoided that arena and immersed themselves in 'men's business', especially of a religious kind. The revolt of the young unmarried mothers is perhaps seen by many Aboriginal men as just another step in the general movement of women away from their domination and control.

IV. Vandalism

In pre-contact days in the desert people spent most of their time in small bands of about fifteen to thirty and the few child members of a group led a playful existence largely free of parental constraint.[8] They were excessively indulged and almost never physically punished. There was little in the way of 'property' and no hard and fast rules about its treatment. The few restraints on children were taboos on certain areas of 'men's country' and prohibitions on accompanying older males in activities with secret-sacred aspects. Once they were considered capable of looking after themselves, children spent a lot of time playing beyond the range of adult supervision and their parents were happy to allow them a great deal of freedom. There was so little of importance to deface or destroy that vandalism never posed a problem.

The traditional situation contrasted greatly with that at the mission, where in both school and dormitory children received their first taste of strict discipline and physical punishment. They were outraged, but they found that their temper tantrums brought more of the same instead of the instant capitulation that ensued when their parents upset them. They also learned about property and its high valuation in European culture, by being taught its proper care and maintenance and receiving beatings if they damaged it. Because school-age children were in the care of teachers and missionaries most of the time, their parents took for granted the caretaking role of the whites in the 'settlement' arena. Parents continued to indulge their children during the time spent together each day in the camp, and felt little or no responsibility for their behaviour elsewhere.

Following the abandonment of the dormitory system shortly before the mission era ended, the children were returned to the care of their parents for the entire time outside school hours. They began to get up to mischief, including the damaging of mission property. Initially this caused little alarm in the community. However, after Jigalong's incorporation and the setting up of the council, what had formerly been 'whitefella property' and 'whitefella business' became Aboriginal communal property, and its protection the responsibility of the community. Furthermore, repairs to windows, light bulbs, buildings, etc. now cost the community money it could ill afford. Children's break-ins and the vandalising of white staff residences caused anger and demands to the council for firm action. The Aborigines were less worried about the crimes themselves than at having the onus of apprehending and punishing the offenders. A problem, masked in the mission era by the disciplinary role played by whites, had suddenly become visibly theirs. There were no traditional precedents and no easy solutions, since for most adults the corporal punishment of their children was, and still is, anathema, while to beat other's children invariably produces hostility and frequently a violent reaction from the other parents.

Since the offences took place in the 'settlement' arena the Aborigines tried to categorize them as 'whitefella business' so that the whites would deal with them, just as the missionaries used to do. But although the whites had drawn attention to the problem, they refused to take action since this would have contravened the principles of self-management and the development of Aboriginal initiatives in the running of their community. Physical punishment had also largely disappeared from the school environment, which has become more relaxed and supportive of cultural differences. Aboriginal parents therefore have been unable to persuade the teachers to fill the disciplinarian role that they have remained reluctant to adopt.

The Aborigines are also confronted by an unprecedented demographic situation. The handful of children in the desert band has become, thanks to a considerable aggregation of people and a high birth rate, a large horde. It consists of many play-groups and peer-groups that roam the camp and settlement areas at will, unsupervised and looking for adventure. As the adults often put it, there are 'too many kids runnin' around and playin' up'. With no generalized policing roles within the society, neither individuals nor the council will take responsibility for the problem. Aboriginal adults continue to place little value or emphasis on material goods, and since the problem of controlling their children is in reality that of protecting property, they do not share the concern of local whites who see the situation as serious and getting out of hand. With each new crisis, there is in the council and community a surge of determination to act decisively and punish the offenders. But the gap between resolve and effective resolution is large, and many Aborigines feel that children are increasingly becoming a law unto themselves.

The Aborigines' reluctance to move decisively against their misbehaving children may derive in part from their wider concerns about the future. They realize that the children are being exposed to many elements of 'whitefella law', and that this poses a threat to the transmission of Aboriginal Law. In the view of adults, Aboriginal cultural survival depends on children's eventual assumption of responsibility for the perpetuation of highly valued institutions, especially those relating to kinship and religion. To ensure this, they must have the cooperation of their children. Despite some involvement of children in the excitement of ritual activities, boys must wait until the commencement of their initiation, around age 16 or 17, before important revelations begin. Adults therefore want to avoid actions that might alienate their children from the Law, and would rather tolerate vandalism, etc. than run the risk of losing the younger generation to the new law.

V. Drinking

There were no intoxicating beverages in the desert culture and therefore no mechanisms evolved to deal with their disinhibiting effects. Jigalong Aborigines first became aware of alcohol and its effects when they took jobs on pastoral properties or when they visited towns between jobs. During the mission era, it was strictly prohibited at the settlement and, because Aborigines lacked their own vehicles, no drinking ever took place there. In the 1970s, however, with the introduction of a cash economy and the purchase of vehicles, people began to obtain alcohol and to bring some of it back to the settlement to share with others. There were no longer missionaries who would have strongly opposed its entry and sternly punished offenders. The rapidly escalating problem of drink-related violence and death became the concern of the council, and ultimately of the whole community. Like the problems of unmarried mothers and children's vandalism, the problem of alcohol consumption had no traditional precedent, but unlike them was seen by the Jigalong people as a serious threat to their Law.

The Jigalong Aborigines are socialized to experience, when sober, powerful feelings of shame or embarrassment if they deviate from society's norms. Conformity is maintained most of the time through self-regulation, underpinned by these strong inhibitory mechanisms. People drink alcohol for a variety of reasons: as a response to boredom, to release tensions built up in everyday life, to enjoy the taste and the sensation of becoming inebriated, or perhaps for its disinhibiting effects. It 'makes them brave' and precipitates behaviour connected with fighting or sexual activity that would never be entertained when sober.

At Jigalong, the essence of other people's reactions to those who are inebriated is avoidance and retreat. This is motivated largely by embarrassment over their shamelessness, but also by the fear aroused when drunk people are violent or are believed likely to become so. Because inebriated people are believed not to be fully in control of, and therefore not responsible for, their actions, there is an attitude of 'poor bugger, can't help it', and often a mixture of pity, embarrassment, amusement (if there is no violence) and refusal to be judgmental towards them. Other individuals and the community at large refuse to invoke the kinds of social control mechanisms they would employ against sober troublemakers. Among Jigalong people there have been several alcohol-related traffic accident deaths as well as fatalities resulting from disputes involving drunk people. These resulted in police visits, community distress, and the jailing of some people. There have been strong pressures from community advisors, police and other outsiders for the council to adopt stern measures against grog-carting and the bringing of liquor and/or drunk people into the settlement (the nearest source being 100 miles away).

The problem is rendered particularly intractable by the prevailing view that inebriated persons are not fully responsible for their actions while drunk - in effect, that they are not the same persons as their sober selves. This prevents the application of sanctions provided in the Law that have long been used effectively against offenders, and that continue to have force despite a clash with the law of the wider society with respect to the permissibility of physical punishment. The proof to Aborigines that drunk people are not themselves is that they sometimes commit violent assaults, or sexual offences regarded as incestuous in that they involve classificatory kin who are 'wrong' for them in kinship terms. This they would never do if sober, when the usual inhibitory forces of shame and embarrassment are in operation.

The council has tried a variety of measures, including handcuffs, a small jail, locally appointed policemen, heavy fines for bringing alcohol onto the reserve, roadblocks, the smashing of wine flagons, public 'trials', firing offenders from community jobs, impounding vehicles, and recently the burning of a vehicle repeatedly used for grog-carting. The aftermath of this last measure illustrates the difficulties confronting the council. The owner, who had not been involved in the offence, complained to the Aboriginal Legal Service. This led to a rebuke to the council from the Nullagine police officer whose patrol area includes Jigalong, and an order for the council to pay compensation to the owner. The upshot was resentment among the councillors who, after being urged repeatedly by police and others to act firmly against such offenders, were punished for doing so. Thus there was a direct clash between the two systems of dealing with offenders (although not in this case between 'traditional' Law and the law of the land according to Europeans). The kind of punishment the Aboriginal men would propose for repeat offenders is spearing and clubbing of a severity which would disable them for a time and thus curtail their mobility. But this traditional punishment would certainly bring about police intervention and charges. Therefore, as with other categories of offence demanding severe physical punishment, the council and aggrieved individuals are reluctant to act as they would like.

Various strategies aimed at the problem of alcohol and related disruptions of community life have been variably applied, none with conspicuous success. As with vandalism, there is often a lull, perhaps without any problems, then a couple of weekends in succession in which the calm is shattered, followed by a flurry of earnest concern, discussion and statements (and perhaps actions) asserting a resolve to do something strong against the people who are seen to be threatening the fabric of the Law. But consistent application of any particular strategy seems hitherto to have been beyond the capability of the council or the community at large, despite the large amount of time spent discussing the problem. It should be noted, too, that often for quite long periods there is no 'drinking problem'; moreover the majority of those who do drink rarely, if ever, cause serious upsets. This fact, too, helps explain why there are problems in sustaining fierce resolve over time.

Recently the community instituted an informal court to deal with offences committed within the reserve and not involving serious bodily harm. Stiff fines are imposed on those found guilty of offences such as grog-carting, and deducted in instalments from social security cheques. The Nullagine policeman, in an attempt to eradicate grog-carting, has promised to clamp down on unroadworthy vehicles driven on main roads. In this case, there is determination to marshall the forces of both Law and law in a combined attack on the problem.

Although the mission failed to make Christian converts, some of its teachings about the faith were retained. In 1983 Jigalong was caught up in the evangelical movement that has swept Aboriginal communities in several areas of Australia in recent years. A small group of Aborigines professing Christian beliefs (but not to the exclusion of the traditional religion) has been formed and meets regularly. One notable feature of its activities is a strong anti-alcohol stance. After six months' abstinence, several fell from grace in July 1983 only to make a quick return to the fold. With the support and encouragement of local white Christians, this group could grow, and its stance on alcohol could provide momentum for community resolve to combat alcohol. The outside force to which Christian teetotallers appeal for strength is spiritual rather than human, and perhaps therefore their strategy does not have the same implications for community self-determination that stationing a police officer at Jigalong would have.

It may be that, beyond these recent developments, the primary need is for a large conceptual leap: for the community to treat drunken people as if they were sober and therefore responsible for their actions, and then to invoke the Law to punish them if they persist in causing trouble. In the absence of strategies that result in the complete exclusion of both liquor and inebriated people from the reserve, this might be the only effective solution. It would require, however, that the community's infliction of physical sanctions on offenders not be subject to police intervention except in extreme cases of grievous bodily harm. Defining the boundaries between acceptable and grievous harm clearly presents another problem, but this is less pressing than the need to achieve the kind of conceptual leap that is being posited here as vital to any successful resolution of the drinking problem.

Conclusion

The three problem areas that I have discussed share some common characteristics: none of them existed traditionally; all in various measures appear to the Jigalong Aborigines to be intractable; and all are resistant to both Aboriginal Law and the law of the wider society. Much greater use could perhaps be made of outside intervention, especially by the police, in the case of vandalism and drinking. But this would mean for the council and community a further erosion of their already diminished capacity to maintain a cherished internal autonomy and the feeling of controlling their own destiny. For all three problems, the will to persevere in any strategy aimed at their solution is weakened by other considerations. In the case of unmarried mothers there is an underlying optimism that eventually the problem will go away; a realization by men that the status of women in the community can never be returned to its condition prior to emigration from the desert; and an appreciation that neither Aboriginal nor European law can deny these young women their 'free agent' status. With vandalism, traditional values of permissiveness restrain parents from punishing their children or allowing other Aborigines to fulfill a disciplinary role outside the bounds of the kinship system; a low cultural valuation of non-religious property weakens the community's reactions to the problem; and, most important, adults fear that chastisement of their children could lead to a turning away from, or outright rejection of, the Law, the perpetuation of which takes first place in their priorities. The most serious problem, that of alcohol and the resultant disturbances to community life, is made more difficult by the general belief that the inebriated cannot be held responsible for their acts.

The powerful legacy of paternalism before 1973 has undoubtedly contributed to the community's felt inadequacy to deal with these difficulties. All the problems developed unseen and suddenly surfaced full-blown on the departure of the missionaries. Shortly afterwards new government policies put pressure on communities to make their own decisions and solve their problems without paternalistic control or assistance from local whites. Thus were closed off avenues of appeal to outside sources in cases which, being resistant to solution by the Law, fell into the 'too-hard basket'.

In my view, the fundamental problem lies in Aboriginal conceptualizations of two distinct realms of power and authority: their own, deriving from the Dreaming, and that of the whites, deriving from some other source.[9] Governed by this dichotomy, the Aborigines refused to see any parallels or convergence between their Dreaming-originated culture and the wholly alien culture of the whites. They made a spatial division between the *maya* 'house' (or settlement area, in the case of the mission) and the ngurra 'camp'. Each domain had its own loci of authority, and within it that authority was paramount. With a measure of common agreement this separation was sustained in both the pastoral station and the mission milieux, and it helped the Aborigines retain a strong belief in their autonomy with respect to their own affairs.

The first threat to this separation was the insistence by government policy that Aborigines assume responsibility for what had formerly been part of the *maya* domain, that of 'whitefella business'. The strategy adopted by the Jigalong people to maintain the dichotomy aimed to insulate the increasingly penetrative bureaucratic machinery of the outside world from the camp, and the means they used was to require the council to mediate between themselves and the wider society. The council was to deal with all 'whitefella business' and report to the camp meetings anything of direct concern to the Aborigines. This insulation strategy has been increasingly undermined as more and more of what once was 'whitefella business' becomes 'Aboriginal business' and thus invades the domain of the camp. It is no longer possible to maintain the clear dichotomy, since the pace of change is necessitating some degree of fusion between the two realms of power and authority.

The only power available to Aborigines was for long that derived from the Dreaming, which in their view is the ultimate source of all knowledge and power. They fully understood both the sources and the methods of mediation in the flow of power from the spiritual realm into that of human beings and the physical world. Through ritual, they controlled their own fertility as well as that of the flora and fauna, and thus in essence controlled society's reproduction.[10] But until recently they had no understanding of the sources of the great power of the whites or access to its administration. Only in the last decade has this situation been transformed, with a limited but significant portion of 'whitefella' power being placed in their hands through the community council. Before this they had had no opportunity to attempt any synthesis of the two separate domains of power. They could learn no adaptive lessons from the Dreaming power realm, and they had no incentive to apply the principles drawn from one source of power in the exercise of the other.

The challenge now is to fuse the two domains in such a way that the heritage of strategies and organizations for the marshalling of resources and channelling of power can be applied to the realm of 'whitefella-become-Aboriginal' business. Certain major rituals require considerable planning, resource-management, personnel-scheduling, and co-ordination of various activities. If the same Law which produces these considerable skills can be extended to embrace also the requirements and activities of non-Aboriginal origin, a very productive fusion could result. Perhaps here also a large conceptual leap is required: one in which the ultimate origins of power become less important than the modes of employing it, be they derived from the Law or whites or newly invented in response to pressing needs. A notion of power as having common properties irrespective of its source could significantly aid the Aborigines. They could yet attain the kind of convergence of two laws and two cultures that provides workable solutions to the problems that have arisen, and no doubt will continue to arise, as the impingement of the wider society intensifies.

Notes

1. This paper is based on field research conducted at Jigalong settlement since 1963, in ten trips totalling almost three years.
2. Many Australian Aborigines use the English word 'law' to refer to their cultural legacy, attributed to the creative activities of ancestral beings in the formative period they call the Dreamtime or Dreaming. Their choice of this term suggests that they perceive parallels between their 'law' and that of whites in terms of obedience to a set of powerful dictates, and of punishment for non-conformity, since in both systems human agents are involved in the punishment process. In this paper, the capitalized 'Law' is used to connote the Aboriginal concept, which at Jigalong is called *Yurlubidi* in the vernacular. For an excellent account of the fundamental and overarching Dreaming concept, see Stanner (1979); Berndt and Berndt (1977).
3. This area, comprising about one sixth of the continent, is the largest single language bloc, and is also characterized by a very high degree of cultural and social homogeneity among the component Aboriginal groups; cf. Berndt (1959), Douglas (1980), Tonkinson (1980).
4. This transformation, and particularly the relationships between the Jigalong people and resident missionaries, is detailed in Tonkinson (1974). See Stanton (1980) for a description of another desert-fringe community.
5. The gap between government policies and their on-the-ground implementation in the context of Jigalong, and problems of adaptation, are discussed in Tonkinson (1977a and 1977b).
6. A detailed reconstruction of the culture of the Aborigines living on the western side of the Gibson Desert prior to European intrusion is given in Tonkinson (1978). On the traditional role of women see also Hamilton (1980), who writes of culturally similar eastern Western Desert peoples, and Berndt and Berndt (1945).
7. An account of this woman's life is given by M. Tonkinson (1985).
8. For a detailed account of Aboriginal socialization, see Hamilton (1981).

9. The conceptual dichotomization of power by the Aborigines of Jigalong is discussed in Tonkinson (1982), where the focus is on the problem of vandalism by children and the problems caused by 'masking' are first outlined.
10. This point is well made by Bern (1979) in his analysis of Australian Aboriginal social formation.

References

BERN, J. (1979)
"Ideology and domination: toward a reconstruction of Australian Aboriginal social formation," 50 Oceania 118-132.

BERNDT, R.M. and C.H. (1945)
"A preliminary account of field work in the Ooldea region, Western South Australia," (Oceania, vols. 12, 4; 13, 1-4; 14, 1-4; 15, 1-3), Oceania Bound Offprint, Sydney.

---------- (1977)
The World of the First Australians, Sydney: Ure Smith.

---------- (eds.) (1980)
Aborigines of the West. Perth: University of Western Australia Press.

BERNDT, R.M. (1959)
"The concept of the tribe in the Western Desert of Australia," 30 Oceania 81-107.

DOUGLAS, W.H. (1980)
"The desert experience: language," in R.M. and C.H. Berndt (eds.), 108-118.

HAMILTON, A. (1980)
"Dual social systems: technology, labour and women's secret rites in the eastern Western Desert of Australia," 51 Oceania 4-19.

---------- (1981)
Nature and Nurture: Aboriginal Child-rearing in North-Central Arnhem Land. Canberra: Australian Institute of Aboriginal Studies.

STANNER, W.E.H. (1979)
"The Dreaming," in White Man Got No Dreaming: Essays 1938-1973. Canberra: Australian National University Press: 23-40.

STANTON, J.E. (1980)
"The Mt Margaret community," in R.M. and C.H. Berndt (eds.), 119-125.

TONKINSON, M. (1985)
"Two women of Jigalong," in I. White, D. Barwick and B. Meehan (eds.), Fighters and Singers: the lives of some Aboriginal women. Sydney: Allen and Unwin.

TONKINSON, R. (1974)
The Jigalong Mob: Aboriginal Victors of the Desert Crusade. Menlo Park: Benjamin/Cummings.

---------- (1977a)
"Aboriginal self-regulation and the new regime: Jigalong, Western Australia," in R.M. Berndt (ed.), Aborigines and Change: Australia in the 70s. Canberra: Australian Institute of Aboriginal Studies.

---------- (1977b)
"Aboriginal community autonomy: myth and reality," in M.C. Howard (ed.), Whitefella Business: Aborigines in Australian Politics. Philadelphia: Institute for the Study of Human Issues.

---------- (1978)
The Mardudjara Aborigines: Living the Dream in Australia's Desert. New York: Holt, Rinehart and Winston.

---------- (1980)
"The desert experience," in R.M. and C.H. Berndt (eds.), 140-150.

---------- (1982)
"Outside the power of the Dreaming: paternalism and permissiveness in an Aboriginal settlement," in M.C. Howard (ed.), Aboriginal Power in Australian Society. Brisbane: University of Queensland Press.

Legal anthropology in the formulation of correctional policy in the Northwest Territories, Canada

Harald W. Finkler

I. Introduction

Complementary to the author's socio-legal research in the Northwest Territories (NWT)[1] and related writings on this subject[2], this paper addresses some of the pertinent issues and considerations inherent in the formulation of a framework for the recognition and application of traditional measures for socio-legal control and socialization in future corrections institutional policy and programs.

This discussion is timely for several reasons. To begin, the findings of the above research have confirmed the disproportionate incarceration of native peoples along with the increasing trend in the commitment of offenders to institutions. Notwithstanding the development of territorial initiatives to provide native oriented policy and programming, and their current emphasis on the development of culturally relevant non-institutional options at the community level, doubts remain as to the effectiveness of their interventions with indigenous offenders and their ability to reduce and prevent the disproportionate incidence of native criminality.

This finding, in combination with current aboriginal development toward a more culturally grounded justice system within the context of land claims and political, socio-economic, and cultural self-determination, has generated a resurgence and demand for the recognition and accommodation of traditional customs and values. One consequence was that, in 1980, at the 2nd Session of the Legislative Assembly of the NWT, a motion was adopted urging "the administration and the Department of Justice and Public Services to develop a strong law reform capability within that Department which will, among other things, review and update existing territorial legislation, examine ways in which aboriginal customs, values and rights can be discovered, recognized and protected by territorial laws, and develop proposals for new legislation to meet the special needs and circumstances of northerners, as directed by the Assembly from time to time".[3]

Furthermore, in its discussion on the development of a constitution for Nunavut (which is the proposed creation of a provincial type government and public institutions in the NWT which reflect and provide for the special needs and circumstances of Inuit and their culture), the Nunavut Constitutional Forum recommended it "continue to study the application of Inuit customary law in Nunavut, propose specific provisions for a Nunavut constitution and, with the results of that work, plan further for the overall administration of justice within Nunavut".[4] Similarly, in its discussion of a proposal for a circumpolar arctic policy during its Third General Assembly in Frobisher Bay in July 1983, the Inuit Circumpolar Conference also affirmed that its "future self determination requires national and international recognition of our economic, political, social and cultural rights and the right to our own judicial system".[5]

If we are to respond to this demand, we need to determine the appropriate grounding or evolution of such policy and program. We need to ascertain whether the demand can best be met by system adjustments to reflect the traditional indigenous system of social control concurrently with the continued operation of the existing territorial correctional framework; or whether it entails the development of an entirely new system based on the traditional normative structure and system of sanctions. It should be emphasized that consideration of either policy must take into account that, whereas the emergence of culturally based justice policies and programming in southern Canada occurred in terms of addressing native needs as a minority group, the demographic reality of the NWT, with its majority native (63.2% in 1980) yet small and culturally diverse, population (totalling 46,069 inhabitants in 1980), necessitates that northern justice policies and programs be primarily oriented to responding to the needs of the northern indigenous offender.

In order to establish whether sufficient grounds exist for the development of justice policies and programs partially or entirely reflecting traditional measures, as a first step we need to examine the traditional indigenous system of social control. To this end, the assessment of studies in the anthropology of law will provide the requisite information in terms of description and analysis of the traditional aboriginal normative structure and mechanisms for dispute settlement. Anthropology's contributions and relevance to the study of law is clearly demonstrated by the range of its inquiry, which includes attempts to answer the following questions:

(1) What are the types of adjudicating or mediating agents operating in society?

(2) What is the basis of their authority to exercise these roles in dispute settlement?
(3) Which disputes are amenable under specific conditions to negotiated compromise settlements and which require adjudication?
(4) Which procedures are taken for each type of dispute under given conditions? (This question implies inquiries into such aspects as apprehension of the accused, locale, evidence, etc.)
(5) How are juridical decisions enforced?
(6) What ex-systemic functions and effects attach to legal processes? (This includes inquiries into the network of social, psychological, economic and political relationships between the parties, their representatives or supporters, and the authorities.)
(7) How does law change?[6]

Accordingly, we will now summarize anthropologists' description and analysis of the traditional system of social control of Inuit society, the target group of much of my previous research, and consider its implication for future socio-legal policy. This documentation provides the data for the subsequent discussion of the issues and considerations involved in the formulation of a framework for the recognition and application of traditional measures for socio-legal control and socialization in future corrections institutional policy and programs.

II. The traditional Inuit system of social control

In the author's earlier review of the anthropological literature[7], the system of social control in traditional Inuit society was based upon values which stressed intra-group cooperation and avoidance of interpersonal conflict. The aim in dispute settlement was to restore the peace and social equilibrium of the community as opposed to seeking justice or punishment. The process was characterized by its flexibility, tolerance and pragmatism, in that the determination of sanctions was not principally dependent upon the question of guilt or responsibility, but rather aimed to curtail unacceptable behaviour and prevent recidivism. Furthermore, reaction to conflict, albeit without the existence of formalized institutions for socio-legal control, entailed an assessment of the offender's personality and situational circumstances, demonstrated an individualized approach to treatment, did not necessarily isolate him from society and refrained from invoking sanctions more disruptive than the crime itself.

A framework for the recognition/application of traditional measures for socio-legal control and socialization in future correctional policy and programs

In focussing on the recognition/application of the traditional normative structure and sanctions in future correctional policy and programming, the previous summary of the description and analysis of traditional Inuit system of social control provides the terms of reference for the following discussion on considerations in policy formulation and alternative approaches to correctional policy and programs. However, I should point out that, while my discussion continues to be primarily directed at future justice policies for the Inuit, the methodology in our approach to this issue could be readily applied to Dene society. Furthermore, several of the issues and policy directions outlined would apply to the northern indigenous population as a whole.

A. Considerations in policy formulation

While past studies in the anthropology of law have provided the requisite background for the formulation of a framework of traditionally grounded justice policies, additional field research is required to assess prevailing community views on this matter. Specifically, responses are necessary to questions on the extent to which traditional law-ways are still practised in northern communities, as well as data which will enable us to distinguish the locations where they continue to exist by community size, ethnic composition, level of homogeneity, isolation, and general traditional orientation, and information about where traditional family/kinship based authority structures are still maintained. Furthermore, in regard to corrections, we need to determine the degree of willingness to retain some traditional physical or other harsh punishments and whether their retention is required to support the recognition and application of customary law.

Any proposed research in this area, however, would have to assess the effects of accelerated social change and development in northern Canada on the traditional measures for socio-legal control. For example, southern influence on and presence in the north has resulted in the imposition of Anglo-Canadian law and formalized agencies for socio-legal control, along with a decline in primary group relationships, traditional family/kinship based authority structures, and an increasing incidence of native criminality. Furthermore, there are indications that Inuit are becoming less willing to maintain offenders in their community and more reluctant to participate in socio-legal control. These and other recent developments pose several difficulties in adapting traditional law-ways to a drastically altered indigenous society.

Nevertheless, at a general level, future field investigations on these questions and related issues will enable us to ascertain the needs and advantages of a plural legal system, and more specifically, provide us with concrete guidelines for a framework of traditionally grounded values and measures in correctional policy and programming. While my socio-legal research in the NWT has not been specifically directed at measuring the prevailing indigenous views on this question, my preliminary thoughts on this subject lead me to believe that we are essentially looking at the merits of two approaches to correctional policy and programming, varying in their level of recognition and application of traditional law-ways.

B. Alternative approaches to correctional policy and programming

Briefly, the first alternative approach or model essentially entails specific adjustments or refinements in the existing territorial correctional framework to reflect and accommodate aspects of traditional indigenous social control. Such an approach may entail legislative amendment to An Ordinance Respecting Corrections Services. The section pertaining to the purpose of corrections would be amended to reflect the recognition of the rights of aboriginal offenders through the provision of differential treatment based on different cultural needs. Such a recognition would clearly acknowledge the demographic reality of the NWT and mandate corrections services to provide traditional, culturally grounded programming primarily oriented to responding to the needs of the northern offender. The implication for programming would be a greater emphasis throughout the system on "group self-determination and the fostering of cultural revitalization and positive self-concept".[8] The system's present thrust of native oriented institutional policy and programming continues to be primarily delivered by regional facilities, such as the Baffin Correctional Centre. Given the limited development of the range of socio-legal services in the NWT, it would be advantageous to revise the Ordinance to include the designation of bush or wilderness camps or outposts as correctional institutions. This would facilitate the increasing emphasis on contracting with natives to provide correction services. Measures directed toward the implementation of more culturally grounded institutional programming, through a recognition of the special needs and circumstances of northern indigenous offenders, should include the following:

> "increasing institutional recognition and support of inmate requests to pursue or discover traditional cultural and spiritual beliefs;
>
> provision of innovative, culturally relevant, intensive short term programs embodied in outward bound, wilderness or survival programs that facilitate the

acquisition of traditional skills, and a sense of self worth, along with emphasizing an inmate's responsibility and accountability for his behaviour;

as an alternative to conventional institutional alcohol treatment programs, the in-house utilization of culturally appropriate alcohol treatment programs, developed and delivered by indigenous persons;

provision of vocational and educational training directly relevant to life on release, or the increasing utilization of community based educational and vocational, as well as recreational and therapeutic resources where appropriate;

increased adoption of a more culturally relevant, holistic therapeutic approach in individual and group counselling;

availability of an effective classification scheme for matching offenders and programs, with increased attention on pre-release planning;

emphasis on the recruitment and training of indigenous staff balanced with ongoing initiatives in cultural sensitization for non-native staff;

commitment by indigenous communities, groups, as well as native organizations to actively participate in the conceptualization and delivery of culturally relevant correctional policy and programming for native offenders; this entails their access into justice planning and programming through mechanisms such as citizen advisory committees".[9]

Such a culturally grounded policy/programming orientation, while not necessarily providing for total application of the traditional approach, would bring about its recognition, through an individualized, flexible and tolerant treatment of offenders with the emphasis on reducing their isolation from society through facilitating the community's access and involvement in the rehabilitative process.

A second approach or model would be the development of an entirely new correctional system, based on the traditional normative structure and system of sanction. This would be legislatively entrenched, not only in the Corrections Ordinance but throughout the penalty provisions of other territorial legislation. As in the instance of Greenland, where it is achieved through codification, the Inuit's individualized, flexible, tolerant, and pragmatic approach to the treatment of offenders, avoiding where possible isolation from society, refraining from invoking sanctions more disruptive than the crime itself, and excluding an unnecessarily strict requirement to relate measures to the gravity of the offence, can be integrated into the sanction provisions of several ordinances. The traditional emphasis on peace maintenance as opposed to punishment or justice, and the goals of rehabilitation of the offender and the protection of society can be included. Within this legislative framework, confinement to an institution would be seen as a last resort, with greater emphasis placed on non-institutional measures directed toward maintaining an offender in the community. In time, similar revisions might be undertaken to the federal Criminal Code so as to reflect more readily traditional law-ways. The planning of institutional models within this approach, in addition to considering the aforementioned directions in culturally grounded institutional programming, could take account of the methods of the Baffin Correctional Centre, whose program is primarily oriented for and delivered by Inuit.

The foregoing represents some preliminary thoughts on this subject. Whether the implementation of any of the above approaches will have the intended effect of preventing crime and reducing recidivism remains to be seen. However, their application will immeasurably reduce the negative or harmful effects of incarceration for indigenous offenders, and moreover, focus on the community's responsibility for socio-legal control.

Notes

1. Finkler and Parizeau, 1973; Finkler 1976; 1981.
2. Finkler, 1982a; 1982b; 1983; 1985.
3. Legislative Assembly Of The Northwest Territories, *Debates*, 2nd Session, 9th Assembly, Tuesday, March 11, 1980, p. 1377.
4. Nunavut Constitutional Forum, 1983:29.
5. "The ICC Resolutions - in brief". The *Arctic Policy Review*. October-November 1983, p. 27.
6. Koch, 1969.
7. Finkler, 1976:10-12.
8. Newby, 1981:62.
9. Finkler, 1982b:19-20.

References

FINKLER, H.W. and A. PARIZEAU (1973)
Deviance and Social Control: Manifestations, Tensions and Conflict in Frobisher Bay. Montreal: International Centre for Comparative Criminology.

FINKLER, H.W. (1976)
Inuit and the Administration of Criminal Justice in the Northwest Territories: The Case of Frobisher Bay. Ottawa: Indian and Northern Affairs.

---------- (1981a)
The Baffin Correctional Centre: A Review of Current Programs and Alternatives. Ottawa: Indian and Northern Affairs.

---------- (1982a)
"Corrections in the Northwest Territories 1967-1981, With a Focus on the Incarceration of Inuit Offenders," 5 Canadian Legal Aid Bulletin 27-38.

---------- (1982b)
Policy Issues in the Delivery of Correctional Services in the Northwest Territories. Paper presented to the American Society of Criminology's 34th Annual Meeting in Toronto.

---------- (1983)
"Violence And the Administration of Criminal Justice in Northern Canada," in K. Johnson (ed.), Insights and Strategies For Confronting Violence: Conference Proceedings. Anchorage: School of Justice, University of Alaska.

---------- (1985)
"The Role of Traditional Inuit Measures for Social Control in Correctional Policy and Administration," in A. Allott and G.R. Woodman (eds.), People's Law and State Law: The Bellagio Papers. Dordrecht: Foris.

KOCH, Klaus-Fredrich (1969)
"Law and Anthropology: Notes on Interdisciplinary Research," 4 Law and Society Review 16.

NEWBLY, L. (1981)
Native People of Canada and the Federal Corrections System. Ottawa: The Correctional Services of Canada.

NUNAVUT CONSTITUTIONAL FORUM (1983)
Building Nunavut. Ottawa, Nunavut Constitutional Forum.

Institutionalizing criminality in Greenland

Elaine J. Schechter

Anthropologists have long studied the law-ways of indigenous peoples, particularly their informal mechanisms of social control (e.g., Pospisil 1971, 1978; Gluckman 1965; Nader 1965; Hoebel 1954; Llewellyn and Hoebel 1941; Malinowski 1926). Inuit traditions such as song duels or drum songs, regulated combat, and forced exile have drawn particular attention (q.v. Kleivan 1971; Balikci 1970; Graburn 1969; Steenhoven 1962, 1966; Gluckman 1965; Birket-Smith 1959; Hoebel 1954; Weyer 1932). But in most Inuit communities, these techniques for dispute settlement have become extinct (Kleivan 1971); and powerful, albeit less colorful traditional forms of social control, such as withdrawal, teasing and negative public opinion, have weakened (Finkler 1976; Chance 1966).

Recently, the literature has begun to address the problems created by conflicts between traditional law-ways of Native North Americans and Inuit, and the alien judicial systems imposed on them (e.g., Bayly 1985; Conn 1985; Brakel 1978; Rosen 1978; Finkler 1976; Strickland 1975; Hippler and Conn 1973; Price 1973; Bahr, Chadwick and Day 1972; Reasons 1972). Many U.S. Indians, who are overrepresented as inmates in penal institutions (Stewart 1964), feel that the police and courts treat them unfairly (Bahr, Chadwick and Day 1972). That they are subject to criminal laws drafted by and for the dominant majority is evident

---

*) An earlier, unrevised draft of this paper, entitled "The Greenland Criminal Code and the Limits to Legal Pluralism," was presented at the Symposia of the Commission on Folk Law and Legal Pluralism in Vancouver, Canada, on August 22, 1983. This unauthorized version was printed without the author's knowledge or consent in Etudes/Inuit/Studies, 1983, Vol. 7, No. 2, pp. 79-93.

when comparisons are drawn between tribal codes and federal and state statutes. In the State of Washington, for example, tribal codes cite only 40 to 60 offenses, while state penal laws enumerate over 2000 (Reasons 1972). The Canadian Inuit have a similar problem: "a system imposed on aboriginal people by the Canadian government and its representatives, without consultation or evaluation as to whether it was appropriate or required any modification to fit the cultural milieu" (Finkler 1976:13).

Drafted 35 years ago by Danish jurists for their former colony (Greenland is now semi-autonomous), the unique Greenland Criminal Code attempts to graft traditional Inuit concepts of rehabilitation onto a Western, and specifically Danish, system of laws and procedures. The philosophy behind even the enlightened Danish penal system is punishment (Serrill 1979), i.e., a repressive means of social control whose object is forced conformity with society's norms (Goldschmidt 1980:118). In contrast to this "conformity model" (ibid.), the object of Inuit customary law is neither punishment nor justice, but the elimination of conflict and the restoration of harmony (Steenhoven 1962, 1966; Hoebel 1954) - a philosophy dubbed "The Arctic Peace Model" by Verner Goldschmidt, the Danish author of the Greenland Criminal Code (Goldschmidt 1980).

The goal of the Greenland Criminal Code is not retribution (the word "punishment" is never used) but rehabilitation. There are no full-time prisons. The most severe sanction served in Greenland is night-time confinement in a correctional institution. Offenders spend day-time hours at regular jobs (earning standard wages) or in regular schools, thus remaining integrated within the society. Youthful offenders might be placed with a family of fishers, hunters, or sheep herders to learn their trade.

Unlike Danish, U.S. and Canadian models, in which justice is, supposedly, equal and "blind," and the punishment is determined by the severity of the *crime*, the Greenland Criminal Code gives judges broad discretion to impose a wide variety of sanctions on the basis of the individual *offender's* personal background. Local district judges are neither lawyers nor a colonial elite, but lay Greenlanders who are to employ their intimate knowledge of the offender's family situation, occupation, and behavior to prescribe an individual program of correction.

Finally, unlike most Euro-American criminal systems, the Greenland Criminal Code provides no protection against double jeopardy. Although the 1979 revision of the Code has limited the court's flexibility regarding how sanctions may be altered, under the Codes of 1954 and 1963, cases could be reviewed again and again, and sentences shortened, lengthened (if the original provided for this possibility), or re-designed to promote the Code's goal - that the offender not repeat the undesirable antisocial behavior (Brøndsted 1973, 1979, 1980; Goldschmidt 1956, 1963, 1970, 1973-74; Udvalget for Samfundsforskning i Grønland 1962).

In this paper I will briefly trace the aspects of the evolution of the Greenland Criminal Code, elucidating how Greenlandic traditions of informal consensus and social control have been maintained, modified or abandoned in the context of the Danish state-level political/legal structure. I will demonstrate that despite a written law and an ideology supporting maintenance of a Greenlandic legal perspective, the administration of justice in Greenland is profoundly and increasingly a product of Danish and European legal thinking. It is, in particular, the powerful centralizing tendencies of the imported Danish bureaucracy that subvert the local autonomy of Greenlandic authorities, and fossilize the very flexibility that the Code's author attempted to codify.

Prior to the Greenland Criminal Code of 1954, Danes living in Greenland were tried according to Danish law, and most Greenlanders according to an assortment of regulations introduced by the Danish Ministries of Justice and the Interior, and other Danish authorities (Bentzon, Goldschmidt and Lindegaard 1950:1-4; Goldschmidt 1956:220-221). Although the Greenland Provincial Councils had accepted a proposed Greenland Penal Law which was a simplified version of the *Danish* Penal Law of 1930, the Danish authorities rejected it, on the grounds that the prison punishment it authorized was neither economically nor humanistically suited to Greenlandic conditions (Goldschmidt 1956:221; 1980:122).

In 1948-49, a juridical expedition of three Danish jurists and legal sociologists was sent to Greenland to conduct research for a code which would incorporate both Greenlandic customary law and Danish concepts of justice. The expedition's goals in codifying Greenlandic criminal law were (1) to preserve and protect the traditional Greenlandic criminal law; and (2) to satisfy the need for a symbol of fairness - i.e., a law which was valid for both Greenlanders and Danes in Greenland (Goldschmidt 1980:123).

The expedition found that, after over 200 years of colonization and missionization, the Greenlandic normative system, in terms of what was considered to be punishable offenses, for the most part resembled the Danish, with some exceptions regarding sexual norms. My own frequent observations in both local district courts and the High Court, albeit over 30 years after the Juridical Expedition, confirm this conclusion. It is true that not all defendants understand the courtroom procedures. But bewildered defendants who do not understand that their acts are defined as criminal - as described by Bayly (1985:287-91) in the Northwest Territories - are simply not seen in Greenland, even though the section defining illegal acts in the Greenland Criminal Code quite closely resembles parallel definitions in the Danish Penal Law.

The Juridical Expedition discovered, however, that the Greenlandic reaction or sanction system was markedly different from the Danish and other Western systems. Concerned largely with general crime prevention, the latter administer a kind of tax system of specific minimum to maximum penalties for specific crimes - the aforementioned repression model.

By contrast, early legal authorities (village councils and district courts) in Greenland reacted not so much to the *offense* as to the *offender.* Sanctions were meted out individually on the basis of a total evaluation of the offender, his family, social background, and social function. They were extremely flexible, and designed neither to prevent crime by others (i.e., general prevention) nor to punish the offender, but simply to prevent recurrence of the undesirable behavior, and thus re-establish harmony in the society - Goldschmidt's aforementioned "Arctic Peace Model." In the small, personal Greenlandic communities, where traditional patterns of hunting, sharing and labor cooperation made individuals indispensable to one another, incarceration would be both impractical and undesirable. Primary social control, rooted in personal familiarity and lack of privacy, could usually suffice. (Goldschmidt 1980:117-118, 122; cf. Christie 1975 for a discussion of primary social control in "the close society.")

When court cases did arise, flexible, creative and often very pragmatic solutions were found to the conflicts. An unemployed chronic thief was given a job and a home-building loan. A man convicted of bestiality with sled dogs was married, with the minister's help, to a woman reputed for her sexual dissipation. When some fishermen assaulted a settlement leader and vandalized his property because the salthouse was not large enough to permit the purchasing and accommodation of their catch, monies were allotted not to build a jail for the perpetrators, but to expand the salthouse (Goldschmidt 1980:126-127).

The important point is that decisions were reached individually on the basis of the offender's situation and *not* on the basis of the offense itself. This separation between the determination of guilt and the determination of sentence was one of the unique elements of traditional Greenlandic law which Goldschmidt codified when drafting the Greenland Criminal Code.

It is also the element that has been most subverted by Danish legal centralism.

Although the Greenland Criminal Code establishes no particular sentences for particular offenses, the Danish-led, centralized prosecution employs unofficial "minimum-maximums" derived from precedents, which the prosecution cites when appealing in the High Court decisions made by Greenlandic lay judges in the local district courts. The sources of these precedents are several internal documents and especially an unofficial card file in the Police Chief's Headquarters in Nuuk/Godthåb, Greenland's capital. (In Greenland and Denmark, the police also serve as the prosecution.) The file was begun in 1970 and by 1982 contained 535 cards, most of which summarized significant cases *according to the nature of the crime* - for example, drunk driving, first, second, third and fourth offenses; illegal fishing; assault (63 cards); homicide (21 cards); sex crimes (26 cards); other criminal code offenses (93 cards); and various special law violations (63 cards), such as liquor control laws.

Imported Danish jurists preparing prosecutions (i.e., indictments) and appeals in Greenland refer to this card file daily, carefully matching crime circumstances and sanctions. Such procedure in effect establishes specific unwritten "*punishments*" for specific *offenses* in a system whose law theoretically postulates individual *treatment* for individual *offenders*. This unofficial standardization of sanctions, which is contrary to the philosophy of the Greenland Criminal Code, in fact reflects trends in *Scandinavian* criminology, which has abandoned the treatment orientation of the 1940's and 1950's, in favor of the "New Classicism" - i.e., the principle of "let the punishment fit the crime." The Danish jurist who wrote the internal documents worked as a prosecutor in the Police Chief's office from 1976 to 1980, and is a firm believer in the New Classicism. (For a prime example of the treatment philosophy, see Stürup 1968; for discussions of the New Classicism, see Christie 1981 and Nielsen 1979).

The Danish jurists in the Greenland Police Chief's headquarters rely heavily on this file because it satisfies their perceived and expressed need for an annotated Greenland Criminal Code, which would provide precedents for them, but which, until very recently, has not existed.

However, in May 1985, the above-mentioned former Danish prosecutor, author of the internal documents used in the Greenland Police Chief's office, published a two-volume work described as "primarily having the character of an annotated criminal code" (Senholt 1984: Preface). A painstakingly careful review of Greenlandic court decisions and their applicability, with references to precedents, this book is now used in conjunction with the file. In his review of the book, a former Greenland High Court Judge assessed it as "a thorough and honest work, although, characterized as it is by its juridical organization and language use, is most likely addressed more to the Danish jurists in the courts and prosecuting authorities than to the Greenlandic lay judges" (Brøndsted 1986:13).

Moreover, when the Danish prosecutors are in doubt as to the interpretation of a paragraph in the Greenland Criminal Code, they do not hesitate to look up the parallel paragraph in the Annotated *Danish Penal Law*. Such citations of a law that is not legally valid in Greenland are permitted in the High Court under the guise of analogies in the prosecution's summations. Yet Greenlandic lay defenders and Greenlandic lay district judges have told me that they *never* refer to the Danish Penal Law because "That law isn't valid in Greenland."

One Greenlandic lay assessor, who served on cases in the High Court, complained to me that the Danish judges also refer to the Danish Penal Law during deliberations, when they feel the Greenland Criminal Code does not suffice. His reaction was to protest by asking ironically, "Why not use the American Penal Law? It's just as valid as the Danish Law here in Greenland!"

It is at this subtle and sophisticated level that the conflict between the Danish and Greenlandic perceptions of justice emerges.

Danish jurists tend to stay only a couple of years in Greenland, and when an eager new prosecutor has arrived, it is not uncommon to hear courtroom citations from a half-dozen Danish law books. As one Greenlandic lay district magistrate remarked to me about the Danish police/prosecutors, "Just when I've gotten one of them trained to our way, they go home and I have to start all over again with a new one ! "

In point of fact, however, most of the tutelage flows in the opposite and expected direction - i.e., from Danish jurists to Greenlandic lay judges. Every two years, Danish jurists from Greenland's High Court and either the Law Committee for Greenland or Denmark's High Court hold a meeting for the Greenlandic lay district judges. Over the years, the emphasis has changed from group discussions of common problems to long lectures by Danish jurists telling Greenlandic lay judges how they are to interpret various laws, paragraph by paragraph, and how they are to write formally correct decisions. While training is necessary, and the intentions admirable, some of the Greenlandic magistrates have complained to me that it is difficult to follow the jargon-studded lectures. They would rather have more group workshops using mock cases than a two-week crash course in law.

The autonomy and flexibility of local Greenlandic police and lay district courts are also severely subverted by the wholesale importation of Denmark's centralized prosecuting authority. In Denmark, *all* prosecutions in local police districts must be cleared at the Police Chief's Headquarters in Copenhagen. But Denmark is a land of 5.5 million people living in 43,069 square kilometers. One can travel from the East Coast to the West by train in just four hours, and overnight postal deliveries are guaranteed.

By contrast, Greenland is an island of 2.18 *million* square kilometers, which is three times the size of Texas and *50 times* the size of Denmark. The distance from the northernmost to southernmost point is 2670 kilometers - equivalent to the distance from Copenhagen to deep into the Sahara. Yet Greenland's population of 50,000, scattered along a 39,000 kilometer coastal region in 122 towns and settlements, could easily fit into Yankee Stadium. As recently as 1978, one could not travel from the West Coast of Greenland to the East without first flying to Copenhagen. No roads link any two towns today, and telephone connections to all settlements were only first completed in 1982.

Yet despite these vast distances, difficult communications and transportation, and regional linguistic and cultural differences, the Danish prosecution is every bit as centralized in Greenland as in Denmark. In recent years, the Danish prosecuting authorities in Greenland's Police Chief Headquarters in the provincial capital of Nuuk/Godthåb have "strived at carrying out more uniform legal praxis by issuing directives to the police regarding which charges should be made and which sentences should be demanded for the various types of cases" (Brøndsted 1986:10).

Furthermore, *all* local police - and they are often Greenlanders - must send their indictments to the Police Chief's Headquarters in the capital for approval. The Danish jurists in the Police Chief's Headquarters can rewrite the charges and suggested sanctions, and send them back to the local municipality for trial in the district court. If the local district court's decision - made by Greenlandic lay judges and assessors - does not suit the Danish jurists in the Police Chief's Headquarters, they can appeal the case to the High Court in Nuuk. There, although two lay assessors are usually Greenlandic, the High Court judge and his deputy judges are always Danish jurists. And, according to one of the Greenlandic lay assessors, the Danish High Court judge's superior legal training can influence the Greenlandic lay assessors to bow to his perceived authority.

In addition, the charges and requested sentences, so carefully prepared and screened by the centralized, Danish-dominated prosecution, are usually accepted by the local Greendlandic district courts, except regarding the size of fines, and, on rare occasions, length of sentences. Fines are determined according to the offense *and* the offender's income, and the Greenlandic lay judges have a deeper understanding of the unstable incomes of hunters and fishermen. Nevertheless, as in Conn's descriptions of Alaskan bush justice (cf. Conn 1985:307-9), most defendants plead guilty, are found guilty as charged, often on the basis of their own confessional testimony alone, and most sentences are identical to the prosecution's demands. As one Danish acting police station leader remarked to me, "We just serve the cases up on a platter for the local court."

This Danish legal centralism has also eliminated the free-wheeling Greenlandic legal autonomy, flexibility, imagination, and pragmatism that Goldschmidt celebrated and attempted to preserve through codification.[1]

For example, the local district court of a remote town in East Greenland sanctioned a man, who had several times fired weapons recklessly within the town, by forbidding him the use of firearms for one year. This unique and hitherto unheard-of sentence caused serious hardship, since the accused's job - and a very unpopular one at that - was to shoot sled dogs running around loose in town. In addition, since all Greenlanders in that area earn or supplement their living through hunting, the loss of the right to bear firearms would have effectively rendered the man a pauper.

Early in 1982, the case was appealed, not only by the defendant, but also by the prosecuting authorities in Nuuk/Godthåb. The latter argued that although one of the possible sanctions listed in Chapter 23, para. 85 of the Greenland Criminal Code is loss of rights, that is interpreted as only including rights for which special permission is needed, such as a driver's license. (See also Chapter 30, para. 114 and 115 of the Code.) In Greenland, certain rights are inalienable, including the right to bear arms. Thus the prosecution was in the odd and paternalistic position of appealing a local decision which it regarded as either illegal or simply too harsh. (Of course, it routinely appeals decisions it considers too mild.) The High Court of Greenland set the local decision aside, thus again limiting the discretionary powers and flexibility of the local Greenlandic judiciary.

Interestingly, this case stands in direct contrast to the Canadian situation, in which any defendant convicted of any serious crime, even one having no connection with guns, also loses the right to bear firearms for five to ten years. As Bayly (1985:289-90) notes, this sanction is a perfect example of conflict between Inuit hunting culture and laws written for urban Canadians.

In its concern to follow precedent and praxis, the Danish-led prosecution in Greenland has also appealed homicide decisions which it considered too harsh. To avoid escalating current praxis, the prosecution in November of 1981 got one murder sentence reduced from eight years in an open correctional institution to seven, and another from seven to five, which is the usual sentence for homicide in Greenland.

Another sign of increasing formalization in Greenland's criminal justice system is the use of trained Danish jurists and lawyers as counsellors in criminal cases. Lay counsellors, both Greenlanders and Danes, usually serve this function, especially in the local district courts where, by "gentlemen's agreement," lawyers normally do not participate in criminal cases. There the magistrates and assessors are all lay-people and usually Greenlanders, and the prosecutor is either a Greenlandic or Danish policeman. Although the latter has no legal training, he has three advantages over the lay defenders: (1) his work as prosecutor is part of his job, not minutes snatched from his spare time or other career obligations; (2) he gets a certain amount of training for this task; and (3) he can seek guidance from the Danish jurists in the Police Chief's Headquarters. The lay counsellors have no legal training and few law books, all of which they have paid for themselves. Although they supposedly can turn to the High Court judge and deputies for guidance, one lay counsellor has told me that the former are too busy with their work to have time to help him.

So the match has been uneven. One Danish jurist employed as a government civil servant attempted to serve as counsellor in the Nuuk local district court, but the policeman/prosecutor marched out of the courtroom in protest. This jurist has since won several cases for defendants in the High Court of Greenland. Private attorneys also occasionally serve as defense attorneys in the High Court, when a defendant (usually a Dane) has been canny enough to request a real lawyer and thus obtain a more professional adversarial defense.

Little by little, however, and for better or worse, resistance to lawyers in the local district courts is being undermined. In November 1982, Nuuk's local district lay magistrate refused to appoint as counsellor a lawyer requested by a Danish defendant. The lawyer's firm responded with a letter citing the Greenlandic Administration of Justice Law, Chapter 5, Section C, Paragraph 23, regarding the two conditions permitting a person to be appointed defender: non-notoriety and adulthood. The lawyer was eventually appointed to the case, serving for the defense in both the local district court in February 1983, and in the High Court in April 1983.

This development reflects the growing complexity, bureaucratization, and formalization of not just the system of justice, but Greenlandic society as a whole. Although the lay counsellors' defense is often weak, the extraordinarily mild sanction system in Greenland provides a safeguard against gross miscarriages of justice. Thus, the admission of lawyers to the role of defender should not be interpreted as a major advance in Greenland's justice system. It is, rather, yet one more sign of development in the society as a whole, and yet one more way in which the administration of justice in Greenland is growing more and more Danish. And since there are less than a handful of Greenlanders who have been educated as jurists, the use of lawyers in criminal cases in Greenland means that these counsellors are Danish and do not speak the defendants' nor the lay judges' nor the lay assessors' mother tongue. Therefore, court procedures which normally take place in Greenlandic (if the prosecutor/policeman is also Greenlandic) have to be carried out in Danish for the sake of the monolingual defense attorney.

Finally, the autonomy, flexibility and creativity of the lay Greenlandic judiciary has been subverted by the importation of Denmark's Department of Corrections and Probation. Until the mid-1960's, it was the duty of the police-/prosecution and local district courts to locate specific individuals and private homes to serve as private probation officers and foster homes for specific offenders. In the late 1960's, this function began to be informally taken over and professionalized by the newly imported Danish Department of Corrections and Probation. In the 1979 revision of the Greenland Criminal Code, these tasks were formally assigned to Greenland's Department of Corrections and Probation, which is under Denmark's Department of Corrections and Probation.

Since the Department of Corrections and Probation took over much of the sanctioning function in Greenland, institutionalization of offenders has steadily replaced the unique system of sending offenders to private homes to live as family members and learn traditional skills (hunting, fishing or sheepherding). As shown on Table 1, the daily average number of offenders in private care fell from 20 in 1976 to 5 in 1982. During the summer of 1982, that figure was only 3.

Table 1

Daily average number of penal measures in pursuance of the Greenland Criminal Code for the period 1974-1985

Sources: Kriminalforsorgen i Grønland 1986; Justitsministeriet 1983:70)

Penal Measure	1974	1975	1976	1977	1978	1979	1980	1981	1982	1983	1984	1985
Psychiatric hospital in Denmark	(9	(10	(10	7	6	7	7	6	4	7	9	8
Psychiatric penal institution at Herstedvester, Denmark				6	7	10	10	12	14	17	13	12
Adult correctional institution in Greenland	19	22	27	36	42	53	48	40	45	49	48	50
Private placements and so forth in Greenland	11	10	20	19	18	20	21*	6*	5*	9*	5	8
Supervision (probation/parole) with provisions/conditions	196	147	153	151	158	169	186	183	193	176	174	210
Total	245	203	216	224	234	268	284	262	272	270	260	299
Under mental observation in Denmark	3	2	4	4	3	4	3	1	2	2	1	2

*) includes 3 to 5 individuals assigned for short periods to Allu, a family treatment center in South Greenland. Thus this daily average figure may be inflated by an estimated 1-1.5

Department of Corrections and Probation leaders explained that they rarely use private homes any more because it has become so difficult to find willing families. Yet my research in Northwest Greenland in the summer of 1982 has revealed that some previous foster families, although willing to serve again, have never been asked. In addition, the local, decentralized Child and Social Welfare Offices of three municipalities in Northwest Greenland (Uummannaq, Ilulissat/Jakobshavn, and Aasiaat/Egedesminde) still use this system successfully for juvenile delinquents between the ages of 15 and 18. These Greenlandic leaders told me that they can still find enough foster families, despite the Department of Corrections and Probation's inability to do so. Furthermore, one remarked to me that her office gets fewer requests than previously from the Department for help in locating foster homes.

The reasons that the Child and Social Welfare Offices are more successful than the Department of Corrections and Probation in using private families are:

(1) Child and Social Welfare clients, although often delinquents convicted of many thefts and vandalism, are younger, less hardened, and more appealing to potential foster parents.

(2) Until recently, the Child and Social Welfare Offices paid a much higher monthly support for their clients. In 1982 the Department of Corrections and Probation paid an honorarium of only 22 Danish kroner (crowns) per day (a mere $2.30!) "for the inconvenience of having a stranger in their home, and for having responsibility for an offender." This payment is symbolic, and according to the Department of Corrections and Probation, "should under no circumstances be regarded as payment for living expenses," since, "The offender shall through his work efforts/income be able to pay for his food and lodging at the host family" (Greenland Department of Corrections and Probation 1982a: Section M, Appendix 1, unpaged). The amount was later raised to 30 kroner, which at $3.15 was still no incentive. And,

(3) The Child and Social Welfare Offices are local, decentralized, and run by Greenlanders who maintain steady contact with potential and actual foster parents in their districts.

In June 1982, the leadership of Greenland's Department of Corrections and Probation passed from a Dane to a Greenlander, who has made concrete efforts to increase the placement of young offenders in private families. On October 1, 1985, after three years' of pleading by the new leader, the Danish Department of Corrections and Probation and the Danish Ministry of Justice in Copenhagen agreed to increase payments to foster families to 65 kroner ($6.85) per day - the same rate paid by Greenland's Child and Social Welfare Offices.

In addition, in 1984, Greenland's Department of Corrections and Probation began a public information campaign, in which staff members from the central office in the capital and the four local offices met with Child and Social Welfare Offices and settlement councils to explain their work and the need for foster families (Kreutzmann 1986; Justitsministeriet 1985:76). Through improved contacts with hunting and fishing settlements, and especially improved cooperation with the local Child and Social Welfare Offices, the use of private foster families increased to 8 in 1985 (see Table 1) and 9 by the beginning of 1986. The Director of Greenland's Department of Corrections and Probation is also aiming at increasing the use of private probation officers, in order to reduce clients' dependence upon office personnel and to help them establish or strengthen lasting personal relationships - with, for example, an uncle, other family member, employer, co-worker, or a friend - in society (Kreutzmann 1986).

Although the purpose of these measures is to avoid building even more institutions, particularly youth institutions, trends appear to be going in the opposite direction. There are currently three adult night-time correctional institutions, with a total capacity of 66 (recently expanded from 44), and two youth institutions housing 14 to 16. The adult facility in Nuuk/Godthåb was opened in 1967 with space for 18 inmates, expanded to 28 in 1976, and to 50 (including 6 detainees) ten years later. The adult institution in Aasiaat/Egedesminde was opened in 1976, and the adult institution in Qaqortoq/Julianehåb, in 1977. Each has an official capacity of 8, but often houses 10. The youth institution in Sisimiut/Holsteinsborg was first opened in 1965, housing 5 to 7, and in the mid-70's was moved to a new building, also housing 7. That building is identical to the youth institution in Ilulissat/Jakobshavn, opened in 1979 and also housing 7. A possible third youth institution has been suggested for Qaqortoq/Julianehåb (Kreutzmann 1986).

Institutionalization has risen sharply in recent years. As Table 1 shows, the daily average number of inmates in adult institutions in Greenland has more than doubled from 19 in 1974 to 50 in 1985. And, as the use of private foster families has dwindled, the use of youth institutions has swelled from a daily average of only 4 inmates in 1977 to 11 in 1985.

As former Greenland High Court Judge Henning Brøndsted (1986:11) points out, "It is a paradox that Greenland, with its tradition of limiting the use of confinement, uses more spaces per capita in Greenlandic facilities and Danish institutions than the number of prison spaces per capita in Denmark and the other Scandinavian countries with the exception of Finland."

The increase in institutionalization also reflects an increase in serious crime, particularly homicide. In the mid-1970's, more than 50 per cent of the population of the adult institutions was convicted for offenses against property. By contrast, of the 49 inmates in the three adult correctional facilities as of December 1, 1985, over half, or 29, were convicted of homicide (23), attempted homicide (4), and assault leading to death (2). Since the sentences of the 23 are long by Greenlandic standards - varying from 2 to 8 years, and averaging 5 to 7 years - these convicts contribute to a serious lack of space in the institutions: "Our institutional system is drowning in murderers," complains the Director of Greenland's Department of Corrections and Probation. "They block up the whole system" (Kreutzmann 1986).

As a result, convicts whose crimes and social problems are severe enough to warrant placement in the adult institutions wind up instead in the youth institutions (Brøndsted 1986:12). According to the Director of the Department of Corrections and Probation, this lack of adequate institutional space has "contributed to the people's loss of trust in the Criminal Code. They don't feel protected enough" (Kreutzmann 1986).

In the interests of protecting society, the Greenland Criminal Code also provides for the exile to psychiatric prison in Denmark of those offenders who are deemed too dangerous or mentally deviant to remain in Greenland's open institutions. As Table 1 indicates, this figure practically tripled from 6 in 1977 to a high of 17 in 1983. In that year, there were also 7 other convicts in mental hospitals in Denmark, pushing the total number of Greenlandic offenders in Danish institutions up to 24, or *33 per cent* of all Greenlandic inmates serving time in adult institutions.

One of these was a 19-year-old who, in May 1982, escaped from Nuuk's night-time correctional institution, killed three youths and raped a woman. His crimes, along with three other murders commited within a two-week period in the wake of Greenland's repeal of alcohol rationing, spurred demands for greater security.

In October 1982, the Greenlandic legislature voted to construct a closed wing in the capital's night-time correctional institution. Renovations were completed early in 1986, resulting in 19 cells (8 for disciplinary problems, 6 for police detainees, and 5 for new arrivals) whose occupants are only permitted out of their cells for two half-hour periods per 24 hours. Since the secure wings have no workshops, it is the stated intention of both the law and the Department of Corrections and Probation that, depending upon their behavior, inmates in the closed wings will also eventually be moved to the open wings and employed outside the institution.

Nevertheless, this measure can be seen - sadly - as a developing nation's first step toward the birth of a prison system. As Greenlandic society comes increasingly to resemble its mother country, it appears almost inevitable that the sanction system will follow suit, with increasingly repressive measures of social control replacing the vanishing Arctic Peace Model.

Notes

1. Goldschmidt later came to acknowledge that his attempt to codify flexibility was in itself a contradiction in terms:

> Something indicates, though, that the Criminal Code's catalogue of sanctions has to some degree restrained the court authorities' imagination and excluded them from what in the Danish perception of justice would b?e called non-traditional solutions, which seen from the Greenlandic point of view, was traditional in the small communities.
>
> Codification of the arctic peace model is in reality a self-contradiction. *Codifying implies in itself a tendency toward conformity,* which means rigidifying something which otherwise had been flexible.

(Goldschmidt 1980:128; emphasis in the original; translation mine)

As one internal document from the Greenlandic Department of Corrections and Probation points out, pursuant to the 1979 version of the Greenland Criminal Code: "There thus exist 14 - and only 14 - possible sanctions!" These are:

1. No sanction (possibly with warning)
2. Fine
3. Conditional release/suspended sentence
4. Conditional release/suspended sentence plus fine
5. Conditional release/suspended sentence plus conditions from the Child and Youth Welfare Office
6. Conditional release/suspended sentence plus conditions from the Child and Youth Welfare Office plus fine
7. Sentence to supervision of the Department of Corrections and Probation
8. Sentence to supervision of the Department of Corrections and Probation plus fine
9. Sentence to supervision of the Department of Corrections and Probation, but beginning with short-term institutionalization
10. Sentence to supervision of the Department of Corrections and Probation, but beginning with short-term institutionalization, plus fine
11. Sentence to a correctional institution for a determined period of time (maximum 10 years)
12. Sentence to a correctional institution for an indeterminate period of time
13. Sentence for an indeterminate period of time to a psychiatrically-administered institution in Denmark under the Danish Department of Corrections and Probation (i.e., Herstedvester)
14. Sentence to a hospital or other institution.

(Greenland Department of Corrections and Probation 1982b: Section O, unpaged, translation mine).

However, the Greenland Criminal Code of 1979 (Chapter 23, para. 85; Chapter 30, para. 114 and 115; and Chapter 31, para. 116-119) also provides for sentencing to loss of rights (not including civil rights), and confiscation. The Department of Corrections did not list these sentences probably because they do not administer them.

References

BAHR, H.M., B.A. CHADWICK and R.C. DAY (1972)
Introduction to Chapter 5, Crime and Deviant Behavior, in Native Americans Today: Sociological Perspectives. New York: Harper & Row.

BALIKCI, Asen (1970)
The Netsilik Eskimo. Garden City, N.Y.: Natural History.

BAYLY, John U. (1985)
Toward the Development of a Northwest Territories Law Reform Capability to Enable the Development of Proposals for New Legislation to Meet the Special Needs and Circumstances of Northern Peoples, in A. Allott and G.R. Woodman, People's Law and State Law: the Bellagio Papers. Dordrecht: Foris: 285-297.

BENTZON, Agnete Weis, Verner GOLDSCHMIDT and Per LINDEGAARD (1950)
Betaenkning afgivet af den Juridiske Expedition til Grønland, 1948-49, Vol. V. Copenhagen. Stencil.

BIRKET-SMITH, Kaj (1959)
The Eskimos. Revised Edition. W.E. Calvert and C.D. Forde (eds.), Trans. London: Methuen & Co. Ltd.

BRAKEL, Samuel, J. (1978)
American Indian Tribal Courts: The Costs of Separate Justice. Chicago: American Bar Foundation.

BRØNDSTED, Henning (1973)
Ruling in Greenland and Forms of Integration in Denmark: The Established Legal Components, in J. Malaurie (ed.), Le Peuple Esquimau Aujourd'hui et Demain. The Hague: Mouton.

---------- (1979)
Personal communication. Interview, August 30, 1979.

---------- (1980)
Den Grønlandske Kriminallovs Anvendelse i Praksis og Sammenstødet mellem Dansk og Grønlandsk Retstradition, in Retfaerd i Grønland. Ärhus, Denmark: Modtryk. Retfaerd Vol. 16: 130-138.

---------- (1986)
Review of Leif Senholt: Den Grønlandske Kriminalret. Nordisk Tidsskrift for Kriminanlvidenskab. Copenhagen. Forthcoming in 1986 (Vol. 73). (Page references refer to the typewritten manuscript, which has 13 pages.)

CHANCE, Norman A. (1966)
The Eskimo of North Alaska. N.Y.: Holt, Rinehart & Winston.

CHRISTIE, Nils (1975)
Hvor Tett et Samfunn? Copenhagen: Christian Ejlers' Forlag.

---------- (1981)
Limits to Pain. Oslo: Universitetsforlaget.

CONN, Stephen (1985)
Alaskan Bush Justice: Legal Centralism Confronts Social Science Research and Village Alaska, in A. Allott and G.R. Woodman, People's Law and State Law: the Bellagio Papers. Dordrecht: Foris: 290-320.

FINKLER, Harold W. (1976)
Inuit and the Administration of Criminal Justice in the Northwest Territories: The Case of Frobisher Bay. Ottawa, Canada: Department of Indian and Northern Affairs.

GLUCKMAN, Max (1965)
Politics, Law and Ritual in Tribal Society. Chicago: Aldine.

GOLDSCHMIDT, Verner (1956)
The Greenland Criminal Code and its Sociological Background. 1 Acta Sociologica 217-265.

---------- (1963)
New Trends in Studies on Greenland Social Life: Criminal Law in Changing Greenland. Folk, Vol. 5, 113-121.

---------- (1970)
The Greenland Criminal Code, with an Introduction by Verner Goldschmidt. American Series of Foreign Penal Codes, Vol. 16. London: Sweet & Maxwell; S. Hackensack, N.J.: F. Rothman.

---------- (1973-74)
Social Tolerance and Frustration: An Analysis of Attitudes Toward Criminals in a Changing Arctic Town. 3 International Journal of Sociology 147-163.

---------- (1980)
Fra Uskreven til Skreven Kriminalret i Grønland. In: Retfaerd i Grønland. Ärhus, Denmark: Modtryk. Retfaerd Vol. 16, 116-129.

GRABURN, Nelson H. (1969)
Eskimo Law in Light of Self- and Group-interest. 4 Law and Society Review 45-60.

GREENLAND DEPARTMENT OF CORRECTIONS AND PROBATION (1982a)
(Kriminalforsorgen i Grønland) Oversigten over Kriminalforsorgens Virksomhed i Grønland. Retlingslinier for Opholdsvaerter. Bilag I. April, Unpaged.

---------- (1982b)
Oversigten over Kriminalforsorgens Virksomhed i Grønland. Foranstaltningsmulighederne. May 7, Unpaged.

HIPPLER, Arthur E. and Stephen CONN (1973)
Northern Eskimo Law Ways and Their Relationships to Contemporary Problems of "Bush Justice": Some Preliminary Observations on Structure and Function. ISEGR Occasional Paper No. 10. Fairbanks: University of Alaska, Institute of Social, Economic and Government Research.

HOEBEL, E. Adamson (1954)
The Law of Primitive Man: A Study in Comparative Legal Dynamics. Cambridge, Mass.: Harvard University Press.

JUSTITSMINISTERIET (1983)
Kriminalforsorgen 1982 (Prison and Probation 1982). Copenhagen: Justitsministeriet, Direktoratet for Kriminalforsorgen (The Ministry of Justice, Department of Prison and Probation).

---------- (1985)
Kriminalforsorgen 1984 (Prison and Probation 1984). Copenhagen: Justitsministeriet, Direktoratet for Kriminalforsorgen (The Ministry of Justice, Department of Prison and Probation).

KLEIVAN, Inge (1971)
Song Duels in West Greenland - Joking Relationship and Avoidance. Folk, Vol. 13, 9-36.

KREUTZMANN, Elisaeus (1986)
Personal communication. Interviews, January and February, 1986. Kreutzmann is Director of Greenland's Department of Corrections and Probation.

KRIMINALFORSORGEN I GRØNLAND (1986)
Statistical materials prepared for the forthcoming (1986) issue, Kriminalforsorgen 1985 (Prison and Probation 1985), to be published in Copenhagen by Justitsministeriet, Direktoratet for Kriminalforsorgen (The Ministry of Justice, Department of Prison and Probation).

LLEWELLYN, K.N. and E. Adamson HOEBEL (1941)
The Cheyenne Way: Conflict and Case Law in Primitive Jurisprudence. Norman: University of Oklahoma Press.

MALINOWSKI, Bronislaw (1926)
Crime and Custom in Savage Society. London: Routledge and Kegan Paul, Ltd.

NADER, Laura (1965)
The Anthropological Study of Law, in The Ethnography of Law. American Anthropologist Special Publication. Vol. 67, Part 2. Washington, D.C.: American Anthropological Association.

NIELSEN, Beth Crothe (1979)
Ny-Klassisk Strafferet i det Taette Samfund. Copenhagen: Institute of Criminal Science, University of Copenhagen, Stencil Series No. 4.

POSPISIL, Leopold (1971)
Anthropology of Law: A Comparative Theory. New York: Harper & Row.

---------- (1978)
The Ethnology of Law. Second Edition. Menlo Park, California: Cummings Publishing Company.

PRICE, Monroe E. (1973)
Law and the American Indian: Readings, Notes and Cases. New York: The Bobbs-Merrill Company, Inc.

REASONS, Charles (1972)
Crime and the American Indian, in H.M. Bahr, *et al.* (eds.), Native Americans Today: Sociological Perspectives. New York: Harper & Row.

ROSEN, Lawrence, Ed. (1978)
American Indians and the Law. New Brunswick: Transaction Books.

SENHOLT, Leif (1984)
Den Grønlandske Kriminalret - Kommentarer til Kriminallov for Grønland, m.v. Bind 1 og 2. Maløv, Denmark: FAVN Forlag.

SERRILL, Michael S. (1979)
A Microcosm of Society. 67 Scandinavian Review 42-49.

STEENHOVEN, Geert Van Den (1962)
Leadership and Law among the Eskimos of the Keewatin District, Northwest Territories. Rijswijk: Uitgererij Excelsior.

---------- (1966)
The Law Through Eskimo Eyes, in People of Light and Dark. M. van Steenel (ed.), Ottawa: Department of Indian Affairs and Northern Development.

STEWART, Omer (1964)
Questions Regarding American Indian Criminality. 23 Human Organization 61-66.

STRICKLAND, Rennard (1975)
Fire and the Spirits: Cherokee Law from Clan to Court. Norman: University of Oklahoma Press.

STÜRUP, Georg K. (1968)
Treating the "Untreatable"; Chronic Criminals at Herstedvester. Baltimore: The Johns Hopkins Press.

UDVALGET FOR SAMFUNDSFORSKNING I GRØNLAND (1962)
Kriminalloven og de Vestgrønlandske Samfund. I. Samfundsvidens?kabelige undersøgelser. København: Udvalget for Samfundsforskning i Grønland.

WEYER, Edward Moffat (1932)

Alcohol control in Alaska Eskimo communities: communal vs. 'official' law

Jane M. Yamashiro

The state of Alaska is one of paradoxes and polarity. It is the largest state in the Union, and when superimposed on the United States, it stretches from coast to coast, spanning three time zones. Yet its population of 500,000 is one of the smallest; 300,000 residents live in Anchorage, an urban city with tall buildings, street lights, running water and the same amenities as any city in the United States. A few air miles out of Anchorage the simplest conveniences like running water are unavailable, and residents live in the harshest of conditions, with the minimum of services from the state or federal government. Many residents of Anchorage have never ventured into the rural areas and do not understand the conditions there. The lifestyle, values and beliefs of the native component of the state's population (roughly 20%, and resident largely in the rural areas) are as foreign to urban Alaskans as if they were those of another country.

One common thread unites all residents of the state, however. Across Alaska, throughout the social stratum, Alaskans engage in high levels of alcohol consumption, with the result that the problems of alcohol have become the focal point of citizens' contact with the criminal justice system. A fundamental difference, however, is that alcohol is seen as the basic cause of Native problems, whereas alcohol use by non-Natives is viewed as the result of other social or environmental problems.

This paper presents an account of Native Alaskans' problems with alcohol and, in so doing, demonstrates that the problems of alcohol management and control are the results of the unresponsiveness of governmental actions, laws and structures to community needs. An historical bias in the treatment of Eskimos and their relationship to alcohol underlies the decisions of the 'official' legal system. The drive to unify the villages into a state system resulted in the breakdown of rural law and order. Moreover, the official structures of social management lack the necessary components to function successfully and have failed to respect the prevailing communal system of law and order.

I. Review of literature

During the execution of the fieldwork of which the results are reported below, the paradoxes of alcohol use and abuse surfaced continually. An extensive review of the existing literature, inasmuch as it lays bare a number of concerns about the approach to and categorization of earlier research findings, helps put this study in perspective. The effects of alcohol have been examined in relation to four general themes: social problems; aggression and criminality; anxiety, anomie and tensions; and possible solutions.

A. Social problems

One of the weaknesses of most alcohol-related research is its basis in a highly emotional and value-ridden belief system. It is seldom possible to perceive alcohol in a customary or value-free context. One of the outstanding features of Western studies of non-Western cultures is the contrast between *alcoholism* - the negative consequences of alcohol use - and *alcohol use* - the ritualistic or random use of alcohol - and the accompanying failure to understand the roles and meanings of its use. In Western culture immense emphasis has been placed on the 'social problems' created by alcohol abuse, with people generally being identified as the fundamental problem (Bacon 1962). However, there is a vast difference between examining the 'problems of alcohol' and the problem of alcoholism. Furthermore, while the literature on Indian or Native American drinking illustrates a wide range of approaches, Heath's (1977) analysis does point out that, when discussing social problems, social scientists tend to examine *causes* for non-Western cultures and *consequences* for Western cultures. (Graves 1967; DuToit 1964; Horton 1943; Honigmann 1979).

A further weakness is excessive generalization. An examination of research on populations as large and diverse as those of Europe shows that the necessary circumspection has been observed in avoiding generalization about drinking habits and patterns. Basically, however, the cross-cultural approach constitutes, for non-Western societies, 'an anthropological perspective' which pays little heed to the diversity within and among ethnic groups (Heath 1974). For example, 'objective' social scientists, operating from a Western methodological perspective, may colour their reporting of Native people by failing to recognize the differences between groups having very different values and philosophies. (Bacon 1973).

B. Relationship of alcohol to aggression and criminality

Studies of non-Western cultures emphasize the negative consequences of alcohol use. It is highly probable that this emphasis arises from the fact that Native drinking came to the attention of colonial administrators concerned with adjudication as a result of its negative consequences. The abundant literature on American Indians, especially that of the eighteenth century, focuses on the 'firewater myth', the belief that calm, peaceful Indians became crazed when they consumed alcohol or 'firewater'. From this literature two major generalizations may be drawn. First, aggression expressed by inebriated individuals, in whatever society, is neither random nor diffuse. Rather it is patterned, in the sense of being directed in a limited number of ways against a limited range of persons. Secondly, drinking and drunkenness will have been commonplace in a society for several years before the pattern of aggression becomes unusual (Heath 1974). Other research suggests, however, that no clear relationship exists between the use of alcohol and expressions of aggression or other criminal acts (Heath 1974; Honigmann 1979).

In the analysis of alcohol use and criminal acts, the focus of current research is on the individual *within* the criminal justice system. Though limited, statistics on Natives arrested, jailed, and paroled are available. However, Native people's interaction with and their modes of relating to the 'system' have not been examined. In Alaska, where English is not the mother tongue of many people, the courts and other institutions generally make no effort to use interpreters or otherwise show sensitivity to cultural values. Furthermore, there is little research examining the relationship of Native communities with state and federal agencies in terms of alcohol-induced violations committed on Indian reservations. An exception is the American Indian Court Judges Association's finding that, whereas fifty per cent of all federal cases arising from violations committed on Indian reservations involve alcoholic intoxication, there has been a failure to prosecute in the majority of these cases. This lack of official action has resulted in communal anger. Evidence to the commission stated:

> The fact remains that the Indian community looks to the Federal Government for the prosecution of serious offenses, and when it is not happening, you have, again, this negative impact ... that's when the whole

> problem starts. The mistrust begins at that level, and when you begin to mistrust the police and the criminal justice system, all the other little sections of the wall begin to crumble (U.S. Civil Rights 1981:28).

Thus the examination of aggression and criminality becomes a complex issue. Although it is acknowledged that aggression does exist and is regarded as anti-social by most people in the Native American community, the lack of government support for control by effective enforcement undermines the stability of the community. Research in this area is sadly lacking.

Another complicating factor is that members of the community consider violent drunken offenders less responsible than sober individuals, and conclude from this that law enforcement should be more consistent and stringent. Whereas Western thinking puts great emphasis on the individual in considering deviant behaviour, the Eskimos in the two communities studied hold quite another view. One of the more significant studies is that of MacAndrew and Edgerton (1969), who postulate that drunkenness is regarded as a partial 'time out' and serves as an excuse for behaviour which is normally not sanctioned. The two communities exhibited this attitude and blamed alcohol and inconsistent application of the laws rather than the individual.

C. Relation of alcohol to anxiety, anomie, and tension

vast differences in emphasis characterize the approaches to ethnographic research illustrated in the published literature. Studies of western societies tend to focus on the results of drinking and drunkenness. In viewing other cultures, however, social scientists tend to emphasize external causes. A common and popular belief is that acculturation, culture change, and stress are causes of drunkenness (berreman 1956; graves 1967; james 1961). Villagers asked in interviews why they drank all felt that rapid culture change had a significant effect on their drinking. Merton (1964) hypothesized that in the cross-cultural person, the tension created by the differences in goals and in the means of achieving those goals were important factors in native drinking.

Hugh Brody (1975) notes the classic dilemma in which the Eskimos of Canada find themselves and which is also that of the Alaska Natives. He points out that the Whites' negative attitude toward individual Eskimos springs from a belief in the stereotype of the 'real' Eskimo.

> There is therefore, a striking contradiction between White attitudes towards Eskimo-ness in general and towards Eskimos in particular: all

> Eskimos are touched with the magic of real Eskimo-ness, although any given Eskimo is likely to be criticized for stupidity, incompetence or delinquency. The source of the contradiction is obvious: the modern individual Eskimo fails to achieve the standard of excellence implicit in the Whites' ideas of the 'real Eskimo'. A majority of Eskimos, perhaps the vast majority of them, are therefore from the White point of view deviants in some degree - they deviate from the canon of perfect Eskimo-ness and fail to live up to part of, perhaps a great part of, the Whites' accepted stereotype. The paradox is brutal: Whites criticize those who respond to pressures the Whites' institutions are dedicated to exerting. (Brody 1975:86).

The literature displays many trends. Some research focuses on cultural systems, viewing alcohol abuse as a type of pathology within the culture, while other work focuses on the individual and views it as a neurotic response to stress (Horton 1943). While a psychoanalytic approach to other cultures may offer solutions for individual drinking habits and problems, its value depends largely on the researcher's understanding of a particular culture's belief system. The classical psychoanalytic approach, without, for example, an understanding of the Alaska Native's notion of status, may be inadequate and even damaging.

Psychiatric studies have claimed that Natives are unable to resolve their 'oedipal constellation'. Their drinking is reported to be obsessive and compulsive, and it is said that the individuals have insufficient ego development. Rather than being perceived as expressions of painful and conflicting experiences, their drinking and alcohol abuse are reduced to character defects indicating social inferiority (Clarke 1975; Devereaux 1948; Hippler 1972).

The most plausible hypothesis is that people drink primarily to lessen anxiety, whatever the cause (Lemert 1962; Kunitz and others 1971). From his research on Navaho drunkenness, Graves (1971) concludes that the roots of the problem lie in the wider society within which Indians are trying to survive. His contention is that, rather than assisting communities to confront the issues, the social service agencies are concerned with helping the Natives *adjust* to their status of inequality and inferiority.

Alcohol is such a recurrent problem in Native American history that it has been researched by anthropologists, sociologists, psychologists, historians, medical and public health professionals, social workers, biologists and physiologists. Religionists such as the Jesuits have cited alcohol as the principal reason for their inability to convert the Indian tribes. That their culture was destroyed by alcohol abuse is a common belief, yet very little has been said about the concurrent impact of other cultural changes affecting the Indians.

Mandelbaum points out that 'alcohol is a cultural artifact', and that the 'form and meaning of drinking alcoholic beverages are culturally defined, as are the uses of other artifacts'. (Mandelbaum 1979). Just as for other cultural artifacts, the form of use is quite explicitly specified, with rules and role behaviour prescribed.

While most researchers look within a cultural context for historical uses of alcohol, Lurie (1979) contends that liquor as a cultural artifact has always been closely related to the *external* interaction between whites and Native Americans, and identifies more clearly the role alcohol has played in American history:

> Liquor was more than a borrowed item like steel traps ... Generous distribution of liquor was soon discovered to be a good way to do business with Indians. It augured a satisfactory contract for both parties ... but, as trade declined, as international boundaries in North America were firmed up to prevent Indians from playing different white nations one against the other, and as severe competition for land set in, the nature of Indian-white relationships changed. Indians still kept their own cultural, social, and political counsel but whites deemed them a nuisance with nothing to offer in exchange to justify their separate existence. (Lurie 1979:137).

Another author describes the role alcohol played between the cultures in these terms:

> Initially, alcohol was introduced to the Indians through the fur trade. However, it quickly came to have far reaching social, economic and political implications for Indians and whites alike. In evaluating its place in history, the popular view has been to stress the role of liquor as the villain and accept the fur trade as an absolute necessity. This is not unexpected since despite the threat of both secular and ecclesiastical punishment ranging from stocks to excommunication, nonetheless efforts to abolish the liquor traffic were unrealistic. For one thing, without a successful fur trade, the solvency of the colony could not be assured. For another, even if the French had ceased to use alcohol in their relations with Indians, there was no agreement with the Dutch or the English that they would also stop the practice. Indian allies were important in the power struggle for the control of North America. The regular distribution of alcohol was a means of maintaining Indian loyalties as well as gaining new friends. (Dailey 1979:117).

D. A cry for solutions

Finally, there must be solutions to the problem. Thus, when the Natives have pleaded for restrictions of the liquor trade, their request has essentially been for a restriction of contact with whites and white culture. Liquor has come to symbolize the contact with whites and its demoralizing effects. But it seldom occurs to the white man that his way of life and business practices produce such a negative effect on the Native people. For him, liquor becomes the scapegoat. (Dailey 1979).

Thus, the problem is complicated by questions of values and morality.

> The question of moral blame here is a very interesting one as it helps us to understand how the Indian could ask the white man to stop supplying him with liquor at the same time as he was drinking it. How can one blame the white man if the Indian sought him out and demanded liquor at any price? Or on the other hand, how can one blame the Indian if the white man continued to supply it even after the former had pleaded with him to stop? (Dailey 1979:125)

Possible solutions are piecemeal and themselves raise many conflicting issues. Alcohol as both symptom and problem is conceptually complex and thus difficult to analyze with a view to the rational prescription of solutions. This difficulty has been at the heart of American policies.

> Self proclaimed friends of the Indian all too often would help their objects of philanthropy according to their image of the Indian rather than through any understanding of Native Americans as people(s) .... [They] share the urge to reform the Indian according to their desires rather than to help Native Americans on their own terms. (Berkhofer, 1978:193)

II. The Alaskan case study

A. The historical context

The purchase of Alaska subjected it to the laws of the United States. U.S. policies have displayed many inconsistencies and a general disregard for the country's Native populations, including the tribes of Alaska. The federal government recognized the Indians of the area neither as members of a sovereign nation nor as citizens of the United States. They were in fact referred to as 'uncivilized Native tribes' who were excluded from citizenship but subjected to the laws and regulations of the United States. (Arnold 1978).

The history of the management and control of alcohol for Native Americans highlights the inconsistent and confusing policies of the United States Government. As a matter of fact, control of liquor has historically been one of the most comprehensive federal activities in Indian affairs. (Strickland 1982). The problem is due in large part to the basic legal structure.

> In constitutional law today, the U.S. is a tripartite society. The citizens of the states enjoy all the personal (or civil) and political liberties afforded by our system of delegated and limited powers. The residents of the territories and possessions are somewhat less secure, because in theory their political franchise may be altered, or even extinguished, if Congress chooses. Citizens of Indian tribes, by contrast, have little civil or political liberty. Their use of property is completely regulated, they are subject to separate laws and administration, and their self-governing powers have been altered at Congress's pleasure (Barsh and Henderson 1980:viii-ix).

Throughout Alaska's early history, concern was focused on the increasing difficulties of governing so vast an area. Even under the administration of the fifth governor (1897-1906), there were still requests from the territory to Washington to design criminal and civil codes and create a more workable judicial system. In 1899 a Criminal Code was enacted at the federal level. In the debates which preceded its enactment the issue of law enforcement was intimately related to the need for revenue. Since alcohol was prohibited, no liquor licenses could be sold. Governor Bradley pointed out that revenue from liquor licenses would pay for government administration and give towns a source of income. Congress accepted this argument, legalized alcohol, and set up a system of licensing for alcohol and other commodities. It was envisaged that the revenue derived from sales of alcohol would go toward the enforcement of the new Criminal Code.

Thus, since the early days, Alaska's development and alcohol have been interlinked. As an economic necessity for the maintenance of civil and judicial order in the land, the protection of alcohol rights has given rise to a continuing paradox. Though the human and social problems resulting from alcohol abuse have been an overriding concern for the territory, the sale of alcohol has been necessary from an economic standpoint in order to manage the very problems it has created.

In terms of the governmental structures which impinge on the villages, mechanisms for the management and control of alcohol are directly related to the confusing nature of the governmental jurisdiction. On one level, there are precedents for strong federal involvement (the state was designated Indian country early in its history) primarily to prohibit the sale of alcohol within its boundaries. Yet the absence of any extensive, federally established reservations system brought the Alaska Natives under territorial law and later, state law.

> Some resolution of disputes and imposition of sanctions for infractions of customary behavioral norms always have been handled locally in villages, using quasi-traditional methods. But even before statehood, Congress delegated authority to teachers employed in federal schools to enforce territorial law in native comunities for the purpose of achieving a greater level of 'civilization'. In 1958 Public Law 280 extended territorial law (and upon statehood, state law) over criminal offenses and civil causes of action in Indian country within Alaska.
>
> Wide acquiescence in the long tradition of state jurisdiction operating side by side with systems of customary controls over internal matters in Native communities may account for the dearth of judicial decisions involving the extent of state and tribal jurisdiction. Still, the principles guiding determinations of whether state jurisdiction properly may be applied in Alaska Native communities are the same as those used when the question arises concerning Indians elsewhere in the United States (Strickland 1982:764).

The federal Indian Reorganization Act of 1934 (also known as the Wheeler-Howard Act) gave the Alaska Native the same status as other Native Americans. This development produced a major change in the villages, putting the governing bodies under the IRA constitution and business charters. The system of governing remained questionable, and its effectiveness was mixed. A 1980 analysis of the Western Alaska villages indicates that only eleven out of 57 villages in the region were governed by the IRA form of government. However, it is one of the many federal legislative actions which has affected the governance of the villages.

The Alaska Native Claims Settlement Act (ANCSA) brought a whole series of new organizations, giving rise to new issues within the villages. The village corporations are not 'villages in the sense of governmental and cultural units. Rather they are vehicles for holding lands distributed under the Act and for administering other benefits under the Act' (Strickland 1982). Although it has produced no real effect on governmental structures, it has had great influence within the villages.

> Tribal governments, as opposed to regional and village corporations, will be the main vehicle for carrying out tribal governing powers. Internal self-government within a village by a municipal government is not appropriate when control of the government becomes diluted by the growth of a non-Native constituency. Also, the Native regional and village corporations are chartered under state law to perform proprietary, not governmental, functions. As long as it is important to native communities in Alaska that they control membership, sanction individual conduct through customary law, and regulate affairs or property that are uniquely tribal, such as descent and distribution and subsistence activity, tribal entities must be kept viable .... Since ANCSA, courts also have continued to uphold the sovereign immunity from suit of Alaska tribal organizations. Congress, too, has anticipated and provided for the performance of governmental functions by Native villages and organized communities in the Indian Child Welfare Act (Strickland 1982:755).

B. Alcohol consumption and crime

It is within this context that the negative consequences of alcohol use must be viewed. Alaska has the fourth highest alcohol consumption rate in the United States according to a 1972 study (Keller 1972). A comprehensive study conducted by the State Office of Alcoholism, Department of Health and Social Services, indicated that the per capita consumption of absolute alcohol in Alaska is very high by both national and international standards (Kelso and Fargnoli 1975). Given that alcohol consumption is excessive, there is a need to call attention to the rate - the amount of alcohol consumption allowed - in relation to the prevalence of problems related to alcohol use.

State policies have aided the expansion of the alcohol business more than its management and control. There are, for example, a larger number and variety of outlets per 1000 persons in Alaska than in most other states; there are only about half as many people for each license in Alaska as the national average. Furthermore, there are fewer hours of prohibited sales than in most states. The state has also facilitated liquor usage by creating a taxation system which favours the liquor industry. State and federal taxes account for 50-75% of the price of alcohol and therefore changes in the tax rate have a considerable impact on price. But the state excise tax on alcohol had not changed in over twenty years until, in 1983, it was raised. The relative price of beverage alcohol rose by 0.3% during the period 1970-75, while that for all other commodities increased by 41.2%.

The incidence of crime in Alaska is very high. Moreover, in comparison with the rest of the United States and with statewide statistics, village Alaska clearly has an exceptional crime rate. While the total adult population of rural districts amounts to only 10% of the state adult population, 35% of the accumulated impact incidents occur in rural districts. Though data on alcohol use are not kept, it is clear that there is a high correlation of crime and alcohol use. According to Native Health Service information, accidents treated on an outpatient basis indicate the high incidence of alcohol-related accidents. Tables 1 and 2 illustrate the correlation.

Table 1
Comparison of Alaska villages, Alaska statewide and United States crime rates

CRIME	Alaska Villages	Alaska Statewide	United States
Homicide	28.4	10.8	8.8
Rape	99.2	51.6	26.4
Robbery	127.6	96.8	195.8
Aggravated Assault	326.0	284.0	228.6
Burglary	936.8	1331.7	1439.4
Vehicle Theft	4467.5	3369.8	2921.3

C. The subject matter of the research

Seaside and Riverside, the communities from which information for this study was gathered, are both Eskimo villages along the Yukon-Kuskokwim Rivers. They are isolated in the sense that there are no roads and that all travel is by aircraft, riverboat or, during the winter, by snowmachines. Another factor contributing to their isolation is the unreliability of the systems of communication due to environmental conditions. These villages are without everyday conveniences such as running water and central heating, taken for granted by most Americans.

The governmental systems which impinge on these villages are the complex and confused systems already mentioned. In addition, since Alaska became a state, the villages have been affected by the movement away from strong federal influence and toward legislative regulation at the state level. These institutional changes, inasmuch as they have produced overlapping and confusion in the lines of responsibility and authority, have put considerable pressure on the villages. It is within this context that three institutions will be examined - the village council, the magistrate system and the police force - each of which has responsibility for the management and control of alcohol use and abuse.

Table 2
1978; native health service; accidents treated on an outpatient basis

	STATEWIDE+	BETHEL**
Percentage of all accidents that were alcohol related	14%	10%
Percentage of all alcohol-related accidents that were injury purposefully inflicted by another	38%	41%
Percentage of all accidents that occur inside the home	17%	13%
Percentage of all injury purposefully inflicted accidents, alcohol-related that occur inside the home	36%	48%
Percentage of all purposefully inflicted accidents that occur inside the home	32%	46%

\+ This represents the statewide native population which included all Native Health Service Units, Urban and Rural

** This represents the service unit region which includes the town and surrounding villages

Data Source: Department of Health & Human Services, Alaska Area Native Health Service, On-Request Report 14. (Conn and Boedeker 1983)

D. Village councils

The village councils were at one time the major institutions of government (Hippler and Conn 1973; Case 1976). Other institutions such as the police, courts and mayors were non-existent. The village council played major roles not only in enacting ordinances but in administering justice to maintain social control.

The councils became concerned about the increasing incidence of crime, violence, and death resulting from alcohol abuse. Hence in 1962, representatives of the Association of Village Council Presidents (AVCP), from 57 villages of the Yukon-Kuskokwim Delta, gathered 'to discuss the interplay between state law and traditional social control meted out by village councils with alcohol-related problems' (Conn 1980). The state's enforcement of the official law was in a very primitive stage. The only representative of the legal system was a single state trooper stationed in Bethel, with jurisdiction over a region of 90,000 square miles. One magistrate was appointed for the same region, but otherwise judges and lawyers had to fly in periodically to deal with felonies. The 1962 meeting resulted in a recognition of the need for a more uniform legal system within the region. At this first attempt of village leaders to discuss common problems they set the objective of standardizing village council rules, but their major concern was the problem of the making and drinking of homebrew.

Ironically, the greatest concern of the villagers - homebrew - was not of concern to the state. The state trooper reported from the state's perspective on homebrew, that he would be unable to assist the villages unless it was made for resale. Those who brewed for their own consumption were within the bounds of state law, and therefore the state could not play any role in enforcing village ordinances.

The problem was obvious yet the state was unsympathetic to the needs of the village. Though the villagers could not legally pass ordinances which conflicted with state law, the state district attorney advised them to make their own rules and to impose their own penalties (Conn 1982). However, should violations occur there could be no recourse to the state for more severe penalties.

Furthermore, it was clear that the state's interest was to be limited to the criminal aspects of drinking behavior and its resources would not be available to assist villages by the provision of services or the setting-up of preventative measures. It was also emphasized at the meeting that, if the village laws were not unified with the official law, and if they, the leaders, chose to enforce their own laws, they would be vulnerable to lawsuits. Thus, on the one hand they were encouraged to make their own laws, while on the other hand they were told that to do so might entail serious consequences.

The implications of these contradictions are evidenced in the records of Seaside, a coastal village of the Delta. Governmental powers were further diluted in this village because its governance was divided between the traditional council (IRA) and the city council. The traditional council often set policy and sought funds from the federal government through the Bureau of Indian Affairs. The city council's function was to engage in self-government by translating village consensus into statutes and ordinances. The city council was governed by the state's second class structure. State revenue sharing and grants from state and federal agencies were used to hire staff and run programs.

The present analysis of city council minutes concentrates on the manner in which policies and practices regarding the alcohol problem were developed. In 1976 members of the Regional Health Corporation approached Seaside and suggested that there might be funds to support an alcoholism program. The council would have two trained employees to work within the community, and the program would stress problems with youth and address the apparent lack of constructive activities for them.

At the same time the council was wrestling with the problem of disruptive behavior induced by alcohol. Although a village ordinance reinforced regulations to maintain a dry community, alcohol continued to be brought in. The council was concerned about the dangers of intoxicated people driving snowmachines in the village. The village had adopted an ordinance covering the operation of vehicles and boats under the influence of alcohol, but there was no clear-cut penalty or redress, nor any institutional supports to enforce the ordinance.

The set rules proposed for the village by the AVCP were more in keeping with the state laws. They dealt with the *consequences* of alcohol use and abuse, but contained no preventative measures. Two ordinances addressed the issue of alcohol and minors, and four rules dealt with alcohol-related conduct, but there were none directed at drinking. There were no rules to keep alcohol out of the village, to prevent the sharing of alcohol with those known to be violent or to prevent the making of homebrew.

In its dual role as a judicial and an executive body, the council heard of problems of stealing, drinking, and gambling. The conflict between the actual role of the council and the expectations of the people created a number of problems. The council minutes record: 'People have their eyes on the council and are ready to criticize them'. The dilemma created by the state was eroding trust in and respect for the village leaders.

In 1977, alcohol and its problems were still the principal issue at council meetings. A village sleep-off center was proposed. There was increased concern about bootlegging. A major concern was the airlines' continued transportation of alcohol to the villages despite the ordinance providing for a dry village. Since alcohol was considered low priority freight, it would remain in Bethel until there was enough freight to merit a trip, and then alcohol shipments would come into the village in large quantities. The individual's right to order alcohol was protected by state and federal laws, overriding the village laws and ordinances. The village council attempted to stop alcohol from entering the village, but these attempts were met with disapproval and lack of support, as they had been forewarned.

The conflict of laws created an atmosphere of ambivalence and distrust. The council was unable to remain united in its efforts to control alcohol. The council minutes of November 8, 1977 read: 'Council members fighting among themselves wanting to keep booze in the village'. A community member epitomized the distrust and confusion in this statement:

> I don't like people or councilmen who do nothing about drinking here. Some drink who are supposed to be helping. Ordering should be stopped by people or the company should quit accepting the orders. Who can help? The people who are councilmen, alcohol program people, or the people themselves? (interview of villager).

The council was clearly unable to stop the obvious source of alcohol. When interviewed about the problems, the mayor in great frustration responded:

> What solutions? We vote ourselves dry, we tell the airlines people to make sure no one brings booze in the village. Troopers tell us we cannot do that. What solution! How can we come with solutions when the airlines keep bringing in the booze.

The council went as far as to provide money to purchase 'booze' in order to find the bootleggers. Its ordinance was strong on out-of-town violators, who were to be forcibly evicted if they didn't leave voluntarily.

By the end of 1977, the council had recognized that the alcohol issue needed to be dealt with by all villages in concert, but they felt every avenue was blocked by the legalities of the 'official' laws:

> All bad things come to all villages. If people work together, this can be solved. The future of the village lies with the councils, if the council just sits back and enjoys the trouble, the village will head for trouble. If we want a trouble-free village, we have to work together. (Council minutes 12/12/77).

This was not an easy task, as at every step of the way they seemed to encounter roadblocks and problems. Every solution they tried to meet village needs seemed in conflict with either a state or a federal law or policy.

The conflict in the roles of the council was exemplified at the same meeting when an uncooperative young man was brought before it by his parents. In keeping with the preventative nature of the council's interest in community members, they listened to the parents and reminded the young man of his role and place in the community. However, the council remained essentially powerless. In the past, had the young man failed to comply with the wishes of the council, he could have been banished, a severe consequence. However, at this time the admonishment was sanctioned by no legal redress nor any strong informal consequence. No official law could support the council, and the village authority was so eroded as to be ineffective.

While the council continued its struggle to translate community wishes into laws, it was well aware of its limitations and the continual erosion of the respect paid to it. Many persons complained at the non-enforcement of council rules and the repeatedly broken laws. State troopers and other agents of the law failed to assist the council and its authority was in serious question. As the council was unable to deal with the inherent conflict, citizens doubted the competence of their elected officials, and criticism of the council was common.

Riverside, a village seven miles by river from Bethel, had a longer history of contact with alcohol. However, its governmental structure led to a very different approach to the control of the use of alcohol.

The Riverside council was representative of all the major organizations and families, and was thus able to maintain consensus and support for the village rules. It recognized early the problems arising from the many new and changing rules affecting the village. It was bombarded with demands from the state and federal agencies to adopt various governmental systems and advisory organizations. Methodically, the council agreed that the various burdens should be allocated amongst all members, viewing the council like a yoke in which to carry the many demands and burdens imposed on them. As a result, whereas Seaside's population demonstrated ambivalence and hostility toward their council members, Riverside exhibited support for the ordinances and the leadership. The rules were clear and were well supported, even by offenders.

Though the village ordinances were essentially the same, the council responded in a more unified manner. When someone within the village brought in alcohol or was known to drink, those members of the council who were also members of his family would talk with him. The concept of 'respect' and 'care' was continually emphasized. Offenders against the liquor ordinance were forced to face the city council as well as the alcohol counsellor. In general, the villagers respected the ordinances, and, though they had no support from the state, the council maintained strict control over the local community to ensure compliance.

Being very close to Bethel, the Riverside council was able to appeal to the flight services not to deliver alcohol to known inebriates or to bring alcohol to the villages. The council's unanimous agreement on its ordinances and the proximity to Bethel made their program more successful.

E. The magistrate

'The role of the council began to disintegrate when the state introduced the magistrate court to rural Alaska' (Case 1977). Awareness of the formal processes by community members, through education and through litigation under the ANCSA, heightened the knowledge that the village council had little authority to enforce local laws. As the council saw its powers eroding, many villages looked to the magistrate to solve their problems. In fact, however, the magistrate system added to the difficulties.

Traditionally the village council was endowed with executive, judicial and legislative powers. With statehood a number of changes came about. Greater awareness of formal judicial processes caused villagers to doubt the legitimacy of the village council as an enforcer of village ordinances. Without respect for or acceptance of the council's powers, a formal village court process could not survive.

The problem was further compounded. Alaska is unique in lacking any legal process whereby local governments may establish local courts. The state legislature, however, created District courts, with law-trained district judges, and with magistrates, most of whom were without legal training. The magistrate's function was to 'hear, try and enter judgment in all cases involving violation of ordinances of political subdivisions' (AS 22.15.120 (7)). As a result of lack of personnel the trying of cases in the villages became more and more difficult. 'Of the 215 villages in Alaska, only approximately 50 have the services of a part-time or full-time magistrate. The remaining 165 villages have no means to judicially enforce their ordinances' (Case 1977).

Riverside is one of the villages without a magistrate. The council therefore found itself forced to exercise both administrative and judicial powers. Though it applied for and continually sought to have a magistrate appointed to the village, in fact the council maintained better control of the village without that institution.

Seaside, however, has a magistrate and consequently has two systems, neither of which is complete or integrated with the other. There are no clear-cut guidelines as to their respective functions or how they should relate to each other. The undefined nature of these lines of authority has deterred both the magistrate and the council from fully exercising their roles. The council in its traditional role had brought before it issues such as misconduct, poor citizenship, and disrespect for family. The capacity to discover and treat problems before they resulted in deviance or violence had been the essence of the Eskimo village justice system. Restitution could also be ensured within the system. However, the Western system has worked separately from the Eskimo village council system and, in fact, has given little heed to it and has made no attempt to integrate the two. The magistrate in any particular village is a resident who is appointed a lay judge of limited jurisdiction by the presiding judge of the Superior Court in each judicial district. The appointment is not subject to any kind of formal approval by any of the other village governing bodies.

The magistrate has jurisdiction to preside over cases arising from violations of local ordinances passed by the village council. He or she can also sentence defendants who plead guilty to state misdemeanors and hear state misdemeanor cases when the defendant consents. Finally, he or she has jurisdiction to hold preliminary hearings to determine whether the state can show probable cause on admissible evidence and to bind over an arrested person to the Superior court on a felony charge. The civil jurisdiction of the magistrate is limited to small claims of $1000 in damages or in property loss. The magistrate also performs various administrative duties as coroner, keeper of vital statistics, notary public, performer of marriages, and custodian of the property of deceased persons (Hippler and Conn 1973).

What little training was available to the magistrate has aimed at making him a better bureaucrat, rather than at assisting his insertion into a comprehensive governmental system within a community. Though there is a magistrate, the other supporting functions and positions such as the attorneys, public defenders, and paralegals are not available at Seaside. The magistrate and former magistrates revealed in interviews that much of their information and direction was sought from Bethel, Anchorage or Juneau. Council minutes reflect the magistrate's unsuccessful attempts to integrate the council and the judiciary. On a number of occasions the magistrate approached the Council and asked that there be a closer working relationship between the two institutions. Though there was agreement that it would be more effective to work together, the inherent weakness in both institutions seemed to prevent any comprehensive changes. Community members indicated that there was no place to get legal advice, and that no lawyers travelled to the villages. The closest contact for legal assistance was in Bethel.

Furthermore, despite Seaside's relatively large youth population, the State has made little attempt to assist the council in enforcing corrections and juvenile law. For drinking offenses people are generally sentenced and released on their own recognizance. Magistrates comment that the same people appear before them repeatedly and that very little is done to assist them through long-term treatment. The ineffectiveness of the corrections system does nothing to alleviate the problems created by alcohol. Former magistrates interviewed felt that they were subjected to unusual pressures and often blamed for the fact that the system was not workable.

> In recent years, the improved application of American due process rights and criminal justice procedure have made it increasingly difficult for the Troopers to comply with the expectations of residents of Native villages. Even when Troopers remove the accused, he is frequently released without bond and freed to return to the village. This practice is usually neither understood nor approved by the people in the communities. They attribute it to lenient judges. It has led to the creation of demands for heavier sentences for people who have been turned over to Troopers (Conn 1976).

Finally, the courts fail to inform the community about sentences. When a trial is held outside the communities, it may not be clear that 'something' has in fact taken place. People who have become violent while under the influence are feared, especially by those who referred him to the police officer. Thus the erosion of trust in the system is repeatedly demonstrated. As stated in the case of *U.S. v Mazarie,* when distrust begins in those areas where safety and trust is paramount, the whole system begins to fall apart.

F. The police

The police had the power to enforce laws requiring each person to conduct himself and use his property in such a way that he would not endanger himself or others. Of the municipal powers classified as governmental, the police power was the broadest. It was the essence of the ability to govern locally (Case 1977).

On the local level, however, the police were not highly organized or firmly supported. Funding was always tenuous - the positions were generally paid for through temporary funding or from revenue sharing. They were generally short-term, and the pay rate was less than the community average. In spite of his broad powers, the local police officer was not held in high esteem. Though the police force was considered of paramount importance to the stability of the community, the state did little to make it functional.

The position of the police officer in Seaside was fraught with difficulty. There was little contact with the state trooper or other law enforcement officers. There was a high incidence of violence in the village. A police trainee reported that 'he received very little help from the Council and he was afraid to do much on many occasions due to inadequate equipment and size sufficient to defend himself in violent situations'. (Conn 1982). His situation was quite desperate. Virtually untrained, he suffered also from the lack of institutional support in the form of lawyers, paralegals, judges, or other police officers or enforcement personnel. He felt a strong desire to serve, but for these reasons could do no more than imitate the model of a professional policeman.

Drinking among police officers was not uncommon. The men faced tremendous social and cultural pressures. In particular, the pressure on young police officers to drink with their peers was immense, especially given their low status. The choice between their temporary employment and long-time friends, relatives and hunting partners was not easy. In their enforcement of alcohol rules in a community where those rules were confused and ambiguous, police officers encountered a lot of criticism. Totally unsupported, they were left alone to make individual decisions on the enforcement of the ordinances. Their lives and those of their families were often threatened by intoxicated community members.

Some of the difficulties confronting the police appear from the review of their functions at the Bush Justice Conference:

> More seriously, however, is the state's responsibility to provide legal assistance to support the local ordinances. For example, A.S. 28-35-040 and 28-35-045 which relate to reckless and negligent driving respectively may be important in enforcing the drinking and driving of both automobiles and snowmachines. The communities, however, may lack the necessary scientific equipment (breath analyzers) to have sufficient proof to charge. Furthermore these ordinances at the local level have little power as the ordinances being 'consistent' with state statutes (Title 28) requires imprisonment as *possible* punishment. Such action requires the municipalities to provide for an attorney and small rural communities would be financially unable to do so. *Basic* legal services such as lawyers, are unavailable to the residents of rural communities (Case 1977:12).

Furthermore, in terms of providing protection, the state police has not been of great support to the villages. It is clearly understood by anyone living in rural Alaska that it does not take many people to keep the community in flux. In a survey of police response to calls, it has been estimated that in most urban areas a police officer responds within the half hour. In rural areas, the responses took anywhere from one hour to over one week! (Conn 1980). Local officials estimate that 14% of the *requests* for police services from outside the community require more than an hour to complete. Many calls are made by telephone or radio, but often requests are sent by planes stopping in the villages. Villages such as Seaside must face the additional problem of inclement weather which precludes regular plane services.

III. What is the true problem?

The State of Alaska '[has given] Alaskan municipalities *regulatory* powers over "dangerous and disorderly conduct" and other powers and functions affecting the general health, safety, well-being and welfare of their inhabitants' (Case 1977). It is obvious from the minutes of council meetings that the state has simply turned over those responsibilities to the municipalties and done little itself to ensure that the rural communities are, in fact, safe. Research into governmental structures of the villages has shown the double bind in which the communities are held. The ambiguous lines of authority confuse the issues, but the state unwittingly continues to undermine the integrity of the community structure. If the villages, though their councils, enact laws to govern their communities in a responsible way, they find these laws in conflict with the 'official' laws. If they try to institute new laws in the forms dictated by state and federal governmental guidelines, it is only to discover that they lack the elements of support necessary to make them effective.

Throughout, the state has remained insensitive to the dire situation it has caused. It continues to ignore the source of the problems, and to attempt piecemeal solutions which only exacerbate the difficulties of alcohol management in rural communities.

The paradox continues. We as a nation were born in a struggle for political liberty - for meaningful self-government according to what we believed to be 'self-evident' truth. Yet this very right of self-government is denied to Native villages by capricious decisions at the state and federal levels. The issue of *alcohol* continues to cloud the fundamental problem. The quest for a means of alcohol management is in reality nothing other than the desperate but determined cry of Native Alaskans for *equal treatment*. They demand simply what all Americans value and jealously defend: the right to establish local governments and to exercise any and all the powers they have reserved to themselves. They seek as a 'self-evident' truth, the right of self-determination. The irony is that this right which we most cherish, the right which Americans are willing to fight to protect, is the very right which is withheld from Native Alaskans. The issue is not alcohol. The issue is management - the governing of one's own destiny. Alcohol confuses the issue. *Alcohol is the scapegoat.*

References

ARNOLD, Robert, et al (1978)
Alaska Native Land Claims. Anchorage: Alaska Native Foundation.

BACON, Seldon D. (1962)
"Alcohol and Complex Society," in D.J. Pittman and C.R. Snyder (eds.), Society: Culture and Drinking Patterns. New York: John Wiley.

---------- (1973)
"The Process of Addiction to Alcohol: Social Aspects," 34 Quarterly Journal of Studies on Alcohol 1-27.

BARSH, R. and J.Y. HENDERSON (1980)
The Road: Indian Tribes and Political Liberty. University of California Press.

BERKHOFER, Robert F., Jr. (1978)
The Whiteman's Indian: Images of the American Indian from Columbus to the Present. New York: Random House.

BERREMAN, G.D. (1956)
"Drinking Patterns of the Aleuts," 17 The Quarterly Journal of Studies on Alcohol 503-514.

BRODY, Hugh (1975)
The People's Land: Eskimos and Whites in the Eastern Arctic. Toronto: Penguin Books.

CASE, David (1976)
Alaska Natives and the Law: A Special Relationship. Anchorage: Alaska Native Foundation.

---------- (1977)
"Twenty Four Ordinances: To Enforce Local Laws through the Alaska "Village" Council (With Comments)." Anchorage: The Alaska Federation of Natives Bush Justice Committee.

CLARKE, Frank (1975)
"Thoughts on Indian Alcoholism," Association of American Indian Physicians Newsletter 3(1) part 12.

CONN, Stephen (1976)
"Strangers in Our Midst: Drunken Comportment and Violent Aggression," Criminal Justice Center, Anchorage: University of Alaska, Unpublished, research manuscript prepared pursuant to a grant from Law and Social Sciences, National Science Foundation.

---------- (1980)
"Alcohol in Village Alaska," Criminal Justice Center. Anchorage: University of Alaska, Working Draft.

---------- (1982)

"Town Law and Village Law: Satellite Villages, Bethel Alcohol Control in the Modern Era - The Working Relationship and its Demise," Paper delivered at the American Society of Criminology meeting. Toronto, November.

CONN, Stephen and B. BOEDEKER (1983)
"An Analysis of Outpatient Accident Trends in Two Dry Eskimo Towns as a Measure of Alternative Police Response to Drunken Behavior," Academy of Criminal Justice Science, Annual Meeting.

DAILEY, R.C. (1979)
"The Role of Alcohol Among North American Indian Tribes as Reported in the Jesuit Relations," in MacMarshall (ed.), Beliefs, Behaviors and Alcoholic Beverages: A Cross-Cultural Survey. Ann Arbor: University of Michigan Press.

DEVEREUX, George (1948)
"The Function of Alcohol in Mohave Society," 9 Quarterly Journal of Studies in Alcohol 207-251.

DuTOIT, Brian M. (1964)
"Substitution, a Process in Culture Change," 23 Human Organization 16-23.

GRAVES, Theodore D. (1967)
"Acculturation, Access, and Alcohol in a Triethnic Community," 69 American Anthropologist 306-321.

---------- (1971)
"Drinking and drunkenness among urban Indians," in J.O. Waddell and O.M. Watson (eds.), The American Indian in Urban Society. Boston: Little, Brown.

HEATH, Dwight B. (1974)
"Anthropological Perspectives on Alcohol: A Review in Cross-Cultural Studies on Alcohol," in M.W. Everett, J.O. Waddell, and E.B. Heath (eds.), Cross-Cultural Approaches to the Study of Alcohol: An Interdisciplinary Perspective. The Hague: Mouton.

---------- (1977)
"A Critical Review of 'The Sociocultural Model' of Alcohol Use," Prepared for Normative Approaches to Alcohol Abuse and Alcoholism. San Diego, National Institute on Alcoholism and Alcohol Abuse, April 26-28.

HIPPLER, Arthur E. (1972)
"Fundamentalist Christianity: An Alaska Athapascan Technique for Overcoming Alcohol Abuse." Fairbanks: University of Alaska, Institute for Social, Economic and Government Research.

HIPPLER, Arthur E. and Stephen CONN (1973)
"Northern Eskimo Law-Ways and Their Relationship to Contemporary Problems of 'Bush Justice'," Fairbanks: University of Alaska, Institute of Social and Economic Research.

HONIGMANN, John J. (1979)
"Alcohol in its Cultural Context," in MacMarshall (ed.), Beliefs, Behaviors, and Alcoholic Beverages: A Cross-Cultural Survey. Ann Arbor: University of Michigan Press.

HORTON, Donald (1943)
"The Functions of Alcohol in Primitive Societies: A Cross-Cultural Study," 4 Quarterly Journal of Studies on Alcohol 199-320.

JAMES, Bernard J. (1961)
"Social-Psychological Dimensions of Ojibwa Acculturation," 63 American Anthropologist 721-746.

KELLER, Mark (1972)
"Multidisciplinary Perspectives on Alcoholism and the Need for Integration and Historical Perspective Notes," in Tongue Archer and Eva (eds.), Proceedings of the 30th International Congress on Alcoholism and Drug Dependence: Switzerland.

KELSO, Dennis and Jack FARGNOLI (1975)
Descriptive Analysis of the Impact of Alcoholism and Alcohol Abuse in Alaska. Five Volumes, Juneau: State Office of Alcoholism.

KUNITZ, S.J., J.E. LEVY, C.L. ODOROFF and J. BOLLINGER (1971)
"The Epidemiology of Alcohol Cirrhosis in Two Southwestern Indian Tribes," 32 Quarterly Journal of Alcohol Studies 706-720.

LEMERT, Edwin M. (1962)
"Alcohol, Values, and Social Control," in D.J. Pittman and C.R. Snyder (eds.), Society, Culture and Drinking Patterns. New York: John Wiley.

LURIE, Nancy (1979)
"The World's Oldest On-Going Protest Demonstration: Northern American Indian Drinking Patterns," in Mac Marshall (ed.), Beliefs, Behaviors, and Alcoholic Beverages: A Cross-Cultural Survey. Ann Arbor: University of Michigan Press.

MacANDREW, Craig and Robert B. EDGERTON (1969)
Drunken Comportment: A Social Explanation. New York: Aldine.

MANDLEBAUM, David G. (1979)
"Alcohol and Culture," in MacMarshall (ed.), Beliefs, Behaviors, and Alcoholic Beverages: A Cross-Cultural Survey. Ann Arbor: University of Michigan Press.

MERTON, Robert K. (1964)
Social Theory and Social Structure. Glencoe, Illinois: The Free Press.

STRICKLAND, Rennard (1982)
Felix S. Cohen's Handbook of Federal Indian Law. 1982 Edition. Charlottesville: Michie Bobbs-Merrill.

U.S. CIVIL RIGHTS (1981)
Indian Tribes: A Continuing Quest for Survival. A Report of the United States Commission on Civil Rights.

The Contributors

Patricia BAINES

holds the B.A. (Leeds), Dip. App. Psych. (Zurich) and M.A. (Cant., New Zealand). In 1980 she began research among the Nyungar Aboriginal communities of Western Australia, and is writing a Ph.D. thesis on intergenerational transmission of Nyungar identity.

John U. BAYLY

studied at the University of Toronto and Osgoode Hall Law School. He is now a barrister and solicitor based in Yellowknife, Northwest Territories, Canada. He was a founding member of the Commission on Folk Law and Legal Pluralism. His law practice is general but centers on native rights law on aboriginal claims issues, and environmental law especially related to oil and gas review and regulatory hearings. He is counsel to the Dene Nation and Metis Association, was the first Executive Director of the Legal Services Board of the Northwest Territories, and was Chairman of the NWT Government Task Force on Spousal Assault.

Diane BELL

is a Professor of Australian Studies at Deakin University, Victoria, Australia. She obtained a Ph.D. in Social Anthropology at the Australian National University in 1980 for research which focussed on the changing role and status of Aboriginal women in Central Australia with special reference to religious practice, and which is described in her *Daughters of the Dreaming* (1983). She is co-author of *Law: the Old and the New* (1980/4). She was for eight years a consultant to various Aboriginal and governmental bodies, preparing submissions, giving advice and appearing as an expert witness in relation to land rights, law reform and customary legal matters. Before taking up her present position she was a research fellow at the Australian National University.

B.K. Roy BURMAN

is Senior Professor at the Council for Social Development, New Delhi. He has studied the tribal communities of India, publishing a series of monographs which began with reports for the 1961 Census of India, and included: *Hundred Years in a Tribal Village: Totopara. Trends of Socio-Economic Change in India 1871-1961* (1969, Institute of Advanced Studies, Simla); *Towards Poverty Alleviation Programmes in Nagaland and Manipura* (1984, Mittal Publishers, Delhi); and *Social-Ecology of the Tribal Communities on Arunachal* (Council for Social Development, 1986). He is currently Chairperson of the Committee on Land Holding System of Tribals, which has published several studies.

Richard CHISHOLM

is Associate Professor of Law at the University of New South Wales, Australia. He is co-author of *Understanding Law* (2nd ed. Sydney, 1984); *Black Children: White Welfare?* (University of New South Wales, 1985); *Australian Family Law* (loose-leaf service Sydney, 1987); and other publications in the area of family law and children's law. He was a founding member of the Aboriginal Legal Service and of the children's rights group, Action for Children. He has been a consultant to the Australian Law Reform Commission on criminal procedure, child welfare and the recognition of Aboriginal customary law.

Stephen CONN

is a Professor of Justice at the University of Alaska. He has worked on the Navajo Indian Reservation, pursued research in Alaskan native villages, and for nearly twenty years conducted Brazil-related research. He holds a Master's degree in international affairs (Columbia University, 1969), as well as a Master's degree in anthropology (UCLA, 1976), for which his thesis was on family law in Brazilian favelas (squatter colonies). He is co-author of *The Law of the People: Dine Bibee Hazaanii, a Bicultural Approach to Legal Education for Navajo Students* (1972, 4 vols.) and *Alaska Natives and the Law* (1977, 7 vols.), and author of *No Need of Gold: Alcohol Control and Alaska Natives* (1986). He has published numerous law review articles on Native Americans.

James CRAWFORD

is the Challis Professor of International Law at the University of Sydney, Australia. He is the author of *The Creation of States in International Law* (1979), *Australian Courts of Law* (1982), and numerous articles on international and public law. He was Commissioner in Charge of a number of Reports of the Australian Law Reform Commission, including *The Recognition of Aboriginal Customary Laws* (2 vols., 1986).

Nathan ELBERG

is an anthropologist specializing in cultural change. He studied at McGill University (Montreal) and the New School for Social Research (New York). He has worked as an applied anthropologist with the Program in the Anthropology of Development (McGill University) and various Native organizations. Current projects include computers in anthropology and ethnology in popular culture.

Harald W. FINKLER

is Chief, Scientific Affairs Division, Circumpolar and Scientific Affairs Directorate of the Department of Indian and Northern Affairs, Canada. Before taking up his present post he was successively a principal researcher with the Internatioanl Centre for Comparative Criminology, Université de Montreal, and a research officer of the Northern Social Research Division, Indian and Northern Affairs. A founding member of the Commission on Folk Law and Legal Pluralism, he has undertaken extensive research into the criminal justice system in Canada's arctic, focussing on the socio-legal impact on northern natives of major resource developments and accelerated social change. He has published many papers on his research, including *Inuit and the Administration of Criminal Justice in the Northwest Territories* (1976) and *The Baffin Correctional Centre: a Review of Current Programs and Alternatives* (1981).

E. Mary FISHER

is a Senior Law Reform Officer with the Australian Law Reform Commission. She was formerly Private Secretary to Senator Peter Baume, the then Federal Cabinet Minister for Aboriginal Affairs, and after joining the Commission she worked from 1983 to 1986 on the Commission's Reference on the Recognition of Aboriginal Customary Laws, publishing a Research Paper, *The Recognition of Traditional Hunting and Fishing Rights* (1984).

Peter R. GRANT

is a barrister and solicitor in practice in Hazelton, British Columbia, Canada. He is legal counsel for the Gitksan Wet'suwet'en hereditary chiefs who have commenced a court action against the Government of British Columbia for recognition of their aboriginal rights of ownership and jurisdiction.

Paul L. HAVEMANN

is Professor and Associate Dean of the School of Human Justice in the University of Regina, Saskatchewan, Canada. He has studied legal ethnography and Commonwealth constitutional law as a graduate student at the School of Oriental and African Studies, University of London. He has been a Senior Lecturer in Law at North East London Polytechnic, and a Visiting Fellow at the Australian National University. He has also been a Principal Investigator under contract to several Canadian federal government departments, evaluating the Native Counsel Project and reviewing conceptual models and ideological biases in recent research literature relating to Canada's indigenous peoples and the criminal justice system. He has published the findings of this research.

Peter K. HENNESSY

is a Principal Law Reform Officer with the Australian Law Reform Commission. He worked on the Australian Law Reform Commission's Reference on the Recognition of Aboriginal Customary Laws for the five years prior to its completion, and during that time published several Research Papers, including: *Aboriginal Customary Law: Traditional and Modern Distributions of Property* (1982); *Aboriginal Customary Law: Problems of Evidence and Procedure* (1983); and *Aboriginal Customary Law and Local Justice Mechanisms: Principles, Options and Proposals* (1984).

Bradford W. MORSE

is Professor of Law at the University of Ottawa. He has been a visiting professor at the University of Hong Kong and Macquarie University. He has worked for a number of local, regional and national Aboriginal organizations in Canada and Australia. He has also written extensively in the general field of Aboriginal Peoples and the law with his latest two books being: *Aboriginal Peoples and the Law: Indian, Metis and Inuit Rights in Canada* (1985) and *Aboriginal Self-Government in Australia and Canada* (1985).

Jeff RICHSTONE

is legal counsel to the Inuit Committee on National Issues. He formerly engaged in a general civil law private practice in Québec. He has authored a number of papers including, *Securing Human Rights in Nunavut: A Study of a Bill of Rights for Nunavut* (1985). He is currently completing a study on the implementation of customary law in Nunavut to be published by *Etudes/Inuit/Studies*.

Rob RILEY

worked for some years for the Aboriginal Legal Service in Australia. A member of the former National Aboriginal Conference, where he represented the Metropolitan Perth Constituency, he was elected National Chairman of the Conference in 1984.

Basil L. SANSOM

is Professor of Anthropology, University of Western Australia. He was awarded a Ph.D. by the University of Manchester in 1970. From 1975 onward he has conducted research among urban and fringe-dwelling Aboriginal communities in the Darwin area, part of which he reported in *The Camp at Wallaby Cross* (Australian Institute of Aboriginal Studies, Canberra, 1980).

Elaine J. SCHECHTER

is a doctoral candidate in the Department of Anthropology, Columbia University, New York. During her five years of fieldwork in Denmark and Greenland, she was affiliated as guest researcher, first with the Institute of Criminal Science of the University of Copenhagen, and later with the Inuit Institute in Nuuk, Greenland. She has published academic papers on Greenland, particularly on alcohol control, and numerous popular articles on events and developments in Greenland as the local correspondent for United Press International.

Robert TONKINSON

is Professor of Anthropology at the University of Western Australia. He previously taught social anthropology at the University of Oregon, USA, and the Australian National University. He has extensive experience of field research, both among Aborigines in the Western desert area of Australia and also in Vanuatu. He has published two books on Aborigines: *The Jigalong Mob* (1974), and *The Mardudjara Aborigines* (1978).

Gordon R. WOODMAN

is a Senior Lecturer in Law and an Associate of the Centre of West African Studies at the University of Birmingham. Formerly he was a lecturer and professor of law at the University of Ghana. He gained a Ph.D. from the University of Cambridge, Britain, for a thesis on customary land law in Ghana, and has published extensively on customary law and legal pluralism, particularly with reference to Africa. He was a founding member and is currently President of the Commission on Folk Law and Legal Pluralism, and is an associate editor of the *Journal of Legal Pluralism*.

Jane M. YAMISHIRO

works in the University of Hawaii, where she currently holds the post of Educational Specialist in the Office of the Chancellor for Community Colleges. She has also worked in Alaska, where she was a Senior Associate at the Center for Equality of Opportunity in Schooling of the Alaska Native Foundation, a Research Associate at the Institute for Social and Economic Research of the University of Alaska, and Education Director, North Pacific Rim Native Corporation.

James W. ZION

is a Hearing Examiner for the Montana Human Rights Commission, an attorney for the Montana Department of Labor and Industry, and a Senior Associate in Native Technical Resource Associates, an Indian-controlled service firm. He is also currently General Counsel to the National America Indian Court Judges Association, and Mentor to the Saddle Lake (Alberta, Canada), Tribal Justice Centre. He has in the past served as Customary Law Project Director of the Federation of Saskatchewan Indian Nations, Solicitor to the Courts of the Navajo Nation, Court Adviser to the Blackfeet Tribal Court, and Resource to the Canadian ad hoc Coalition at the IVth Russell Tribunal, Rotterdam, The Netherlands. He has published *The Navajo Peacemaker Court Manual* (1982), edited the *Navajo Reporter* (Vol. 3), and written various articles on Indian justice.

Kolibri 360 GmbH
Ferdinand-Jühlke-Straße 7
99095 Erfurt, Deutschland
produktsicherheit@kolibri360.de